ENGLISH PLACE-NAME SOCIETY

VOLUME LXXI FOR 1993-94

General Editor

VICTOR WATTS

THE PLACE-NAMES OF LINCOLNSHIRE

PART FOUR

THE SURVEY OF ENGLISH PLACE-NAMES

undertaken with the approval and support of

THE BRITISH ACADEMY

THE PLACE-NAMES OF LINCOLNSHIRE

By

KENNETH CAMERON

in collaboration with

JOHN FIELD and JOHN INSLEY

PART FOUR

THE WAPENTAKES OF LUDBOROUGH AND HAVERSTOE

NOTTINGHAM

ENGLISH PLACE-NAME SOCIETY

1996

Published by the English Place-Name Society

Registered Charity No. 257891

ISBN 0 904889 46 7

The camera-ready copy for this volume
has been prepared by Mrs E. Pattison
on equipment provided by
Allied Breweries plc
and
Advent Desktop Publishing Ltd

Printed in Great Britain
by Woolnough Bookbinding, Irthlingborough, Northants

CONTENTS

The collection from unpublished documents
of material for the Lincolnshire volumes has been
greatly assisted by grants received from the
British Academy

This volume is dedicated to Kathleen Major, FBA
for all her help and encouragement

PREFACE

The fourth part of *The Place-Names of Lincolnshire* covers the Wapentakes of Ludborough and Haverstoe. Once again I have to thank my friends in the Lincolnshire Archives Office for their constant help during the years in which I have been collecting material there. In particular must be mentioned Mr Nigel Colley and Mr Peter Noon. The text of the volume itself shows how many Collections have been searched and the time and energy spent by members of the staff to place it all at my disposal.

My friends Mr John Field and Dr John Insley have helped greatly in the preparation of the volume that again their names appear as collaborators on the title page. Once more Mr Field prepared the first draft of the field-names of each parish and in doing so made many suggestions of etymology which have been silently incorporated into the text. With his wide experience in the study of field-names he has been able to make suggestions I might never have thought of and only he will actually know his contributions to this volume. Dr Insley has read the whole of the text and with his expertise in the field of personal names and in philology generally he has made a considerable contribution which enhances the scholarship of the book.

My grateful thanks go to Mrs Anne Tarver who has drawn the detailed map of the parishes of the two wapentakes, and also to an unnamed friend who has checked the text at least twice and saved me from numerous errors. She accompanied me on numerous trips around the area on what we like to call "practical place-names", checking the topography of individual places and providing a photographic record. Particularly important has been the field-work in Hawerby, Fulstow and Marsh Chapel.

Once again the text itself was prepared for press by our former Publication Officer, Mrs M.D. Pattison, whose experience and knowledge in handling difficult place-name material has earned the admiration of the Society's editors and members for many years. Again, I stand greatly in her debt, especially for her endless application and patience.

University of Nottingham Kenneth Cameron

ADDITIONS to the ABBREVIATIONS and BIBLIOGRAPHY printed in THE PLACE-NAMES OF LINCOLNSHIRE PARTS 1-3

AH	Documents in the Allison and Helmer Deposit in LAO
BD	Documents in the Burton and Dixon Deposit in LAO
BPLeases	Bishop's Possessions Leases in LAO
ContGerm	Continental Germanic
DCLeases	Dean and Chapter Leases in LAO
EHN	O.S. Anderson, *The English Hundred Names*, 3 vols, Lund 1934-39
Em	Documents in the Emeris Collection in LAO
FMap	Haiwarde's Map of Fulstow and Marsh Chapel in private hands; copy in LAO
FSurv	Survey of Fulstow and Marsh Chapel, Revesby Abbey 2/B/1-2 in LAO
GrimsCB	Grimsby Court Books i-xvi in SHARO
Hen	Documents in the Heneage Collection in LAO
MC	Marsh Chapel Parish Documents in LAO
MiscSewer	Miscellaneous Serwer Documents in LAO
PM	The Peterborough Museum Collection in LAO
RevesbyA	Documents in the Revesby Abbey Collection in LAO
SewerAlf	Alford Sewers Deposit in LAO
SewerLouth	Louth Sewers Deposit in LAO
SHARO	South Humberside Record Office in Grimsby

SPNNf — John Insley, *Scandinavian Personal Names in Norfolk*, Uppsala 1994

TSJ — Tweed, Stephens and Jourdain Collection in LAO

NOTES ON ARRANGEMENT

(1) Following the names Ludborough and Haverstoe Wapentakes, the parishes in the Wapentakes are set out in alphabetical order.

(2) Each of the parish names is printed in bold type as a heading. Within each parish the names are arranged as follows: (i) the parish name; (ii) other major names (i.e. names of sizable settlements and names of primary historical or linguistic interest), each treated separately in alphabetical order; (iii) all minor names (i.e. the remaining names recorded on the 1906 edition of the O.S. 6 in. map, as well as some names that are 'lost' or 'local', *v. infra*), again treated in alphabetical order but in a single paragraph; (iv) field-names (which include other unidentified minor names) in small type, (a) modern field-names, normally those recorded since 1750, with any older spellings of these names in brackets and printed in italics, (b) medieval and early modern field-names, i.e. those recorded before about 1750, printed in italics, the names in each group being arranged alphabetically.

(3) Place-names no longer current, those not recorded on the editions of the 1 in. and 6 in. maps are marked '(lost)', This does not mean that the site to which the name refers is unknown. Such names are normally printed in italics when referred to elsewhere.

(4) Place-names marked '(local)' are those not recorded on the 1 in. and 6 in. O.S. maps but which are still current locally.

(5) The local and standard pronunciations of a name, when of interest and not readily suggested by the modern spelling, are given in phonetic symbols in square brackets after the name.

(6) The early spellings of each name are presented in the order 'spelling, date, source'. When, however, the head-form of a name is followed only by a 'date and source', e.g. CHURCH CLOSE (lost), 1760, 1796, 1798 *Hen* and 1828 Bry the spelling in 1760, 1796, 1798 *Hen* and 1828 Bry is the same as that of the head-form.

(7) In explaining the various place-names and field-names summary reference is often made, by printing the elements in bold type, to the analysis of elements which will appear in the final volume of the Lincolnshire County Survey, and more particularly to *English Place-Name Elements* (EPNS 25, 26) and to *Addenda and Corrigenda* to these volumes in *English Place-Name Society*

Journal 1. In many of the minor names and field-names the meaning is so obvious as to need no comment or so uncertain as not to warrant it. For personal-names which are cited without authority, reference should be made for Old English names to Redin, Searle and Feilitzen, for Old (Continental) German to Förstemann PN and Forsner, and for English surnames to Bardsley and Reaney (for details of these sources *v.* Abbreviations and Bibliography in *The Place-Names of Lincolnshire*, Part 1 (EPNS 58).

(8) Unprinted sources of the early spellings of place-names are indicated by printing the abbreviation for the source in italics. The abbreviation for a printed source is printed in roman type. The exact page, folio or membrane is only given where the precise identification of an entry is of special importance or value, as e.g. under the Strait Bank in Covenham f.ns. (a) *Hill* 22/1/9/3/1.

(9) Where two dates are given for a spelling, e.g. Hy2 (e13), 1190 (m13), the first is the date at which the document purports to have been composed and the second the date of the copy that has come down to us (in many cases the latter is a Cartulary, ecclesiastic or lay). Sources whose dates cannot be fixed to a particular year are dated by century, e.g. 11, 12, 13, 14 etc. (often more specifically e13, m13, l13 etc., early, mid and late 13th century respectively), by regnal date, e.g. Ed1, Hy2, Eliz, Jas1 etc., or by a range of years, e.g. 1150-60, 1401-2 etc., although this last form of date may alternatively mean that the spellings belong to a particular year within the limit indicated.

(10) The sign (p) after the source indicates that the particular spelling given appears in that source as a person's surname, not primarily as a reference to a place.

(11) When a letter or letters (sometimes words or phrases) in an early place-name form are enclosed in brackets, it means that spellings with and without the enclosed letter(s), words or phrases occur. When only one part of a place-name spelling is given as a variant, preceded or followed by a hyphen, it means that the particular spelling only differs in respect of the cited part from the preceding or following spelling. Occasional spellings given in inverted commas are usually editorial translations or modernisations and whilst they have no authority linguistically they have chronologically.

(12) Cross-references to other names are given with *supra* or

infra, the former referring to a name already dealt with, the latter to a name dealt with later in the text.

(13) Putative forms of personal names and place-name elements which appear asterisked in the concluding volume of this survey are not always asterisked in the text, although the discussion will often make it clear which are on independent record and which are inferred.

(14) In order to save space in presenting the early spellings of a name, *et passim* and *et freq* are sometimes used to indicate that the preceding form(s) occur respectively from time to time or frequently from that date of the last quoted source to that of the following one, or to the present day.

ADDENDA AND CORRIGENDA

Volume 58

xxxiv s.v. Sewer. Part 2 was edited by A.E.B. Owen and not by A. Mary Kirkus.

Volume 64/65

2-3 s.n. Binbrook. Gillis Kristensson, *English Studies*, 1965, 155, suggests that the first el. of Binbrook is OE *binn(e)* 'a manger', used in a transferred topographical sense of 'a valley' appropriate enough for the site of the village. The meaning would then be 'the brook in the valley'.

67 s.n. Waterhill Wood. Seven lines from bottom read "held" for "hend".

76 s.n. Newstead Priory. Add *Ruholm locus iuxta ancolne* 1156-57 *HarlCh* 51.H.1.

87 s.n. Caistor. A 17th century form of *Thwancastr(e)* has been noted: *Thongcaster* 1623 *MiscDep 16.*

104 s.n. *Wardnoth.* Three lines from bottom read *nomine Warnott.*

141 s.n. Harborough Grange. The head form should read HABROUGH GRANGE.

145-6 s.n. *le Moldfanch(e).* The reference to the appellative use, p. 146 top line, should read *Stayn Moure ... cum le Moldfang adiecente.*

147 s.n. *Stayn Moure.* It is now clear that the etymology of *Moure* is wrong. It was not realised at the time that this is the same word as *maure* 'a salt-hill, a saltern', discussed under *Cauthernsome Lane* in Marsh Chapel p. 119 in the present volume. The Habrough name is the first instance noted of *moure, maure* used in a f.n., a further example being *Lady moure* 1446 Cl in Tetney parish in Bradley Wapentake. We may postulate a ME *moure, maure* in the sense 'a salt-hill, a saltern', though the etymology of the word is still obscure. Two further examples have been noted in Tetney - *Pynders Mawer als Pynders Close* 1626 *MiscDep 161,*

three Parcells of Lands called the Mawers 1671 *ib.*

157 s.n. *Scalawe.* *v.* The Scallows Hall *infra* in addenda to Volume 66, 4.

205 s.n. *Briniglandes.* For *Bryning* read *Brȳning.*

208 s.n. *Manesloth.* Mr A.E.B. Owen has noted a further example in *Bard* ff. 145v-146 in Sutton on Sea LSR: *iuxta Northdic in West Sexesmanneslot.* The charter will be printed in a forthcoming LRS volume to be edited by Mr Owen.

Volume 66

4 s.n. The Scallows Hall. *v.* Scallow, Part 4, 13-14, where it is pointed out that the etymology suggested for The Scallows Hall is wrong. The name should no doubt be interpreted as 'the hill with a shieling', *v.* **skáli**, **haugr**. Two further examples of this compound have been noted in Part 4, 102 and 111-12.

47 s.n. Kingerby. The first form should, of course, read *Chenebi* (2x) 1086 DB.

81 s.n. North Gulham. Mr A.E.B. Owen notes that in "south Lincs and the Isle of Ely goole/gull regularly means a breach in a bank, sometimes man-made (cf. indexes to *Holland Sewers* vols 2 and 3), more often natural". He refers us to H.E. Hallam's article on "Goll Grange" in Cowbit (LAAS v, p. 8) with the definition "the great hole caused by the flood as it whirls around the pool formed just inside a broken sea-bank or fen bank. It is usual (in repairing it) to make a large bulge in the new bank to avoid the goule". Mr Owen wonders whether Gulham alludes to such a feature in the R. Ancholme.

93 s.n. *del See de Ouresby* (p). Mr Owen draws attention to a prominent family of this name in Grimsby recorded as early as 1315. No doubt the Owersby forms refer to members of this family. Reference to **sǣ** in the sense 'marsh' should, therefore, be deleted.

136 s.n. Tealby, line 4. The bibliographical details to the edition of the Confraternity Book of Reichenau are: *Das Verbrüderungsbuch der Abtei Reichenau*, ed. J.

Autenrieth, D. Geuenich and K. Schmid, MGH Libri: Memoriales et Necrologia, Nova Series 3, Hanover 1979.

136 s.n. Bully Hill. Bully Hill is marked on the OS map in the parish of Tealby, but as 1824 O shows, it is really the name of the prominent round barrow to the east of High Street just in the modern parish of Kirmond le Mire LSR. In the adjacent parish of Binbrook, p. 11, the forms *Bolehowegate* etc. are recorded and it is likely enough that the two are to be associated. The f.n. would then mean 'the road, way to Bully Hill'. The f.ns. should, therefore, be transferred to Bully Hill, p. 136.

184 s.n. Red Chalk Hill. Mr A.E.B. Owen notes that this must refer to an outcrop of the red chalk stratum, one of many in the southern Wolds. He points out that Red Ochre, even if popularly called "red chalk", is geologically quite different.

Volume 71

30 s.n. *The Great micke.* Add *micchelemare* c.1200 *DC* and *v.* **micel, (ge)mǣre**.

62 s.n. Bratton Ho. This is apparently *Waythe Lane Ho.* 1828 Bry.

119 s.n. *Cauthernsome Lane.* On the word *maure, v.* Addenda vol. 64/65 p. 147.

147 s.n. North Coates Clow. This has been wrongly derived from **clōh**. It should be referred to *clow* 'a dam for water', 'a sluice or floodgate'. For the history of the word *v.* NED s.v. *clow* sb[1], 1a.

155 s.n. Rothwell. A further example of *Thwancastr(e)* for Caistor is - *iuxta Thuancastr'*.

164 s.n. *le Broth de Svyneop.* Delete this reference. It has been correctly included under Swinhope Brats p. 162.

PHONETIC SYMBOLS

p	*p*ay	j	*y*ou	ɔ	p*o*t
b	*b*ay	x	lo*ch* (Scots)	ɔ:	s*aw*
t	*t*ea	h	*h*is	ɔi	*oi*l
d	*d*ay	m	*m*an	e	r*e*d
k	*k*ey	n	*n*o	ei	fl*ay*
g	*g*o	ŋ	si*ng*	ɛ	jam*ais* (Fr.)
ʍ	*wh*en	r	*r*un	ɛ:	th*ere*
w	*w*in	l	*l*and	i	p*i*t
f	*f*oe	ʧ	*ch*ur*ch*	i:	b*ea*d
v	*v*ote	ʤ	*j*u*dg*e	ou	l*ow*
s	*s*ay	ɑ:	f*a*ther	u	g*oo*d
z	*z*one	ɑu	c*ow*	u:	b*oo*t
ʃ	*sh*one	a	m*a*nn (German)	ʌ	m*u*ch
ʒ	a*z*ure	ai	fl*y*	ə	ev*er*
þ	*th*in	æ	c*a*b	ə:	b*ir*d
ð	*th*en			?	wa*t*er (Cockney, glottal stop)

Phonetic symbols are enclosed in square brackets: [ ].

The symbols used in the expression of Brit and PrWelsh forms are those used in LHEB.

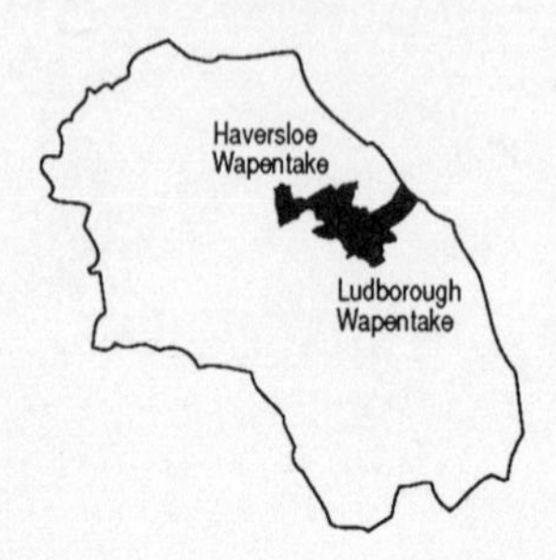

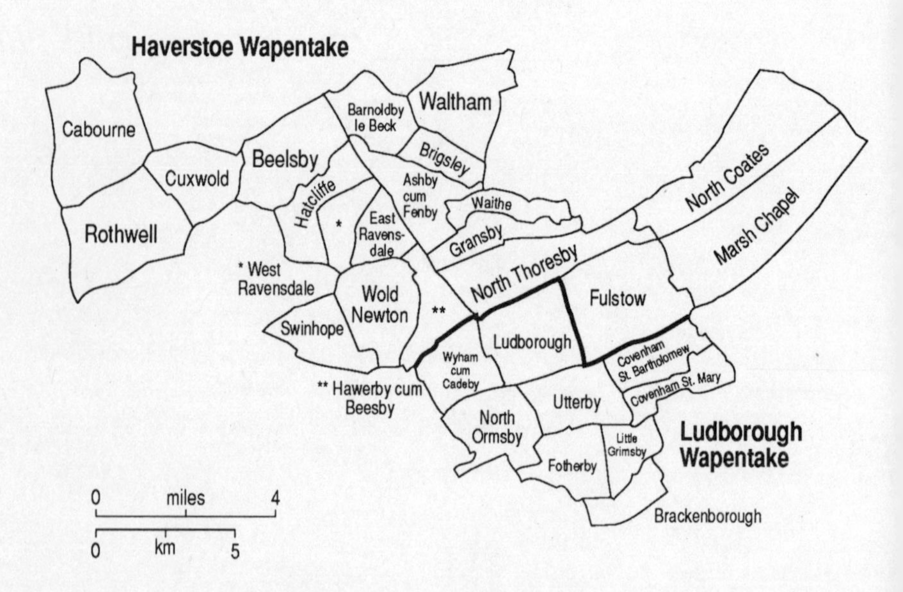

Based upon the 1963 Ordnance Survey four miles to one inch map, with the permission of the controller of Her Majesty's Stationery Office. © Crown Copyright.

Ludborough Wapentake

LUDBOROUGH WAPENTAKE

Ludeburc c.1115 LS, *-bur* 1265 Misc, *-burgh'* 1304 *DCAcct*, 1316 FA

Ludburc 1200, 1209 P, *-burg'* 1254 ValNor, 1276 RH, *-burgh* 1281 QW, 1327 *SR*, 1530 Wills ii, 1535 VE iv, 1602 *SewerLouth, -burghe* 1610 *ib, -boroughe* 1625 *Anc, -brough* 1526 Sub, 1663 *SewerLouth, -borht* 1537 LP xii, *-brovgh* 1610 Speed

Lueburc 1168, 1169 P, *-burga* 1202 Ass

Lubur 1202, 1203 P, *-burc'* 1202 Ass, *-burg'* 1238-41, 1242-43 Fees

Lutbur 1210 P

Lutheburg 1291 Tax, *-burgh'* 1298 Ass, *Loutheburgh'* 1298 ib, 1332 *SR*

Luthburgh 1428 FA

Lotheburgh(') 1343 NI, 1374, 1396 Peace

Lodeburg 1287 Ipm

Lodburgh' 1329 *Ass*

The forms are preceded or followed by some form of Latin *wapentagium* etc., though some later forms refer to Ludborough *Deanery*.

The wapentake takes its name from Ludborough *infra*, where its meeting-place must have been, though the exact site is unknown.

Brackenborough

BRACKENBOROUGH

Brachenberg 1086 DB, *-berch* c.1155 (1409) Gilb (p), *-bergha* c.1155 (1409) ib (p), *-berge* eHy2 (1409) ib (p), *-berga* Hy2 (1314) Ch, *Brachingberge* 1160-66 (1409) Gilb (p)

Brakenberga 1150-60 Dane (p), *-berge* 1200 P (p), 1202 Ass (p), 1207 Cur (p), 1218 Ass (p), 1219-27 Fulstow (p), 1303 FA, 1314 Ch, *-berg* 1274 *Alv*, 1288 Ipm, *-berche* 1166-75 Fulstow (p), *-berch* c.1200 (1409) Gilb (p), 1275 RH, *-bercg* lHy2 Dane (p), *-berhe* 1212 Fees (p), *-bergh*(') 1227 Cur (p), 1278 Ch, 1281 QW, 1299 Pat, 1306 Ipm *et freq* to 1428 FA, *-berge*

1272 Ass, *Brakynbergh* 1375 Ipm, *Brakingeberewe* 1272 FF
Bracunbergh', Bracumbergh' 1242-43 Fees
Brekenberga 1188, 1190, 1191, 1192, 1193, 1194 P all (p)
Brackenberg l12 Dane (p), *-berge* 1220 Cur (p)
Brackenburga c.1200 (1409) Gilb (p), *Brakenborgh* (sic) 1343 NI, *Brakynbrugh* 1517 LouthCA, *Brakyngburgh* 1431 FA, *Brakingburgh* 1486 Ipm
Brakenborough 1495 Ipm, *-burghe* 1543 LP xviii, *-burthe* (sic) 1550 Pat, *-borowe* 1565, 1567, 1614, 1615 *Harm, -bury* 1571 *MiscDon 64, Brackenburgh* 1655, 1674 *LindDep 42, -otherwise Brackenborough* 1700 *ib, -brough* 1706 *Hen, -borough* 1639, 1655, 1671, 1697 *ib et passim*

'The bracken-covered hill', *v.* **brakni**, **berg**, a Scand. compound. It is possible, however, that there was an OE ***bræcen**, cognate to ***brakni**, but the distribution pattern of p.ns. in Bracken- suggests a Scand. origin for ME **braken** 'bracken, fern'. Subsequent confusion with **burh** 'a fortified place' has taken place, hence the modern form Brakenborough. The name is represented today by Brackenborough Hall, which stands on a prominent hill.

Fellows-Jensen, SSNEM 152, draws attention to an identical name, Breckenbrough, PN YN 275, and to the Danish p.n. Bregnebjerg. Comparable also is Brackenber PN We 2 165.

BRACKENBOROUGH HALL is referred to as *That Capitall Messuage or Mancon House* 1700 *LindDep 42* and is *Brackenboro' House* 1824 O, *Brackenborough House* 1830 Gre, cf. *Hall Yard etc.* 1760 *Hen.* BRACKENBOROUGH WOOD is *Brackenborough Holt* 1828 Bry and is *the wood* 1697 *LindDep 42, the great -, little wood* 1700 *ib.* CHURCH CLOSE (lost), 1760, 1796, 1798 *Hen*, 1828 Bry; it was situated just beside the Hall. MOAT, cf. *Moat F.m* 1828 Bry; it is just to the west of the modern Hall. OAK HOLT (lost, approx. TF 335 905), 1828 Bry, *v.* **holt**. SHEPHERDS HO (lost, TF 335 902), 1828 ib.

Field-Names

Forms dated Hy2 (1314) and 1314 are Ch; 1327, 1332 are *SR*; 1353 *Cor*; 1495

Ipm; 1497 *StJ*; 1535-46, 1576-7, 1597-8 *MinAcct*; 1671, 1674, 1697, 1698, 1700 and 1782 *LindDep 42*; 1707, 1709, 1710, 1732, 1737, 1744, 1760, 1788, 1796 and 1798 Heneage; 1717, 1719 Hungate; 1864 *Terrier*.

(a) Arliss Cl 1760, 1796, 1798 (*Arlis his Furr close formerly in the Tenure or occupation of William Arlis deceased* 1697; named from the *Arliss* family, cf. John *Arlis* 1594 *BT*, William *Arlisse* 1707); N. -, S. Ash Garth 1760, North, South - 1796, 1798 (*Ash Close* 1698, *the Ash garth* 1700, *v.* **æsc**, **garðr**); Bottom Cl 1760, 1796, 1798; Bracken Hill 1760, 1796, 1798 (*Braken hill* 1698, *Brakenhill Close* 1700, *v.* **brakni**, **hyll** and cf. Brackenborough *supra*); East -, West Brick Cl 1760, 1796, 1798; Brooks Pingle, - Waste 1760 (named from the *Brook(e)s* family, cf. Joshua *Brookes* 1736 *BT*); Broughton Cl 1864 (presumably named from the *Broughton* family); Burnets East Cl, - West Cl, - Yard 1760 (named from the *Burnet(t)* family, cf. Frank *Burnett* 1732); Clay Cl 1760, 1796, 1798 (1737); Collison (sic) 1760, Collison Cl 1796, 1798 (*Collison* is presumably a family name); Corn Cl 1760, 1796, 1798, Lt - 1796, 1798 (*ye Corn Close* 1737); The Corner 1796 (once a house); Cow Cl 1760, 1796, 1798 (- *close* 1700); East Cl 1796, 1798; Gt -, Lt East Fd 1760, 1796, 1798 (*le Est Feldes* 1495, *Estefeld* 1576-7, *Eastfeild'* 1597-8, *the East Field* 1697, *little East Feild* 1700, *East Field* 1717, 1719, cf. *the East feild Closes* 1674, *v.* **ēast**, **feld**, one of the great fields of the village); Fotherby Parson's Cl 1796, 1798 (from the adjacent parish of Fotherby); (E. -, N. -, South) Furze Cl 1760, Furze Cl 1760, 1796, 1798, - in 2 parts 1796, East Furze Cl 1796, - Furze Cl 1798, Furze Pce 1796, North Furze or Fallow Cl 1796, 1798, South - or Corn Cl 1796, 1798 (*v.* **fyrs** and cf. Corn Cl *supra*); Grimsby Rd 1760; Grove 1760; Gunniss's Brick Yd 1788 (no doubt named from the *Gunniss* family, and cf. East -, West Brick Cl *supra*); Hassack Cl 1760, 1796, 1798 (*Hassack close* 1697, probably from the surn. *Hassack*); Hill Cl 1760, 1796, 1798 (*v.* **hyll**); Hills 1760, 1796, 1798; Lt Holt 1760, 1796, 1798, Low - 1796, 1798 (*v.* **holt** and cf. Brackenborough Wood *supra*)); (E. -, Middle -, W.) House Cl 1760, (East -, Middle -, West) House Cl 1796; Gt -, Lt Ings 1760, 1796, 1798 (*v.* **eng**); John Lings 1782 (possibly from the surn. *Ling(s)*, or *v.* **lyng**); Little Cl 1760, 1796, 1798; Low Fd 1760, 1796, 1798 (*the Low Feild* 1674); Market Cl 1796, 1798; New Plant 1760, Plantation of Oaks 1796, New Plantation 1798; Newmans 1760, 1796, 1798 (*new munn close* 1700, probably named from the *Newman* family, cf. Thomas *Newman* 1641 LPR); Old House Garth 1760, - Close & Garth 1796, the House - 1798 (not near a house on Plan); Ozier Holt 1796, Ozyer - 1798 (*v.* **oyser**, **holt**); Parson's Cl 1760; Pingle 1798, - East 1760, East Pingle 1796, 1798, Pingle north of the road 1796, the Pingle south of the Road 1796, West Pingle 1796, 1798 (*v.* **pingel**); Poor House Yard 1760, - etc. 1796, 1798; Gt -, Lt Pudge Hole 1760, - Podge Hole 1796, 1798 (*Loftes Inges otherwise*

Pudge hole 1674; perhaps alluding to a pit for the excavation of *pug* 'clay used for brick-making', *v. pug-hole* NED s.v. *pug* sb[3] and cf. Gunniss's Brick Yd *supra*); Scott Cl 1760, 1796, 1798 (named from the *Scott* family, cf. William *Scott* 1674 *BT*); Shaw Cl 1760, 1796, 1798 (named from the *Shaw* family, cf. Thomas *Shaw* 1700); Stripe 1760, 1796, 1798 (a narrow strip, *v.* **strīp**); West Cl 1796, 1798; E. -, W. White House Grd 1760, 1796, 1798; Wilsons House Grove Gard.[n] etc. 1796, Wilson's House Grove, Gard.[n] etc. 1798 (named from the *Wilson* family, cf. Robert *Wilson* 1744, Stephen *Wilson* 1796).

(b) *the becke* 1674 (*Brakynburghbek'* 1497, *v.* **bekkr**); *Bennetts close* 1697 (named from the *Bennet* family, cf. *M*[r] *Benett* 1710); *Lady Bowles close* 1697, *the two Bowles closes* 1700 (named from the *Bo(w)les* family, cf. Joseph *Boles* 1710); *Burton Inges* 1674 (named from the *Burton* family, cf. William *Burton* 1599 *BT*); *Comptons clay close* 1697 (*formerly in the Tenure or occupation of Richard Compton* 1697 and cf. Clay Cl in (a) *supra*); *Duchenges* 1314 (perhaps from **duce** 'a duck' and **eng** 'a meadow', in the pl.); *in campis de Brachenberga* Hy2 (1314), *in campo ville de Brakenbergh'* 1353 (*v.* **feld**); *the Geldinge close* (sic) 1674, *Goldinge close* 1697, *Golding Closes* 1700, - *Close* 1709 (forms from 1697 to 1709 appear to be from the surn. *Golding*, but the earliest reference so far found is to Richard *Goulding* 1775 *BT*; the 1674 spelling suggests a derivation from ME *geldyng* 'a castrated horse'); *Huberts Close* 1674 (presumably from the surn. *Hubert*); *the Laine* 1674, *the lane* 1700; *le landelawes* 1535-46 (probably to be taken literally, though the precise application of the term is uncertain); *Lofts-Ings* 1671 (probably from the surn. *Loft(s)* with **eng**, and cf. Gt -, Lt Pudge Hole *supra*); *Attemare* 1327, *atte Mare* 1332 both (p) (*v.* **(ge)mǣre** 'a boundary'); *the Mill Close* 1674; *Rods-Ings* 1671 (*v.* **eng**); *Walgraves Furr close* 1697 (*now or late in the Tenure or occupacon of Thomas Waldegrave* 1697, cf. Furze Cl in (a) *supra*, but note *furr* is a common dial. form of *far* in L); *le West Feldes* 1495, *the little Westfeild* 1671, *the little west feild* 1674 (*v.* **west**, **feld**, cf. Gt -, Lt East Fd in f.ns. (a) *supra*).

Covenham

COVENHAM

Covenham a1067 (c.1240) Whitby, (3x) 1086 DB, 1090-96 (c.1240) YCh ii, 1100-15 (m13) ib ii, 1100-15 (c.1400) Whitby, Hy1 (c.1400) ib, a1135 (c.1240) ib, 1136 (1312) YCh ii, 1145-48 (c.1240) Whitby, 1174-79 (c.1240) YCh ii, 1212 Fees, 1219, 1226 FF, 1231 Welles, 1238-43 Fees, 1254

ValNor, 1270 Pat, 1271 FF, 1276 RH, 1281 QW *et freq*, *Covanham* 1577 *Terrier*

Couenham 1086 DB, Hy2 (1409) Gilb, lHy2 Dane, 1191, 1192 P, l12 RA v, 1201, 1202, 1203, 1204 P all (p), 1231, 1246 FF, 1282 *Ass*, c.1300 *Monson et passim* to 1424 *Foster*, *Kouenham* 1187 (1409), Hy3 (1409) Gilb

Choveneham 1082 (1303) Pat

Couenam c.1115 LS

Covenom c.1155 (1409) Gilb

Coveham c.1115 LS, 1237, 1242-43 Fees, 1254 (14) Percy

Coueham 1191, 1193, 1194, 1195 P, 1196 ChancR, 1197, 1198, 1199 P, 1199 Memo, 1200, 1206, 1207, 1208, 1209, 1210, 1211, 1212, 1214 P, 1567, 1614 *Harm*, *Koueham* 1230 P *Couam* (*u* = *n*) 1383 Peace, *Conam* 1427 Cl, 1457 Pat, 1507 Ipm, 1526 Sub, 1601, 1625 *Terrier*, *-ame* 1574 *AD*, *-ham* 1519 DV i, 1532-33 ECP, *Coneham* 1576 LER

According to Ekwall, DEPN s.n., this is 'the homestead at a recess', *v.* **cofa**, **hām**. There does not seem to be any marked topographical feature here, which would fit the description of 'cove, a recess in the steep side of a hill, etc.', so it is more likely that the first el. is an OE pers.n. **Cōfa*, the probable first el. also of Coventry, PN Wa 160-61. Covenham, therefore, appears to mean 'Cōfa's homestead, village', *v.* **hām**.

Forms in *Conam* etc. show a loss of medial syllable and must represent a local pronunciation, apparently not heard today, but which is found in local documents into the 18th century.

COVENHAM ST BARTHOLOMEW

Covenham Sancti Bartholomei 1254 ValNor, - *Sancti Barth'i* 1291 Tax, - *Sancti Bartholomei* 1428 FA, - *Bartholmew* 1597, 1604 *BT*, - *Bartlemew* 1613 *ib*, - *St Bartholemew* 1661 *ib*, - *St Bartholomew* 1671 *Terrier*, 1824 O, 1828 Bry, *Couenham S. Bartholomei* 1270 RRGr

Conham Bartholemei 1461 Pap, - *Bartholomew* 1531 Wills iii, - *Barthme* 1562 *BT*, - *S. Bartholomew* 1723 SDL, *Connham Bartholme'* 1566 *BT*, *Conam Brthollmew* 1601 *Terrier*

The church is dedicated to St Bartholomew.

CAWTHORPE (lost)

Caletorp c.1115 LS, a1135 (c.1240) Whitby, 1175-84 *AddCh*, 112 RA v, 1226 FF (p), *Kalethorpe* Hy3 (1409) Gilb

Calthorp(') 1100-15 (m13) YCh ii, 1224 FF, 1227 RA i, Hy3 (15) Whitby, 1281 QW, (- *iuxta Couenham*) 1288 *Ass*, c.1300 *Monson*, 1319 *FF*, 1335 Percy, 1357 *Cor et passim* to ("by" *Covenham*) 1457 Pat, 1538-39 Dugd vi, 1547 Ormsby, 1556 Pat, 1574 *AD*, *-thorpe* 1335 Pat, 1391 *MM*, 1406 Pat, 1416 Ormsby, 1505 *MM*, 1538-39 Dugd vi, *-torp* 1212 Fees, 1219 FF (p), *Kalthorp*(') 1227 RA i, 1252 (14) Percy, *Kaltorpe* 1233 RA ii, *Calthrop* 1309, 1417 *MM*, 1553-55 ECP, *-thorup* 1577 *Terrier*, *North Calthorp'* c.1300 *Monson*

Cauthorp(*e*) 1335 Percy, 1559 *Harm*, 1696 *Tur*, 1715, 1718, 1761, 1835 *SewerLouth*, *-throppe* 1571 *Yarb*, *-thrope* 1574 *AD*

Chalthorp 1459 Ormsby

Cawthorp(*e*) ("or" *Calthorp*) 1477 Hast i, 1526 Sub, 1556 Pat, 1564 *MM*, 1565, 1566, 1567 *Harm*, 1573 *AD*, 1576 Saxton, 1586 *Foster et freq* to 1836 *SewerLouth*, *-thrope* 1585 Admin, *-thropp* (*by Covenham*) 1610 *DCLB*, 1671 *Red*, *-throp* 1703 *Terrier*

Cawlthorp 1507 Ormsby, c.1520 *MM*

Cowthropp 1668 *NW*

This appears to be identical with Cawthorpe Kest and Little Cawthorpe LSR, as well as Calthorpe Nf, DEPN s.n. Each is 'Kali's secondary settlement, dependent outlying farmstead' from the Scand. pers.n. *Kali* and **þorp**. It was presumably an outlying settlement of Covenham itself. Its site is unknown but it may well lie beneath the recently constructed Covenham Reservoir. From the 14th century onwards the forms show vocalisation of [l] to [w] in all three L examples.

BULL BANK, 1863 *LindDep Plan*, *a road called bullbank* 1812 *Terrier*, forming in part the boundary between Covenham St Bartholomew and Fulstow. The name is self-explanatory and Bull Bank is still a prominent raised road. COVENHAM GRANGE, 1535-37 LDRH, 1824 O, 1830 Gre and note *Covenham - Firma grangiæ* 1537-38 Dugd v; it was a **grange** of Kirkstead Abbey. HILL TOP FM is probably *Crowsticks* 1828 Bry. MANOR HO,

1797 *EnclA*. MIDDLE LANE (lost), 1828 Bry, 1863 *LindDep Plan*, *Midle Lane* 1834 *SewerLouth*; it led from Covenham St Mary to Hill Top Fm. NORRIS CORNER is named from the *Noris*(*s*) family, cf. Fred *Norris* 1933 Kelly. PLOUGH INN, *Plough* 1828 Bry. RECTORY, *the personage house* 1601, *ye Parsonage* 1634, 1664, 1706, 1724, - *parsonage* 1668, 1671, *the Parsonage* 1686, *the Parsonage house* 1697, *y^e^* - 1745, *Rectory House* 1812, 1864 all *Terrier*. SOUTH SYKE, - *Bottom Road*, 1797 *EnclA*, 1828 Bry, *South Sike Bottom Road* 1863 *LindDep Plan*, *le Suth sike* c.1300 *Monson*, *the southe sike* 1601 *Terrier*, - *South Sicke* 1739 *SewerLouth*, - *Sike* 1742 *ib*, *South Syke* 1797 *EnclA*, and *sowthsyk furlong* 1577, *ye South Sicke close* 1664, - *Sike close* 1668, 1671, 1724, - *Syke closes* 1686, - *sike close* 1706, - *Sike Close* 1745, *the southe sike gate* 1601[1], all *Terrier*, *South sike yate* 1732 *SewerLouth*, *the South Sike Gates* 1752 *SewerAlf*, 'the south ditch', *v*. **sūð**, **sīk**; there is a deep ditch, leading to the Louth Navigation today, on the south side of the road from the village to Covenham Grange. WESTFIELD HO is *Covenham Mill* 1824 O, 1830 Gre, *ye mill* 1697, - *milne* 1724, *ye Mill* 1745 all *Terrier*, cf. *Mulnewone* (for -*wong*) 1314 Ch (*v*. **vangr** 'a garden, an in-field'). The modern name commemorates one of the open fields of the village and is *campo occident'* 1420 *Goulding*, *the west feld* 1577, - *feild* 1601, *ye west Feilde* 1638, - *feild* 1724, - *field* 1686, - *Westfield* 1697, *the west Field* 1745 all *Terrier*, *Covenham Westfield* 1797 *EnclA*, *the Westfield* 1864 *Terrier*, self-explanatory, *v*. **west**, **feld**. WINDMILL, 1797 *EnclA*, now demolished and replaced by MILL HO, a restaurant.

COVENHAM ST MARY

Couenham B. Marie 1265 RRGr, - *Mary* 1625 *BT*

Covenham Sancte Marie 1254 ValNor, - *S. Marie* 1279 RRGr, - *Beate Marie* 1280 RSu, - *Sancte Marie* 1428 FA, - *Marie* 1535 VE iv, 1559 Pat, - *Mary* 1601 *BT*, - *St Mary* 1824 O, - *S^t^. Mary* 1828 Bry

Connham Mare 1574 *BT*, *Conham Mare* 1577 *Terrier*, *Conham St. Mary* 1723 SDL

The church is dedicated to St Mary.

COLD HARBOUR, - *Harbor* 1828 Bry; the site of the farm is exposed to east winds. FEN BRIDGE, *Austen fen bridges* 1732, - *brid* (sic) 1736, *austin fen brig* 1742, *awston fenn bridge* 1745 all *SewerLouth, austen fen bridge* 1752 *SewerAlf*, named from Austen Fen in the adjoining parish of Grainthorpe LSR. It is on the parish boundary. INGS LANE. NEWBRIDGE LANE, *New bridge Lane* 1663 *MiscSewer, the new bridge Lane* 1686, *newbrigg lane* 1690, *new brige lane* 1697, *newbridge Lain* 1745 all *Terrier, New Bridge Lane* 1828 Bry, 1837 *SewerLouth*, 1863 *LindDep Plan, Newbridge Lane Road* 1767 *EnclA* and cf. *new bryege* (sic) 1577, - *brigge* 1601 both *Terrier*, (*the*) *new bridge* 1732, 1726, *the New brigs* 1739, *new brig* 1742, *the New brig* 1745 all *SewerLouth*, self-explanatory; the Scandinavianized forms in *brig* etc. are noteworthy. POULTON DRAIN, 1833 *SewerLouth*, 1863 *LindDep Plan, poulton dike* 1745, cf. *Poūton* (sic) 1664, *Pouton* 1668, 1671, 1674, *poulton* 1690 all *Terrier, Poulton* 1825 *SewerAlf, Polton* 1835 *SewerLouth* and *Poulton bank* 1610 *ib.* This appears to be an old p.n. 'the farmstead by the pool', *v.* **pōl**, **tūn**, cf. Poulton Ch, Gl, K, La (DEPN s.n.), but the forms are late and no certainty is possible. POUND (lost, approx. TF 338 942), 1828 Bry, self-explanatory, *v.* **pund**; the more usual name in L is Pinfold. TREASURE LANE, 1863 *LindDep Plan, treaser lane* 1739 *SewerLouth, treasure lane* 1752 *SewerAlf*, obscure.

Field-Names

In (a) are included names from both Covenham St Bartholomew (CSB) and Covenham St Mary (CSM). Early forms of unspecified location are listed with Covenham St Bartholomew (b) names, as are those occasional spellings found in CSM Terriers for names well represented in Terriers for CSB. Spellings dated Hy2 (1409) and Hy3 (1409) are Gilb; 112 RA v; 1219 are FF; 1250-51 RRG; c.1300 *Monson*; 1308 *MM*; 1314 Ch; 1332 *SR*; 1374, 1383 Peace; 1417, 1420, 1421 *Goulding*; 1497 *StJ*; 1537-9 LDRH; 1577[1], 1601[1], 1634, 1638[1], 1664[1], 1668[1], 1671[1], 1686[1], 1697[1], 1706, 1724, 1745[1], 1812, 1864[1] are *Terrier* (CSB); 1577[2], 1601[2], 1625, 1638[2], 1664[2], 1668[2], 1671[2], 1686[2], 1690, 1697[2], 1703, 1745[2], 1822, 1864[2], are *Terrier* (CSM); 1590 *MiscSewer*; 1610, 1644, 1648, 1665, 1669, 1686, 1697[3], 1712, 1715, 1718, 1726, 1732, 1736, 1739, 1742, 1745[3], 1835, 1837, and 1839 are *SewerLouth*; 1752, 1825, 1838 are *SewerAlf*; 1776 *Tur*; 1797 *EnclA*; 1799 *Harm*; 1804, 1811, 1823, 1832, and 1839 are *DCLeases*; 1863 *LindDep Plan.*

(a) Acre Flg 1797 (*v.* **æcer**, **furlang**); Addle Croft 1797 (*addlecroft* 1742, from dial. *addle* 'a dunghill' (OE **adela** 'filth'), and **croft**); Andrew's Hill 1797 (from the surn. *Andrew(s)*); Bakers Cl 1797 (named from the *Baker* family, cf. John *Baker* 1332 *SR*); for laying a Bridge over the Beck 1837, the beck 1864[2], The Beck 1863 (*v.* **bekkr**); Bottoms Cl 1797 (cf. *the bottom close* 1577[2], y^e *bottom closes* 1601[2], *v.* **botm**); Burnt Cl, - Cl or Bone Acres 1797; Butteram Bridge 1752, Boterham bridge 1835 (*Butteram bridg* 1732, *butteram* - 1736, *Butteram bridje* 1742, *Buttram brig* 1745, *v.* **brycg**; the forms are too late to propose a convincing etymology for *Butteram*, but, since *ham, am* are frequently found as late reflexes of **holmr**, the name *might* mean 'raised land amidst marshes which provides rich pasture', *v.* **butere**, **holmr**); Cabbage Garth 1797 (*v.* **garðr**); Cawthorpe East Field 1804 (cf. *Calthorup feld* 1577[2], *Calthrop* -, *Cawthorp feild* 1601[2], *Cawthorp field* 1601[1], *Calthrop Fielde* 1638[1], named from the lost *Cawthorpe supra*); Coney Green 1797 (*v.* **coningre** 'a rabbit warren'); Covenham Eastfield 1797, the East and West Fds of Cawthorpe and Covenham 1776 (*in oriental' campo* 1420, *the est feld* 1577[1], *the Este felde* 1577[2], *the east feild* 1601[1], y^e - 1668[1], 1668[2], y^e *eastfeild* 1664[2], 1671[1], 1671[2], y^e *East field* 1686[1], 1690, 1706, *the* - 1686[2], y^e *Eastffeld* 1697[1], *the East feild* 1697[2], *East* - 1703, y^e - 1724, - *Field* 1745[1], *the Est field* (sic) 1745[2], y^e *East feild of Couenham Ma'* 1601[2], *Covenham St Marys eastfield* 1664[2], *v.* **ēast**, **feld**); Covenham St Mary westfield 1822[1], - West field 1864[2] (*the weste felde* 1577[2], *the westfeilde* 1601[2], *the west feild* 1625, 1703, y^e - 1664[2], 1668[2], 1671[2], *the west field* 1686[2], y^e *West field* 1690, *the West feild* 1697[2], - *Field* 1745[2], *v.* **west**, **feld** and cf. Westfield Ho *supra*); Covinham Sike Gates 1752, Covenham Syke 1797, 1799 (*Couenham syke* 1417, *Connham sycke* 1577[2], *Conam sike* 1601[1], *Conham* - 1601[2], *Covenham sykes* 1610, - *sike* 1668[2], 1703, - *Sicke* 1664[2], - *sick* 1671[2], - *syke* 1690, *Coven-sike* 1697[2], *Couenham sike* 1745[2], *v.* **sík**, cf. Syke Cl *infra*); the Cow Pasture 1797; Craikmoor Pingle 1797, craikmoor pingle 1812 (from **kráka** 'a crow, a raven' and perhaps **mōr** 'marsh', with **pingel**); Fladels Cl 1797 (*fleydayles* 1664[2], *fleadales* 1668[2], *the fleydales* 1671[2], the first el. is uncertain; the second is **deill** 'a share, a portion of land', as elsewhere in this parish); Four Acres 1797; Fur Cl, the Furr Cl 1776 (*fur(r)* is often a dialect form of *far* in L but cf. the foll.); Furze Cl 1797; the Goat 1835 (1703, 1745[2], y^e *gote* 1601[2], y^e *goate* 1664[2], y^e *goate* 1664[2], y^e *Goate* 1671[2], *the Goote* 1712, 1718 *the gote, the gote banck* 1745[3], *v.* **gotu**); Good Acres Homestead 1797 (probably from the surn. *Goodacre*); Great Cl 1797; High Bridge 1825 (cf. *terram Petri de Ponte* Hy3 (1409), *ad pontem, atte brigg'* 1332 (p), *v.* **brycg**); Hinds Cl 1797 (named from the *Hind* family, cf. William *Hynde* 1580 *Inv*); Hoe Cl 1797 (*Hou* Hy3 (1409), *v.* **haugr**); Home Cl 1797; ye Hors Bridge (sic) 1752; Ings sewer 1863 (*v.* **eng**); Ingwell Hills Cl 1797; Land Cl, - Pingle 1797 (*Land Close end* 1668[1], - *End* 1745[1], - *close End* 1671[1], *land close end*

1697[1], 1724, *the Land Close yate* 1686[2], *y[e] land close gate* 1690, - *Close gate* 1697[2], *land Close-gayt* 1703, *ye Landclose gate* 1745[2], *v.* **land** in the sense 'a strip of arable in the common field', **clos(e)**, **pingel**, **ende**, **geat**); Lawers Cl 1797; Lokings Cl, - Garth, Locking Pingle 1797 (named from the *Locking(e)* family, cf. William *Lockinge* 1642 LPR); Long Cl 1797; Long Pingle 1797 (cf. Pingle *infra*); Louth Rd (*lowthe gayt* 1597[1], *Lowth way* 1625, self-explanatory, *v.* **gata**); Lurborough Lane End (sic) 1797 (*Ludborugh laines end* 1668[1], *Ludbrough lanes* - 1697[1], 1706, 1724, *Ludbrough Lain End* 1745[1], leading to the parish of Ludborough); High -, Low Mare 1797 (*v.* **(ge)mǣre** 'a boundary, land on a boundary', as elsewhere in this parish); John Motley's Nine Acres 1863 (named from a member of the *Motley* family, cf. George *Motley* 1825. The land may have been a medieval assart comprising nine selions, cf. perhaps *Niacros* (sic) Hy3 (1409), *v.* **nigon**, **æcer**); Munsh or Monks Gdn 1797 (Alvingham Priory held land here); Myers Cl, - Corner, Myers or Willows's Cl 1797 (probably from the surn. *Myers* cf. *pratum Willi le Mire* c.1300, *v.* **mýrr** and Willows Cl *infra*); Narferth Lane 1752; New Drain 1863 (from Utterby); Norman Leys (Close) 1797 (near the parish boundary; *Norman(s)* is found elsewhere as a variant of *No Man's* for boundary land, e.g. Normans Hill, PN Wa 357, *v.* **nān-mann**); North Park 1797; North Syke 1797, 1864[1], north syke close 1812 (*north syk* 1577[1], *y[e] north Sicke* 1671[1], *the North Syke* 1686[1], 1697[1], *the North Sicke* 1739, *y[e] North Sike* 1745[3], *The north Sike Close* 1668[1], 1671[1], *The North-syke* - 1697[1], *The North sike close* 1706, *The north* - 1724, *The northsike Close* 1745[1], *north syke gayt* 1577[1], *the Northe Sike gait* 1601[1], *north sicke gate* 1625, *ye North syke* - 1686[1], - *North Syke gate* 1697[1], *ye north sike* - 1706, 1745[1], *ye north side* - (sic) 1671[1], - *sidegate* (sic) 1724, *v.* **norð**, **sík** 'a ditch, a stream', **gata**, cf. South Syke *supra*); Old Garth 1797 (*v.* **garðr**); Pan Cl 1797 (perhaps cf. *Panewange* Hy3 (1409), *v.* **vangr**); Parker's Home Cl (named from the *Parker* family, cf. Robert *Parker* 1605 *Inv*); Petty Croft 1797 (probably from the surn. *Petty*, with **croft**); Pingle, Pingle Furze 1797 (*v.* **pingel**, **fyrs**); the Rectorage Garth (sic) 1822[1] (*v.* **garðr**, cf. Rectory *supra*); the Samrides, Ploughed Sumrides 1797 (perhaps alluding to a stream flowing in summer, *v.* **sumor**, **rið**); the Sands Cls 1804, 1818, 1823, 1832, 1839 (*v.* **sand**); Sheep Gate Cl 1797 (*v.* **shep-gate**); Shift Cl, - Willows 1797 (cf. The Willows *infra*); 6 Acre or New Bridge Cl, Six Acres 1797; South Cl (Bottom) 1797; the Strait Bank 1752, the Strait, Strait Cl 1797, the East & West Straits 1838 (*Cawthorpe and Covenham straighte* 1590, *the great stone strayhte* 1610, *Strait* 1686[2], *y[e] strait* 1690, *the Strait* 1697[2], (*the*) *Strate* 1736, 1739, 1742, 1745[2], - *bank* 1742, *the Strait banck* 1739, 1745[3] and note the appellative use in *certaine other straightes in some of the said towneshipps* 1590. The name occurs in several parishes in north-east L, though the noun is not recorded in dictionaries. Its sense, however, is clear from a reference dated 1774 *Hill* 22/1/9/3/1.

Lorborrow (i.e. Ludborough) *has a right to run water into Fulstowe and comes into it at 3 different places, where in Fulstow there are Brick Tunnells called Streights.* There follows a description of their size. *Straight, Streight, Strait* etc. is apparently a developed sense of *strait* NED B sb.); Sutcope Lane (sic) 1839 (*Settecope* Hy3 (1409), *v.* **set-copp** 'a flat-topped hill'); Syke Cl 1797, Sykes Sewer 1863 (*the syke, syk furlong* 1577[1], *the sike* 1601[1], *y[e] sike, - furlong, y[e] sik Lane* 1634, *Sykes Close* 1686[1], *the Sikes* 1736, *v.* **sīk** and cf. North Syke and South Syke *supra*); 3 Acre Cl or Oat Cl 1797; Three Acres 1797; Town end Cl 1797; The Town Street 1864; Utterby Road 1797 (self-explanatory); (Middle -, North) West Cl 1797; Wilkinsons Cl 1797 (named from the *Wilkinson* family, cf. Robert *Wilkinson* 1575 *Inv*); Willows Cl 1797 (probably named from the *Willows* family, cf. Edward *Willows* 1797; *v.* also Myer's Cl *supra*); the Willows 1776 (*yarbrught wylloyes* (sic) 1577[2], *Yarbroughe willoughes, - willowes* 1601[2], *Yarbrough Willows* 1664[2], 1668[2], *a little pingle called by the name of willows* 1703 (*v.* **wilig** and cf. *y[e] willas bridg* (b) CSB *infra*; presumably these were willows on the boundary with Yarburgh LSR).

COVENHAM ST BARTHOLOMEW

(b) *Almaresholm* 1219, *Armerholm'* c.1300, *alomer hedland* 1577[1], *Allimer headland* 1686[1], *Allimore headland* 1697[1], *Allimere headland* 1706, *Allimers headland* 1724, *allemar Headland* 1745[1] (from the ME pers.n. *Almar* (from OE *Ælfmǣr* or OE (Angl) *Aldmār*) and **hēafod-land**); *toftum voc' arderntoft'* 1417 (*v.* **toft**; the first el. is probably a surn.); *at aslam* (sic) 1601[1]; *Austen medow* 1601[1]; *bartil(l)mew hedland* 1577[1], *Bartlemew headland* 1601[1], *Bartholomew - 1634*, *Bartholomews -* 1668[1], *St Bartholomews -* 1671[1], *Bartholowe -* (sic) 1686[1], *Barthol. head long* (sic) 1697[1], *Bartholomews headland* 1706, *- head Land* 1724, 1745[1] (named from St Bartholomew's church and **hēafod-land**); *Ryc' barton close* 1577[1]; *Biscopecroft* 1314 (*v.* **biscop**, **croft**; the Dean and Chapter of Lincoln Cathedral held land in Covenham); *bottom gayt, - hyll, - wong* 1577[1], *bottom gaite* 1601[1], *bottome gate* 1625, *Bottom -* 1664[2], *Bottam Gate* 1668[2], *bottom gate* 1703 (*v.* **botm**, **gata**, **hyll**, **vangr**); *braymors* 1577[1], *Bramiers* (sic) 1601[1], *Bramers* 1671[1], 1686[1], 1697[1], 1745[1], *Brmers* (sic) 1724 (*v.* **breiðr** 'broad', **mōr**[1] in the sense 'marshland', the second el. confused with **(ge)mǣre** 'boundary, boundary land' in some forms); *Bryal* (?) *park Stock* 1742; *iuxta riuulum de Caldewelle* Hy3 (1409) (*v.* **cald**, **wella**); *the Car* 1601[1] (*v.* **kjarr**); *Caster bank* 1697[1], *Caster bank* 1706, *Caster Bank* 1745[1] (the reference to Caistor is uncertain); *Ceppeland* 1250-51; *y[e] Church bank* 1638[1], *church bancke* 1664[1], *y[e] church Bancke* 1664[2], *church banke* 1668[1], *a church banck* 1671[1], *a Churchbank* 1686[1], *Church bank* 1690, 1703,

1745[2], *a Church-bank* 1697[1], *Church Bank* 1697[2], *y[e] Churchbanks* 1706, *y[e] Church bankes* 1724 (described as a *bancke belonging to y[e] Church* 1638[1]), *y[e] church greene* 1668[1] (*v.* **grēne**[2]); *y[e] churchway* 1664[1], *y[e] church way* 1671[1], *the Church* - 1686[1], 1697[1], *y[e]* - 1706, 1724, *kirkyate de Couenham* 1374 (p), (*v.* **cirice, kirkja, geat**); *Rob[t] Clarkes Close* 1671[1], *Henry Clarke Close* 1686[1], *Clarks close* 1697[1], *a Close late Robert Clarke* 1706, *Robert Clark Close* 1724; *campum de Couenham* Hy2 (1409), *Couenhamfeld'* 1497, *Conam fielde* 1601[1], *Covenham feild* 1610, 1703, *Couenham field* 1745[2], *Covenham St Bart field* (sic) 1668[1] (*v.* **feld**); *Conisam Cros yeat* 1745 ('the road to *Conisholme Cross* (in Fulstow *infra*)', *v.* **gata**); *Conisome Lane* 1742 ('lane leading to Conisholme (LSR)'); *Covenham closes* 1610; *in pratis de Couenham* 1308 ('in the meadows of Covenham', *v.* **mǣd**); *Cuke furr* 1577[1], *Cooke furres* 1601[1] (probably named from the *Cook* family and **furh** in the pl.; Robert *Cook* is named in 1577[1]; cf. also Robert *Cook* 1575 *Inv*); *Damwell, Dam wels* 1577[1], *Damwels* 1601[1], 1634, *Damwells* 1601[1], *Damwils* 1634, *Damrills* (sic) 1638[1] (*v.* **damme (dammr)** 'a pond', **wella**, cf. Damwells in Ludborough *infra*); *Dettmere gren* 1577[1], *Detmergrene* (sic) 1601[1], *Depney greene nowke* 1634, - *Nouke* 1638[1] (*v.* **grēne**[2]; the variety of forms *Dettmere, Depney*, further confused by *Depmere* in (b) CSM *infra*, allows no certain explanation); *Will' Dixson Close* 1745[3]; *Elkington Horne* 1601[1] (described in the Terrier as being between Cawthorpe & Wragholme); *Robert Elrishe close end* 1601[1] (Robert *Elrishe* is named in the document); *Eybank* 1715, *the Eay bank* 1742 (*v.* **ēa** 'river', **banke**); *the flintins* 1601[1]; *Fulstow hedge* 1601[1], 1625, 1671[1], 1724, 1745[1], - *Hedg* 1638[1], - *hedg* 1686[1], 1697[1], - *Hedge* 1706, *fulstow stret* 1577[1], *Fulstow strete* 1601[1], *Ful stow streete* 1638[1] (from the neighbouring parish of Fulstow with **hecg** and **strǣt**); *y[e] furlong meare, y[e] Towne side* 1638[1] (*v.* **furlang, (ge)mǣre**); *the furres* 1625, *y[e] Furrs* 1634 (*v.* **furh** 'a furrow' in the pl.); *the garewong* 1577[1], *gare wong* 1686[1] (*v.* **geiri** 'a triangular plot', **vangr**); "grange in" *Cawthorppe* 1537-9 (it was a **grange** of Alvingham Priory); *greatley mare, - meare* 1577[1], *Great la mare* (sic), *Greatlamare* 1601[1], *great-lamare* 1625, *great la mere* 1634, 1638[1], *Greatley mare* 1668[1], *great La mare* 1686[1], *Great lea mere* 1697[1], *Greatly Mare* 1706, *Greatle mare* 1724, *greatleamear* (sic) 1745[1] (*v.* **grēat**, dial. **lea**, *ley* (OE **lēah**) 'grassland, pasture') with **(ge)mǣre**); *Grenegate* 1601[1], *greene gate* 1625, *Grene gate* 1634, *greene* - 1638[1] (*v.* **grēne**[2], **gata**); *ad aulam* 1332 (p), *Hall furs* (sic) 1668[1], *hall furrs* 1697[1], 1724, - *forrs* 1745[1] (*v.* **hall, furh**); *the hall hedland* 1577[1], *the Haull headland* 1601[1] (*v.* **hēafod-land**); *Hare wong* 1668[1], *Harewong* 1671[1], *Hare wong bank* 1697[1] (*v.* **hara** 'a hare', **vangr**); *3 stong Caled the harpe* 1577[1], *the harp* 1601[1] (probably alluding to the shape, cf. Fulstow f.ns. *infra*); *haslo* 1577[1] (perhaps 'the hazel-covered hill', *v.* **hæsel, haugr**); *the haull garthe* 1601[1] (*v.* **hall, garðr**); *a headland and his fellow* 1601[1] (presumably referring to two adjacent headlands, with *fellow* in the sense 'a match, a counterpart', cf. for the same name PL L **2** 12, PN L **3** 12); *the hey -, the heye -, the hye gayt* 1577[1], *Heigate, Heygate* 1601[1], *y*[e] *hie gate* 1634, *y*[e] *high -* 1634, 1638[1], 1668[1], 1724, 1745[1], *- Gate* 1724, *the high gate* 1686[1], *the high-gate* 1697[1], *y*[e] *highgate* 1697[1], 1706 (*v.* **hēah** in the sense 'important', **gata**); *Hill* 1668 (described as *3 lands*); *hommer hill* 1601[1] (*v.* **hyll**); (*short*) *hunters* 1577[1], 1577[2], *land lienge on -, - in hunters* (sic) 1601[1], *short hunters* 1625, *hunters* 1690, *a place called huntus* 1745[2] (obscure; the name occurs in both CSB and CSM Terriers); *William Kerman Close* 1745[1]; *kow le close* 1601[1] (*v.* **cū, lea** (OE **lēah**) 'grassland, pasture'); *Lache* Hy3 (1409), *y*[e] *lack* 1634 (*v.* **læcc** 'a stream, a bog'; the 1634 form appears Scandinavianized); *Langemare* Hy3 (1409) (*v.* **lang, (ge)mǣre**); *Lariwate* Hy3 (1409) (obscure); *letforth* c.1300 (*v.* perhaps **(ge)lǣt** 'confluence', **ford**); *Lodney barrs* 1718 ('bars or toll-gates of Ludney (in Grainthorpe LSR)', *v.* **barre**); *y*[e] *Low sike* 1634, *y*[e] *Low Sike* 1668[1], *y*[e] *low Sicke* 1671[1], *y*[e] *low Syke* 1686[1], 1697[1], *y*[e] *Low sike* 1706, *y*[e] *low Sick* 1724, *ye low Sike* 1745[1] (*v.* **sík**); *Mastall or the theryng ground* (sic) 1577[1], *Marstele* 1577[2] (for *Mastal* cf. *Mill Mastal butts* in Goxhill f.ns. (b) and *le Marstal'* in Killingholme f.ns. (b), PN L **2**, 133 and 209, where it is suggested that this is derived from OE ***mær(e)stall** 'a pool' or the like; Mr John Field draws attention to the fact that *theryng* is listed as a synonym in Norfolk of *tathing* (Adams 163). This seems to refer to the folding of sheep in an enclosure for eight to ten days in order to bring about an improvement of the soil by the dung, urine and trampling of the animals. Presumably *theryng ground* was such an enclosure); *neel furrs* 1577[1], *neale furrs* 1601[1] (*v.* **furh** in the pl.; the first el. is no doubt the surn. *Neal*); *new close* 1625, *New-close* 1634, *new close end* 1668[1], 1671[1], 1686[1]; *Nordfen* Hy3 (1409) (*v.* **norð, fen**); *The north close* 1664[1]; *the northe dike* 1601[1] (*v.* **norð, dík**); *the northfeld* 1577[1] (*v.* **norð, feld**); *parson slackes* 1577[1], *the person -* (sic) 1601[1], *parsons slackes* 1625, *Parson -* 1634, *Parson-slacks* 1638[1], *y*[e] *parsonage slackes* 1668[1], *Parsonage slacks* 1697[1], *- Slacks* 1724, *ye Parsonage Slacke* 1745[1] (*v.* **persone, slakki**, the latter being rare in L, cf. *Potterdale slacke* and *Elbrough Slack* PN L **2**, 27 and 132); *Richard Peacokes close* 1601[1]; *peers hyll* 1577[1] (the reading is doubtful), *Peers Haile* 1601[1] (*v.* **halh**; the first el. is perhaps the pers.n. or surn. *Peers*); *pinder bank* 1697[1], *Pinder -* 1724 (*v.* **pindere**, as an occup. n. or surn.); *the quenes stret* (sic) 1577[1]; *Raulotemares* Hy3 (1409) (from the ME pers.n. *Raulot*, an *-ot* derivative of OFr *Rau(l)f*, itself derived from Frankish *Radulf*, and the pl. of **(ge)mǣre** 'a boundary, boundary land'); *Regate* 1250-51; *Rimstone* 1601[1], *Ry...ston* 1577[1], *y*[e] *Furlonge called Rumpston* 1638[1]; *Rose leas* 1601[1], 1668[1], 1724, *a Close cald Rose leas* 1671[1], *Rose Leas* 1686[1], *a close called Rose leas* 1697[1], *Rose Leas* 1706, *- Leays* 1745[1] (perhaps from the surn. *Rose* and the pl. of **lea** (OE **lēah**) 'grassland, pasture'); *Sand gayt* 1577[1], *Sandgate, -gaite* 1601[1] (*v.* **sand, gata**); *Scallow* 1686, 1706, 1745[1], *skawlow hill* (sic) 1577[1], *Skallo hill* 1601[1], *Scallow* - 1625, 1671[1], 1724, *Skallow hill*, - *Hill* 1686[1], 1697[1], 1706, 1745[1] (perhaps 'hill with a shieling', *v*. **skáli**, **haugr**, with tautologous **hyll**, cf. Scalehaw Hill, PN YW **6** 161, though in PN L **3**, 4, s.n. The Scallow Hall, it is probably wrongly suggested that the meaning is 'the bald hill', *v*. **skalli**, **haugr** and note also *Scalawe* PN L **2** 157. Probably 'the hill with a shieling' is the more likely of the two interpretations); *Simundedeile* 1314 (*v*. **deill**; the first el. is the ME pers.n. *Simund*, probably from ON *Sigmundr*, though it should be noted that in the 14th-cent it could stand for an Anglo-French form of *Simon*); *Skypwythland*, *ter' nuper Thome de Skypwyth'* 1421 (*v*. **land**); *Slede de Couam* (sic, for *Conam*) 1383 (p) (*v*. **slǣd** perhaps in the dial. sense 'low flat marshy ground'); *Stonfurlang* 1219, *Stanfur(r)s* 1577[1], *Stanfurres*, *Stanfoures* 1601[1], *stanfoures*, *ye stanfurs* 1634, *ye stanfoures* 1638[1], *Stanforrowes* 1668[1], *standfurrow* (sic) 1686[1], *Standfurrows* 1697[1], *Standforrows* 1706, *Standforrows* 1724, 1745[1], *Standfowers* (sic) 1745[1], (*v*. **stān**, **furlang**, **furh** (in the pl.); the same name is also well-evidenced in CSM f.ns. (b)); *Stewant* Hy3 (1409) (obscure); *the stintinges* 1601[1], *y^e^* -, *the stintings* 1625, 1634, 1638[1] (*v*. **stinting** 'a portion of common meadow set apart for one man's use'); *the Stock* 1577[1] (*v*. **stocc**); *ye Tack land* 1638[1]; *thew close* 1601[1]; *Thoresholm* 1250-51, c.1300, *thursom* 1577[1], *Thursholme*, *thursome* 1601[1], *Thorsam* 1686[1], *thurshom* -, *thursom gayt*, *thurson yayt* 1577[1], *Thoresome gate* 1634, *Thorsam Gate* 1668[1], 1724, - *gate* 1745[1], *Thorsham* - 1697[1], *Thoram* - (sic) 1706 (the first el. is the pers.n. ON *Þorir*, ODan *Thorir*, *Thurir* with **holmr** 'a piece of higher land in marshes' and **gata**); *Thoruoithesich* 112 (*v*. **sīc**; *Thoruoithe-* might be a scribal error for *Thoruorthe-*, in which case it would be from the ON pers.n. *Þorvarðr* or **Þorfrøðr*); *the town end* 1697[1], *ye Townes* - 1724, *ye towns End* 1745[1]; *Two Marfoures* 1638[1] ('the two boundary-furrows', *v*. **marfur**); *Utterbe hedge* 1577[1], *Utterby Hedg* 1638[1], *utterby hedg* 1697[1], *Vtterby hedge corner* 1625 (*v*. **hecg**; Utterby is an adjoining parish); *la Waise* Hy3 (1409) (*v*. **wæsce**); *Walbodecroft* 112 (*v*. **croft**; the first el. is a pers.n., ContGerm **Walbode*); *John waters close* 1601[1]; *Water Webster close* 1601[1] (named from one *Walter Webster*); *le West dik'* 1308 (*v*. **dík**); *Wekin* -, *Wykyn holue gayt* 1577[1], *Wikam Holme* 1601[1], *Wak engholme*, *Wekenholme*, *Weken holme gate* 1634, *winkingholme* 1668[1], 1745[1], *winkingholme* 1671[1], *Winking holm* 1686[1], 1697[1], *Winkingholme* 1706, 1724 (obscure; the name is also recorded in CSM f.ns. (b) *infra*); *ye wilas bridg* 1732, *the Willas brigs* 1739, *Willas brig* 1742 (*v*. **brycg**, perhaps cf. the Willows in (a) *supra*); *Wrong Landes* 1577[1], *wronglandes* 1601[1] (*v*. **vrangr**, **land**).

COVENHAM ST MARY

(b) *alamar headland* 1625 (*v.* **hēafod-land** and *Almaresholm* in (b) CSB *supra*); *bartholmew headland* 1625, *St Bartholomews headland* 1664[2], *Barthelemews* - 1668[2], *Bartholomews headland* 1671[2], *Bartlemew headland* 1690, *Bartholomew head-land* 1697[2] (the same name occurs in CSB f.ns. (b) *supra*); *Blackdyke* 1610, *blacke dike* 1625 (*v.* **blæc**, **dík**); *Boddam hill, Bottom Hill* 1664[2], *boddam hill, Bottam Hill* 1668[2], 1671[2], *Boddam hill* 1671[2], *bottom* - 1686[2], 1690, 1697[2], *Bottomhill or Bear hole* 1745[2]; (cf. *bottom gayt* etc. in CSB (b) *supra*); *buth gate* 1703; *Calthorup sycke* 1577[2], *Calthorp -, Calthrop syke, Cawthrop sike* 1601[2] (*v.* **sík** and *Cawthorpe supra*); *Connham gate* 1577[2] ('the road to Covenham', *v.* **gata**); *Cottger wong* (sic) 1703 (*v.* **vangr**; *Cottger* is a variant of *cottager*); *Daue hyll* 1577[2], *Davy hill* 1601[2], *dauils* 1625 (*v.* **hyll**); *depemer grene noucke* 1577[2], *depmer green nooke* 1601[2] (*v.* *Dettmere gren* in (b) CSB *supra*); *ye Feilde of Covenham St Marie* 1638[1]; *Goute mare* 112, *Goake mare* 1664[2], 1668[1], 1671[2], *Goak mar* 1686[2], *Gockmare* (sic) 1690, *goake mear* 1697[2], *a place Called gockmore* 1745[2] ('Gauti's boundary, land on a boundary', from the ON pers.n. *Gauti*, ODan *Gøti* and **(ge)mǣre**; the first el. has later been replaced by ME *gōk* 'a cuckoo', probably as a result of popular etymology); *the Grene* 1577[2], *greene gate* 1625 (*v.* **grēne**[2] 'a grassy spot, a village green'); *Thomas Hardy close* 1625; *Honedayle* (for *Houedayle*) 1250-51, *Le Heuedaylle* 1308, *head daile* 1625 (*v.* **hēafod**, **deill**; *Houedayle* is probably a Scand. compound from **hǫfuð**, cognate with OE **hēafod**, and **deill**); *high gate, heighgate* 1625, *ye high gate* 1664[2], 1690, 1697[1], - *Gate* 1668[2], *high Gate* 1671[2], *the high gate* 1686[2], 1745[2] (*v.* **hēah**, **gata**; the name occurs also in CSB f.ns. (b)); *the hye waye* 1577[2], *the highe way* 1601[2], *the high waye* 1638[1], *ye highway* 1664[2], - *high way* 1668[2], 1671[2], *the high way* 1697, 1703, *highway* 1690; *Koue lees* 1577[1], *Cow leas* 1601[2], *Cow leas* 1668[2], *Cowlease* 1671[2], *Cow Leas* 1686[2], *Cow lease* 1690, *Cow Leeze* 1697[1], *Cow leaze* 1703, *Cowleas* 1745[2] (*v.* **cū**, **lea** 'grassland, pasture', in the pl.; cf. *kow le close* in (b) CSB *supra*); *Lambe Coates* 1664[2], 1671[2] (self-explanatory); *low mer hyll* 1577[1], *loumer hyll* 1577[2], *loomer hill* 1601[2], *Lumber hill* 1668[2], *Lumber hill* 1671[2], 1686[2], *Loumber hill* 1690, 1697[2], *Lombury hill* 1703, *Lounbrough hill* 1745[1] (the forms are too varied to suggest a convincing etymology); *louthe wathe* 1577[2], *louth wath* 1601[2] (presumably 'the ford leading to Louth (LSR)', *v.* **vað**); *low Sicke* 1625, *the low syke* 1686[2], *ye low syke* 1690, *low sike* 1697[2], *ye low sike* 1703, *ye Low Sike* 1745[2] (*v.* **sík**); *the mareforde* (sic) 1577[2], *ye Marfare* 1601[2], *the marfur* 1625 ('the boundary furrow', *v.* **marfur**); *the mares* 1577[2] (*v.* **(ge)mǣre** 'a boundary', in the pl.); *the North field* 1686[2]; *north street* 1625; *the parsonage* 1625, *ye Parsonage house* 1664[2], *ye Parsonage* 1668[2], 1671[2], *The Parsonage House* 1686[2], - *house* 1690, *The Parsonage House* 1745[2] (of Covenham St Mary); *ye parsonage medow*

1671[2]; (*the lytell*) *preste mare* 1577[2], y^e *preestmare*, y^e *litle preest mare* 1601[2], y^e *preist mare* 1664[2], 1668[2], *preist mare* 1671[2], *preise mare* (sic) 1686[2], *priest mere green* 1703, *priestmare green* 1745[2] (*v.* **prēost, (ge)mǣre**); *One Grein calld Reisman* 1690; *the resome gate* 1625; *Sant mare heade londe* 1577[2], *one headland called St Mary headland* 1601[2], *St Marys Headland* 1664[2], 1668[2], *St Marys headland* 1671[2], *Snt Mary Head Land* 1686[2], *St Mary's headland* 1690, *St Mary head land* 1697[2], *S^t marys headland* 1745[2] (*v.* **hēafod-land**, belonging to the church of St Mary); *shorte bute* 1577[2] (*v.* **sc(e)ort**, **butte** 'a strip of land abutting on a boundary, etc.'); *standfurres, standfurs greene* 1625, *Stanforrows* 1664[2], *Standfurrows* 1668[2], *Stand-forrows* 1671[2], *stan foures* 1686[2], 1690, 1697[2], *Stan-furrows* 1703, *Stanfurrows* 1745[2] (*v.* **stān**, **furh**; there are numerous references to the same f.n. in CSB f.ns. (b) *supra*); *stret* 1577[1], *the Strete* 1577[2], *the street* 1601[2], *Street* 1625 (*v.* **strǣt**, but the significance is not clear); *Thorshall* 1577[2], *Thoresall* 1601[2]; (*the*) *too mares* 1577[2], *two mares* 1601[2], 1671[2], 1697[2], *Two* - 1668[2], *Two Mares* 1686[2] (*v.* **(ge)mǣre** and cf. *the mares supra*); *Wad* Hy3 (1409), *ye Wath stead* 1664[2], - *wath steads* 1668[2], - *stead* 1671[2], *Coningham Wathstead* 1686[2], *Covenham* - 1697[2], *Covenham wath stead* 1745[2] (presumably 'the place where there is a ford', *v.* **vað**, **stede**; this compound is not recorded in Sandred); *Wekenholme, wekeholme gate* 1577[2], *Wekinholme, Wek holme gate* 1601[2], *wekenholme* (*gate*) 1625 (there are a number of references to this name in CSB f.ns. (b) supra); *whyrle beck* 1577[1], *Wharelbekes* 1577[2], *Wharlebeckes* 1601[1], 1601[2], *wharlebecks* 1625, *Wharle becks* 1638[1], *whalebeckes* 1664[2], *Whalebekes* 1668[2], 1671[2], *whallbeckes* (sic) 1671[2], *Wharlebeck* 1686[2], *Wharle beck* 1690, *Wharlebeke* 1697[1], *wharle-becks* 1703, *Wharlbeck* 1745[2] (the first el. is uncertain, but perhaps we may compare ME *wharlwyl, whorlwyl* 'whorl, small flywheel on the spindle of the spinning wheel to maintain or regulate speed', which occurs in the plant designations *whorl-flower* and *whorl-grass*, as Dr John Insley suggests. The meaning would then be 'the stream where the whorl-flower or whorl-grass grows', *v.* **bekkr**); *Winkingholme* 1664[2], *Winkeingholme* 1668[2], *winkeing holme* 1671[2], *Winckhorne* (sic), *Winkkin horne* (sic) 1686[2], *Winkinholme* 1690, *winkinghome* (sic) 1697[2], *winkingholme* 1745[2] (there are numerous references to the same name in CSB f.ns. (b) *supra*); *Would goote* 1644, - *Gote* 1648, - *Goat* 1665, 1669, *the Would goate* 1686, *the would Goat* 1697[3] (*v.* **wald**, **gotu**).

Fotherby

FOTHERBY

Fodrebi (3x) 1086 DB

Foderby 1242-43 Fees, 1288 *Ass*, 1295 RSu (p), l13 (14) Percy,

1304 *DCAcct*, 1328 Banco, 1343 Cl, 1346 FA, 1394 Cl, 1428 FA, 1551 Pat, *-be* 1519 DV i, *Fodderby* 1343 Ipm
Fotrebi c.1115 LS, a1184 (1409) Gilb, *-by* lHy2 (1409) ib, c.1200 RA iv, 1227 Pat, 1260 Cl, 1272 FF, 1287, 1288 Orig, 1536 LP xi, *Fottrebi* c.1200 RA iv
Foterby Hy2 Dugd vi, Hy2, a1170, 1180-90, a1184 (1409) Gilb, 1210-15 RA iv, eHy3 (1291) Ch, a1224 RA iv, 1242-43 Fees, 1250 FF, 1250 RA iv, 1254 ValNor, 1256 FF, 1261, 1266, 1268, 1269 RA iv, 1269 FF, 1272 *Ass*, 1276 RH, 1287 *Ass*, 1291 Tax, 1295 Ass, 1297 Pat, 1297 *HarlCh*, 1298 Ass, 1303 FA *et freq* to 1495 IBL, *-bi* Hy2 Dane, l12 RA iv, 1202 Ass, 1210-20 RA iv, 1219 FF, 1212 Fees, 1239-50 RA iv, *-bia* 1212 Fees, *Foterebi* 1202 Ass, 1207 Cur, *Fotirby* 1343 NI, *Fotterby* 1231 FF, 1271 RRGr, 1526 Sub
Fothrebi 1207 Cur
Fotherby 1272 *Ass*, 1343 Ipm, m14 *AD*, 1373, 1374 Peace, 1538-39 Dugd vi, 1548, 1552 Pat, 1579 *Terrier*, 1610 Speed, 1672 *DCLB*, *-bie* 1509 Wills i, 1557 InstBen, a1567 LNQ v, 1563 InstBen, 1576 LER, 1601 *Terrier*, 1605 *DCLB*, *-bye* 1535 VE iv, 1554 Pat, 1576 Saxton, 1588 *DCLB*, 1606, 1611 *Terrier*

Ekwall (DEPN s.n.) states that this is "OScand *Fōtar-bȳr* 'Fōt's BY'. ON *Fótr* had the gen. *Fótar* by the side of *Fóts*." The gen.sg. *Fóts* certainly occurs in Foston Kest and Fosdyke Holland, besides Foston, PN Db 560, Lei, DEPN, and PN YE 91. Fellows-Jensen, SSNEM 47, points out that *Fótar* is not found in any of the instances of the pers.n. quoted in Lind. The gen.sg. *Fóts-* certainly occurs in these names, even though the gen.sg. *-ar* is "normal for the appellative *fótr* m. 'foot'." She suggests as an alternative explanation that the first el. is OE *fōðer* 'cartload, fodder' or the cognate Scand *fóðr.* Lind only records ON *Fótr* as a byname (LindB 89) from the medieval period, so that it is difficult to see how the (rare) gen. forms in *fotz-*, *fots-* noted here can be of decisive relevance for the first el. of Fotherby. Fellows-Jensen is aware of the fact that it is difficult to explain the numerous early forms in *Foter-*, *Fotre-* as being from *fōðer, fóðr,* and tentatively suggests a third alternative, that we are perhaps concerned with the appellative *fótr* 'foot', used in some topographical sense referring to the site of Fotherby at the foot of the Wolds. She considers that this "would account for the occurrence of the primary gen. *Fótar-* in this name, while the p.ns. containing the by.n. *Fōtr* have the secondary gen. *Fóts-*". It is difficult to see what the topographical application of 'the **bȳ** of the foot' might be, for a number of villages along the same line here could well be so described. In fact, as Dr Insley points out, the problem is more apparent than real. The early OWScand gen.sg. of *fótr* was indeed *fótar,* but this was replaced in medieval byname forms by *fóts* (A. Noreen, *Altisländische u. altnorwegische Grammatik,* 4. Aufl., Halle, 1923, Paragraph 414, Amn. Noreen contrasts later *uxafóts* with early *þyrnefótar*). In Danish, *fōts* is usual, and is the original form, for the West Scandinavian *fótar* evolved through analogy with the *u-* and *o-* declensions, as Dr Insley notes. Gen.sg. *Fótar-* in Fotherby is therefore a specifically West Scandinavian form, while *Fóts-* in Foston is the usual Danish form. Given these considerations, there are no obstacles to interpreting Fotherby as 'Fōt's farm, village', *v.* **bȳ.**

BARTON STREET, 1697 *DCLeases,* 1764 *EnclA, the street* 1606 *Terrier,* the name of a presumed pre-Roman track leading to Barton upon Humber. CHALK COTTAGES, cf. *ye Calk pitts, the calk pites* 1697 *DCLeases,* self-explanatory. CHURCH LANE, 1697 *ib,* 1864 *Terrier, ye Church way* 1697 *ib, the -* 1709 *ib, ye Church Way* 1712 *ib,* and cf. *atte Kyrke* 1327 *SR* (p), *atte Kirk'* 1332 *ib* (p), *ad eccl'iam de foterby* 1329 *Ass* (p); it would appear that ON **kirkja** has been replaced by **cirice** in later forms. FOOTSEY PLANTATION, cf. *Fotsey hill, - green, - headland* 1697 *DCLeases*; the forms are too late to suggest a convincing etymology. FOTHERBY GRANGE, 1830 Gre, "grange in" *Fotherbye* 1537-39 LDRH, *Fotherby, firma grang'* 1538-39 Dugd vi; it was a grange of North or Nun Ormsby Priory. GLEBE FM. INGS LANE, 1828 Bry, cf. *the Inges* 1611 *Terrier, ye Inngs* 1697 *DCLeases, the Ings* 1745 *Terrier,* 1776 *BRA 833, Fotherby Ings* 1713 *LindDep 55, v.* **eng** 'meadow, pasture', in the pl. The lane forms part of the boundary with Utterby. LOW FIELD PLANTATION, cf. *Low fields* 1858, 1865 *DCLeases*; Low Field Cottages are in North Ormsby. MANOR HO. MAWER FM (local) is named from the family of William *Mawer* 1842 White. MAY WOOD. MILL HILL, *miln hill* 1697 *DCLeases,* cf. *ad Molend'* 1327 *SR* (p), *atte miln'* 1332 *ib* (p), *ye Miln close, -*

Milndale 1697 *DCLeases*, self-explanatory. MOTOR HOLT is on the disused railway. NEW BARN (lost, approx. TF 297 919), *New* B^n 1828 Bry. PEPPIN LANE, cf. *pipin* 1697 *DCLeases*, obscure; earlier forms are needed to suggest an etymology. SHORT LANE. TOP BARN. VICARAGE, y^e *Vicaridge* 1606, *the Vicarage of Fotherbye* 1611, *the Vicarage house* 1635, *The* - 1638, - *Vikeridge house* 1674, *one vicceridge house* 1697, - *vikeridge house* 1703, y^e *Vicarage House* 1712, *The* - 1745, *the* - 1822, *There is no Vicarage House* 1864 all *Terrier*, in 1864 it is said to have been sold by auction in 1853.

Field-Names

Forms dated 1180-1200 (1409) and a1184 (1409) are Gilb; 1210-15, 1239-45, 1244-49, 1250, and 1261 RA iv; 1304 *DCAcct*; 1327, 1332[1] *SR*; 1329 *Ass*; 1332[2] *FF*; m14 *AD*; 1353 *Cor*; 1383 Peace; 1497 *StJ*; 1535-46, 1543-5, and 1576-7 *MinAcct*; 1548 Pat; 1588 *DCLB*; 1606, 1638, 1709, 1712, 1745, 1781, 1822 and 1864 *Terrier*; 1697, 1854, 1857, 1858 and 1864 *DCLeases*; 1713 *LindDep 55*; 1753 *HD*; 1764 *EnclA*; 1838[1] *Pad*; 1838[2] *SewerAlf*.

(a) An Ash Holt 1838[1] (*v.* **æsc**, **holt**); Bean Cl Lane 1764 (cf. y^e *Beam close* (sic) 1697); Brackenburg Lane (sic) 1764 (leading to Brackenborough); Brook Cl 1864; East End Nooking 1764 (*v.* **ēast**, **ende**, **nōking**); The Eleven Acres 1854, 1857; Low -, Top Furze Hill 1838[1] (*v.* **fyrs**); Gravel Pit Lane 1764; three Closes ... commonly called or known by the name of Holts or Holts Cl 1753 (perhaps from the surn. *Holt* or *v.* **holt**); Incrofts 1822 (1745), the - 1864, Incroft 1858, 1865 (*v.* **in**, **croft**); little Grimsby and North Elkington Rd 1764, Little Grimsby Road Cl 1864 (cf. *Grimesbimaregate* 1210-15 'the Grimsby boundary road', *v.* **(ge)mǣre**, **gata**); Louth Rd 1764 (*Louth gate* 1697, *v.* **gata**); 9 Acres 1854, 1857; the North Fd 1764 (one of the great fields of the parish, cf. the South Fd *infra* and *in campis de Foterby* in (b) *infra*); Orchard Cl 1854, 1857; Paddock 1854, 1857; the Parish Beck 1864 (y^e *Beck*, *beck bridg*, y^e *beck wath*, y^e *crooking of the Beck* 1697, *v.* **bekkr**); A Plantation of Ash and other Trees 1838[1]; the Pond 1764; East -, West Railway Cl 1864 (the reference is to the East Lincolnshire Railway); The Six Acres 1854, The 6 - 1857; the South Fd 1764, Fotherby South Fd 1781 (one of the great fields of the parish, cf. the North Fd *supra*); the South Wold 1764 (*v.* **sūð**, **wald**); the Stone Pitt (Lane) 1764; Fotherby Strait 1838[1] (y^e *straight close* 1697); The Ten Acres 1864 (area: 10.3.24); Two Acres 1857; Utterby Rd 1764; Walk 1858, 1865 (*v.* **walk**); West Cl

1864; North -, South White Pit 1838[1]; A Close, called the Wold 1838[1], Wolds 1858, 1865 (*ye would* (*side*) 1697, cf. *Waldesende* 1210-15, *v.* **wald**).

(b) *ye Abbygate* 1697 (presumably 'the road to North Ormsby Priory', *v.* **gata**); *Acregates* 1697; *Akredich* 1210-15 (*v.* **æcer, akr, dīc, dīk**); *Acselmare* (*four lands*) 1697 (the first el. is probably a surn. *Axcell*, probably from the ON pers.n. *Asketill* with **(ge)mǣre** 'a boundary, boundary land'; for the surn. *v.* Reaney s.n. *Axcell*); *Allen street* 1697 (*Allen* is probably a surn.); *Andersons Inngs* 1697 (named from the *Anderson* family, cf. John *Anderson* 1641 LPR, Thomas *Anderson* 1650 *Inv*, and **eng** 'meadow, pasture') *barfes mare* 1712 (the first el. is *barf* a dial. form of **beorg** 'a hill', in the gen.sg. presumably with **(ge)mǣre** 'a boundary, land on a boundary'); *attebel* 1304 (p) (for a discussion *v.* Utterby f.ns. (b) *infra*); *Bennett close* 1697 (named from the *Bennett* family; *Mr Bennett* is mentioned in the document); *ye bound stones* 1697; *brading* 1697 (*v.* **breiðr, eng**); *Bramhills* 1697 (*v.* **brōm** 'broom', **hyll**); *the bull peece* 1638, *Bull Piece* 1712, *-peice* 1745 (*v.* **pēce**); *ye Butts* 1697 (*v.* **butte**); *Capel* 1180-1200; *Castelstede* 1239-45, 1244-49, 1250, *Castylstede* 1239-45 (*v.* **castel, stede**; for this compound *v.* Sandred 98-99; it is referred to in the text as a *toft*); *ye common* 1697; *ye Common furrow* 1697 (presumably a furrow forming a boundary, *v.* **furh**), *the Corn field* 1709; *Cropper mouth* 1697; *ye Dale, the -, ye Dales* 1697, *dale Acres, dale acres slack* 1697 (*v.* **deill, æcer, slakki**); *Danschedich* 1210-15 ('the Danish ditch', *v.* **Danskr, dīc**); *Dod head land* 1697 (*v.* **hēafod-land**; *Dod* is probably the surn. *Dod*, *v.* Reaney s.n.); *donner Noaking* 1697 (*v.* **nōking, (nōk, -ing**[1]); the first el. may be a surn.); *Dowkinge* 1535-46, *dowkynge* 1543-5, *pastur' ... vocat' dowkinge* 1576-7 (the first el. is uncertain; the second is **eng**); *Duuecroft* 1239-45, 1244-49, 1250 (*v.* **croft**; the first el. is probably **dūfe**); *in campis de Foterby* 1180-1200 (1409), a1184 (1409), *campos de -* 1383, *feildes of Fotherbye* 1588, *the Common Field* 1745 (*v.* **feld**, cf. the North Fd, the South Fd in (a) *supra*); *ye folk pittes* 1697 (alluding to pits of some kind to which the whole community had access, *v.* **folc, pytt**); *Forketres* m14, *ye four trees* 1697 ('the forked trees', *v.* **furca, trēow**); *fowell noaking* 1697 (*v.* **nōking**; the first el. may be **fūl** 'foul' or **fugol** 'a bird', the second **wella**); *Fray Close* 1712 (presumably from the surn. *Fray*); *Fulstow close* (*hedge*), *Fulstow hedge* 1697 (*v.* **hecg** and cf. *that close called Fullstowe* in the adjoining parish of Little Grimsby. The situation of these closes is not known, but presumably they might be on their common boundary; the parish of Fulstow is some miles to the north of Fotherby, but the fields might well represent an endowment relating to Fulstow, though none has been noted in the sources searched); *ye furr lea* 1697 (*v.* **fyrs, lea**); *Goulding, Goulding thorne* 1697 (*v.* **þorn**; *Goulding* may be a surn., but the earliest reference so far noted is Richard *Goulding* 1775 *BT*); *ye grass headings*

1697 ('headlands laid down to grass', in contrast to ploughed headlands, *v.* **hēafod**, **-ing**^{1}, cf. *y*^{e} *headings infra*); *Halle Croft* 1261, *ye Hall Farme* 1712 (*v.* **hall**); *Hanah farme yarde* 1712; *Hawcroft* 1697 (*v.* **haga**^{2}, **þorn**); *y*^{e} *headings* 1697 (*v.* **hēafod**, **-ing**^{1}); *one lea ... called a headland, one lea more called a headland* 1697 (*v.* **hēafod-land**, cf. *grass headings supra*); *y*^{e} *high close* 1697; *del Hil* 1210-15 (*v.* **hyll**); *Hilly gares, - Garse, y*^{e} *Brow of Hilly gares* 1697 (*v.* **geiri**); *Holbech* 1210-15 ('the stream running in a hollow', *v.* **hol**^{2}, **bece**^{1}); *y*^{e} *Hole gate* 1697 (*v.* **hol**^{2}, **gata**); *Kendales* 1697; *Vuer Ku Scippenes* (checked from manuscript) 1261 ('the cow-sheds', *v.* **cū**, **scipen**, with **ufer** 'over'); *Langmore* 1697 (*v.* **lang**^{1}, **mōr**^{1}); *y*^{e} *leas* 1697 (*v.* **lea** (OE **lēah**) 'a meadow, a piece of meadow-land'); *Louthkedic* 1180-1200 (1409) (*v.* **kjarr**, **dīc**); *in marisco de Foterby* 1180-1200 (1409) (*v.* **mersc**); *atte mare* 1327, 1332 both (p), *Foterby Margate* 1497, *y*^{e} *Mare bank* 1697 (*v.* **(ge)mǣre**, **banke**; *Margate* is 'the boundary road', *v.* **(ge)mǣre**, **gata**); *de Medithorn̄* 1332 (p) (*v.* **þorn**); *Mickelgrene* 1210-15 (*v.* **mikill**, **grēne**^{2}); *Northpratis* 1210-15 (1409) (i.e. '(in) the north meadows', *v.* **norð**, **mǣd**); *Oak clogge* 1697 (perhaps from **clōh** 'a dell', in a Scandinavianised form); *the over whart furrows* 1697 ('the transverse furrows', i.e. at right angles to those adjacent, or to those ploughed in the preceding season, *v.* **ofer**^{3}, **þvert**, **furh**); *ye pingle* 1712 (*v.* **pingel**); *Redwalls* (sic) 1638, *Red hall Leas* 1712, *Reddal Lees* 1745 (possibly 'a (pasture) nook overgrown with reeds', *v.* **hrēod**, **halh** with **lea** 'grassland, pasture' (OE **lēah**)); *Ridd* 1697; *Romer(side)* 1697; *Rowell firrs* 1697 (named from the *Rowell* family, cf. John *Rowell* 1796 *BT*, with **fyrs**); *Long Ryalls* 1697 (*v.* **ryge**, **halh**); *Scottlemores, -mare* 1697; *atte Sedyk'* 1327 (p) (*v.* **sǣ** **dík**, but this can hardly be a local surn. since Fotherby is not a coastal parish); *Seggebecke, Seggebrigge, Seggewra* 1210-15 (from **secg**, in a Scandinavianised form, with **bekkr**, **brycg** (also Scandinavianised), and **vrá**); *Sisor gate* 1697 (presumably 'scissor gate', but the allusion is obscure); *y*^{e} *stintings, the stintinges* 1697 (*v.* **stinting**); *y*^{e} *stone gates* 1697 (*v.* **gata**); *Streye Lande* 1548 (perhaps 'land left without an heir', such property passing to the lord, *v.* **estraieure**, **land**); *Suddales* 1697 (*v.* **sūð**, **deill** in the pl.); *the comon suer* 1606 ('the common sewer', the term (for the drain carrying domestic waste water for the entire settlement) noted in NED as coming into existence c.1600); *one Close Caled Tatum yard* 1712 (named from the *Tatum* family, cf. Richard *Tatom* 1674 *BT*); *Thorndale* 1210-15 (*v.* **þorn**, **deill**); *y*^{e} *townend* 1697 (*v.* **tūn**, **ende**); *turgraves* 1697 ('peat diggings', *v.* **turf**, **græf**); *tyle Kiln close* 1697; *Utterby Beck(s)* 1697 (*v.* **bekkr**, Utterby is the adjoining parish to the north, cf. the Becks in Utterby f.ns. (a)); *y*^{e} *west green* 1697 (*v.* **west**, **grēne**^{2}); *the West Lane* 1697; *Little West pasture* 1697; *White Close* 1697; *y*^{e} *Willow close* 1697; *Woodales* 1697 (*v.* **wudu**, **deill**); *in Le Wra de Foterby* 1332^{2} (p) (*v.* **vrá**).

Little Grimsby

LITTLE GRIMSBY

Grimesbi (3x) 1086 DB, c.1115 LS, l12 (13) *Kirkst, Grymesby* 1160-66 (1409) Gilb, *Grimesby* 1268 Ch

Parva Grimesbia c.1115 LS, 1212 Fees, - *Grimesby* 1209-25 LAHW, 1229 Cl, 1236 RRG, 1242-43 Fees, 1254 ValNor *et passim* to 1346 FA, - *Grimesb'* 1238-43 Fees, - *Grimesbi* 1212 ib, *parue Grymesby* Hy2 (1409) Gilb, *parua Grymesby iuxta Foterby* 1288 *Ass,* - *Grymesby* 1335 *HarlCh,* 1369 *FF,* 1395 Peace, *Parua* - l12 RA ii, - *Grimesby* 1387 Peace, - *Grimmesby* 1307 *Kirkst, parva Grymesby* 1291 Tax, *Parva* - 1303, 1402, 1428 FA, 1535 VE iv, - *Grimmesby* 1296 RH, - *Grymmesby* 1303 FA, 1326 Orig, 1428 FA, *Parua Grimesby* 1387 Peace, - *Grymesby* 1395 ib, *Grymmesby Parua* 1519 DV i, *Grymysby Parva* 1526 Sub, *Grymesbie Pa* a1567 LNQ v

parua Grymsby l12 (1409) Gilb, *Parva Grimsby* Hy2 Dugd vi, c.1221 Welles

"Little" *Grimesby* 1226 FF, 1314 Ch, 1315 Ipm, - *Grymesby* 1335, Pat, 1368 Ipm, 1434 Pat, - *Grimmesby* 1326 Ipm, - *Grymmesby* 1326 Fine, - *Grymmesbie* 1552 Pat

"Little" *Grymsby* 1543 LP xviii, 1551 Pat

Litell Grymesby 1462 Pat, *lytillgrymesby* 1497 *StJ, Littell Grimsby* 1538-39 Dugd vi, 1610 *BT, littel Grymsbe* 1579 *Terrier, Lytle Grymsbye* 1593 *Thor, Litle Grymsbye* 1590 *BT,* - *grymsby* 1594 *ib, Litlegrimsbie* 1597 *ib, Little Grimsbye* 1585 *Anc,* - *Grymsby* 1629 *BT,* - *Grymesbye* 1675 *MiscDon 287*

Grimsby S Mary 1695 Morden

'Grim's farmstead, village', *v.* **bȳ**. The first el. is the ON pers.n. *Grímr,* ODan *Grīm,* which is common in independent use in L, *v.* SPNLY 105. It also occurs in (Great) Grimsby (LNR), in contrast to which *Little* Grimsby is named.

THE BELT, a plantation, so-named from its shape. GORSE (lost, TF 332 924), 1828 Bry; it is marked on the modern map, but is not named. HIRD'S FM, named from the family of William *Hird* 1842

White. INGS LANE, cf. *the Enges* 1497 *StJ*, *v.* **eng** 'meadow, pasture' in the pl.; the lane forms the boundary with Utterby. LITTLE GRIMSBY GRANGE, "grange of" *Lyttell Grymesbye* 1537-39 LDRH, *Littel Grimsby, firma grang'* 1538-39 Dugd vi, "the grange of Little" *Grymsby* 1543 LP xviii, "manor or grange of Little" *Grymesbye* "next" *Brakenbarthe* 1564 Pat, *The Grange Cappitall Messuage and Tenement* 1675 *MiscDon 287*; it was a **grange** of the Priory of North or Nun Ormsby. LITTLE GRIMSBY HALL. POUND (lost, approx. TF 328 916), 1828 Bry, the site of the village pound, *v.* **pund**. SQUARE PLANTATION is actually rectangular today. WOODHOUSE FM.

Field-Names

Forms dated Hy2 (1409) and 112 (1409) are Gilb; 112 (13) *Kirkst*; 1268 Ch; 1369 *FF*; 1497 *StJ*; 1543 LP xviii; 1558-79 ChancP; 1579 *Terrier*, 1675 *MiscDon 287*.

(b) *the Agardykes* 1497 (*v.* **dīk**; the first el. is perhaps the surn. *Agar*, for which *v.* Reaney s.n. *Edgar*); *Aver-Hill* 1675 (probably 'oat hill', *v.* **hafri**, **hyll**); *one close of land ... called Base Bullen* 1675; *the Beane close* 1675 (*v.* **bēan**, **clos(e)**); *the bek', the Bekfurlange* 1497 (*v.* **bekkr**, **furlang**); *Bew holme* 1675 (the first el. is perhaps the surn. *Bew*, *v.* Reaney s.n., with **holmr**); *Bonneacres* 112 (1409), *Boneacr'* 1497, *Bone acre* 1675 (*v.* **æcer**); *in Bramare* 1497 (from **brād** 'broad', with **(ge)mǣre** 'a boundary, land on a boundary' but cf. *langmare infra*); *Church closes* 1675 (*v.* **cirice**, **clos(e)**); *the Clovendyke* 1497 (*v.* **dīk**; the first el. is probably **(ge)clofen** 'forked, divided'); *Collisons close* 1675 (no doubt from the surn. *Collison*); *Cornley feild* 1675; *Cowcroft* 1497 (*v.* **cū**, **croft**); *crosse mare* 1497 (*v.* **cros**; the second el. is **(ge)mǣre** 'a boundary'); *Eglymare* 1497 (*v.* **(ge)mǣre**; the first el. is possibly **īgull** 'a hedgehog' or perhaps, more likely, the ON pers.n. *Egill*); *the Estfurres* 1497 (*v.* **ēast**, **furh** in the pl.); *Great Fatt pasture, the little Fattclose or pasture* 1675 (alluding either to a fattening enclosure or to a pasture with rich herbage); *a campo* Hy2 (1409), *in campis de Grimesby* 112 (13) (*v.* **feld**); *that close called Fullstowe* 1675 (the reference to Fulstow is unclear, since it is not an adjoining parish); *Fyrre Close* 1543, *the litle Furclose* 1675 (*v.* **fyrs**, **clos(e)**); *grenehyll, Grenehyll, Shortgrenehyll* 1497 (*v.* **grēne**[1], **hyll**); *Hopthorn'* 1497 (the sense of *Hop-* here is uncertain, *v.* **þorn**); *Lamb close* 1675 (*v.* **lamb** and cf. the foll. n.); *lampaster* 1497 ('lamb pasture', *v.* **lamb**, **pasture**); *that close called a lane* 1675; *langmare* 1497 ('the long boundary (land)', *v.* **lang**[1], **(ge)mǣre**). Mr John Field notes that 'the long marsh' is suggested for the same form in Kilnwick PN YE 160, adducing **marr**[1] as the second el. He comments that the dialectal development to *mar*(*e*) of both **(ge)mǣre** and **marr** presents a difficulty in interpreting numerous f.ns. in L, including some in previous parts of this survey, e.g. *Blackmare* in East Halton, PN L **2**, 155, *Enedmare* in Killingholme ib, 206, which should therefore be reconsidered with this possibility in mind, together with similarly formed names in other places where the topography is appropriate. He also points out that *Kokermat* (probably for *Kokermar*) 1309 (e14) in Goxhill, **2**, 132, has among its later forms *Cockermarr* 1601, *Cocker Moor* 1693, and *Cocker Meer* 1718, perhaps complicating the uncertainty. It should be noted, however, that marshy ground in Little Grimsby is not a particularly notable feature. Nevertheless, there are many f.ns. in north L where medieval spellings in *-mare* must represent **(ge)mǣre**, e.g. in compounds with numerals as in *tvamar' gate* **2**, 74, *thremares* **2**, 157, 212, *Manimares* **2**, 156; with the names of places in *Littletoftemare* **2**, 208, *Gosetunmare* **2**, 207, *Croxton mare* **2**, 236, *la mare de Melton'* **2**, 236, *mar' de Vlseby* **2**, 297, *Kukewaldemare* **3**, 29, *Wichammare* **3**, 78, *maram de Kinnerebyi* **3**, 57, as well as *þverthemar* 'lying across' **2**, 297, *Brendmar* 'burnt' **2**, 128, *namannesmare* 'no man's' **2**, 209 and at least six examples of *long mare* **2**, 225 etc. It is worth noting that *super Mare* in Croxby **3**, 30 is paralleled by *super diuisam* making the meaning of *Mare* here absolutely clear. While **marr** 'marsh' is perhaps to be reckoned with in north L, by far the greater number of spellings in ME *mare* seem certainly to be reflexes of OE **(ge)mǣre** 'a boundary, land on or forming a boundary'. Unfortunately, very few of the f.ns. recorded in medieval documents are found in Tithe Awards where their sites can be identified. The problem is further complicated, as noted above, by the fact that where f.ns. apparently representing **(ge)mǣre** are only recorded from the 16th century onwards they are also represented by such forms as *mer, mere, mear, moor*(*e*), *more* etc. Clearly, certainty is never going to be possible in some cases, but the overwhelming evidence from north L points to a source in OE **(ge)mǣre**); *larkfurlange* 1497 (*v.* **lāwerce**, **furlang**); *the Ley feild* 1675 ('the fallow field', *v.* **lǣge**, **feld**); *atte Mare de Parua Grymesby* 1369 (p) (*v.* **(ge)mǣre** 'boundary', but cf. foll. f.n. and *langmare supra*); "the marsh of" *Grimesby* 1268; *North' Felde* 1497, *Northfeild* 1675 (one of the great fields of the parish, *v.* **norð**, **feld**, cf. *the South' felde infra*); *Okemarsyde* 1497 (*v.* **āc**; the second el. is probably **(ge)mǣre**, but cf. *langmare supra*); *the landes of the Priour ... of Ormesby* 1497; *Rewels* 1497; *Routhenges* Hy2 (1409) (perhaps a Scand. compound from **rauðr** 'red' and the pl. of **eng** 'meadow', with reference to the colour of the soil); *the South' felde* 1497, *Southfeild* 1675 (one of the great fields of the parish, *v.* **sūð**, **feld**, cf. *North' Felde supra*); *Sowmare* 1497 (perhaps *v.* **sūð**, **(ge)mǣre**, but cf. *langmare supra*); *Stoneleigh Mills* 1558-79; *stretmare* 1497 (*v.*

strǣt, **(ge)mǣre**); *the Comyn strete* 1579 (*v.* **strǣt**); *Tempest close* 1675 (probably from the surn. *Tempest*); *ad Tuincros maris* l12 (1409) (*v.* **twegen**, cf. *crosse mare supra*); *the Vickerage of littell Grymsbe* 1579; *Great west pasture, little -, middle west pasture* 1675 (*v.* **west**, **pasture**); *Wray* 1497 (*v.* **vrá** 'a nook, corner of land'); *yerburgh' heghe* 1497 (probably the hedge between Little Grimsby and Yarburgh (LSR), *v.* **hecg**).

Ludborough

LUDBOROUGH

Ludeburg 1086 DB, 1253 Ipm, *-burc* c.1115 LS, Hy2 (1409) Gilb, *-burgh* 1295 *Ass,* 1316 FA

Ludburc 1177, 1204 P, eHy3 RA iv, *-burg*(') 1223, 1233 Welles, 1249 RRG, 1253 Ipm, 1254 ValNor, 1262 Lib, 1275 RH, *-burgh*(') 1327 *SR*, 1406 Cl *et passim* to 1610 Speed, *-burghe* 1535 VE iv, 1576 Saxton, 1596 *BT, -bourgh* 1353 *Cor,* 1577 *BT, -brough* 1594 *ib*, 1625 *Terrier, -borough* 1600 *BT*, 1676 *BRA 1125 et passim*

Luburc 1191, 1192, 1195 (p) P, 1196 ChancR, c.1200 RA iv, 1212 Fees, 1271 FF, *-burg*(') 1210 ib, 1218 Ass, 1222, 1234 FF, 1238-41, 1242-43 Fees, 1260 Cl, *-brug'* 1254 ib

Lutheburc l12 RA iv, *-burch* 1266 ib, *-burg'* 1253 Ipm, 1269 FF, 1269 RA iv, 1281 QW, 1326 Fine, 1326 Orig, *-burgh*(') 1297 *FF*, 1298 Ass *et passim* to 1402 FA

Loutheburgh 1297 Pat, *-burgh'* 1332 *SR*

Luthburg(') 1281 QW, 1291 Tax, 1352 Pat, 1354 *Cor*, 1375, 1378 Pat, 1382 Peace, 1428 FA

Louthburgh(') 1338 Misc, 1381 Peace, 1454 *LCCA*, 1488 *FF*

Lodeburg' 1276 RH

Loburg' 1260 Cl

Lotheburgh(') 1343 NI, 1343 Cl, 1354 *Cor*, 1356 Pat, 1373, 1374 Peace, *-borou* 1343 Ipm

Lugborough 1595 *FMap*, 1595 *FSurv*

Ekwall, DEPN s.n. Lud R, states that Ludborough is on the Lud and that the p.n. means 'burg on R. Lud' or 'burg belonging to Louth'. Ludborough is in fact *not* on the Lud, but a meaning 'the fortified place belonging to or associated with Louth', *v.* **burh** is certainly possible, for the two places are only just over five miles apart. Forms in *Luth*(*e*)-, *Louth*(*e*), etc, recorded from the late 12th century, certainly suggest that the name was influenced by those for Louth. Nonetheless, Ludborough must have an important place in its own right, since a wapentake was named after it, and though the meeting-place is not known it was presumably at the **burh** at Ludborough. Furthermore, the village is strategically placed close to the junction of Barton Street and the Roman road leading from the coast to Lincoln, cf. Lincoln Gate *infra*.

Both Louth itself and Ludney (LSR) are named from the R. Lud, itself from OE ***hlūde** 'the loud one', that is 'the noisy stream'. There is, however, a further p.n., Ludford, which has similar early forms to Ludborough in *Lud*(*e*)-. For this name Ekwall, DEPN s.n., suggests a meaning 'the ford on the way to Louth', the places being about eight miles apart but on what must have been an old routeway. Like Ludborough, Ludford is not on the Lud; it is actually a ford over the R. Bain. Ludford is in the wapentake of Louthesk 'the ash-tree at Louth', where the meeting-place must have been situated. The second el. of Louthesk is from **eski** 'a place growing with ash-trees' or a Scandinavianized form of OE **æsc**. The importance of Louth in AS Lincolnshire is, therefore, eminently clear. Further it is recorded as early as 790 (c.1100) ASC (F) in the form *Hludensis monasterii*. Ekwall may be correct in suggesting that Ludborough means 'the fortified place belonging to or associated with Louth'.

However, an alternative interpretation which suggests itself is that Ludborough means 'Luda's fortified place', from the OE pers.n. *Luda*, well-evidenced in English p.ns. The occurrence of two names in *Lud*(*e*) in the neighbourhood of Louth would then be coincidental, unless Ludford itself means 'Luda's ford'. No certainty is possible.

BARTON STREET, - *Road* 1775 *EnclA, the strete* 1578 *Terrier*, cf. *Stretedayle* a1184 (1632) *Dods* (*v.* **deill**); this is the name of a presumed pre-Roman trackway along the eastern edge of the Wolds leading to Barton upon Humber and found in other parishes in this Wapentake, *v.* **strǣt**. BLACK HORSE, 1828 Bry, - *Inn* 1830 Gre. COLD HARBOUR is not in an elevated situation but is in an isolated position open to east winds.

CONEY MIRES, *Conam myres* 1674, *Connamires* 1686, 1690, 1693, *le Cona mires* (sic) 1697, *Conammires* 1703, *conamires* 1706, 1724, *Cona-mires* (sic) 1745 all *Terrier*, it seems likely that the first el. is *Conam*, a common local spelling of the nearby Covenham *supra*, the second being **mýrr** 'a mire, a bog, swampy ground'; the modern form would then be due to popular etymology, the first el. being associated with **coni** 'a rabbit'. No evidence has been found for the association with Covenham. DAMWELLS, *damwells* 1578, *-welles* 1625, *Damwells* 1706, 1745 all *Terrier*, 1775 *EnclA*, *Dam swels* (sic) 1697, *Damwels* 1703, *-wells* 1724 all *Terrier*; this is probably 'the springs by the pond' or the like, *v.* **damme (dammr), wella**. Beside the farm, recently demolished, is a pond which presumably gave rise to the name. GLEBE FM. LINCOLN GATE, *Lincolngate or Sparkamires* 1686, *- gate or spark a mires* 1690, *- or spara mires* (sic) 1693, *Lincoln gate* 1697, 1703, 1724, 1745 all *Terrier*, *- Road* 1775 *EnclA*, 'the road to Lincoln', *v.* **gata** and probably part of the Roman road, Margary 272; for the alternative name *v. Sparke meeres* in f.ns. (b) *infra*. LIVESEY ROAD, part of the main road from Louth to Grimsby. The manor of Ludborough was acquired by Joseph *Livesey* "after 1785" AASR xlii, 208. LUDBOROUGH VALE. MANOR HO. PEAR TREE LANE, 1828 Bry; the boundary with Utterby. THE PLATT. RECTORY, *the parsonadge howse* 1578, *a parsenage howese* 1625, *the parsonage house* 1668, *ye parsonage* 1674, *the Parsonage house* 1690, 1693, 1703, 1706, *- House* 1724, 1745, 1788 all *Terrier*, *Rectory* 1828 Bry, 1830 Gre. STATION RD is earlier *the churche lane* 1578, *- Church lane* 1822 both *Terrier*.

Field-Names

Forms dated Hy2 (1407) are Gilb; a1184 (1632) *Dods 135*; c.1200 *DC;* 1311, 1325 are Ipm; 1327, 1332 *SR*; 1374 Peace; 1578, 1625, 1674, 1686, 1690, 1693, 1697, 1703, 1706, 1724, 1745, 1822 *Terrier*, 1775 *EnclA*; 1850 *TA*.

(a) The Acre Paddock 1850 (cf. *de Acres de Lotheburgh'* 1374 (p), *v.* **æcer**); Audby Lane 1775 (*Audbye lane* 1625, *Audby Lain* 1697, *- lane* 1724, *Oatby-Lane* 1745, leading to Autby in North Thoresby parish *infra*); Land in a Close called the "Cottagers Plot" (sic) 1850; Fulstow Rd 1775; Great Grimsby

Rd 1775 (*grimsby Gate* 1697, *Grimsby gate* 1697, 1703, 1706, 1724, - *Gate* 1745, self-explanatory, *v.* **gata**); Grass Leas called Hermitage Leas 1775 (probably alluding to land formerly occupied by *Sir Robert Fen hermet of Ludborough* 1530 Wills ii); Ings 1775 (*the Enges* 1625, *the Ings* 1697, 1745, y^e - 1706, *v.* **eng** 'meadow, pasture' in the pl.); Louth Rd 1775 (*Louth gate* 1697, 1703, 1724, *louth* - 1706, *Louth-gate* 1745 'the road to Louth (LSR)', *v.* **gata**; the name is used today of the main road to Louth); the North Fd 1775 (1745, *the North Feild* 1578, - *field* 1697, *the north feild* 1703, - *field* 1706, y^e *North* - 1674, 1724, *North Field* 1745, one of the great fields of the parish, *v.* **norð**, **feld**, cf. the South Fd *infra*); John Patchett's Cl 1822; the South Fd 1775 (*the Sowthfeld* 1578, *Southe felde* 1625, y^e *South field* 1674, *the South Feild* 1697, - *south feild* 1703, - *South field* 1706, 1745, - *Field* 1724, one of the great fields of the parish, *v.* **sūð**, **feld**, cf. the North Fd *supra*).

(b) *Andromeere* (sic) 1578 (*v.* **(ge)mǣre**; the first el. is probably the pers.n. or surn. *Andrew*); *Autbie hedge* 1578, *audbye hedge* 1625, *Audby hedge* 1686, 1703, 1706, - *hedge* 1686, 1690, 1693, - *Hedge* 1697, *Audby-hedge* 1724, *Aunby hedge* (sic) 1674, *Oatby-Hedge* 1745 ('the boundary hedge with Autby', *v.* **hecg** and cf. Audby Lane *supra*); *the Bee-Gardens* 1745; *the Bergarth* 1578 (*v.* **garðr**); *a furlonge Called Blackhelles* 1625, *Black buts* (sic) 1686, *Blackhill buts* 1690, *Blackhils* (*Buts*) 1693, *Black Hills, black Hils* 1697, *blackhills* 1703, 1706, 1724, *Blackhill* 1674, *Black hils* 1686, *Blackhils* 1690, *Black Hills* 1745 (*hell*(*e*) is an occasional spelling for *hill*(*e*) in 16th and 17th century forms in north L); *Blakeland* c.1200, *Blakelanndes* 1578 (the first el. is **blāc** 'pale, bleak' with **land**); *long bramer* 1578, *Long* - 1674, *long Bramar*(*r*) 1686, *a forlonge Called longbramer* 1625, *Long Bramergate* 1674, *Long Braman* (sic) 1690, *Long Braman* (*gate*) (sic) 1693, *Short Bramer, Bramers hedland* 1578, *shorte bramer* 1625, *Bramers* 1697, *Brame* (sic) 1703, *bramer* 1706, 1724, *Bramer*(*s*) 1745, *Long Bramer gate* 1674 (*bramer* is an English formation 'the wide boundary, boundary land' from **brād** and **(ge)mǣre**, and cf. *braymor* in Covenham St Bartholomew f.ns. (b) *supra*); *Bull dale* 1697, *bull dale* 1703, *bulldale* 1706, 1724, *Bull-Dales* 1745 (*v.* **bula**, **deill**); y^e *Buttes* 1578, *the butes* 1625 (*v.* **butte**); *cardayle* a1184 (1632), *Cadalledalle* 1625, *Cawdwell dale* 1674, *Cawdale* - 1697, 1703, *Cowdales* - 1706, *Cowdale-dale* 1724, *Cow-dale-Dale* 1724 (obscure; the a1184 form may not belong here); *Caudewycke dale* 1578 (perhaps named from the family of Robert *Colwicke* 1591 *BT*, *v.* **deill**); *Codes greene* 1578 (from **grēne**[2] and probably the surn. *Cade*, cf. William *Cade* 1578, which is common in the parish); *ad crucem* 1327, 1332 (p) (*v.* **cros**); *Dawson furres* 1578 (presumably from a surn. and the pl. of **furh**, *furr* being a common form of *furrow* in north L); (*the*) *dyke forlonge* 1578, *dicke forlande*, - *furlonge* 1625, *dike furlong* 1674, *Dike forland(s)* 1686, 1690, 1693, *Dike forland hedge* 1686, *Dikeforland (hedg)* 1693, *dike forland (hedg)*, *- furland (hedg)* 1703, *- furlong (hedge)* 1724, *dikefirland (hedge), dikefurland (hedge)* 1706, *dicke Firland, dick Forland Hedge, - Forlong hedg* 1697, *Dike Furlong (hedge), - furlong (hedge)* 1745 (*v.* **dīk**, **furlang**; *forland* and *furland* are common forms of *furlong* in north L); *ad campum de Ludeburc* Hy2 (1409) (*v.* **feld**); *fremares* 1625, *Firemore* 1690, *Firmor* 1693, *Freemare* (sic) 1697, *fremore* 1703, *Freemore* 1706, *freemore* 1724, *Free More* 1745 (obscure); *furr Close nuyoke* 1578 (*v.* **fyrs**, **clos(e)**, **nōk**); *Gare meare* 1578 (*v.* **geiri** 'a triangular plot of land', **(ge)mǣre**); *godsgrene (bankes)* 1625, *gods green* 1674, 1693, *Gods green* 1686, *- Green* 1697, *Godsgreen* 1690, 1703, *Gods--green* 1706, 1724, *Gods-Green* 1745 (this is presumably self-explanatory, a complimentary nickname); *the grene* 1625 (*v.* **grēne**²); *The Hall Farm* 1745; *the hallgarthe* 1625 (*v.* **hall**, **garðr**); *Haver Cloose* 1578 (*v.* **hafri** 'oats', **clos(e)**); *Headland and fellow* 1690, *- & fellow* 1693 (for the same name, *v.* Covenham St Bartholomew f.ns. (b) *supra*); *Hole* 1578, 1693, *The -* 1690, *ye hole* 1674, *The -* 1686, *the -* 1703, 1706, *howle, howele* 1625. *the Hoale* 1697, *ye hoale* 1724, *the Holes* 1745 (*v.* **hol**¹ 'a hollow'); *Howbecke* 1578, *howbecke* 1625, *How beck* 1674, *howbeck* 1706, *Howbeck* 1724, 1745, *Hawbeck* 1697, 1703, *Hawbeck bank* 1686, 1690, *Hawbeck beck* (sic) 1693 ('the stream running in a hollow', *v.* **hol**², **bekkr**, with **banke** in 1686 and 1690, replaced erroneously by **bekkr** in 1693); *Howdales (Close)* 1625, *Howdale Skirt* 1674, 1686, 1693, *Hawdale -* 1690, *Howdale Flash* 1697, 1745, *- flash* 1703, *howdale Flash* 1706, 1724, *- Flags* 1697 (*v.* **deill** 'a share'; the first el. is uncertain but may be **haugr** 'a mound' etc. The affix is from ME flashe compared by MED with OFr *flache* and denoting 'a watery or marshy place, a swamp, a pool or puddle'. Cf. however, ODan **flask** 'low-lying area, meadow, which has been or is subject to flooding'); *Igell meere* 1578, *Iglemore* 1674, 1690, 1693, 1697, 1706, 1724, *Iglemoore* 1686, *Iglemor* 1703, *Egegellmorhelle* (sic) 1625 (the 1578 form suggests that this is from ON **ighil** 'leech' with **mere**¹ 'a pool' and if so the later spellings have been influenced by *moor*); *Inforth greene* 1578 (*v.* **grēne**²); *kyrk forlonge* 1578, *Kirk furlong* 1674, *- forlands* 1686, 1693, *- forelands* 1690, *the Churchefurlonge* 1625, *Church forlong* 1697, *- furlong* 1703, 1706, 1745, *Church-furlong* 1724 (the interchange of *kirk* and *church* is worthy of note); *Kittle more* 1674 (probably for *Little - infra*); *Lath close* 1703, 1724, *lath-close* 1706, *Lathe Close* 1745 (*v.* **hlaða** 'a barn'); *Law more Hastings* (sic) 1697, *Langmor Haustings* 1703, *Langmore headings* 1745, *Lang More Dale* 1745 (*v.* **lang**, **mōr**¹); *lewdedayle* a.1184 (1632) (*v.* **deill**; the first element is apparently ME *lewede* 'common', but its significance is not clear here); *Litlmoor end* 1686, *Littlemore end* 1690, 1693, *little more* 1697, *littlemore* 1703, 1706, 1724, *Little More* 1745 (self-explanatory; cf. *Kittle more supra*); *the lordes Weste* *wonge, The lordes wange* 1625 (*v.* **vangr** 'a garden, an infield' and foll.; cf. *West Wong infra* and foll.); *Lords dale* 1697, *lords* - 1703, 1706, *Lords-dale* 1724 (this was presumably a share or portion of land (*v.* **deill**) belonging to the lord of the manor); *Ludbruchefeld* 1551 Pat (*v.* **feld**); *lugmore dale* 1703, *Lugmare* - 1706, *Lugmore* - 1724 (probably from ME *lug(ge)* 'a pole, stick' and **(ge)mǣre**, in the sense 'a boundary marked by a pole'); *one land called the lynge* 1578 (*v.* **lyng**); *the Margate* 1578 ('the boundary road', *v.* **(ge)mǣre, gata**); *Marshall garth* 1674 (named from the *Marshall* family, cf. John *Marshall* 1642 LPR, and **garðr**); *Mathew dale hedge* 1697, *mathew-dale hedge* 1706, *Mathewdale* - 1724, *Mathew Dale's Hedge* 1745 (presumably from the surn. *Mathew and* **deill**); *Melinges* 1578, *a furlonge Called Mealinges* 1625, *Mealings* 1697, 1703, 1724, 1745, *mealings* 1706 (the first el. is possibly ME *mēle*, here 'meal made from pulses or other seed', the name denoting a meadow set aside for production of the same, with **eng** in the pl.); *a furlonge called the Great micke* (sic) 1625, *Mickle moor gate, - side* 1686, *Michaelmore Gate, - Side* 1690, *- gate, - side* 1693, *Micklemore* 1697, *Miclemore* (*strome*) 1706, *Micklemore* (*strome*) 1724, - (*Strome*) 1745 (leading to Micklemore in North Thoresby, *v.* **gata**; *strome* is perhaps from **straumr** 'a stream'); *Middeby* 1311 (p) (literally 'middle in the village', *v.* **mid**, **miðr**, **ī**, **bȳ**, cf. PN L **2** 19); *Milner Garth* 1686, *- Garth end* 1690, *- garth end* 1693 (*v.* **garðr**, the first el. being the (occupational) surn. *Milner*); *mylln furlonge* 1578, *the Melle forlonge* 1625, *Mill Furlong* 1697, *- furlong* 1703, *miln furlong* 1706, 1745, *Milln furlong* 1724 (*v.* **myln**, **furlang**; *mell(e)* is an occasional variant of *mill(e)* in north L); *new close* 1703, 1706, *new-close* 1724, *New Close* 1745; *Great Noke* 1686, *- nook* 1690, *- Nook* 1693, *the great nooking* 1697, 1703, *- nookeing* 1706, 1724 (*v.* **nōk**, **nōking** (**nōk**, **-ing**[1])); *y*[e] *oate close* 1706, *the Oat close* 1724, *- Close* 1745; *y*[e] *Oxgang* 1703 (*v.* **oxgang**); *padehowle* 1625, *Padhole* 1674, *Pade hole* 1686, 1690, 1693, *paid hole* 1697, *padehole* 1703, 1706, *Pade-hole* 1724, 1745 (*v.* **padde** 'a toad', **hol**[1] 'a hole, a hollow'); *the parsons headland* 1697, 1703, 1706, *Parsons headland* 1724, *Parsons head lands* 1745 (*v.* **person, hēafod-land**); *les Pihtles* 1325 (*v.* **pightel** 'a small enclosure, a croft', rare in north L where the usual term is **pingel**); *Ralf Close* 1690, *the* - 1693, *Ralph close* 1697, 1706, *- Close* 1703, 1745, *Ralph-close* 1724 (from the pers.n. or surn. *Ralph*); *Rowemeere* 1578, *Rowmere* 1625, *Rowmore Gate* 1697, *Rowmer gate* 1706, *Rowmars* - 1724, *Rowmar's Gate* 1745, *Romer side* 1686, 1693, *Romersicle* (sic) 1690, *Romer gate* 1703 (Dr J. Insley suggests that this is possibly 'boundary at a row (of houses, hedges or the like)', *v.* **rāw, (ge)mǣre**); *Rustie greene gate* 1578, 1625, *Rusty Green* - 1697, *rusty green* - 1706, *Rusty-green* - 1745, *rusty green* 1697, *Rusty* - 1703, 1706, 1724, *Rusty Green* 1745 (*Rustie* is obscure); *Saltergate* 1578, *a lanke Called the Salter gate* (sic) 1625, *Salterbank* 1686, *Saltier bank* (sic) 1690, *Saltren bank* (sic) 1693,

Salter - 1697, 1724, *salter banck* 1706, *Salters bank* 1703, *Salter's* - 1745 (*v.* **gata** 'a road', **banke** with **saltere** as occup.n.; *bank* is sometimes used of a road in north L; *lanke* 1578 may be an error for *banke*); *Scrume* 1686, *Scrowm* (sic) 1690, *Scrown* 1693, *Strooe* (sic) 1674 (obscure); *Segg gate* 1697, *Seggate* 1703, *Segg-gate* 1706, 1724, *Seggs gate* 1745 ('road to the sedge-bed(s)' *v.* **secg** (in Scandinavianized form), **gata**); *Skyttlemeeres* 1578 (Dr J. Insley suggests that *Skyttle-* is from a Scandinavianized form of **scite** 'dung' and **hyll**, with the pl. of **(ge)mǣre**); *Sparke meeres* 1578, *Sparkeconemires* 1625, *Sparkamyres* 1674, *Sparkamire* 1686, *Spark a mires* 1690, 1693, *Sparkamires* 1697, 1703, 1706, 1724, *Sparka mires* 1745 (the 1625 form suggests association with Coney Mires *supra*, but the development of the name is not clear and early spellings are needed to suggest an etymology: *v.* also Lincoln Gate *supra*); *Story maredayles* (reading uncertain) a.1184 (1632) (perhaps 'boundary shares of land', *v.* **(ge)mǣre**, **deill**: *Story*, if the correct reading, is for *Story* and represents *Storþ* from **storð** 'brushwood'); *Syndur mayre*, - *meere* 1578 (*v.* **sundor** 'apart', **(ge)mǣre**); *Thoersbye foute stete* 1625, *Thorsby footsteet* (sic) 1674, *Thoresby foot street* 1686, 1690, *Thirsby* - 1693, *Thorsby Street* 1697, 1745, - *street* 1724, *thorsby street* 1706, *Thoresby* - 1703 (alluding to a footway to the adjoining parish of North Thoresby, *v.* **strǣt**); *the forlonge called thorn-Acres, Thornacres* 1578, *Thorn ackers* 1625, *Thorne acre* 1674, *Thorn Acres* 1686, 1690, 1693, *thorn* - 1697, 1703, 1724, 1745, - *acres* 1706, *Torn Achres* (sic) 1690 (*v.* **þorn**, **æcer**); *the thorn close* 1578, *the thorne* - 1625, *Thornclose* 1674, *Thorn close* 1686 - *Close* 1697, 1745, - *Close end* 1690, 1697, 1703, - *close end* 1693, *thorn close* (*end*) 1706, 1724; *Three mayres* 1578 ('three boundaries', *v.* **(ge)mǣre**); *ye three Oxgang* 1724, *the-three-Oxgangs* 1745 (*v.* **oxgang** and cf. *ye Oxgang supra*); *the towne dales* 1578 (*v.* **deill**); *Tubwelle heade* 1625, *Tubwell* 1674, 1686, 1690, 1693 (*v.* **wella**; the first el. may be ME *tubbe* 'a tub'); *Utterby hedge* 1674, 1686, 1706, 1745, - *hedg* 1690, 1693, 1703, - *Hedge* 1697, *Utterby-hedge* 1724 (the hedge with the adjoining parish of Utterby); *Waingraue dale* 1697, *Waingrave* - 1703, 1706, *Waingraves-dale* 1724, *Waingraves Dale* 1745 (*Waingrave* may well refer to Waingrove Ho in the adjacent parish of Fulstow); *water galls* 1578, *Watergalls* 1625, *Water galle* 1674, - *gales* 1686, *Watergoles* (sic) 1690, 1693, *water gauls* 1697, *Watergales* 1703, *watergalls* 1706, 1724, *water galls* 1745 ('the wet spongy ground', *v.* **wæter**, **galla** and cf. dial. *gall* 'a barren spot in a field, spongy ground'); *le Wdedayle* a1184 (1632) (*v.* **wudu**, **deill**); *ye west clooses nuycke* 1578 (*v.* **nōk**); *Westdales* 1578, *the westedayle* 1625; *the westdale close* 1578, 1625, *Westdale Close* 1674, 1693, - *close* 1690, *Westdale* (*Close*) 1703, *West dale close* 1686, *west dale* (*Close*) 1697, - *dale, west-dale Close* 1706, *westdale*(*-close*) 1724, *West-Dale, West Dale Close* 1745 (*v.* **west**, **deill**); *the hyghway to Westdale furres* 1578 (*v.* **furh** in the pl.); *Westeng* a1184 (1632), *West* *inges* 1578 (*v.* **west, eng**); *West Wong* 1703, (*y^e*) *West wong* 1706, 1724, *the west-wong* 1745 (*v.* **west, vangr**, cf. *the lordes* (*Weste*) *wonge supra*); *Wheat close* 1690, 1703, - *Close* 1697, 1745, *wheat close* 1706, *wheat-close* 1724, *Wheat Close* (*side*) 1693; *Wyttmeere, wytmeere* 1578, *Whitmore* 1625, 1697, 1703, 1706, 1745, *Whittmore* 1724 (*v.* **hwīt** 'shining', **mere** 'a pool', the later forms being influenced by *moor*); *The Wind-Miln* 1745; *Short yarnet Hill* 1578, *Shorte yarmicle helle* (sic) 1625, *Short garnat hil* 1674, - *Yernall hill* 1686, - *yernill hills* 1690, - *yarnell hill* 1693, - *hills* 1697, 1703, *Short yarnall* - 1706, *short yarnell* - 1724, *Short yarnett Hills* 1745 (obscure).

North Ormsby

NORTH ORMSBY

(*æt*) *Vrmesbyg* 1066-68 (c.1200) ASWills

Ormesbi 1086 DB (3x), 1086 ib (p), c.1115 LS, 1164 (16) Riev, 1166 RBE (p), 1177 P (p), c.1189 LAAS v, 1199 CartAnt, 1199 ChR, l12 RA ii, l12 (13th) *Kirk*, 1202 Ass, 1204 P, 1205 Cur *et passim* to 1218 Ass, *-by* 1147-66, 1150-60, eHy2, 1160-66. a1170, c.1170, Hy2 all (1409) Gilb, Hy2 (1314) Ch, c.1260 (1409) Gilb, 1210 FF, 1217 Pat, c.1218 RA ii, 1219 Cur, 1219 Ass, 1222 FF, 1223, 1224 Cur, 1227 Ch, 1228 Pat, 1229 RA iii, 1229, 1230, 1231 Cl *et freq* to 1526 Sub, - *iuxta Ludeburgh'* 1289 *Ass*, *-b'* 1178-83 (c.1250) YCh xii, 1238-41 Fees, *-be* 1538 LP xiii, *-bie* 1552 Pat, *Ormysby* 1428 FA, 1457 Pap

Hormesbi 1212 Fees, *-bia* 1212 ib

Ormesby Monialium 1293 FF, *Noneormesby* 1376 Pat, *-bye* 1516 (1545) *AOMB 217*, 1552 Pat, *Nonne-* 1545 LP xx, 1551 Pat, - *Ormesby* 1538 *AOMB 211*, 1548 Pat

Nunormesby 1386 Peace, 1477 Hast i, 1498 Ipm, 1531 Wills iii, 1554 Pat, *Nun Ormesby* 1399 Pap, 1768 *Harm*, *Nune Ormesby* 1535 VE iv, *Nunnormesbye* 1553 Pat, *Nunn-* 1560, 1565 ib, *Nune-* 1552 PrState, 1558 Pat, *Nunormesbie* 1556 InstBen, 1562 Pat, a1567 LNQ v, 1576 LER, *-ormisbe* 1606 *BT*, *-ormsby* 1678, 1713 *ib*, *Nun Ormsbye* 1538-39 Dugd vi, - *Ormsby* 1662, 1725, 1757 *ib*, *Nuns Ormesby* 1424 IBL

Northormesby 1355 *FF*, 1373, 1374, 1376 Peace, 1437 Cl, *North* - 1328 Banco, 1438 *Cragg*, 1467 WillsPCC, 1610 Speed, 1671 *BT*

'Orm's farm, village', *v.* **bȳ**, the first el. being the ON pers.n. *Ormr*, ODan *Orm*. The earliest reference shows contamination by OE **Wyrm*, cf. J. Insley, *Ortnamnssällskapets i Uppsala Årsskrift* 1987 49 for OE **Wyrm*, which forms the first el. of Ormston La, hitherto taken to contain ODan **Urm*. It is *Nun* from the Priory of Gilbertine nuns, founded in the 12th century, and *North* in contrast to South Ormsby LSR.

BARTON STREET is *the Street* 1779 *Young*, the name of an ancient presumed pre-Roman trackway leading to Barton upon Humber. DOGDYKE. THE FOUR TREES (lost, approx. TF 279 934), 1828 Bry, cf. *Fourtrees piece, Back of Fourtrees* 1842 *TA*. MANOR HO, 1842 White. MILL FM, cf. *molendino de Ormesby* 1374 Peace, *Nun Ormsby, firma molend'* 1538-39 Dugd vi, *Ormsby Mill* 1824 O, *v.* **myln**. NORTH FIELD (lost, approx. TF 300 927), 1779 *DCLeases*, 1828 Bry, *the North Fields* 1859 *DCLeases*, one of the open fields of the village. NORTH ORMSBY ABBEY. *Ormsby Abbey* 1828 Bry, *Ormesbey Abbey* 1830 Gre. Presumably *Ormesbie Abbey* a1577 LNQ v is a reference to the Priory. ORMSBY PLANTATION is *Middle Wood* 1828 Bry. THE SLATES, presumably from the pl. of ON **sléttа** 'a smooth, level field'. It is situated in a saucer-shaped piece of land, with slopes both to east and west. THE VICARAGE, *ther was a vicaridg house ... wch was ruinate in the time of John Lawson who was Vicar there about 15 yeares agoe but never was rebuilt since soe it remains ruinated* 1664 *Terrier*, *the house being downe and have bene downe about sixteen years* 1668 *ib*, cf. *one small Close cald the vicarage yard* 1697 *ib*. WOOD BARN, cf. *Ormsby Wood* 1824 O, 1830 Gre, - *W^d^* 1828 Bry, - *wood* 1842 *TA*, cf. *Wood Closes* 1779 *DCLeases*.

Field-Names

Principal forms in (a) are 1842 *TA*. Spellings dated 1147-66 (1409), eHy2 (1409), Hy2 (1409) are Gilb; Hy2 (1314) Ch; 112 (13) *Kirkst*; 1296 *Ass*; 1343 NI; 1374 Peace; 1538 *AOMB*; 1561 *Harm*; 1697 *LindDep 55*; 1779, 1817, 1859, 1867 *DCLeases*; 1799 Young.

(a) The acre pce (*v.* **æcer**, **pece**); Bailiff's house & garden; Barn Cottage stackyard & plantation; Bean pce (*v.* **pece**); Bull pce 1842, 1867 (*v.* **pece**); Burmans plat (named from the *Burman* family, cf. Thomas *Burman* 1576 *BT*, *v.* **plat**[2]); *Cherry Garth* 1779, 1817, 1859, 1867, - *garth* 1842 (*v.* **cheri**, **garðr** 'an enclosure', as elsewhere in this parish); Church paddock, East church paddock, Church yard (cf. *atte kirk* 1343 (p), *atte Kirke de Ormesby* 1374 (p), *v.* **kirkja**); Clay pce (*v.* **pece**); Corn croft (*v.* **corn**, **croft**); Cow cl; Eighteen acres; Eleven acres; Ely north paddock, - south paddock (named from the *Ely*(*e*) family, cf. Edward *Elye* 1611 *BT*); the Fallow Fd 1779 (*v.* **falh** 'ploughed land'); Five acres; East -, West forty acres; Furze land (*v.* **fyrs**, **land**); Grass Road; Grumble wood pce, - wong (alluding to Grimble Wood, in North Elkington LSR, *v.* **pece**, **vangr**); Hanging hill; Hanson cl (named from the *Hanson* family, cf. Richard *Hanson* 1677 *BT*); the Headings 1779 (*v.* **hēafod**, **-ing**[1]); Hingham's fd (probably from the surn. *Ingham* or *Hingham*); Home cl (2x), North home Cl, South home cl; Hunger hill (cottage and sheds) (a common derogatory name, *v.* **hungor**, **hyll**); Kemps paddock (named from the *Kemp* family, cf. Thomas *Kemp* 1755 *BT*); Little Fd 1779, 1817, 1842, - fd 1859; Little Flg 1779; Long Flg 1779; Low ends; Low fd (*Ormsby lowfeild* 1697); Martis hill; Common Mears 1779 (*v.* **(ge)mǣre** 'a boundary, land on a boundary'); Middle Flg 1779 (*v.* **furlang**); Mill & paddock; Great -, Little miller's cl; the Minster Cl 1779, 1817, Minster cl 1842, - Cl 1859, Ministers - (sic) 1867, Minster five acres 1842, Ministers - 1867 (alluding to ownership by the Dean and Chapter of Lincoln Minster, with occasional erroneous alterations to *Minister*); Ox cl (v. **oxa**); Ozier plantation (*v.* **oyser**); Paddock (2x) 1867; Pease Garth 1779, - garth 1842, Peas Garth 1817, 1859 (*v.* **pise**, **garðr**); Pit cl (*v.* **pytt**); Plantation (*freq*); Road bailliffs Cottage & Garden; North -, South skimmings (obscure); South Fd 1779, 1817, - fd 1859; South Flg 1779, Part of stone paddock; Stone pit walk (*v.* **stān**, **pytt**); Temple pce (*v.* **temple**, **pece**); East -, West thirty acres; Thorn Free plot 1842, - Tree Plat 1867 (- *Free* 1842 is uncertain, the *f* having been altered from some other letter; it is probably for *Tree*, *v.* **þorn**, **trēow**, **plot**, **plat**[2]); Pce above Tutty's (*v.* **pēce**; *Tutty* is presumably a surn.); Twelve acres; Twenty acres; Twenty six acres; Warney furze (*v.* **fyrs**); The warren of North Ormsby 1799, The warren, The warren with barn brickyard and sheds 1842 (*v.* **wareine**); West paddock; Pce above whiles (*v.* **pece**; *while* is probably a surn.).

(b) *Alegcroft* 1147-66 (1409) (*v.* **croft**; the first el. is obscure, though perhaps a corrupt form of some Continental Germanic pers.n., e.g. Old Saxon *Athallêk* might be thought of, though this is highly tenuous, as Dr J. Insley points out); *Cringelbec* 1147-66 (1409), *Chrungesbec' (with -s-* for *-l-*) Hy2 (1409) (*v.* **kringla** 'a circle', **bekkr**, a Scand. compound); *Dragedale* Hy2 (1409) (*v.* **dalr**; Dr J. Insley suggests that the first el. may be ODan **dragh* 'narrow tongue of land connecting two areas of land', originally 'tongue of land over which ships could be drawn', *v. Danmarks Stednavne* 13 61 (Drejø). He notes, however, that the etymologically identical byname, ON *Dragi*, might be considered); *Durewardethorn'* Hy2 (1409) (*v.* **þorn** 'a thorn tree'; the first el. is OE *duruweard*, ME *dōr(e)ward* 'gate keeper, porter', perhaps used as an occupational byname); *Engdale* Hy2 (1409) (*v.* **eng** 'meadow, pasture', **deill**); *Engecroft* Hy2 (1409) (*v.* **eng**, **croft**); *in campis de Ormesby* eHy2 (1409), *in campis et brueria de Ormesby* Hy2 (1314) ('in the fields and waste of Ormsby'); *Flintouh'* eHy2 (1409) (*v.* **flint**, **haugr** 'a (burial) mound, a hill'); *a grangia sua* 1147-66 (1409), *grangiam de Ormesby* 112 (13), *one Grange* 1561 (no doubt a **grange** of North (Nun) Ormsby Priory); *atte Grene de Ormesby* 1296 (p) (*v.* **grēne**[2]); *Higelmare* 1147-66 (1409), *-mara* Hy2 (1409) (this should be compared with *Ygelmare, hihelmare* in East Halton f.ns. (b), PNL 2, 158, where it is wrongly suggested that the name means 'the boundary land where leeches are found' from ON **igli** and OE **(ge)mǣre**. Dr John Insley points out that ON ***igli**, despite its inclusion as an entry in EPN I, is not the correct form. We are rather concerned with ODan ***ighil** 'leech', which is well attested in Denmark in minor names in wet areas, *v.* J. Kousgård Sørensen, *Danske sø- og ånavne* 3 224-31. Mr John Field suggests that the second el. is rather ON **marr** 'fen, marsh', said to be common in parts of Yorkshire, *v.* particularly PN YE 327 and also PN YN 329, PN YW 7 223. A word meaning 'marsh, marshy ground' would fit better with ***ighil** 'leech', and would also fit in with the frequency of the element ***ighil** in Danish minor names whose second elements denote bodies of water. The East Halton example, therefore, probably means 'the marsh, marshy ground where leeches abound'; *v.* also Mr Field's note on *langmare* in Little Grimsby f.ns. (b) *supra*); *le Shepegate* 1538 (*v.* **shep-gate** 'pasturage or right of pasturage for a sheep', common in north L); *Thremares* Hy2 (1409) ('the three boundaries', *v.* **þrēo**, **(ge)mǣre**, cf. Common Mears in (a) *supra* and Three mayres in Ludborough f.ns. (b) *supra*); *Westlanges* eHy2 (1409) (*v.* **west**, **lang**[2] 'a long strip of land' in the pl.).

Utterby

UTTERBY

Uthterby 1150-60 (1409) Gilb, *Vthterbi* 112 RA ii

Utterby Hy2 (1409) Gilb, c.1221 Welles, 1242-43 Fees (p), 1244

Cl, 1254 ValNor, 1263 FF, 1276 RH, 1281 QW, 1287 Ipm, 1291 Tax, 1295 Pat, 1316 FA *et freq, - iuxta Ormesby* 1292 *FF, -bye* 1551, 1552 Pat, 1567 *Harm*, 1574 *AD*, 1576 Saxton, 1582, 1589 *BT, -bie* 1551 WillsStowe, 1562, 1569 *BT*, 1576 LER, 1607 *PM*, 1625 *Terrier*, 1628 *BT, Uttirby* 1343 NI, 1413 Fine, *Uttyrby* 1428 FA, 1430 IngCt, 1454 WillsPCCC, *Hutterby* 1287 *Ass*

Uterbi Hy3 (1409) Gilb (p), *-b'* 1238-43 Fees

Vttrebi 1195, 1197 P (p)

Vtrebi 1106 ChancR (p), *-by* 1288 *Ass*

Vtterby e13 RA ii, 1209-35 LAHW, 1272, 1287 *Ass*, 1292, 1294 *FF*, 1295 RA ii, 1297 CoramR, 1327 *SR*, 1328 Banco, 1332 *SR et passim* to 1443 *DCAcct*

Vterby 1295 RA ii

Ekwall (DEPN s.n.) interpreted this name as 'the outer farm, village', from a Scand. **Ytri-býr*, this also being the etymology of Itterby in Bradley Wapentake LNR. He takes ON **ytri** to have been subsequently replaced by the corresponding OE **ūterra** 'outer, more remote'. It is, however, difficult to see what significance 'outer, more remote' has here, unless it should denote Utterby's relationship to North Ormsby. Dr John Insley suggests that it might be more plausible to suggest that initial *Uth-*, *Vth-* in the two earliest forms is an inverted spelling for *Uht-*. If this is the case, it may be suggested that the first el. is the OE pers.n. **Ūhthere* or *Ūhtrēd*. The spirant would have been lost through progressive assimilation, which could have been accompanied by shortening of the initial vowel. If we are concerned with OE Ūhtrēd, a name which is relatively frequently attested in late Old English and early Middle English, the development would have been **Uhtrēdebȳ*> *Uhtreby*> *Utterby*.

BANK LANE. BARTON STREET, 1697 *LindDep 85*, named from the presumed pre-Roman trackway along the eastern edge of the Wolds leading to Barton upon Humber and found in other parishes in this wapentake. CHAPEL LANE. CHEQUERS FM, cf. *the Chequers* 1671, 1698, 1739 *LindDep 55*, 1839 *TAMap*, *Checker Close* 1721, *Cheeker Close* (sic) 1746, 1751 *LindDep 55*, *North -*, *South Chequers close* 1838 *TA*, no doubt from the chequered appearance of the ground, *v.* **cheker**. CHURCH LANE. GOWT FM, *Gowt Close* 1838 *TA*. GOWT PLANTATION, 1838 *ib, v.* **gotu**, in L apparently in the sense a sluice. GRANGE FM, *The Grange* 1839 *TAMap*, cf. *grangie de Utterby* Hy2 (1409) Gilb, *Utterbye graunge* 1535-46 *MinAcct*, "grange of" *Utterbye* 1537-39 LDRH, *Utterby, firma grang'* 1538-39 Dugd vi, *Utterbye Grange* 1539 LP xiv, *Utterby graunge* 1543-35 *MinAcct, Utterbye Grange* 1552 Pat, *the Grange of Utterby* 1630 *LindDep 55, messuag' siue grang' de Utterby* 1630 *ib, Utterby Grange* 1828 Bry, 1830 Gre; this was a **grange** of North Ormsby Priory. GRANGE LANE, *The* - 1839 *TAMap*. THE GREEN (local), *Green* 1828 Bry, *Town Green* 1838 *TA*, self-explanatory, *v.* **grēne**[2]. GROVE FM. HOLY WELL, HOLY WELL LANE, *Hollíwell Lane* 1694 *LindDep 55, - Land* (sic) 1697 *ib, Holy Well Lane* 1839 *TAMap*, self-explanatory, *v.* **hālig**, **wella**; there is still a prominent spring on the west side of the gate leading to Randall House. INGS LANE, *the Ings Laine* 1713 *LindDep 55*, cf. *the east Ings close* 1636, *Theastings Close* (sic), *the West Inggs Close* 1661, *the West Inggclose* 1698 all *ib*, 'the meadows, pastures', *v.* **eng** in the pl. Ings Lane forms the boundary with Little Grimsby. MANOR HO, *the Messuage or Mannor house* 1636, *that Capitall Messuage ... in Utterby ... called or known by the name of Ormsby Mannor house* 1698, *the Manor House* 1699, cf. *manerium de Utterby vocat' Nun Ormesby* 1630 all *LindDep 55*. NORTH GRANGE, 1839 *TAMap*; it is north of Grange Fm. OAK PLANTATION is *Goat Close Plant^{n}* 1828 Bry. PARSONAGE (lost), *Pars^{e}* 1828 ib. PEAR TREE LANE, forms the boundary with North Ormsby. PORTER'S YARD, presumably named from the *Porter* family. RANDALL HO, 1838 *TA*, cf. *in valle cuius nomen est Rauendale* Hy2 (1409) Gilb, *great Randle* 1661, 1698, *little Randall* 1671, 1698 all *LindDep 55, Little Randall* 1838 *TA, two Randall Closes* 1713 *LindDep 55*, 'the valley where ravens are found', *v.* **hrafn**, **dalr**, a Scand. compound, the same name as East and West Ravendale *infra*. ROUND HO (local), *Octagon Cottage Garden and Orchard* 1838 *TA*; the original house, octagonal shaped, still stands, but is today called Round House. STONE BRIDGE (local), *Utterby Stone Bridge* 1697 *DCLeases, Stone bridge* 1839 *TAMap*, cf. *Stonebrigg Close* 1661, *stone Briggclose* 1698 both *LindDep 55*, self-explanatory. UTTERBY HO, 1839 *TAMap, Hall* 1828 Bry. WHITE HO.

Field-Names

Principal forms in (a) are 1838 *TA*; forms dated Hy2 (1409) are Gilb; eHy3 (1632) *Dods 135*; 1287, 1288 *Ass*; 1294 *FF*; 1327, 1332 *SR*; 1390 Cl; 1497 *StJ*; 1607 *PM*; 1614 *Harm*; 1636, 1661, 1671, 1673, 1687, 1689, 1694, 1697, 1698, 1699, 1713, 1721, 1739, 1746, 1747, 1750, 1751 *LindDep 55*; 1697 *DCLeases*; 1839 *TAMap*.

(a) Anthony's Pingle (2x) (from the surn. *Anthony*, with **pingel** 'a small enclosure'); Back garden; Back Yd; Barn & Crew Yd (i.e. 'farm yard'), the Barn Close 1750 (1739, 1747), East -, West Barn Cl 1838; the Becks or Grest Becks & Little Becks 1838, the Beckfield 1750 (1747), Beck cl 1838 (*Beckfields* 1687, *the Beck field* 1739, 1747 (area 100 acres), *the Great Becks* 1739, 1747, *Little Beck* 1739, - *Becks* 1747, *Beckfeild Walke* 1661, 1698, cf. Utterby Beck *infra*, *v*. **bekkr**); (Gt -, East Little -, West Little) Bilches (*Close of pasture called Andersons Bilshoes* 1671 (named from the *Anderson* family, cf. William *Anderson* 1608 *Inv*), *great Bilshoes* 1671, 1698, *Great Bilshoe* 1697, *Ormesby Bilshoes* 1671, *Ormsby fout Bilshoe* 1697, - *foot Bilshoes* 1698 (*v*. **fōt** and the neighbouring parish of North Ormsby), *the becke Bishoe* 1673 (*v*. **bekkr**); no explanation can be offered for Bilches/*Bilshoe(s)*); Blayd's cl (from the surn. *Blayd* or perhaps *Blades*, cf. Charles *Blades* 1824 *BT*); Borman cl (named from the *Borman* or *Burman* family, cf. William *Burman* 1695 *BT*, William *Borman* 1822 *BT*); Brick cl (cf. *the Brick-kiln Close* 1739, *the Brick Kiln Close* 1747); Cabbage Garden (3x); Calf cl; Carr cl (*Carr Close* 1661, *Care Close* 1698, *v*. **kjarr** 'brushwood', later 'a bog, a marsh, especially one overgrown with brushwood'); Church Croft and Garden (*ad ecclesiam* 1327, 1332 both (p), *Churchcroft* 1661, *Church-Croft* 1687, (*the*) *Church Croft* 1698, 1721, 1747, *the Church-Croft* 1739, *v*. **cirice**, **croft**); (Plantation in) Church Paddock; Church yard (Btm) (cf. *Churchclose yeard* 1661, *Church close yard* 1698); Clover cl; Cobbys Home Cl; Collingwood cls, - Garth (Garden) (named from the *Collingwood* family, cf. Henry *Collingwood* 1671 *LindDep 55*, *v*. **garðr**); (East -, West) Corn Cl, East -, West Corn Cl Btm (*the home Corne Close* 1671); Cottage underlet; Cottagers cl (2x), Cottagers Gardens (*the Cotchers close* 1636, 1698, - *Close* 1671, *Cotcher close* 1698, *the Cotcher Close* 1713; *cotcher* is a common L form of *cottager*); Cow cl, - Hills (*Cow-hill Close* 1661, *Cow hill Close* 1698, *Cow Hills* 1721, *the Cowhills* 1729, 1747); Crab Garth (Great Moat) (cf. *the Crabtree close* 1636, *Crabtree Close* 1661, *the* - 1697, *the Crab-Tree Closes* 1689, *Crabtree close* 1698, *v*. **crabbe**, **trēow**, **garðr**); (Gt) Dairy House cl; Davisons Homestead (named from the *Davison* family, cf. Thomas *Davison* 1667 *BT*, Thomas *Davison* 1838 *TA*); Dovecote cl (*the douecoate close wherein the* *ould douecoat did sometyme stand* 1636, *Doue coate Close* 1661, *the Dovecoate Close* 1689, 1721, - *Dove Coat Close* 1697, *Dovecote Close* 1729, *the Dovecoat Close* 1747, *v.* **douve-cote**); Drove cl; Far cl; First -, 2nd -, 3rd -, 4th Far Walk (*v.* **walk**); Farrows Orchard (named from the *Farrow* family, cf. William *Farrow* 1818 *BT*, William *Farrow* 1842 White); Fenerick's Home Garth (probably named from the *Fenwick* family, cf. Thomas *Fenwick* 1672 *BT*, Elizabeth *Fenwick* 1819 *ib*, common in the parish and *v.* **garðr** 'an enclosure', as elsewhere in this parish); Footh path Plantation (sic); Forest cl; Four acres; Fourteen acres (Btm, - Grass); Furze, Great Furze cl (*Firrclose* 1661, *Firclose* 1698, *v.* **fyrs**, **clos(e)**; Garden & Plantation; Garing cl (*v.* **geiri** 'a triangular plot of ground', **-ing**[1]); Garth (*v.* **garðr**); Bottom -, Gt -, Top George cl (from the surn. *George*); Gibsons cl, (- Orchard) (from the surn. *Gibson*); Goose Pasture (*v.* **gōs**, **pasture**); Gorse cover (*v.* **gorst**, **cover(t)**; the occurrence of both *Gorse* and *Furze* (*supra*) in the same parish is noteworthy); Great Cl; Great Orchard; Hill cl; Hobbing Garth (2x) (probably from the surn. *Hobbing*, with **garðr**, but Dr J. Insley compares ME *hobing* 'hawking with a hobby', so that this may be an enclosure from which such activities took place); Hog cl; Far -, Nr Holt (*v.* **holt**); Home cl (or Garth), Home Garth, Home yd (*v.* **garðr**, **geard**); Horse cl (2x) (*the Horse close* 1636); Horsley cl (presumably from the family name *Horsley*); Hotchin's cl (from the surn. *Hotchin(s)*); House on the Waste; Howdens Garth (named from the *Howden* family, cf. George *Howden* 1836 *BT*); Hut Garth (a hut is marked on the *TAMap* 1839); the Key Cl 1750, Key cl 1838 (*Key Close* 1739, 1747); Kitchen Garden yard etc.; Laith cl (*v.* **hlaða** 'a barn'); the Lark Firrs 1751 (*larkfirr Close* (sic) 1661, *the Close called Larkfurrs* 1687, *Larkfir Close* 1698, *Lark Furrs* 1721, *the Lark Furz* 1739, 1747, *Lark Firrs* 1746, *v.* **lāwerce** 'a lark', **fyrs**); Leaze cl(s) (*v.* **lea** 'meadow, pasture' (OE **lēah**) in the pl.); the Low Cl 1750 (1739) (cf. *the Willowe or Lowe Closes* in f.ns. (b) *infra*); Malstons 20 acres (named from the *Maltston* family, cf. Maximilian *Maltson* (sic) 1759 *BT*, John *Maltston* 1813 *ib*); Meadow Cl, - pce; Gt -, Lt Michaelmas Holes (*Micklemoorehole Close* 1661, *Micklemor-Hole* 1687, *mickellmorehole close* 1698, *v.* **mikill**, **mōr** with **hol**[2] and **clos(e)**); the Milnfield 1751, Mill Fd 1838 (*Milnefeild Close* 1661, *the great Milne feild wher the Milne lately stood* 1673, *the West Mil-feild* 1687, *milnefeild close* 1698, *Milnfield* 1721, *the Mill-Field* 1739, *Milnfield* 1746, *the Mill Fielld* 1747, *v.* **myln**, **feld**, cf. *the Millers house* 1671, 1698); Mourning cl (obscure); Mustard Seeds (*the Mustard seed close* 1636); the Myers Cl 1750 (1739, 1747), Myers cl and Hovel, Far -, Nr Myers, Middle Myers cl 1838 (*Myers Close* 1661, *the Mires Close* 1671, 1739, 1747, *mires close, the mires close(s)* 1698, *the Mires Closes* 1713; this is no doubt ON **mýrr** 'a mire, swampy ground'. On *TAMap* a pond is marked here and it is still there today); Neds cl (Orchard); Firstnew Walk (sic), Second -, Third new Walk (probably alluding to a sheep-walk, *v.* **walk**); Nine acres; North East pce (cf. *the North East feild* 1661, 1687, 1698, - *Feild* 1671, *the north East feild* 1673); Oat cl (*Oate close* 1661, 1698); Occupation road (i.e. a green lane or access road, originally through the open fields); Orchard and Paddock (cf. *the old Orchard* 1699); Ox cl with Barn (*Oxe Close* 1671, *v.* **oxa**); Pinfold (*v.* **pynd-fald**); Low -, Top Pingle, Pingles (*v.* **pingel**); Plantation (several), Plantation Gowt (*v.* **gotu**); Plough cl; Rape Cl (alluding to the arable crop, oil-seed rape, *Brassica campestris oleifera*); the South Redings 1750, Reedings, (High end) Broad Reedings 1838 (*Utterby Redynge* 1390, *Utterby Reedinges* 1614, *the Readings* (*close*) 1636, *the greate Readinge, Reading Close, Redinge Close, The two Reeding Closes* 1661, *great Readinge, Readingclose* 1698, *the Great -, the South Readings* 1739, 1747, *v.* **hrēod** 'a reed', **eng** 'meadow, pasture'; a pond is marked on *TAMap* in High end Broad Reedings and is still there today); Rye Grass Btm; Seeds cl; Seven pound cl; the Shepherds Cl 1751 (1746, 1747), Shepherd cl 1838 (*the Shepherds close* 1636, *Sheppard Close, North Sheppard close* 1661, *Noth Sheppard close* (sic) 1698, *the Shepperds Close* 1721, *the Shepherd's* - 1739, named from the *Sheppard* family, cf. Ellen *Shepparde* 1614 *Inv*, William *Sheppard* 1661); Shift cl North, - South (the sense of *shift* here, as elsewhere in L f.ns., is uncertain; the term occurs also in Shift Car in Bonby (PN L **2**, 60) and *a Shift Acre* in South Ferriby (ib 116), where the sense "each of several crops in a course of rotation" is suggested from NED; as all the references are to meadow land, another sense, that of "shifting severalty", i.e. an annual arrangement of changing occupation of grassland, may also be considered); Six acres; Slead pce (cf. *the sleede,* PN L **3** 156, where it is noted that ME *slāde, sled*(*e*) can denote 'low lying ground, a valley, a flat grazing area, a stream'); South East pce (*v.* **pece** and cf. North East pce *supra*); Swittle Green (perhaps an error for *Spittle* -, *v.* **spitel**); Thorougfare Pingle (sic) ('a small enclosure beside a road', *v.* **thoroughfare**, **pingel**); Three acres; Great Tidings, Tidings cl (*Tithing Close* 1607, *the new Tidinge Close* 1661, *newtidinge close* 1698, *the Tidings* 1713, *the Tythe piece* 1747, from **tēoðung** in the sense 'land set aside for the payment of tithes'); Tile Kiln cl & Hovel (*the tile Kilne Close* 1671, *the tile kilne close* 1698); Tilneys Paddock (from the surn. *Tilney*); Triangular Plantation (alluding to the shape); Twelve acres; Utterby Beck 1839 (*v.* **bekkr** and cf. the Becks *supra*); Vegetables; Nr -, North -, West Walk (Plantation) (cf. Firstnew Walk *supra*); Well's cl (from the surn. *Wells*); West Lane cl 1838, West Lane 1839 (this is the now unnamed lane leading west from the village); West pce (*v.* **west**, **pēce**); Wilkinsons home cl (named from the *Wilkinson* family, cf. Peter *Wilkinson* 1706 *BT*).

(b) *Atte Bele* 1387, *Attebele* 1287, 1288, - *de Vtterbi* 1294 all (p) (this topographical surn. has also been noted in Fotherby f.ns. (b) *supra* and six times in Burgh le Marsh (LSR) between 1293 and 1395 and once in Welton le Marsh (LSR) in 1343. It is discussed by Kristensson, SMETT 19-20, who draws attention to Ekwall, Studies[2] 159-63 and DEPN s.n. Belaugh. There Ekwall considers a number of p.ns. in Bel- and presupposes an OE **bel* of unknown meaning to explain them. He suggests that this word may be connected with ON *bil*, Danish dial. *bil* 'interval, space', perhaps originally 'interspace' and believes that a possible meaning might be 'a piece of dry land in fen'. The same word occurs in Beald Fm & Drain (PN C 223-4), with a number of ME spellings *Bele*, for which Ekwall's suggested meaning would be topographically apt, as Reaney points out. The same can be said for the L examples of this word, for all four parishes in which they have so far been noted are ones in which a name denoting a piece of dry land in fen or marsh would be natural enough. It may be noted that in considering the meaning of *Bele*, Smith's discussion of the OE **bēl**[1] (EPN s.v.) can be disregarded, for Ekwall was no doubt right in wondering, NoB xlv 139, whether **bēl** occurs in any of the names considered by Smith); *Cawthorpe hedge* 1636 (the boundary (*v.* **hecg**) with the lost *Cawthorpe* in Covenham St Bartholomew); *Detmore Close* 1661, *Dettmore close* 1698 (*v.* **mōr**[1]; the first el. is uncertain, but is possibly **dēop**, with final consonant dissimilated as in Deptford K); *the East feild* 1636 (*v.* **ēast**, **feld**); *Hirst Close* 1661, *hurst close* 1698 (*v.* **hyrst** or the derived surn.); *the Inn yarde* 1636; *the Land-Close* 1687, *the Land-Close* 1687, *the Land Closes* 1694, 1697, 1698 (*v.* **land**); *Lawmire Closes* (sic) 1671, *Lowmire Close* 1673, *Lawmire close* 1698, *West Low Mire* (sic) 1671, *west Lowmire* 1698 (cf. Myers cl *supra*); *vtterby Margate* 1497 ('Utterby boundary-road', *v.* **(ge)mǣre**, **gata**); *newclose* 1661, *new close* 1698; *the north feild*, *the north and south feild* 1636; *Oxleys Close* 1661, *Oxleyes Close* 1698 (possibly from the surn. *Oxley* or *v.* **oxa**, **lea** (OE **lēah**) in the pl.); *Rookesby close* 1698 (named from the *Rooksby* family, cf. *Annas Rouksbie* 1597 *BT*); *one Close called Skipwith foure Acres* 1671, *Skipwith fouracres* 1698 (named from the *Skipwith* family, cf. *Elinoure Skypwith* 1577 *Inv*, William *Skipwith* 1630 *LindDep 55*); *Stile Croft* 1671, *Style* - 1698; *Tousedaile* 1390 (a piece of meadow, *v.* **deill**; the first el. seems obscure, but Dr John Insley suggests that we might think of a Scand. stream-name **þōsa* connected with the IE root **ta*(*u*)- 'dissolve', cf. A. Janzén's remarks on Tosån in Bohuslän, *NoB* 23 (1935), 32-35, and the discussion of Taasinge in *Danmarks Stednamne* 23, 63-66. For the spelling *-ou-* for /o:/ in late ME, *v.* Jordan, para 53); *vian de Couenham* Hy2 (1409) ('the way to Covenham'); *the Willowe or Lowe Closes* 1636, *the Willow Closes or Low Closes* 1697, *Willow Close* 1661, *The Willow Closes* 1687, *the* - 1689, *the Willow Close* 1721, 1747, *the Willow-Close* 1739 (cf. the Low cl in f.ns. (a) *supra*); *Yredaile* eHy3 (1632) (probably 'the Irishmen's share or allotment of land', *v.* **Íri**, **deill**, a Scand. compound).

Wyham cum Cadeby

WYHAM CUM CADEBY

Wyham cum Cadeby 1561, 1562 *BT*, 1712 *Terrier*, 1749 *BT*, *Wyham with Cadeby* 1848 *TA*, *Cadeby cum Wyham* 1680 *BT*

WYHAM

Widun (2x) 1086 DB

Wihum c.1115 LS, Hy2 (1409) Gilb, a1184 (1409) ib (p), 1210-12 RBE (p)

Wihom 1147-66 (1409) Gilb (p), 1185-87 Dane (p), *Wyhum* R1 (c.1331) *Spald i*, 1221 Guis (p), 1245 RRG, 1245 FF, 1250 (1409) Gilb (p), 1254 ValNor *et passim* to 1397 Pat, *Wihum* 1295 RA ii, *-hom* 1303 FA, 1332 *SR*, 1399 Pat, 1428 FA, *-home* 1551 Pat

Wihun 1147-66 (1409) Gilb (p), *Wyhun* 1233 Ch (p), 1233 RA ii, 1241, 1247 RRG

Wium Hy2 Dane (p), Hy2 (1409) Gilb, Hy2 (1314) Ch, 1200 Cur (p), 1202 ChancR (p), 1202 Ass, 1212 Fees, 1218, 1219 Ass (p), 1222 FF (p), 1238-41 Fees, *Wyum* 1200 Dugd iii, c.1200 RA iv (p), 1219 FF (p), 1230 P *et passim* to 1328 Banco, 1428 FA, *Wyom* 1199 (1330) Ch, 1272 *Ass*, 1381 Peace

Wiun 1187, 1188, 1190 *et freq* to 1212 all P (p), 1201 OblR (p), 1202 Ass (p), 1211, 1214 P, 1219 Ass, *Wyun* c.1215, c.1218 RA ii, 1226 FF, 1226 Welles, 1238 Cl, 1240 FF, 1240 Cl (p), *Viun* 1219 Ass, *Wion* 1202 Ass (p)

Wiam 1200 (c.1331) *Spald i*, 1276 RH, *Wyam* 1526 Sub, 1579 *Terrier*

Wiham c.1200 RA iv, a1219 Welles, *Wyham* Hy2 (1409) Gilb, 1272 FF, 1294, 1312 Pat, 1346 FA, 1401 RRep, 1595, 1596 *BT*, 1601 *Terrier et freq*, *-hame* a1219 Welles

Wyorme als Wyham als Wyam 1676 *BRA 125*

'At the heathen shrines', from the dat.pl. **wīhum** of OE **wīh**, **wīg**. Wyham is situated on the slope of the edge of the Wolds rising from the 150 foot contour and overlooking the lower land towards the coast, an excellent site for a number of shrines. This is the most northerly example of a place-name commemorating Anglo-Saxon paganism.

CADEBY

Cadebi 1086 DB, *-by* 1426 Cl, 1431 FA, 1461, 1561 Pat, (- *next Wyam*) 1666, 1673 *LindDep 95*, 1671 *ib*, 1688, 1699 *BT et passim*, Cadby 1410 *Foster*, 1445 AASR xxix

Catebi c.1115 LS, *-by* 1155-58 (1334) Ch, Hy2 Dane (p), c.1200 RA iv, 1212, 1238-41 Fees, 1245 FF, 1254 ValNor, 1260-70 *Foster*, 1281 Ipm, 1291 Tax, 1295 Ipm, 1296 RSu, 1303 FA *et freq* to 1438 *Foster*, *Kateby* c.1200 RA iv, e13 ib ii (p), 1202 Ass, eHy3 (1409) Gilb, 1242-43 Fees, 1270 RRGr, 1275 RH, 1322 Pat, 1374 *Foster*

North Cateby 1287 *Ass*, 1307, 1318, 1319 *Foster*, *Northe* - 1359 *ib*, *Northecateby* 1282 *FF*, *North-* 1349 Pat

Catteby 1222 FF

Katesby 1276 RH

'Káti's farm, village', *v.* bȳ. The first el. is the Scand. pers.n. ON *Káti*, ODan *Kati* found also in South Cadeby LSR, Cadeby Lei and Cadeby PN YWR **1**, 63. It is sometimes *North* Cadeby in contrast to *South* Cadeby, both of which are extinct villages. Cadeby is represented today by Cadeby Hall *infra*. In 1327 and 1332 *SR* it is assessed in Haverstoe Wapentake.

BARTON STREET is *the high way or streete called Lowth streete* 1601 *Terrier*, Barton Street is the name of a presumed pre-Roman trackway from Louth to Barton upon Humber, sometimes in early documents called Louth Street. CADEBY HALL, 1842 White and is *Cadeby Ho* 1824 O, 1828 Bry, - *House* 1830 Gre; it is earlier referred to as *the Cappitall Messuage or Mannor howse of Cadeby* 1666, *the Mannor and graunge of Cadeby* 1671, - *Graunge of Cadeby* 1673, *the mannor and Graunge of Cadeby* 1685, *the Capitall Messuage or Mannor house of Cadeby* 1709 all *LindDep 95* and cf. *Graunge of Cadeby* 1666 *ib*; it is possible that here **grange** is an example of the later dial. use of the word 'a homestead, small mansion or farm-house, especially one standing by itself', a sense quoted from L, *v.* EDD s.v. 2. CADEBY PARK. CHALK HO, so-named from its situation on chalky ground. JOBS OLD HO (lost, approx. TF 273 947), 1828 Bry. JOBS WALK (lost) 1828 ib. This and Wyham Lane are continuations of the same road from Ludborough westwards past Top Fm to the west boundary of the parish. SALTER'S LANE, *Salters Lane* 1828 Bry, the name of a short stretch of road from Ludborough Vale to the parish boundary. SHOP COTTAGE. SIX HOUSES. TOP FM. The reference is to Cadeby, cf. Wyham Top *infra*. WYHAM GORSE. WYHAM HO is *Hall* 1828 Bry. WYHAM LANE (lost), 1828 *ib*, cf. Jobs Walk *supra*. WYHAM TOP, *The Top House* 1824 O.

Field-Names

Principal forms in (a) are 1849 *TA*; forms dated Hy2 (1314) are Ch iii; Hy2 (1632) *Dods 135*; c.1215 RA ii; 1219 Ass; 1276 RH; 1307, 1312, 1318, 1319, 1359 *Foster*, 1308 Cl; 1319 (c.1331), 1330 (c.1331) *Spald i*; 1322 Ipm; 1381 Peace; 1579, 1601, 1693, 117, 1703, 1712, 1724, 1822 *Terrier*, 1666, 1667, 1673, 1737 *LindDep 95*.

(a) Allenbys Btm (from the surn. *Allenby* with **botm**); Bonsor Hill, Bonsor hill Pen fd (*Bonsor* is probably a surn.; cf. Pen Fd *infra*); Cadeby far -, first Cl; Church & Church Yd (cf. *selio Iacet abuttans super Gardinum ecclesie de Northcateby* 1312); Clay Cl; Croft (*v.* **croft**); Far -, Near fd; Field; Glebe; Hall lane; (The) Holt, The holt; Home Cl, - fd, - hill; House cl & Paradise (*v.* **paradise**, probably here having the sense 'a pleasure garden'); Land fd (*v.* **land**); North -, South Btm (*v.* **norð**, **sūð**, **botm**); Large -, Small Ox Cl (*v.* **oxa**, **clos(e)**); Paddock (*v.* **paddok**); Pen fd (adjoins Bonsor Hill Pen fd *supra*, *v.* **penn**[2]); Plantation; Ploughed fd; Public Road (cf. *iuxta communem viam de Northcateby* 1312); the Rectory House 1822, Rectory house & Garden 1849, *Pars.e* 1828 *Bry* (cf. *one mansyon house* 1579, *the house of the same parsonage* 1601, *the parsonage now in the possession of the Lady Anne Ellys of London* 1693, *the Parsonage house* 117, *the parsonage house ... not in the possession of any minister* 1703, *the parsonage house* 1712); Road; Sand pit fd (*v.* **sand**, **pytt** and cf. *Sandehille* 1312); Seed pce (*v.* **sǣd**, **pēce**); Sheep Walk (*the Sheepe walke* 1666, 1667, *the Sheep walk* 1673, *Cadeby Sheep Walk* 1737, *v.* **shepe-walk** 'range of pasture for sheep'); Spring fds & Plunket fds (*v.* **spring**; *Plunket* is probably a surn.); Thorney cl 1822, Thorny Cl 1849; Top house & Garden; Far -, Middle -, Near Walk, Walk next Binbrook (*v.* **walk**); (Large -, Small) Wheat Cl; Wood Cl (*v.* **wudu**, cf. *super boscum* 1219, *super siluam* 1330 (c.1331), *le wodedale* 1330 (c.1331) (*v.* **deill**), and *wodewang* 1330 (c.1331) (*v.* **vangr**, *v.* **wudu**); Far -, Nr Wyham Walk (*the sheepwalke called Wyham Would* 1601, *v.* **walk**, **wald**).

(b) *gardinum Agnetis* 1219 ('Agnes' garden', *v.* **gardin**); *duos Akirhefedes* 1318, - *akirheuedes* 1319 ('two selion heads', *v.* **æcer**, **hēafod**); *le biscopwang* 1330 (c.1331) ('the bishop's infield', alluding to the bishop of Lincoln, *v.* **biscop**, **vangr**); *Bisteldale* 1330 (c.1331) (*Bistel* may well be '(the place) by the enclosure', *v.* **bī** 'by, beside', **stell** 'an enclosure' with **deill** 'a share of land' or **dalr** 'a valley'; the site is unknown); *Duodeim'* (sic) *selio Iacet qui dicitur Boutte* 1312 (*v.* **butt**); *bramdeile* 1330 (c.1331) (probably from **brōm** 'broom', **deill**); *britdeile* 1330 (c.1331) (*v.* **deill**; the first el. is obscure, unless it is ODan *bryti* 'a manorial bailiff'); *small Cherry Holt* 1712 (*v.* **cheri**, **holt**); (*le*) *damwang* 1330 (c.1331) (*v.* **damme** (**dammr**) 'a pond', **vangr** 'a garden, an infield', as elsewhere in this parish); *Depedale* c.1215, 1219, 1312 (*v.* **dēop**, **dalr**); *doggedale* 1330 (c.1331) (*v.* **dogga**, **deill**); *de columbar' Johis de Wihum* 1330 (c.1331) ('John of Wyham's dovecote', *v.* **douve-cote**); *Le Dyke* 1312 (*v.* **dīk**); *estrestannondale* 1330 (c.1331) (this is to be taken along with *mikilstannoudale* and *Westerstannondale infra*. Clearly *estre-*, *mikil-* and *wester-* denote 'the more easterly, the big and the more westerly *Stannondale*' respectively. The latter probably means 'the stony share of land', the first el. being ME *stanen* (**stǣnen**) 'stony', the second **deill** 'a share, a portion of land (in the common field)', presumably a large share subdivided into at least three); *in campis de Kateby* Hy2 (1632), *campum de Katesby* 1276, *in campis de Northe Cateby* 1359, *in campum de Cateby* 1381; *in campis de Wium* Hy2 (1314), *in campum de Wyom* 1381, *the fieldes of Wyham* 1601 (*v.* **feld**); *Flynthwange* 1312 (*v.* **flint**, **vangr**); *furlanges* c.1215, *Furlanges* 1219 (*v.* **furlang**); *Graiwang* c.1215, *Graiawang'* 1219, *grawang* 1330 (c.1331) (*v.* **grǣg**[1], **vangr**); *Grangewaud'* 1219 (*v.* **grange**, **wald**; it was probably a grange of Spalding Priory which held land here); *le Grenegatehende* 1312 (*v.* **grēne**[1], **gata** with **ende**[1]); *hawismarforthewang* 1319 (c.1331), *Hawismarforthewang* 1330 (c.1331) (probably 'Hawis' boundary furrow', *v.* **marfur**, with **vangr**; the first el. is the ME (OFr) feminine pers.n. *Haueis*, ultimately from Frankish *Hadwīdis*); *hidirbisteldale* 1319 (c.1331), *hiderbisteldale*, *hidrebisteldale* 1330 (c.1331) ('the nearer part of *Bisteldale* (*supra*)', *v.* **hider** 'nearer'); *Hole* 1312 (*v.* **hol**[1]); *Hullebusc* c.1215,

Hullebosc (sic) 1219 (*v.* **busc**; the first el. is probably the ME pers.n. or surn. *Hulle*, ultimately a pet form of *Hugh*); *Lamcroftfeld* 1330 (c.1331) (*v.* **lamb**, **croft**, with **feld**); *Lanethorne* (sic), *Lanethorne fourlanges* 1312; *Leirlandes* c.1215, 1219 ('clay selions', *v.* **leirr, land**); *Lidh* c.1215, *Lind* (sic) 1219, *Le Lyethe* 1312 (probably from **hlið** 'a slope'); *Liteldale* c.1215, *Litledale, Litlesdale* 1219 (*v.* **lytel, deill**; if *Litles-* is correct, the first el. may be a derived nickname); *super uiam que uadit uersus Linc'* c.1215, *viam que vadit versus Lincolniam* 1219 ('the way that leads towards Lincoln'); *Lodale* 1312; *Lynggedallefourlanges, Lynggdalefourlanges* 1312 (*v.* **lyng, deill**, a Scand. compound with **furlang**); *atte Mare de Cateby* 1308 (p) ('at the boundary of Cateby', *v.* **(ge)mǣre**); *le marlepit* 1330 (c.1331) (self-explanatory); *mikilstannoudale* (sic) 1330 (c.1331) (in view of the certain readings of *estrestannondale* and *westerstannondale* here *-stannou-* is presumably an error for *-stannondale*, though the reading itself is certain, *v.* **mikill** and *estrestannondale supra*); *Molendin' meum vent'cum* 1307 ('my windmill', *v.* **wind-myln**); *le Northcrofte* 1312 (*v.* **norð, croft**); *in campo aquilonari* c.1215, *in Boriali campo de Northcateby* 1312 (*v.* **norð, feld**); *Northklyff* 1312 (*v.* **norð, clif** and cf. *southklyff* infra); *the pond yards* 1712; *the Preists Close* 117, *the Priest or ...rlong Close* 1712, *the Priests Close* 1724 (*v.* **prēost**; the partly illegible alternative 1712 form may be *Furlong Close*, cf. *furlanges supra*); *Scortebuttes* c.1215, *Scortebutes* 1219, *scorebuttes* (sic) 1330 (c.1331) (*v.* **sceort** in a Scandinavianized form, **butte**); *loco qui uocat' serlewe* 1330 (c.1331) (obscure); *le sik'* 1330 (c.1331) (*v.* **sík**); *in campo australi* c.1215, 1219; *in campo Australi de Northcateby* 1312 (*v.* **sūð, feld**, cf. *in campo aquilonari supra*); *southklyff* 1312 (*v.* **sūð, clif**, cf. *Northklyff supra*); *Stockemare* 1312 (*v.* **stocc, (ge)mǣre**); *Swanstanges* c.1215, *Swanestang'* 1219 ('the herdsman's roods of land', *v.* **swān**[2], **stǫng** and cf. Swanland Dale Mearfur, PN L 2 23); *Toindale* (sic, and checked from the MS) c.1215, *Tornedale* 1219 (*v.* **þorn, deill**; *Toin-* is no doubt an error for *Torn-*); "a toft called" *le Uphalle* 1322 ('the upper or higher hall', *v.* **upp, hall**); *super boscum Mathei Vanin* c.1215, *boscum Mathei Wanin* 1219 ('Matthew Vanin's wood', *v.* **wudu**); *Westerbisteldale* 1319 (c.1331), *Westerbiseldale* (sic), *Westerbisteldale* 1330 (c.1331) ('the westerly part of *Bisteldale'*, *v.* **westerra** and *Bisteldale supra*); *Westerstannondale* 1330 (c.1331) (*v.* **westerra**, and *estrestannondale supra*); *le West Welle* 1312 (*v.* **west, wella**); *Westwude ende* c.1215, *Westwde ende* 1219 (*v.* **west, wudu**); *toftum Wigodi* c.1215, 1219 (*v.* **toft**; the first el. is a Latinized form of the ME pers.n. *Wigod*, from ODan *Wīgot*, OSwed (runic) *Vīgautr*); *Wyham Wonge* 1601 (*v.* **vangr**); *le Wylues* 1318, 1319 ('the willows', from the pl. of **wilig** 'a willow'); *Wyncebygarthe* 1312 (*v.* **garðr** 'an enclosure'; the first el. is probably a surn. from Winceby LSR).

Haverstoe Wapentake

HAVERSTOE WAPENTAKE

Hawardeshou (3x) 1086 DB, c.1115 LS, 1238-41 Fees, 1275 RH, 1298 Ass, 1316 FA, *-ho* 1168, 1169, 1170, 1185, 1191 P, 1201 ChancR, 1206 P, *-how* 1202 Ass, 1281 QW, 1288 Ipm, *-howe* 1295 *NCot*, 1327 *SR*, 1329 *Ass*, 1431 FA, *-h'* 1202 P, *Hawardishou* 1219 Fees, *Hawardshowe* 1428 FA, *Hauwardeshowe* 1332 *SR*, *Hawordshow* 1385 Peace

Hawardeho 1230 P, lHy3 *NCot*, 1298 Ass, *Hawardhou* 1242-43 Fees, 1265 Misc, 1338 Pat, *-hou* 1275 RH, 1281 QW, *-howe* 1396 Peace, *Awardeho* 1230 ChancR

Haiwardho 1185 RotDom, *Haywardeshow* 1275 RH

Hawurtheho 1200 P, *Hawrteho* 1201, 1202 ib

Hauevers-sto 1537 LP xii

Havesto 1610 Speed

The forms are preceded or followed by Wapentake or Deanery, usually in a Latin form, *v.* **vápnatak, wæpengetac**.

Haverstoe is 'Hawarth's mound', from the ODan pers.n. *Hawarth*, ON *Hávarðr* and **haugr** 'a mound, a burial mound', a Danish compound. In the same wapentake is Hawerby, 'Hawarth's farm, village', *v.* **bȳ**, and the coincidence is too great to avoid the conclusion that both are named from the same man. The site of the wapentake meeting-place is almost certainly a mound in the parish of Hawerby. Mr A.A. Garner first drew attention to the presence of a round barrow, close to the road from Grainsby to Wold Newton at TF 254 977. Mr Ian George, Sites and Monuments Officer at the Lincoln City and County Museum, informs me that the barrow was formerly some 53 feet in diameter and up to 5 feet high in the late 1970s, but has recently been almost levelled by ploughing. It is situated close to the parish boundary between Hawerby and Wold Newton in a field later called Beacon Field, *v.* Gt -, Lt Beacon Field in Hawerby f.ns. (a) and the barrow itself is no doubt *Horby beacon* in 1703, the site of *Pit Clump* 1824 O. Personal examination confirms that there is little trace of it today. It seems highly likely that this pre-historic round barrow was the meeting-place of Haverstoe wapentake. As Mr Garner pointed out, the site commands a fine view of the Humberside levels.

Haverstoe was subsequently joined with Bradley to become known as Bradley Haverstoe Wapentake.

Ashby cum Fenby

ASHBY CUM FENBY, 1595 *BT*, 1601 *Terrier*, 1617, 1660 *BT*, 1664 *Terrier et freq*, *Asbye cum Fenby* 1658 *BT*, *Asbie cum Fenby* 1577 *Terrier*, - *fenbie* 1580, 1589, 1591, - *Fenbie* 1600, 1603, 1607, - *Fenby* 1603 all *BT*, *Ashbye cum fenbye* 1594 *ib*, - *Fenbye* 1601 *LCS*, 1627 *BT*, - *Fenby* 1635 *ib*, *Ashby cum Fennby* 1718 *Haigh*.

ASHBY

Achesbi 1086 DB

Aschebi (3x) 1086 DB, (2x) c.1115 LS

Ascbi c.1115 LS

Askebi 1196 ChancR. 1202 Ass (p), 1204 P, *-by* 1202 FF, 1205 Cur, 1207 FF, 1210 Cur, 1210-12 RBE, 1226-28, 1242-43 Fees, 1254 ValNor, 1257, 1262 FF, 1280 Ch, 1281 QW, 1291 Tax, 1295 Ipm, 1303 FA *et freq* to 1428 ib, *-bi* 1238-41 Fees, - *Iuxta Grymmesby* 1287 *Ass*, "near" *Grimesby* 1335 Cl, - "by" *Fanneby* (sic) 1299 Pat, - "near" *Fenneby* 1300 Cl, - *juxta Fanneby* 1300 Orig, - "by" *Waltham* 1328 Banco, - "near" *Briggesle* 1334 Cl, - *juxta Briggesby* (sic) 1346 de l'Isle, *Haskebi* 1212 Fees, *-by* 1256-57 RA x

Askby 1276 RH, 1388 Peace, 1402, 1431 FA

Ascheby 1275, 1276 RH, *Asheby* 1303 FA, 1557 Pat, *-bie* 1557 InstBen, 1576 LER, *Ashbye* 1595 *BT*, - *iuxta Fenby* 1623 *Hill*, 1635 *BT*, *-by* 1595 *ib*, 1601 *Terrier et passim*, - *in fenby* 1728 *MiscDep 16*

Asseby 1526 Sub, 1539-40 Dugd iv, *Assby* 1535 VE, 1553 Pat, *Asbye* 1561 *BT*, 1576 Saxton, 1610 Speed, 1658 *BT*, 1675 Ogilby

Fellows-Jensen, SSNEM 31-32, points out that there are six p.ns. Ashby in L. The forms of each are similar and it is clear that they are Danish compounds 'the farm, village where ash-trees grow', *v.* **askr**, **bȳ** It is possible, however, that the first el. is the ON, ODan pers.n. *Aski* found occasionally in independent sources in L. Indeed, Sandred, JEPN 19, 9-10, assumes this pers.n. as the first el. of Ashby in Flegg Hundred (Nf).

There are also five Ashbys in Nth and three in Lei, the forms of each indicating that the first el. is OE **æsc** 'an ash-tree', cognate with ODan **askr**. This would suggest that they are partial Scandinavianizations of earlier English names, perhaps Ashton 'the farm, village, estate where ash-trees grow'. Fellows-Jensen, SSNEM 32, suggests that the L Ashbys are probably comparable and that they too may be Scandinavianizations of earlier English names. Whilst this is formally and theoretically possible, Danish influence is so strong in L that it would hardly be wise to look upon the Lincolnshire Ashbys as being other than their forms suggest, pure Danish compounds. Ashby, here, is probably to be interpreted as 'Aski's farmstead, village', *v.* **bȳ**. Ashby is occasionally described as being near Brigsley, Fenby, Great Grimsby and Waltham *infra*.

FENBY

Fendebi 1086 DB
Fenbi hundred 1086 DB
Fembi c.1115 LS
Fenbi 1190, 1191, 1192 P, *-b'* 1204 ib, 1238-41 Fees, *-by* 1231 Cl, 1231 Ch, 1242-43 Fees, c.1276 LNQ vii, 1311 Pat, 1312 Fine, 1312 Orig, 1327 *SR*, 1328 Ipm, 1347 *Cor et freq*, *-be* 1498 Pat
Fenneby 1261 FF, 1275, 1276 RH, 1295 Ipm, 1311 YearBk, 1311 Ipm *et passim* to 1362 ib, *Feneby* 1338 *HarlCh*
Fanneby 1299 Pat, 1300 Orig, *-bie* 1556 CA

'The farm, village in the fen', *v.* **fenn**, **bȳ**, an Anglo-Danish hybrid with the first el. OE **fenn**. It is most likely to be a partial Scandinavianization of an earlier OE p.n., perhaps Fenton, with a similar meaning. The name is represented today by Fenby Fm, which lies in what must have been a fenny area on the lower slope of the Wolds.

ASHBY HILL, perhaps cf. *del Hill'* 1327 *SR* (p), *del hill'* 1347 *Cor v.* **hyll**, the name of the steep slope of the Wolds between the

100 and 200 foot contours. ASH HOLT, perhaps cf. *ash grene* in f.ns. (b) *infra*. BARTON STREET, cf. *the Highe strete* 1577, - *high street* 1601, 1664 all *Terrier*, Barton Street is the name of the presumed pre-Roman trackway from Louth to Barton upon Humber, found in a number of parishes in this wapentake. FAR YARD. FENBY WOOD, east of Fenby Fm, 1856 *Yarb* and is *Fenby Close* 1824 O, 1772 *Yarb*, 1843 *TA*. FENBY WOOD, west of Fenby Fm, is *Cottagers Plat* 1824 O, 1843 *TA* and - *Plot* 1843 *ib*, *v*. **plat**, **plot**. GLEBE FARM HO, cf. *ye gleab close* 1679, *the Old Glebe* 1822, 1834, 1837 all *Terrier*. HALL FM, cf. *atte hall' de Askeby* 1360 *Cor* (p), *v*. **hall**. MOOR HO, MOORHOUSE FM, *Ashby Moorhurst* (sic) 1824 O, *Moorhouse* 1843 *TA*, - *Farm* 1853 *MiscDon 348*. NORMAN WELLS HO, cf. *Low* -, *Top Normanwells* 1843 *TA*; this is on the boundary with Grainsby parish and *Norman* may be a rationalisation of **nānmann** 'no man', indicating spring(s) claimed by more than one parish or owner, *v*. **wella**. SOUTH FM (local). SYKES FM, probably named from the family of John *Sykes* 1842 White, 1843 *TA*. It is now called Thoroughfare Farmhouse. WRAY ALMSHOUSES, *Alms Houses* 1843 *TA*, named from the Wray family, formerly lords of the manor. Note, *There is in the said Parish an Hospital founded by the Lady Wray for six poor Widows or Widowers who have each a convenient appartment and £30 per Ann' payable out of certain Lands in Barnoldby-le-Beck in this county* 1791 *Terrier*. Cf. also *Wray lande* 1577, *wraye land* 1601, *Wray Lands* 1662 and *Christopher Wray knighte* 1577 all *Terrier*.

Field-Names

Principal forms in (a) are 1843 *TA*. Forms dated 1327 and 1332 are *SR*; 1347 are *Cor*; c.1370 are *Extent*; 1388 and 1395 are Peace; 1435 Pat; 1577, 1601, 1612, 1627, 1632, 1638, 1662, 1664, 1679, 1690, 1697, 1703, 1709, 1724, 1762, 1791, 1822, 1834, 1837 are *Terrier*; m17, 1718, 1720, 1784 are *Haigh*; 1705, 1722, 1772 are *Yarb*; 1708 are *Td'E*; 1744 are *MiscDep 118*; 18 are *MiscDep 16*.

(a) Ashby Cl (*Ashby closes* m17); Back Garth; Beck Cl, a different field from Middle beck (*the becke* 1577, *the Beck* 1577, 1664, *the Becke* 1601, *the beck* 1664, *ye Beck* 1690, *the Beck furlonge* 1577, - *furlong* 1664, *the Beke Furlong* 1601, *v*. **bekkr**, **furlang**, named from Waithe Beck); Bennett's Ploughed

Cl (2x) (from the surn. *Bennett*, cf. William *Bennet* 1723 *BT*); Blythe Cl (4x) (from the family of John *Blyth* 1775 *BT*); Bullivent Cl (from the *Bullivant* family, cf. John *Bulivant* 1670 *BT*); Car Cl (*v.* **kjarr**); Carrd Cl (sic) (3x) (perhaps from the surn. *Card*, *v.* Reaney s.n.); Church Yard; Coney Greens (*v.* **coni** 'a rabbit', **grēne**[2] in the pl.); Low -, Top Corn Cl; Cow Cl; Crooks (*crok hyll, croke gate, croke furres* 1577, *Crooke gate, - Furrs, Croke furrs* 1601, *Crook furs* 1664, 1690, *Crake gate, - hill* (sic) 1664, *Crook gate, - hil* 1690; the *TA* Crooks is the name of a field in a marked bend on the boundary of the parish, *v.* **krókr** 'land in a bend'; cf. the appellative use of *crook* in *One Crook of medow, ii Crokes of medow* 1601 *Terrier* (Brigsley)); Crowston's Low Mill Croft 1784 (cf. Crowston's Mill Croft in Brigsley f.ns. (a) *infra*); Deborah Cl; Dodson Cl (2x) (from the surn. *Dodson* cf. Edmund *Dodson* 1777 *BT*); Dove Cote Cl; Elbow Cl (2x) (presumably this alludes to the shape; it lies on the parish boundary and on *TAMap* it is not particularly distinctive); Ewe Cl; Fandels; Fenby Orchard, - Walks; Fir Cl; Garth (*v.* **garðr**); Gunnel's Yard 1822, Gunnell's yard 1834, Gunnill's Yard 1837 (named from the family of Edward *Gunnel* 1728 *BT*); Gt Havercroft (*great habercroft* 1664, *v.* **hafri** 'oats', **croft**); Little Hawcroft (*great hawcrofte, hawcroft* 1577, 1601, *Hawcroft* 1664, 1690, *great Hawcroft hedg* 1664, *Great Haw croft* 1690, *v.* **haga**[1] 'a hedge, an enclosure', **croft**); Hog Plot (several) (*v.* **plot**); Home Cl (4x), Home Fd (4x); Horse Cl; House & Garth (2x); Janett's Home Cl; Lea Cl (*The Lay-close* 1697, *Lay-close* 1703, *v.* **lǣge**, **clos(e)**); the Little Park 1822, 1834, 1837, Little - 1843; Low Cl (2x); Major Plot (probably from the surn. *Major* with **plot**); Manby Walk (*v.* **walk**; *Manby* is probably a surn.); May Cl(s) (probably named from the family of Mary *May* 1817 *BT*); New Pce (*v.* **pece**); Norlands (perhaps from **norð** and **land**; it lies in the extreme north-west corner of the parish); Nymph Walk (3x) (*v.* **walk**; the significance of *Nymph* is unclear, though it may possibly stand for ME *nimfete* 'the white water lily (*Nymphæa alba*)'); Oat Fd (several); the Old Corn Cls 1822, 1837, the old Corn cls 1834; Old Park; Old Road House & Buildings; Paddison's Pce 1822, 1837, - pce 1834, Paddison Pce 1843 (named from the *Paddison* family, cf. John *Padison* 1642 LPR, with **pece**); Palmer leys (no doubt from the surn. *Palmer* with **lea** (OE **lēah**) in the pl.); a Field called the Park 1822 (cf. Old Park *supra*); Parsonage house 1762, The Parsonage House 1791 (*the parsonage house* 1664, *The Parsonage house* 1679, *A* - 1697, *ye Parsonage hous* (sic) 1703, cf. *the parsonage lande* in (b) *infra*), Rectory House 1822, Rectory-house 1834; The Pinfold (*v.* **pynd-fald**); Pingle (5x) (*ye Pingle* 1697, *v.* **pingel**); Plough'd Cl; Seeds Pce (*v.* **pece**); Seven Acre; Shop Cl (*Shop-close* 1697, *v.* **sc(e)oppa** 'a booth, a shed'); Six Acre; Sixteen Acre; Stamp Cl (Plantation) (from the surn. *Stamp*, cf. John *Stamp* 1808 *BT*); Stoker Cl (perhaps from the surn. *Stoker*); Stone Briggs (*v.* **brycg**, in a

Scandinavianized form and in the pl.); Street Fd 1822, 1834, 1837, 1843, - Plantation 1843 (*Street furlong* 1690, cf. *ye Street in Fenby Field* 1690, *v.* **strǣt**; the reference is uncertain, for it is not near the ancient trackway Barton Street); Three Acre (2x); Town End pce ('piece of land at the end of the village', from **tūn**, **ende**[1] with **pece**); Tup Garth (*v.* **tup** 'a breeding ram'. **garðr**); Turnpike Cl (2x) (*v.* **turnepike**); Twelve Acre; Waith Road 1791 (*Waithe road* 1697, *Waithe-Road* 1703 'the road to Waithe (*infra*)'); Water Garth (*v.* **wæter**, **garðr**).

(b) *the Acres* 1577 (*v.* **æcer**); *Asby feelde* 1627 (*v.* **feld**); *Ashby Cow Pasture* 18; *ash grene* 1577, *Ashe greene* 1601, *Ash green* 1664, *Ashgreen* 1690 (*v.* **æsc**, **grēne**[2]); *bond gate* 1664, *Bendgate* (sic) 1690 (*v.* **gata**; the first el. is possibly ME *bond(e)* 'bondman' from ODan *bondi* 'peasant proprietor'); *the bottom Close* 1718; *the Butt marfer, the buttes under ye towne* 1577, *the buttes* 1601, *a little stighe cominge to the butt marfa* (sic) 1601, *butt Marfarr* 1664, *But Marfar* 1690, - *marfar* 1697 (*v.* **butte**, **marfur**); *Carriver Land* 1690 (Dr John Insley suggests that the first el. is Fr *carrefor(es)* 'a cross-roads, intersection', cf. ME *carfouk*); *the checker pice* (sic) 1577, *the Checker pece* 1601, *the checker peec* (sic) 1664, *ye Checquer piece* 1690 (*v.* **cheker**); *the crabbe hyll* 1577, *the Crabbe hill* 1601, *ye Crab hil* 1690; *in Le Croftis*, - *Croftes* 1327, - *Croftes* 1332, *de croftes de Askeby, inthe croft* - 1347, *in the Croftes de Askeby* c.1370, *othe Crofts de Askby* 1388, *in the Croftes de Askeby* 1395, *atte Croftes* 1435 all (p), *croftes landes, Croft wyllowes* 1577, *Crofte willes* (sic) 1601, *Crofts willows* 1664; *Croft* - 1690 (*v.* **croft**); *deale sicke greene* 1612, *the dale sick* 1664, *Dalesike* 1690 (*v.* **dalr**, **sík**); *the East fyelde, the east fyeld* 1577, *the East feild* 1601, *the east field* 1664, *ye East Field* 1690; *ye East Side of ye sayd town* 1662 (*v.* **ēast**, **feld**); *fenby churchwaye* 1577, *Fenby church way* 1664, - *Church way* 1690 (*v.* **cirice** and cf. the forms in *Kirk-*, s.n. *Atte Kyrke infra*); *campum de Fenneby* 1276 RH, *campis de ... Fenby* 1431 *AD*, *fenby fyelde* 1577, *Fenby feild, fenby fyelde* 1601, *Fenby field(s)* 1612, - *feeld* 1638, - *feild* 1662, 1664, - *field* 1664, 1690 (*v.* **feld**); *Great Fenby Green* 1705, 1744, *Little* - 1705, 1722, 1744, *fenby-Green-head* 1638, *Fenby greene (head)* m17, *Fenby Green heads* 1703 (*v.* **grēne**[2]); *Fenbye hedge* 1612 (*v.* **hecg**); *Fenbie short Butts* 1709, *Fenby short Butts* 1724 (*v.* **butte**); *Fenbie short Furlong*, - *long furlong* 1709, 1724, *Fenby Short furlong* 1724 (*v.* **furlang**); *fenbye mylne* 1577, *Fenby milne* 1601; *fenby styghe* 1577, *Fenbie Stighe* 1601 (*v.* **stīg**); *ye West field of Fenby* 1690 (all named from Fenby); *forth hedg* 1664 (*v.* **forð** 'in front', **hecg**); *grymsbye gate* 1577, *Grymsby gate* 1601, *Grimsby* - 1664 ('the road to Grimsby', *v.* **gata**); *ye High street* 1690 (this may well be a reference to Barton Street); *Howfa hyll, Howfa hedg* 1577, *howfa hill* 1601, *howfah hill, Hompha hill* (sic) 1664, *Howsah hil* (sic), - *hedge*

1690; *in Le Hyrne* 1327, *in the hirne* 1332 both (p) (*v*. **hyrne**); *Atte Kyrke* 1327, *ad ecclesiam* 1332 both (p), *Short Kyrk landes, longe kyrklandes* 1577, *Longe kirkland, Short kirklands* 1601, *Kirkland, Long kirk lands* 1664, *Long kirk lands* 1690 (*v*. **kirkja**, **land**, cf. the forms in *Church-* s.n. *fenby churchwaye supra*); *lenges furlonge* 1577, *Lenges furlonge, - medowe* 1601, *Lengs furlong, - Meadow* 1664 (no doubt from the surn. *Leng*); *Long furland* 1690 (*v*. **lang**[1], **furlang**); *Long meadow* 1690; *lowe lande* 1577, *- land* 1601; *morysse gate, morysse grene, morysse oddes, morysse southe greene, morisse thornes* 1577, *beneath morris, morice gate, - greene, morris oddes, morris Thorns, Morris southgreene* 1601, *upon Morric(e), Morrice-gate, Morrice green, - South green* 1664, *Morrice gate, - green, - Thorns, - southgreen, Moris gate* (sic), *Morris oddes* 1690 (perhaps from ME **mōrisch** 'moist and soft, spongy', though this is purely speculative, with **gata**, **grēne**[2], **þorn**; *oddes* may allude to a topographical feature, ON **oddi** 'a point or tongue of land' or may be ME **odde** 'odd, the odd one of three &c.', perhaps having the sense of 'remnant'); *the new enclosed peice of ground* 1720 (*v*. **pece**, it was in Fenby); *the parsonage lande* 1577, *- land* 1601, 1664, *the Parsonage heading* 1664, *ye -* 1690 (*v*. **land**, **hēafod**, **-ing**[1], cf. foll. n.); *the parsons land* 1577, 1601, *- headyng* 1577 (*v*. **hēafod**, **-ing**[1]); *the pear garthe* 1577, *the peare garth* 1601, *peargarth* 1664, *Peargarth* 1690 (*v*. **peru**, **garðr**); *pettam* (*greene*) 1577, *Pettam* (*greene*) 1601, *pettam* 1664, *Pettam* 1690 (perhaps *v*. **pete** 'peat', with an uncertain second el.); *Ratcliffe lands, Ratcliffe medowe* 1577, *Ratclife land, Ratcliffe meadowe* 1601 (named from the *Ratcliffe* family, cf. *Mr Ratcliffe* 1577); *Rowson lande* 1577, *Rawson land* 1664, *ye lands now or late Rowsons* 1690 (named from the *Rowson* family, cf. Robert *Rowson* 1610 *BT*); *Saundersons land* 1664, *Saunderson's -* 1690 (named from the *Saunderson* family, cf. Lawrence *Saunderson* 1596 *Inv*, Robert *Saunderson* 1642 LPR); *Sharpethorne hedge* 1612 (perhaps alluding to the common sloe or blackthorn (*Prunus spinosa*), with its many stout thorns, rather than to the hawthorn, commonly used for hedging, *v*. **scearp**, **þorn**, with **hecg**); *little Short landes* 1601 (*v*. **sceort**, **land**); *Smiths lands, - Meadow* 1664 (named from the *Smith* family, cf. Christopher *Smithe* 1573 *Inv*, John *Smith* 1642 LPR); *ye South bank* 1690; *the stone* (*Close*), *the stone furlonge* 1577 (*v*. **stān**, **furlang**); *Tharrolde lande* 1577 (named from the *Tharrold* family, cf. John *Tharrold* 1591 *Inv*); *Short tofte* 1577, *- Tofte* 1601 (*v*. **sceort**, **toft**); *the hyeway at the Towen Ende, the Towen' ende* 1577, *ye highe way at the towne end* 1601 (*v*. **tūn**, **ende**[1]); *welsyk* 1577, *Welsike* 1601, 1664, 1690, *welsyk hyll, welsyke heale* 1577, *Welsyke hill, - head* 1601, *- Hill* 1664, *- Hil* (sic) 1690 (*v*. **wella**, **sīc**, **sík**, with **hēafod**, **healh** and **hyll**); *the west fyelde* 1577, *the weast feild* 1601, *ye West Field* 1690, *W. Field* 1703, *the West Field* 1708 (*v*. **west**, **feld**); *the west field of Fenby* 1664; *ye West side of ye sayd towne* 1662; *the whomstall* 1664 (*v*. **hām-stall** 'a homestead' cf.

the Parsonage house *supra* in (a)); *Woodall Headings* 1577, *Wooddall headinges* 1601, *woodall headings* 1664, *wooddale* - 1690 (this is perhaps from the surn. *Woodall*; for *headings* v. PN L **2** 14); *woodhyll furlong* 1577, *Woodhill furlonge* 1601, *Woodhill Furlong* 1690 (*v.* **wudu**, **hyll**, with **furlang**).

Barnoldby le Beck

BARNOLDBY LE BECK

Bernulfbi 1086 DB, 1196 ChancR, *-by* 1230 Cl
Bernoluebi 1178 P
Bernoleby 1202 Ass (p), 1231 Ch, 1231 Cl
Bernolesbi 1202 *HarlCh*, 1202 (1342) Pat
Bernoldeby 1234 FF
Bernolbi 1204 P, *-by* 1220-40 *Foster*, 1254 ValNor, 1280 RSu, 1281 QW, 1287 Ipm, 1293 *NCot*, 1293, 1294 *Ass*, 1294 RSu, 1296 Cl, 1298 *Ass*, 1304 Cl, 1308 *NCot*, 1314 Inqaqd *et freq* to 1526 Sub, *-b'* 1238-41 Fees, *Bornolby* (sic with *Bo-* for *Be-*) 1275, 1276 RH, *Bernalby* 1240 FF (p), 1298 ChancW
Bernoldby 1322 Pat, 1327 *SR*, 1344, 1348 Pat, 1406, 1408, 1415 Cl, *Bernaldeby* 1255 Pap
Barnolby 1387, 1393 Pat, 1393 *HarlCh*, 1472 AD, 1535 VE iv, 1548, 1557 Pat, 1623 *Hill*, *- le Beck* 1706 *Terrier*, *-be* 1394 Pat, *-bie* 1576 LER, *-bye* 1601 *Terrier*, *Barnalby* 1380 AASR xiv, 1428 FA, 1498 Pat, 1639 *Foster*, *- in the Beck* 1715 *Terrier*, *-bey* 1509-10 LP i, *-bye* 1548 *Anc*, 1644 LAAS ii
Barnoldby 1408 Hast i, 1601 *LCS*, 1644 LAAS ii, 1723 SDL, *- upon Becke* 1662, *- upon ye Becke* 1668, 1671 all *Terrier*, *- le Beck* 1770, 1816 *MiscDon 140*, 1822 *Dixon*, 1822 *Terrier et passim*, *Barnaldby* 1410 Fine, 1638 *Terrier*
Barneby 1402 FA, 1610 Speed, *- by the Beke* 1675 FMB i, *Barnabye* 1576 Saxton, *-by* 1653 *ParlSurv*, 1695 Morden

It is to be identified with *Bernetebi* c.1115 LS and *Barnetbie* a1567 LNQ v, where Barnoldby has been confused with Barnetby le Wold, PN L 2, 8-10.

'Bernulf's farm, village', *v.* **bȳ**. The first el. is in all probability the ON pers.n. *Biǫrnúlfr*, recorded independently in DB from Yorkshire, *v.* Feilitzen 200, rather than the cognate OE pers.n. *Beornwulf*, especially taking into consideration the heavy

Danish influence in north L.

It is later *in the Beck*, *v.* **bekkr** 'a stream' and it is noteworthy that the form *le Beck* has not been noted before the early 18th century. *v.* also the comparative forms for Becklands *infra*.

BARTON STREET, 1671, 1686, 1691, 1706, 1715, - *Streete* 1668 all *Terrier*, this is the name of the pre-Roman trackway from Louth to Barton upon Humber, found in other parishes in this wapentake. BECKLANDS, *The* - 1895 *BD*, and cf. *the becke* 1601, 1624, 1638, - *Becke* 1634 all *Terrier* and cf. Barnoldby le Beck *supra*. BEDLAM HILL, 1828 Bry, presumably a derogatory nickname, "alluding to the Royal Bethlem Hospital in London, an old-established institution for the insane" Field 17. GLEBE FARM COTTAGE, cf. *Glebe Lands on the East side of the town* 1706 *Terrier*, *v.* **glebe**. THE GRANGE, apparently a late use of **grange**, found elsewhere in north L, for a homestead, a small mansion, especially one standing by itself. HUNTSMAN'S OBELISK. Part of the inscription on the obelisk states "This monument was raised by his many friends, as a token of their regard, and to mark the spot where William Smith, huntsman to the Earl of Yarborough, fell on the 11th of April 1845". The site was given by a friend "on the 6th Day of April 1861". MANOR HO, 1828 Bry. MOUNT PLEASANT WEST. NEW FM. OAKLAND HO. PARSONAGE FM (lost), *Pars^e^ F.^m^* 1828 Bry. THE RECTORY, *a parsonage house* 1601, 1638, 1715, - *howse* 1624, *A parsonage house* 1706, 1712, *one parsonage House* 1718, *One Rectory House* 1864 all *Terrier* and cf. *The Old Rectory House now a dwelling house* 1864 *ib.* THE SHIP, 1828 Bry. SUNK FM. TEAM GATE DRAIN, 1824 O, cf. *Team Gate* 1828 Bry. The Drain forms the boundary with Bradley. On Bry, *Team Gate* apparently marks a point on the road to Bradley. WELBECK HO, *Welbeck Cottage* 1828 Bry. WELBECK SPRING, *a place called Welbecks* 1770 *EnclA*, *Welbecks* 1820 *EstMap*, *Wellbeck* 1824 O, *Well Beck* 1828 Bry, 'the stream rising from the spring', *v.* **wella**, **bekkr**, a compound found elsewhere in north L, cf. Welbeck Spring PN L 2, 234. There is a deep hollow here with a spring rising from it and flowing to join Team Gate

Drain. Within the present generation, the hollow was full of water and was used for bathing.

Field-Names

Forms dated 1296 are Cl; those dated 1220-40 are *Foster*, 1294, 1298, 1329 *Ass*, 1326, 1393 *HarlCh*, 1327, 1332 *SR*, 1394 Pat; 1395 *FF*, 1601, 1624, 1634, 1638, 1662, 1668, 1671, 1686, 1691, 1706, 1712, 1715, 1718, 1822, 1864 *Terrier*, 1723 SDL; 1770 *EnclA*.

(a) Beelsby road 1770 (*Beelesby gate marforth* 1601, - *mearforth* 1624, *Beelsby-gate* 1634, *a Marforth called Beelsby gate mearforth* 1638, 'the road to Bealsby' *v*. **gata** 'a road', **marfur** 'a boundary furrow', as elsewhere in this parish and common in north L); Low -, Top Bradley Btm 1864 (from the neighbouring parish of Bradley); Little Church Fd 1864 (cf. *atte Kirke* "of" *Bernelby* 1296, *atte Kirke* 1298, - *Kirk'* 1332, *atte Kyrk'* 1393, - *de Bernelby* 1395, *atte Kyrke* 1394, *ad eccl'iam de eadem* [*Bernelby*] 1326, *ad ecclesiam* 1327 all (p), *v*. **kirkja**); Cow Cl 1864; the East Fd 1770, 1822 (*the Este felde* 1601, - *East-field* 1624, - *East Fielde* 1634, - *field* 1638, *the Eastfield* 1662, *the field on ye East side of ye sayde towne* 1668, - *side of ye Towne* 1671, - *on the East side of the town* 1706, 1715, *Glebe Lands on* - 1712, *the field on* - 1715, *ye Field on the East Side* - 1718, *v*. **ēast**, **feld**, one of the great fields of Barnoldby, cf. the West Fd *infra*); Home Cl 1864; a place called the Marams 1770 (obscure); Low -, Middle -, Top Moor 1864 (*v*. **mōr**[1]); the Street Road 1770 (cf. Barton Street *supra*); Gt -, Lt Waltham Plot 1864 (*waltham closse* 1601, *Walthome Close* (sic) 1668, 1671, *Waltham close* 1634, 1638, - *Close* 1686, 1706, 1712, 1715, 1718, *Waltam hedge* (sic) 1691, cf. foll.); Waltham road 1770 (*Waltham gate* 1601, 1634, 'the road to Waltham', *v*. **gata**); the West Fd 1770, 1822 (*the weste felde* 1601, - *West field* 1624, - *fielde* 1634, 1638, *the Westfield* 1662, *ye westfield* 1668, *the west field* 1671, *ye Field on ye West side of ye Town* 1686, *ye West Field* 1691, *the field on the West side of the town* 1706, 1712, 1715, *ye Field on ye West Side of the Town* 1718, *v*. **west**, **feld**, one of the great fields of the parish, cf. the East Fd *supra*); Low -, Top Willow Dyke 1864 (cf. *willow dycke hedge* 1601, *Willow-dike hedge* 1624, self-explanatory, *v*. **dīk**).

(b) *Beketwra* 1220-40 (William *Beket* is named in the document, *v.* **vrá** 'a nook, a corner of land, etc.'); *Brigsley knowle* 1624 (*v.* **cnoll** 'a hillock'), *Brigsley marforth* 1601, - *meareforth* 1624, *a mearforth called Brigslye street* 1634, *Brigsly Mearforth* 1638 (*v.* **marfur**), *Brigsley wongue* 1671, 1718, *Brigsly Wongue* 1686, *Brigsley wonge* 1691, 1706, - *Wong* 1712 (*v.* **vangr** 'a garden, an infield', each named from Brigsley *infra*); *a certayne greene called Daliger grene, dolgargreene* 1601, *a certaine greene called Dalingers* 1624, *a certaine greene Called Dalligers* 1634, - *called dalligers* 1638, *Dallygers* 1671, (*upon*) *Daligers* 1686, 1706, *Dalligers* 1691, *Daligers* 1712, *the* - 1715, (*on*) *Dalingers* 1718 (obscure); *the feilds gate* 1601 (*v.* **feld**, **gata**), *ye fielde meare* 1624, *the fieldes* - 1634, *the fields* - 1638 (*v.* **feld**, **(ge)mǣre** 'a boundary'); *Atte Grene* 1294, 1327, *atte* - 1332 (p) (*v.* **grēne**[2]); *one wonge ... called Harp wonge* 1601, *Harpewong* 1624, *Harpe wong* 1634, 1638, *Harp Wongue* (described as *A wongue*) 1668, *Harpe wongue* 1671, *Harp Wongue* 1686, *Harpe Wonge* 1691, 1718, *Harp wong* 1715 (referring to the shape, *v.* **hearp**, **vangr** 'a garden, an in-field'); *de Hille* 1327, *del Hill' de Bernelby* 1329, *del Hill'* 1332 all (p) (*v.* **hyll**); *a pece of medow ground commonly called Kirkin* 1601, *Kirkin* (sic) 1634, *kirkin* 1638, *the kirkine* (sic) 1662, *Kirk inge* 1668, *kirkine* 1671, *ye Kirking* 1686, 1718, *Kirking* 1691, 1706, *a parcel of meadow commonly called Kirkin* 1712, *the Kirking* 1715, *a parcel of land, called Kirkin, given to the Minister* (*as it appears*) *that he may strew the Church in summer* 1723 (*v.* **kirkja**, **eng**, and for a similar endowment, *v.* Beanfield, in Sawbridgeworth, PN Hrt 303); *att Mare de eadem* [*Bernelby*] 1298 (p) (*v.* **(ge)mǣre**); *the pinfold* 1712, *the pinnfold* 1715 (*v.* **pynd-fald**); *One Land comonly caled ye Tippet* 1668, *ye Typpitt* 1671, *ye Tippet* 1686, *One Land Commonly called ye Tippit* 1691, *the Tippit* 1706, 1712, *the Tippett, the tippit* 1715, *One land commonly cald ye Treppit* (sic) 1718 ('a long, narrow piece of land', figuratively alluding to the strip of cloth worn as an extension of a hood or sleeve; the term is also used as an appellative in *A Tippit of arable* 1691, 1706, cf. *hood & typett* PN L **2** 289, The Tippet, ib **1** 203); *a common marfurth called Tormor marforthe* 1601, *Turmore Mearforth* 1624, - *meareforth* 1634, *Tormore* - 1638 (presumably where turves were cut, from **torf**, **turf**, **mōr**[1], with **marfur**); *a greene called wymore* 1601 (*v.* **mōr**[1]; the first el. is obscure; without earlier forms no convincing suggestion can be made).

Beelsby

BEELSBY

Belesbi (3x) 1086 DB, (3x) c.1115 LS, 1130 P (p), 1180 ib, 1188, 1190, 1191 all (p) ib, a1191 Dane (p), 1192, 1193 *et freq* to 1200 P all (p), 1200 Cur (p), c.1200 RA iv (p), c.1200 Dane (p), 1201 P (p), 1202 *HarlCh et passim* to 1259 Ipm, *-bia* 1212 Fees, *-b'* 1185 Templar (p), 1227 ClR (p), 1238-43 Fees, *-by* l12 (m13) *NCot* (p), 1202 Ass (p), 1205 FF (p), 1206 OblR (p), 1219 Welles, 1222 Cur, 1231 Ch, 1231 FF, 1242-43 Fees, 1250 FF, 1252 Cl, 1254 ValNor, 1272 *Ass*, 1276 RH, 1281 QW, 1284 *HarlCh*, 1291 Tax, 1295 Pat, 1304 Ipm *et freq* to 1549 Pat, *-bye* 1576 Saxton, 1610 Speed, *-bie* 1591 Beelsby

Bilesbi 1086 DB (corrected from *Blesbi* with *i* interlined, through confusion with Bleasby in the previous entry)

Bellesby 1234 FF, 1235 IB, 1327 *SR*, 1553 Pat

Belysby 1242-43 Fees, *Belisby* 1296 *AD*, 1328 Banco, 1346 Pat, 1364 Cl, 1526 Sub

Belebi 1198 Cur (p), 1202 Ass (p), 1202, 1203 P (p), *-by* 1268 Ch, 1291 Tax

Billesby 1331 Pat, 1519 DV, *Byllesby* 1535 VE iv, *Bylisby* 1397 Pat, *-be* 1498 ib, *Bylsby* 1538 LP xiii

Beylesby 1539-40 Dugd vi, *Beilesby* 1626 *FLIrnham*

Bielsby 1576 LER, *Beelesby* 1601 *Terrier*, *Beelsbie* 1647 *Td'E*, *-by* 1673, 1690 *Terrier*, 1698 *FLIrnham et freq*

According to Ekwall, DEPN s.n., this is 'Beli's farm, village', from the ON pers.n. *Beli* and **bȳ**. Fellows-Jensen, SSNEM 35 s.n., points out that this is a very rare Scand. pers.n., though it is found in later 12th and 13th century sources in L, *v.* SPNLY 51-52. She further points out that the first el. has secondary OE gen.sg. in *-es*.

BARF FM, *Beelsby Barf Fm* 1828 Bry, cf. *the South Barfs* 1698 *FLIrnham, South Barfe, The Barfe* 1699 Beelsby, *Barfs* 1848 *TA*, from **beorg** 'a hill, a mound', dial. *barf* 'a long low ridge or hill' (EDD), common in L, cf. Howsham Barff, PN L 2, 78. BEELSBY COVER (lost), 1824 O and is *Barf Fox Cover* 1828 Bry, *Fox Cover* 1848 *TA* (no. 91). BEELSBY HO is *Mr. Sowerby's Farm* 1848 *TAMap*. BEELSBY MILL, 1828 Bry, *Mill* 1824 O, cf. *Millhouse & Mill and Close* 1699 Beelsby, *that Water Mill house* 1717 *LCC*, *water Corn Mill* 1753 *ib.* BEELSBY TOP, 1824 ib, 1848 *TA*. BRATTS LANE (lost), 1828 Bry, cf. *closes called* ...

Bratts 1699 Beelsby, *Bratts* 1848 *TA*, from **brot** 'a small piece of land', *brat* being a common form in L. It is the lane marking the boundary with Irby, from New Fm and the junction of the road leading south-west to Beelsby village. CLINT INGS (lost), 1828 Bry, from **klint** 'a cliff, a steep hill' and the pl. of **eng** 'meadow, pasture', a Danish compound. It denoted the area to the north-west of Flint Hills, where there is a steep rise. DYKE WALK (lost), 1828 Bry, *Dyke Close Walk* 1848 *TA*, from **dīk** and **walk**, the latter common in L, denoting land used for the pasture of animals, especially sheep. It was the name of part of the track running south-west from the road from Bratts Lane to the village. ELSTON HILL (local), 1848 *TA*. ELSTON HO (local), named from the local *Elston* family, cf. William *Elston* 1790 Beelsby. HALL FM (local), *Hall* 1828 Bry and is *M^r. Coale's Farm* 1848 *TAMap*. LONGFOSS HO (local), cf. *Long Foss* 1848 *TA*, cf. *Lower Fosse* 1699, Beelsby, 'the long ditch', *v.* **lang**[1], **foss**[1]. Though Smith, EPN s.v., says **foss**[1] is frequently found in early sources in YE and L, this is the first instance noted in north L. RECTORY, *the Rectory howse* 1679, *The Parsonage house* 1686, *one Brick and Tiled Dwelling House ... inhabited by labourers* 1822 all *Terrier*. UPPER WOLD BARN (lost, approx. TA 200 010), 1828 Bry. WALK HO (lost, TA 200 018), 1828 Bry, cf. *Dyke Walk supra*. WELL GARTH (lost), 1828 ib, *Wellgarth Walk* 1848 *TA*, *v.* **wella**, **garðr**. It denoted the area west of Beelsby Top and north of *Dyke Walk*.

Field-Names

Principal forms in (a) are 1848 *TA*; forms dated 1271-2 are *Ass*; 1346 Pat; 1375 Peace; 1601, 1679, 1686, 1822 *Terrier*; 1699 Beelsby; 1717, 1721, 1753 *LCC*.

(a) Blacksmith Shop; (Gt) Calf Cl; Church Cl; Cinque foin Cl (*v.* **sainfoin**); Clover Cl and Little Milkings (*Little Mickling* 1699, *v.* **mikill**, **eng**); Mr Coate's Fm (Christopher *Coates* is named in the document); Corn Pce (*v.* **pēce**); Cottage pastures; Cow Holme (*v.* **holmr** 'a water-meadow, higher dry ground amidst the marshes', as elsewhere in this parish); Cow House; Crab tree walk (*v.* **walk** 'a sheep walk', as elsewhere in this parish); Croft (*v.* **croft**); Dove Cl Walk (*v.* **walk**); Field (*in campis de Belesby* 1271-2, 1375, *v.* **feld**); Furze Hill (*v.* **fyrs**, **hyll**); Garth(s) (*v.* **garðr**); Hardy leys (named from the

Hardy family, cf. Robert *Hardy* 1628 Beelsby and **lea** (OE **lēah**) 'meadow, pasture', in the pl.); High fds; Home Cl; Home Walk & Cow pasture; Horse Holme (*v.* **holmr**); Intack (*v.* **inntak**); Land fd, Bottom land - (*v.* **land**); Lane Barfs (from dial. *barf* (OE **beorg**) 'a hill'); Little Holme (*v.* **holmr**); Joiners Shop and Yard; First -, Second -, Third long fd; Lords Fds; Gt -, Hither Lowfield, Low Fds, - fds (*Little -, Old -, South Low Field* 1699); Low Garth Hill & little fd (*v.* **garðr**); Milking Barfs (cf. Barf Fm *supra*), Gt Milkings (*Great Mickling* 1699, *v.* **mikill**, **eng**, and cf. Clover Cl in f.n. (a) *supra*); Orchard (cf. *a little Orchard* 1601); Out walk (*v.* **ūt**, **walk**); The Pasture; Plantation; Quarry; Seed Holme (*v.* **holmr**); (Near) Seed walk (*v.* **walk**); Bottom South fds; Swales; Swallow walk fd (*v.* **walk**); Swikes; The Walk (*the Walk* 1699, this is different from Walk Ho *supra*, cf. *Sheep walke* 1717, - *walk* 1721, *v.* **walk**); Well Garth (this is different from *Well Garth supra*, though the name is the same); West fd (*West Field* 1699, *v.* **west**); The wood and New Cl.

(b) *Cony Grees* 1699 (*v.* **conigre** 'a rabbit warren'); *Foster's Piece* 1699 (*v.* **pēce**; John *Foster* is named in the document); *Great Holme* 1699 (*v.* **holmr**); *the mansion howse* 1601, *One Capitall Messuage or Mannor House* 1721; *North Walk* 1699 (*v.* **walk**); *Potten Fosse* 1699 (cf. Longfoss Ho *supra*); *Thorpe by Belesby* 1346 (p) (*v.* **þorp**); *Roberts Close* 1699 (from the surn. *Roberts*); *Tuppinge Low Field* 1699 (*v.* **tup**); *Wilmore Low Field* 1699 (doubtless from the surn. *Wilmore*).

Brigsley

BRIGSLEY

Brigeslai (2x) 1086 DB, *-lea* 1196 ChancR, *-l'* 1204 P, *-le* e13 (Ed 1) *Newh*, 1219 Ass, 1290 RSu, 1300 Abbr, 1312 Pat, 1428 FA, *-lay* IB, *-ley* 1490 Cl, *-leye al's Briggeslye* 1620 *LCS*, *Brygesley* 1406, 1408, 1415 Cl, *-lay* 1531 Wills iii, *Brygslay* 1539 LP xiv, *-ley* 1505 Ipm, 1577 *Terrier*, 1594, 1599, 1603 *BT*, 1601 *Terrier*, *Brigsley* 1593, 1623, 1664 *BT*, 1664 *Terrier et passim*

Brigesla c.1115 LS, 1194 CurP, 1213 Abbr

Brighesla c.1115 LS

Brighesle 1212 Fees

Brichisle 1212 Fees

Briggesle 1202, 1207 FF, 1275, 1276 RH, 1281 QW, 1291

HarlCh, 1299 Cl, 1299 Pat, 1300 Cl, 1300 Orig *et freq* to 1361 Cl, *-lee* 1295 Ipm, 1316 FA, *-ley* 1327 *SR*, 1349 *Cor*, 1388 Pat, 1388 Peace, 1423 Fine, 1526 Sub *et freq* to 1718 *Haigh*, *-lay* 1576 Saxton, 1610 Speed, *-lye* 1554 Pat, *-ly* 1679 *Terrier*, *Bryggesle* 1291 Tax, *-leye* 1361 Ipm, *-lay* 1395 Peace, 1431 FA, *-ley* 1401-02 ib, 1425 Cl, 1450 Pap, 1460 Pat, 1535 VE iv

Bruggesley 1374 Peace

Bridgsley 1680 *Haigh*, 1695 *BT*, *-ly* 1697, 1709 *ib*

Brigelai 1086 DB, *-lega* 1210-12 RBE, *-leya* 1226 Welles, *-le* 1219 Ass, 1338 Pat, *-l'* 1254 ValNor, *-ley* 1454 Cl, *Brigelle* 1242-43 Fees, *Brigley* 1313 Inqaqd

Brighela c.1115 LS

Brichelai 1202 *HarlCh*, *-lay* 1342 Pat

Briggel' 1202 Ass, 1219 Welles, 1242-43 Fees, *-leye* 1281 QW, *-le* 1202 Ass, 1304, 1338 Pat, 1428 FA, *-lee* 1332 *SR*, *-lay* 1373 Peace, *Briggelle* 1275 RH

Bridgeley 1657 *Rad*

Ekwall, DEPN s.n., interprets Brigsley as originally OE *brycg-lēah* 'the wood, the glade by the bridge', "later Scandinavianized, *gs* being introduced for the palatal *cg* which was unknown in Scandinavia". Fellows-Jensen, SSNEM 202-03, draws attention to forms in *Briges-* and in *Brige-* and argues convincingly that these seem to reflect a variation between genitival and non-genitival composition. Clearly, the evidence indicates that both forms were in use side by side. She further points out that it seems unlikely that "the p.n. Brigsley has been Scandinavianized in DB", since *Brige-* is a regular reflex of OE **brycg** in that Survey. However, she points out that the scribe of the LS "regularly employed the spelling *gh* to indicate the voiced plosive [g] before *e*, but he could also indicate the same sound by *g*. In the light of the early 13th century forms in *Briche-* and *Brigge-* and the modern form Brigsley, therefore, it seems reasonable to assume that the LS spelling represents a genuine local Scandinavianized form of the p.n." This is sound common sense. We can assume that Brigsley means 'the wood, the glade of the bridge' side by side with 'the wood, the glade by the bridge', *v.* **brycg**, **-es**[2], **lēah**, the first el. of the modern name in a Scandinavianized form. The bridge is presumably one over what is today called Waithe Beck, which forms the boundary of the parish and Ashby cum Fenby.

Brigsley is the only certain example of the el. **lēah** in a major p.n. in the North Riding of Lindsey. Indeed it is infrequent in the whole of the county and in this it is probably comparable to Norfolk and Suffolk. The situation of Brigsley close to a bridge suggests that in spite of it being an isolated example of **lēah** the likely sense of the word here is 'a glade, a clearing' and topography would seem to support this interpretation.

BRATTON HO, *late the Property of Mrs Brattan, deceased, and known as Brattan Farm* 1854 *Haigh.* The land here is called Peaselands, for which *v.* the Pease lands Cl in f.ns. (a) *infra.* BRIGSLEY COVERT. BRIGSLEY TOP. LINGMARES LANE (lost), 1828 Bry, probably 'the boundary land where heather grows', *v.* **lyng, (ge)mǣre.** This was the name of the road forming the north-west boundary with Waltham, now called Cheapside Road. MANOR HO is *Old Hall* 1828 Bry, cf. *atte hall'* 1332 *SR* (p). NORMAN CORNER, on the boundary with Waltham; for earlier comparative forms, *v.* Norman Corner in Waltham *infra.* WAITHE LANE 1850 *TA, Waythe Lane, Waythe Lane Ho* 1828 Bry, the lane leading to Waithe.

Field-Names

Forms dated e13 (Ed 1) are *Newh*; 1275, 1276 RH; 1327, 1332 *SR*; 1577, 1601, 1626, 1634, 1638, 1674, 1679, 1690, 1697, 1700, 1703, 1712, 1718[1], 1762 *Terrier*, 1656, 1675, 1680, 1683, 1687, 1688, 1699, 1705, 1710, 1713, 1718[2], 1719, 1725, 1740, 1742, 1743, 1753, 1754, 1756, 1774, 1782, 1784, 1788, 1793, 1803, 1804, 1808, 1831, 1837, 1839[1], 1840, 1854, 1860, 1863, 1875 *Haigh*; 1696, 1722, 1792, 1832, 1839[2] *PT*; 1733 *Nelthorpe*; 1850 *TA*; 1851 *TAMap*.

(a) the Beck Drain 1854 (*v.* **bekkr**); One other Close called Black-Swine Glebe 1762 (*a Furlonge called blackswyne* 1601, *one close commonly called Black Swine* 1712, *One Gleab Close call'd black swine* 1718[1], *v.* **blæc, swin**[2] 'a creek, a channel'); Booths Cl 1863 (probably from the surn. *Booth*); the Bottom Cl 1782; Little Bowlands 1756, 1782, 1863, Great - 1863, Close ... called Bowlands 1784 (*v.* **boga, land**); Brigsley Cl 1782 (*Briggesley Close* 1718[2]),

Brigsley Lane 1832, 1840; Cottage Lane 1851; Cross Lane 1850; Crowston's Mill Croft 1784 (the same name occurs in Ashby cum Fenby f.ns. (a)); Duck Pool Plat 1784; the bottom east Cl 1788, the Bottom East Cl formerly by mistake called the Top West Cl 1837, the Top east cl 1788, The Top East Cl formerly by mistake called the Bottom West Cl 1837 (cf. the bottom west Cl *infra*); Lower -, Upper Grange Cl 1754, 1875, lower-Grange-Cl, upper-Grange-Cl 1793, lower -, upper Grange Cl, upper grange and ... Lower Grange Cl 1804, Lower -, the Upper Grange Cl 1837 (*Close called Great Grange* 1719, *Great Grange* 1740, *Lower -, Upper Grange Close* 1742, *v.* **grange**); Grimsby Road 1850 (*grymsby gate* 1577, *Grymsbye gayte* 1601, *Grimesby gate* 1626, 1638, *Grimsbee -* 1634, 'the road to Grimsby', *v.* **gata**); the Homestead 1784; the Ings Cl 1782, the East -, the West Ings 1784 (*the Ings* 1655, *the Ings Close* 1718[2], *Two ... Closes Called Ing Leys & Bothams* 1719, *Ings, Leys & Bottoms* 1740, *v.* **eng, lea, botm**); the Long Cl or Coxhill Cl (sic) 1831, Long Cl or Goxhill Cl 1875 (*Long close* 1719, 1740, *the Long Close* 1742, *v.* **lang**; the alternative name is from the *Goxhill* family, cf. Joseph *Goxhill* 1840; *v.* also Micklemow *infra*); Martin's Mill Croft 1784 (from the surn. *Martin* with **myln, croft**, cf. Thomas *Martyn* 1707 *BT*); Bottom Mickleholme 1756, bottom Mickle Holme 1782 (*v.* **mikill, holmr**); Close of pasture ... called ... Micklemow (sic) 1753, - called ... Micklemen (sic) 1808, Micklemew (sic) 1831, Micklemore Cl 1792, Close formerly called Micklemoor but now called the Long Cl 1832, - called Long Cl 1839[2], - called the Micklemore but then called the Long Cl 1840, Micklemore 1875 (*myckelmore, - gote, - playne* 1577, *mickellmore* 1601, *Micklemare close* 1634, *a close ... called Micklemare* 1638, *Micklemore* 1655, 1696, *Close of Meadow ... called Micklemere* 1743, *fur Micklemow* (sic) 1688, *micklemore Close* 1722, *v.* **mycel, mikill, mōr**[1] with **gotu** and **plain**); Mickle more Corner 1792, Close formerly called Micklemore Corner but then Little Cl 1840 (*micklemore Corner* 1722, cf. prec. n. *Corner* implies a piece of land set at right angles to *the Micklemore*); the Mill Croft Cl 1782 (1718[2]), Little -, North Mill Croft 1784 (*melchroftes* (sic) 1577, *millcroftes* 1601, *Mill croft* 1655, *v.* **myln, croft**, the earliest form appears to have been influenced by ME *milch(e), mielch, melch(e)* 'juicy, sappy'); the New Plat 1756, the new Platt 1782, - Plat 1784 (*the New Plat* 1700, *ye Newplatt* 1703, *v.* **plat**); One Close of Pasture called Nordham Glebe 1762 (*ye nether nordam forlonge, ye upper Nordam furlonge* 1577, *nordame, a Forlonge called Vppernorde* (reading uncertain) 1601, *a place called Northome or Nordam, a certaine furlonge called ye furlonge aboue Nordam* 1626, *Northolme close* 1634, *a place called Northolme or Nordam* 1638, *Close call'd Nordams* 1718[1], *v.* **norð, holmr, glebe, furlang**); the Pease lands Cl or the farr Peaselands 1774, peaselands cl or the Farr peaslands 1803, a certain plot of land formerly called ... Pease Lands 1837,

Peas Land Cl 1839[1], Pease Land Cl 1860 (*Long peacelandes* 1577, *longe -, short peaslands* 1601, *long -, short peaselandes close* 1634, *low peaslands* 1680, *Peaslands Close or the farre Peaslands* 1656, *Pease Land Close or the Farr Peaselands* 1675, *Pease Land Close or the Farr pease Lands* 1705, *Peaselands Close* 1710, *Pease Land Close or the Farr Peaslands* 1713, *peas Land Close, One other Close of pasture ground ... called or known by the Name of Peas Land* 1725, *Pease lands* 1733, *v.* **pise** 'pease', **land**); Pindar Cl 1792, Pinder Cl but now called Hill Cl 1832, Close formerly called Pinder Cl but now called hill Cl 1839, formerly called Pinder Cl but then called Hill Cl 1840 (*Pinder Close* 1696, *pinder* - 1722, *v.* **pyndere** 'a pinder', perhaps as a surn.); Sackington (sic), Stackington 1863; Stack Yard 1863; Thistle Lands 1863 (*thyslandes, Long Thys landes, Shorte Thyslandes* 1577, *long thislandes, a Furlange called shorte this landes* 1601, *v.* **þistel, land**); Townsend Cl 1831 (*Townsend close* 1719, - *Close* 1740, *the Townsend Closes* 1742, 'close(s) at the end of the village', *v.* **tūn, ende**[1], **clos(e)**); Road to Wash Dyke 1850; the bottom west -, the Top West Cl 1788, The Bottom West Cl formerly by mistake called the Top East Cl, The Top West Cl formerly ... the Bottom East Cl 1837.

(b) *Aldike, Aldyke* 1577, *aldack* (sic) 1601 (*v.* **ald, dīk**); *barnat Accar* (sic) 1577 ('the selion at the burnt place', *v.* **bærnet, æcer**); *Brough Close* 1719, 1740 (possibly from the surn. *Brough*); *the commons* 1601; *the Cooke land* 1601, *Jhon* (sic) *Cookes headlande* 1626 (named from a member of the *Cooke* family and *v.* **land, hēafod-land**); *the corne close* 1655, *Corn Close* 1719, 1740; *Cottager platt* 1655 (*v.* **plat**); *Mr Carys Micklemore* 1700; *Mr Creseys close* 1697, *Mr Cresy's Cottage, - Orchard, - Old walk* 1700, *Mr Cresys Cottage, - Micklemore, - Orchard, - Oldwalk* 1703 (named from a member of the *Cressey* family, cf. Arthur *Cressey* 1655); *ye East Felde* 1577, *The East Feald* 1601, *the east fielde* 1626, 1634 (*v.* **ēast, feld**, one of the great fields of the parish, cf. *ye West Felde infra*); *close ... called Eastlong sometime Peasland* 1683, - *Eastlong and Peasland* 1687 (*v.* **ēast, lang**[2] 'a long piece of land' and the Pease Lands Cl in (a) *supra*); *Elly Close* 1655; *in camp' de Brigesle* e13 (Ed 1), *in campis de Briggesle* 1275, *in campo de Briggisle* 1276, *the comon field* 1634, *the common fielde, ye open field of Briggesley* 1638, *the feilds of Brigsley* 1655 (*v.* **feld**); *Furze Close* 1719, 1740 (*v.* **fyrs**); *the east -, the west gayrs* 1601 (*v.* **geiri** 'a triangular plot of land'); *the gootstead* 1601, *the goat sted close* 1634 (*v.* **gotu** 'a watercourse', but probably in L 'a sluice', **stede**; the compound *gotestead* is not recorded in Sandred); *Hawley Ings* 1719, 1740 (*v.* **eng**); *high Platt* 1719, *High-Plott* 1740 (*v.* **plat, plot**); *Holmflitts* 1655 (*v.* **holmr**; the second el. may be **flēot** 'a stream', in the pl.); *how hyll* 1601, *How hill* 1626 (probably from **haugr** with **hyll** added later); *Atte Kyrke* 1327, *atte Kirkeyat* 1332 both (p) (*v.* **kirkja**, **geat**); *two Closes ... called Land Closes* 1699, *Land Close* 1719, 1740 (*v.* **land**); *one close sometime called green close, and commonly called the Parsonage Close, the Parsonage garth, or the ground where the house formerly stood, the Parsonage house with all the building thereto belonging have been long time down* 1712, *A Parsonage Garth* 1718[1] (*v.* **garðr**, the Parsonage itself is referred to as *the mansion howse* 1601, and *About a Stong of Ground wth the houses demolished* 1690, *no Houses* 1697); *under Ryes mare* 1626, *a furlonge called under Ryes mare* 1634, *furlonge called -* 1638 (from **(ge)mǣre** or **marr**[1], perhaps with **hrīs** 'brushwood'); *ye comon Ryver* 1577, *a common -* 1601; *the Walke* 1655 (*v.* **walk**); *ye Waltham Road* 1700, 1703 (from Waltham *infra*); *ye West Felde* 1577, *The west Fealde* 1601, *the west field* 1626, *- fielde* 1638, *ye west feild* 1674, *- Feild* 1679 (*v.* **west**, **feld**, one of the great fields of the parish, cf. *ye East Felde supra*); *the little wray* 1655 (*v.* **vrá** 'a nook, a corner of land').

Cabourne

CABOURNE

Caburne (9x) 1086 DB, 1155-60 Dane, l12 RA iv, 1238-41 Fees, 1276 RH, 1289 *Foster*, 1291 Tax, 1316 FA *et passim* to 1610 Speed, *Ka-* 1200 Dugd iii, c.1200 RA iv, 1201 Cur, 1201 Abbr, 1202, 1219 FF, 1519 DV, *Caburna* c.1115 (4x) LS, 1130 P (p), c.1155, 1160-66 Dane, *Ka-* 1157-63 ib, e13 (1409) Gilb (p), *Caburnia* 1143-47 Dane, c.1150 *TYR*, 1185 Templars, 1190 (1301) Dugd vi, *Ka-* c.1150 (Ed1) *Newh*, 1150-60 RA iv, 1150-60 Dane, *Caburn(')* 1199 P, 1212, 1242-43 Fees, 1254 ValNor, 1284 RSu, 1288 Ipm, 1289 Abbr, 1328 Banco *et passim* to 1707 *Terrier*, *Ka-* c.1160 (Ed1) *Newh*, 1199 (1330) Ch, l12 (Ed1) *Newh*, e13 RA iv, 1202, 1219 Ass, 1220 LAHW, 1230 Welles, 1234 FF, 1242-43 Fees *et passim* to 1447 *Foster*

Cauburn' 1242-43 Fees, *Cawborne* 1428 FA

Caborn 1303, 1346 FA, 1472 WillsPCC, 1526 Sub, *-borne* 1319 *FF*, 1428 FA, 1438 Cl, 1445 AASR xxix, 1483 *CampbRoll*, 1535 VE iv, 1547, 1550 Pat *et passim* to *- alias Chaborne* 1741 *PT*

Kabourn 1350 Pat, *Ca-* 1783 *Nelthorpe*, 1822 *Terrier*, *-bourne* 1338 Hosp, 1341 Pat, 1715 *Terrier et passim*, *Ka-* c.1414 AASR xxix

Kayburne 1553 Pat, *Cayborne* 1557 ib, *-born* 1606 *Terrier*
Chaburn' 1193, 1194 P (p), *-burne* R1 (c.1331) *Spald i*

'The stream frequented by jackdaw', *v.* **cā, burna**. as suggested by Ekwall, DEPN s.n. The stream is almost dried up today, so that it is impossible to determine its characteristics. *v.* also *toftam Thome ad Bec* in f.ns. (b) *infra*.

BADGER HILLS, 1824 O, cf. - *Fox Cover* 1828 Bry, *1st* -, *2nd* *Badger Hill* 1833 *Yarb.* CABOURNE HIGH WOODS. CABOURNE HO is *Hall* 1828 Bry, cf. *at Hall* c.1414 AASR xix. CABOURNE LODGE, 1841 *TAMap.* CABOURNE MILL (lost), *Cabourn Mill* 1824 O, 1828 Bry, *ye wynde mylln* 1577, *the wynde Milne* 1612, - *Miln* 1625, *the Miln* 1601, - *miln* 1606, - *Mill* 1707, cf. *Mill hill* 1638, 1674, 1686, *Mil-hill* 1662, *Mill Hill* 1697 all *Terrier, Mill Plot* 1793, - *Platt* p1811, - *Plat* 1833, *Mill Slack* p1811, - *Slacks* 1833 all *Yarb, v.* **myln, plat**^{2} 'a small piece of ground'. **slakki** and for the last *v.* Deep Dale Plot in f.ns. (a) *infra.* CABOURNE MOUNT is *Storks Fm* 1828 Bry, presumably from a local family name. CABOURNE PARVA is *Barn* 1824 O, *Wold Bn* 1828 Bry. CABOURNE VALE. CABOURNE WOLD, *the Wold* 1793 *Yarb, Wold* p1811 *ib, v.* **wald** and cf. Cabourne Parva *supra.* GLEBE FM is *Parsonage Fm* 1828 Bry and cf. *the vicaredge headland* in f.ns. (b) *infra.* NEW CLOSE WOOD, cf. *New Close* 1833 *Yarb.* New Close Wood is mainly in Great Limber parish; for early forms *v.* PN L 2, 223. PELHAM'S PILLAR. The *Pelham* family, Earls of Yarborough, owned an estate in Cabourne, *v. Yarb* 5/1/17, 1793. ROUND WOOD. SAND PIT, *the Sande Pittes* 1601, *Sand pit* 1606, *Sand(e) pittes* 1625, *the Sand pits* 1707 all *Terrier,* self-explanatory.

Field-Names

Forms dated c.1150 are *TYR*; 1150-60, 1160-70 Dane 256; Hy2 (Ed1), l12 (Ed1), e13 (Ed1) *Newh*; 1190 (1301) Dugd vi; l12 (13), eHy3 (13) *Alv*; l12 (Hy4), Hy3 (Hy4) *GCB*; c.1200, e13 RA iv; R1 (1318) Ch; 1202 FF; Hy3, 1536 *HarlCh*; 1275 RH; 1289 Abbr; 1300, 1328[1], 1532, 1605, 1609 *Foster*, 1319 *FF*; 1327, 1332 *SR*; 1328[2] Banco; 1341, 1350 Pat; c.1414, 1445 AASR xxix; 1537

AOMB; 1539 LP; 1577, 1601, 1606, 1612, 1625, 1638, 1654, 1662, 1674, 1686, 1690, 1697, 1706, 1707, 1712, 1715, 1822, 1864 *Terrier*, c.1760 *Monson*; 1793, p1811, 1814, 1833 *Yarb*; 1831 *Brad*.

(a) Abbey Dale Plot 1793, - dale platt p1811 (a valley) (*Abbey-Dale* 1638, *abbie dale* 1654, *Abbey-dale* 1662, *Abbye dale* 1674, *Abbye daile* 1686, *Abby* - 1697, *Abbot Dale* 1601, 1625, - *dale* 1606, *Abbott* -, *the Abbot* (sic) 1612, cf. *Abbey Close* 1606 and *messuagium Abbatis de Grymesby* 1328[1]; the two names Abbey Dale and *Abbot Dale* seem to refer to the same piece of land and *Abbey dale platt* p1811 is on one slope of a valley so that *dale* appears in fact to be for **dalr**. There is no real evidence to show which *abbey* is referred to and it could be either Newsham Abbey or the abbey at Wellow, Grimsby); Bart lands 1793, Burtlands p1811 (*Bretlandes* 112 (Hy4), *bretlandes* Hy3 (Hy4), *v.* **land**; the first el. is uncertain); Barton Lane Plat 1833 (cf. *Barton streete* 1638, - *street* 1654, 1662, - *Street* 1674, 1686, - *Streate* 1697, leading to Barton upon Humber, but clearly not the same Barton Street as occurs in other parishes in this wapentake); Blue Dale 1833; Bowlings 1833; Bransby Plot 1793, - Platt p1811 (from the surn. *Bransby*, cf. John *Bransby* 1751 *PR*); Caistor Plat, - Top Cl 1833 (from the adjacent parish of Caistor); Calkhouse Platt p1811 (*v.* **plat**[2], **plot**); Caster Gate Plot 1793, Castor gate Platt p1811, Caster Road 1822 (*viam de Cast'* 112 (13), 112 (Ed1), *castergate* e13 (Ed1), *via de Castre* c.1200, e13, *viam de Cast'* e13 (Ed1), *publicam stratam de Castria* eHy3 (13), *uiam de Castre* Hy3, *super publicam stratam de Castria* eHy3 (13), *viam de Castre* 1202, *super viam de Kast'* Hy3 (Hy4), *castorgate, Cayster gate* 1577, *Caister gate* 1601, 1606, 1612, 1625, 1638, 1662, 1674, 1686, 1697, *the streete called Caister streete* 1601, *Caster gate* 1654, *Castre* - (sic) 1707, 'the road to Caistor', from **gata** 'a road' with **plat**, **plot**); The Coney Cl c.1760, Coney - 1793, 1833, the - 1831, Cony - 1814 (perhaps the same as *Conigre close* 1606, *v.* **conigre** 'a rabbit warren' and **coni**, **clos(e)**); Coney Gate Plot 1793, - gate Marfur Platt p1811 (a different field from Coney Cl; it is derived from **coni** 'a rabbit' and **gata**, a compound found elsewhere in L, having the same sense 'a rabbit warren' and cf. *de novo warenn' in Kaburn* 1275, *v.* also **marfur** and **plat**[2]); the Corne Fd c.1760; Cornered Cl 1793; Cottagers Plot 1793; Cow Cl 1814, 1833; Cow Gate Plot 1793, - gate Platt p1811, (Middle -, Top) Cow Gate 1833 (from **cow-gate** 'pasture, or right of pasture, for cows', with **plot** and **plat**[2]); Croft 1833 (*v.* **croft**); Cuckswold Hill Plot 1793, - hill Platt p1811, Cuxwold Plat 1833 (*v.* **plat**[2]); the Coxwould Road 1831 (from the adjoining parish of Cuxwould); Deep Dale Plot 1793, Deepdale-end Platt p1811, Deep dale (Slack) 1833 ('the deep valley', from **dēop** and **dalr**, with **plot**, **plat**[2] and **slakki** 'a shallow valley, a hollow in the ground', an OWScand word, rare in the East Midlands); Eleven Acres (2x) 1833; the Fallow Fd c.1760; Far Cl

1833; First -, Second -, Third Cl 1833; Little Firth 1793, Firth Platt p1811 (*ye furth* 1654, *- Furth* 1662, *the -* 1686, 1707, cf. *the forthsteade more* (sic) 1601 (perhaps *v.* **(ge)mǣre** 'a boundary'), *the forthsteade* 1606, 1612, *the firth steade* 1625, *ye Furth-stead* 1638, *ye Furthestead* 1662, *ye furthstead* 1674, *the furth stead* 1686, *ye Furth Stead* 1697, perhaps from **fyrhðe** 'a wood, woodland, wooded country', in some later sense such as recorded in MED s.v. *frith* (2) 'a park, a woodland meadow', 'an enclosure' and in EDD s.v. *firth* 'a wood, plantation, coppice', 'unused pastureland'. The field is situated south of the road to Caistor, west of the village, on a valley slope at approx. TF 132 014, and of the recorded meanings 'unused pastureland' is probably most appropriate. In the majority of the 17th century forms it is compounded with **stede**, but *firthstead, furthstead* does not appear in Sandred); Fourteen Acres 1793; Fox Cover 1833; Frent hill, - Plat 1833 (*v.* **hyll, plat**); Funnaby Btm 1793, Fonaby - 1833, Furnaby Btm Platt p1811 (*v.* **botm, plat**; it is not near Fonaby in Caistor); Haven Botton p1811; Hendon Hill (sic) 1793, Hundon Hill p1811 (*Hunden hill* 1638, 1662, 1674, *hunden -* 1654, 1686, *Hundon -* 1697, named from Hundon Manor in the adjacent parish of Caistor, cf. *Hundunegate* in (b) *infra*); the Holme Cl Paddock 1831 (*v.* **holmr**); Home Cl p1811, 1814, 1831, 1833 (it is near a house); Horse Cl 1814, 1833, - Pasture 1833; House Cl 1833 (several, all around Cabourne Ho); Intack 1833 (*v.* **inntak**); Low Lings p1811 (*v.* **lyng**, and cf. *ye South-lings* in (b) *infra*); Littleton Hill Plot 1793, - Platt p1811 (presumably from a local family); First long Fd 1833; The Low Cl c.1760, Low - 1793, p1811, 1833, Low Cl Plat p1811, Low Cl Paddock 1831; Meadow Cl 1833; Middle Fd 1833; Nine Acres 1833; Norman Lays 1793, Nomans Leys p1811, Norman - 1833 (it is on the parish boundary and derived from **nān-mann** and **lea** (OE **lēah**) 'meadow, pasture' in the pl.; *No Man's*, normally used of land of unknown or uncertain ownership on or near a boundary, is occasionally altered, as 1793 and 1833, to *Normans*); Overdale Btm Plot 1793, - btm Platt p1811 (perhaps to be identified with *Orredale* 112 (13), eHy3 (13), *Horredale* Hy3 (Hy4), a compound of ON *orri* 'black grouse (*tebrao tetrix*)' and **dalr**, as Dr John Insley suggests; *v.* **botm, plat²**); Paddock 1814, 1833; Pen Cl 1833 (*v.* **penn**); Pig Garth 1833 (*v.* **garðr**); Plantation Cl 1833; Pond Cl 1831, 1833; Pullythorne 1793, Pully Thorn p1811 (*polrunthorn* (*daile*) Hy2 (Ed1), *pullerthornis* (reading uncertain), *pullerþornheuedland* 112 (Ed1) (*v.* **hēafod-land**), *polirunthornidaile, polrunthordayle* (sic) e13 (Ed1) (*v.* **deill**), *Pullerthornes, Puluerthorndayle* Hy3, *Polethornes* Hy3 (Hy4), *pulla thorne headland* 1577, *Pullathorne headland* 1601, *- headlande* 1606, 1625, *- headland* 1612, *Pullie-thorne headland* 1638, *Pulli(e)thorn headland* 1654, *Pulli(e)thorne headland* 1662, *Pullie thorne headland* 1674, *Pullythorn headland* 1707,

Pullithorn furlong, - headland 1686, *Pullithorne furlong, - headland* 1697; the forms are too varied to suggest the etymology of the first el., but the compound may refer to some species of thorn, *v.* also **hēafod-land, deill, furlang**); Rassel Cl 1793, Russel - 1814, Russell - p1811, 1831 (named from the *Russell* family, cf. William *Russel* 1738 *Monson*); Riby Road 1814, 1833, - Road Plat 1833 (*uiam de rieby* eHy3 (13), *ad viam de Ryby* Hy3 (Hy4), *Ryebigate, Ribyegathe* eHy3 (13), *Ryby gate* 1577, *Rybie* - 1601, 1606, 1612, 1625, *Ribie-gate* 1638, *Ribie gate* 1662, *Riby* - 1674, 1686, *Ryby* - 1707, 'the road to Riby', *v.* **gata**); Rigg p1811 (*v.* **hryggr**); Rooks Dale Plot 1793, Rooks dale Stack Platt p1811 (presumably from the *Rook* family, though the earliest reference noted is to Harry *Rook* 1912 *PR*); Rothwell Gate Plot 1793, - gate Platt p1811, Rothwell Lane 1833, - Road 1814, the Rothwell Road 1831, Rothwell Road Plot 1793, - Road Platt p1811, - Road Cl 1833 (*via de Rowelle* l12 (Ed1), *iuxta viam de Rowel'* Hy3 (Hy4), *Rowthwell stret* 1577, *Rothwell streete* 1601, 1606, 1625, - *Street* 1707, - *gate* 1601, 1606, 1612, 1625, 1654, 1674, 1686, 1697, 1707, *Rothwel* - 1638, 1662, *v.* **strǣt, gata**); Rothwell Slack Plot 1793, - Slack Platt p1811 (*v.* **slakki**; named from the adjacent parish of Rothwell); Round Hill Cl 1833; Sainfoin Plot 1793, Saint foyn Platt p1811 (*v.* **sainfoin**); Sand Bank Platt p1811, Bottom -, Top Sand Bank 1822, Sand Cl 1833, Sands 1793, p1811 (cf. *the Sande Holes* 1601, *the sande holes* 1606, *Sande* - 1612, *Sand hooles* 1625, *ye Sand-holes* 1638, *Sand-holes* 1662, *Sand holes* 1686, *Sandholes* 1697, *the Sand holes* 1707, *v.* **sand, hol**[1] and cf. Sand Pit *supra*); Sherlock Cl 1793, p1811 (named from the *Sherlock* family, cf. William *Sherlock* 1738 *Monson*); Sixteen Acre Cl 1833; Smithfield Ings (*v.* **eng**), - Meadow 1793 (*Smethfeld* 1289, *Smythfylde, Smytheffylde, Smythefyld* 1445, 'the smooth field', *v.* **smēðe, feld**); Smock Mill Cl 1833; Sorbut Hill Plat p1811; South Mill plott p1811; Low Stack yard Platt p1811 (cf. *stack garth* 1612, *Stackgarth* 1625, *v.* **stakgarth** (ON **stakkgarðr**)); (Park) Stone Pit Plot 1793, Stone Pit Platt p1811 (*the stone Pit* 1606, - *pitt* 1612, *ye Stone pit* 1638, - *stone pit* 1662, - *Stone Pit* 1674, *the stone Pits* 1686, 1697, *the Stone pitt* 1707, *Stonnypytt hyll* 1577, *Stone pit hill* 1601, 1654, *stone pit* - 1625, 1686, *Stone-pit* - 1638, *Stonepit Hill* 1674, *Stone pit Hill* 1697, *Stonepit-hill* 1707, *v.* **stān, pytt** and cf. *super quarerium* Hy3 (Hy4)); Street Flg 1793, - Platt p1811 (*streete furlong* 1606, 1625, *the Streete* - 1612, 1638, *ye streete furlong* 1674, *street* - 1686, *the Street Furlong* 1697, - *furlong* 1707, *v.* **strǣt, furlang** and cf. *ad publicam stratam* l12 (13), *The streete* 1601, *the* - 1606, 1612, 1625, *ye strete* 1577, *ye Streete* 1638, *y^e* -, *the Streete* 1674, *the street* 1686, *ye Street* 1697, *the* - 1707, a reference to the ancient trackway, called High Street, from Horncastle to Caistor, and Middlegate Lane from Caistor to South Ferriby); Summer Haul p1811 (*v.* **sumor, halh**); Summer Layers p1811 (from **sumor** and ModE *layer* 'a field of grass or clover', presumably here denoting one used in summer, *v.* further Cowleares in Wold Newton f.ns. (a) *infra*); Swallow Btm 1833, Swallow Fd Platt p1811, Swallow Gate Plot 1793, - gate Platt p1811, Swallow Plat 1833, the Swallow Road 1831 (*uiam de Swalue, swaluegathe, swaluegate* l12 (13), *Swallowe gate* 1601, *Swallow* - 1612, 1707, 'the road to Swallow (an adjacent parish)', *v.* **gata** and **plat**[2]); Three Corner Pce 1833; Top Fd 1833; Town Cl 1833; Town end Plot 1833 (*Towne end* 1601, 1606, *the towne* - 1606, *y^e* - 1638, 1674, - *Towne end* 1686, *the* - 1697, *the Town's* - 1707; the Town Street 1831; Twenty two Acres 1833; Under Hill 1833; Vicarage House 1822, 1864 (*ye Vycarage, the Vicarage* 1577, *the vicaredge* 1601, 1606, - *vicaredge howse* 1606, *the vicarage* 1625, *ye Vicaridge house* 1686).

(b) *acredic, ackerdic* Hy3 (13) (*v.* **æcer**, **akr**, **dīc**, **dík** and *ye acerdikes* PN L **2**, 13); *toftam Thome ad Bec* Hy3 (Hy4) (cf. *attebeck' de Caburn* Hy3, *atte Becke de Caborne* 1319, *Attebecke* 1327, *attebek de eadem* [*Caburne*] 1328[1], *atte Beche* "of" *Caburn* 1328[2], *atte beck'* 1332, *atte Bek* "of" *Cabourne* 1341, - "of" *Kabourn* 1350 all (p); this is presumably the stream from which Cabourne is named); *blabargh* c.1414 ('the cheerless, bleak hill', *v.* **blá(r)**, **berg** and for an identical name Blabers PN L **3**, 66; this is almost certainly a Scand. compound); *usque ad brochau* c1150 (*v.* **haugr**); *Buldailes* eHy3 (13) (*v.* **bula**, **deill**); *Caister hedge* 1674, 1686, 1697 (the boundary hedge with Caistor, *v.* **hecg**); *de Carleton'* 1332 (p), *Carleton plasse, Carletone Thyng* 1445 (named from the *Carleton* family, cf. Roger *de Carleton'* 1332, with **place** and **þing** 'possession, property'); *terram Eccl'ie de Kaburn* Hy3; *Kyrke bryge* c.1414 (*v.* **kirkja**, **brycg**); *the Commons* 1601, 1606, 1612, 1625, 1662, 1686, 1697, *y^e* - 1638, 1674, *ye commons* 1654; *Coxwould Headlande* 1601, *Cowkold headland* (sic) 1606, *Coxwould* - 1612, *Couxwould* - 1625 (named from Cuxwould and **hēafod-land**); *iuxta paruam crucem* Hy3 (Hy4) ('the little cross', *v.* **cros**); (*fee of*) *Esthalle* c1200, e13 (*v.* **ēast**, **hall**); *meta camporum caburnie* c1150, *in campis Caborniæ* l12 (13), *in campis de Kaburne* l12 (Hy4), *campis de Caborne* 1445, *apud Caybornefelde* 1536, *Caybornefeld'* 1537, *Caybornefeld* 1539, *Claybournefeilde sive Caborne feilde* 1609 (*v.* **feld**); *delleheuedland* l12 (Ed1), *dalleheuedland* e13 (Ed1) (*v.* **hēafod-land**); *iuxta thedic* l12 (13) (*v.* **dīc**, **dík**, preceded by the definite article); *ye East close* 1638, *the east clossess* (sic) 1674, 1697, *the East Closess* (sic) 1686; *the East Feilde* 1601, *the East-field* 1707, *the East Field* 1715 (there appear to have been only two open fields in the village, East and West being later divisions); *ad maram fiscedik* l12 (Ed1) (*v.* **fisc**, **dík**); *uallem quandam que a uulgo foxdale uocatur* c1150, *Foxdale* 1150-60, *foxdale* Hy2 (Ed1), e13 (Ed1) (*v.* **fox**, **dalr**); *froskehole* c.1414 (*v.* **frosc** 'a frog' in a Scandinavianized form, **hol**[1]); *Fulnabie gate* 1638, *fulnabie* - 1654,

Funnabie - (sic) 1662, *Fulnabye* - 1674, *fulnaby* - 1686, *Fulnaby* - 1697, 'the road to Fonaby (in Caistor parish)', *v.* **gata**); *portam grangie sue* Hy2 (Ed1), - *sue de caldecotes* e14 (Ed1), *ab oriente grangie p'dci conuent'* eHy3 (13) (*v.* **grange**; the references are to two granges, the first two forms refer to that of Newsham Abbey, the third to that of Alvingham Priory, that of Newsham being once called 'the cold, exposed cottages', *v.* **cald**, **cot**); *t. Johīs de la Grene* Hy3 (Hy4) (*v.* **grēne**[2]); *Haynhoudale* Hy3 (Hy4); *heades gate* 1577, *The headegates* 1601, *headgates* 1606, *they* - (sic), *the headgates* 1612, *The* - 1625, *ye head-gate* 1638, 1662, - *head gate* 1654, *ye hedgate(s)* 1674, *ye headgate* 1686, *the* - 1697, *the heading gate* 1707 (*v.* **hēafod**, **gata** and cf. Headgates PN L **2**, 53); *heuedland*, *Euedland* 112 (13), *Le Heuedland* c.1200, e13, *ye headland* 1577, *the* - 1674 (*v.* **hēafod-land**); *Hic Kededepittes* c.1200, *Hickedodepittes* e13 (checked from MS) (obscure); *ye hygh gate* 1577; *holegathe*, *Holegate* 112 (13) ('the road running in a hollow', *v.* **hol**[1], **gata**); *Hundunegate* Hy3 (Hy4), *Hunden gate* 1662, 1674, *hunden* - 1654, 1686, *Hundon* - 1697, *hunden street* 1638, *Hunden streete* 1674 ('the road to Hundon Manor (in Caistor parish), *v.* **gata**, **strǣt**, and cf. Hendon Hill in (a) *supra* and *Hundone mare* Hy3 (Hy4), *v.* **(ge)mǣre** 'a boundary'); *unum toftum ... vocatum Kakelrowse* (sic in transcript) 1445 (obscure); *Keylbye gate* 1577, *Keylbie* - 1601, 1612, *Keilbie* - 1606, 1625, *Kealebie* - 1638, 1654, *Kealbie* - 1662, *Kealby gate* 1674, *Keeleby* - 1686, 1697, *Keilby* - 1707 ('the road to Kealby', *v.* **gata**); *lambecotedale* Hy3 (Hy4) (*v.* **lamb**, **cot**, with **deill**); *Edmund Lamming Close* 1625; *Lauerdraiks* (sic) 112 (13) (perhaps 'the lord's paths', *v.* **hlāford**, **hraca**); *linland* 112 (13) (*v.* **līn** 'flax', **land**); *litelhoulanges*, *litelhaulanges* eHy3 (13) ('the little mound'. *v.* **lȳtel**, **litill**, **haugr**, to which has been added **lang**[2] 'a long strip of land' in the pl.); *maltekotes* e13 (Ed1) (perhaps 'the sheds for processing or storing malt', *v.* **malt**, **cot**, cf. *malthous* MED s.v. *malt* 2 and Löfvenberg 128 s.v. *Malthus*); *michelbergh*, *mikelbergh* 112 (13), *mikelberg* eHy3 (13), *mikelbergstygþ* eHy3 (13) (*v.* **micel**, **mikill**, **berg**, with **stīg**, **stígr** in one form); *Sr Thomas Monnsonne Close* 1601; *Nettleton furlong* 1638, 1674, 1686 (*v.* **furlang**); *de via de Netelton'* Hy3 (Hy4), *Nettleton gate* 1601, 1612, 1625, 1638, 1686, 1697, 1707, *a gate called* - 1606 ('the road to Nettleton (an adjacent parish)', *v.* **gata**); *Nithdale* Hy3 (Hy4) (Dr John Insley suggests that the first el. is ME *nith* (OE *nīð*) 'wickedness, badness' in some uncertain sense); *Northeuedland* Hy3 (Hy4) (*v.* **norð**, **hēafod-land**, and cf. *heuedland supra*); *in aquilonali campo* eHy3 (13), *the North feild* 1601, 1625, 1638, - *Feilde* 1606, 1612, 1662, *ye North Feild* 1654, *ye Northfeild* 1674, *the North field* 1686, 1706, 1707, 1712, *y^e* - 1690, *the Nor' Field* (sic) 1715 (*v.* **norð**, **feld**, one of the open fields of the parish, cf. *y^e south feyld infra*); *one toft called Parkgarth* 1532 (*v.* **parke**, **garðr**); *Pugkedale* Hy3 (Hy4) (obscure); *Restedic* 1150-60, 1160-70, *restedic* Hy2 (Ed1), *Rescedich* (*c*=*t*) R1 (1318), *Restedikes, restdike* e13 (Ed1) (the readings are uncertain) (*v.* **dīc, dík**); *Rossedale* 1160-70, 112 (13), *Rossedale* 1202; *la mare de Rowell'* Hy3 (Hy4), *Rowthwell meare* 1577, *Rothwell meare* 1601, 1638, 1654, 1697, - *Meare* 1606, 1612, 1625, - *mere* 1674, - *mear* 1686. - *Mear* 1707, *Rothwel meare* 1662, 'the boundary with Rothwell (an adjacent parish)', *v.* **(ge)mǣre**); *scortbuttes* eHy3 (13), *Scortebutes, Scrotbutes* (sic) Hy3 (Hy4) (*v.* **sc(e)ort, butte**, with the first el. in a Scandinavianized form); *one sheepwalk for five hundred sheepe of the large sorte* 1605 (*v.* **shepe-walk**); *Sniepfeld* 112 (Hy4) (*v.* **feld**); *in australi campo* eHy3 (13), *in campo australi* 1300, *ye south feyld* 1577, *the South Feild* 1601, - *Feilde* 1606, *ye South-feild* 1638, 1662, - *South feild* 1654, *the* - 1674, 1686, - *field* 1697, 1706, 1712, - *Field* 1707, 1715 (*v.* **sūð, feld**, one of the open fields of the parish, cf. *the North feild supra*); *ye South-lings* 1638, - *South lings* 1654, *ye Southlings* 1674, *the South Lings* 1686, 1697 (*v.* **sūð, lyng** 'heather'); *spelhau daile* 112 (13) ('the speech mound', from **spell, haugr**, with **deill** 'a portion of land', cf. *þingdaile infra*); *suthberg* 112 (Ed1), *Suthberch* 112 (Hy4), Hy3 (Hy4), *Suthberche* Hy3 (Hy4), *Sudberhyll* 1577, *Sudburd Hill* (sic) 1601, 1697, - *hill* 1606, 1654, 1686, *Sudbur* - 1612, *Sudber* - 1625, *Sudburde* - 1638, - *Hill* 1662, *Sudbarde* -, *Sudbar* - 1674, *Sudburd-hill* 1707 ('the south hill', *v.* **sūð, berg**, with the addition of explanatory **hyll** in later forms); *per viam de Suthdale usque ad regale cheminum* 1202, *sudale, suddale, suthdale* 112 (13) (*v.* **sūð, dalr**); *Suthlandes* Hy3 (Hy4), *Sudlands* 1638, 1654, 1662, 1674, 1686, 1697 (*v.* **sūð, land** 'a selion' in the pl.); *suthlanges* 112 (13), *le Southelonges* 1300 (*v.* **sūð, lang**[2]); *þingdaile* Hy2 (Ed1), *þingdayle* e13 (Ed1) (*v.* **þing** 'an assembly, a council, a meeting', **deill**, cf. *spelhau daile supra*); *Thornton dale* 1601, 1638, 1662, 1697, *thornton dale* 1674, *Thornton daile* 1686, *Thornton-dale* 1707, *Thornton land* 1577, 1612, 1625, *a land called* - 1601, 1606 (named from the *Thornton* family, cf. Gilbert *de Thorneton'* 1289 *Foster*, Alan *de Thorneton'* 1300 *ib*, with **deill** and **land**); *under the towne syde* 1606; *John Underwoodes close* 1606; *the vicaredge headland* 1601, *ye Vicaridge head-land* 1638, *ye vicaradge headland* 1654, *ye Vicaridge* - 1662, *ye vicaridge* - 1674, *the* - 1686, *the Vickridge* - 1697, *the Vicaridge head-land* 1707, *the Vickaridge land* 1686, *the vicars headlande* 1606 (*v.* **hēafod-land**); *Wandailes* 112 (13), eHy3 (13) ('shares of land', *v.* **wandale, wandaile** in the pl.); *certa terras in Caborne nomine Warnott* 1445 (land held by *warnoth* tenure; for a full discussion, *v.* PN L **2**, 104); *Well lankes* Hy3 (Hy4) (from **wella**, probably with **lang**[2]); *the West Field* 1715; *Westgathe* (sic) 1150-60, *Vestgate* Hy2 (Ed1), e13 (Ed1) (*v.* **west, gata**); *Westlandes* 112 (Hy4) (*v.* **west, land**); *ye white house land* 1638, *the white howse* - 1654, *ye white house (land)* 1662, *ye White* - 1674, *the white house land* 1686, 1697; *ye Wilks lands* c.1414 (*v.* **land**; *Wilks* is presumably a surn.); *Wodgarthe* 1300 (*v.* **wudu, garðr**).

Cuxwold

CUXWOLD (now included in the parish of Swallow, Bradley Wapentake)

Cucuwalt (10x) 1086 DB, *Cucvalt* 1086 ib, *Cucuwald* c.1115 LS, 1163 RA i, lHy2 Dane, *-vald'* 1196-98 RA v, *-waud'* 1202 Ass

Cukewald(') 1146 RA i, 1159-81 (e13) *NCot*, 1166 RBE (p), lHy2 (e13) *NCot*, lHy2 Dane (p), 1190 (1301) Dugd vi, l12 RA iv, 1200 CartAnt, 1212 Fees, 1214 Cur, c.1221 Welles, 1235 Cl, 1238-41 Fees, 1262 Ipm, 1265 Misc, 1281 *NCot*, *-waud(')* 1186-1200 Dane, 1218, 1219 FF, 1242-43 Fees, *Kukewalda* lHy2 (1409) Gilb, *-waud* 1249-50 RRG, *-wold(')* 1287, 1288 RSu, 1295 Ch

Cuchewald c.1150, eHy2, 1159-81 (e13) *NCot*, Hy2, lHy2 (1409) Gilb, 1181-85 (e13) *NCot*, lHy2 Dane, l12 (e13) *NCot*, lHy2 Dane, l12 (e13) *NCot*, *-uuald* 1153-54 (e13) *ib*

Chuckewald 1177 P, *Chukuald* Hy2 LN (p)

Cukwaud 1219 Ass, *Kucwald'* c.1300 RA iii, *Cukwald* 1401-02 FA, *-wolde* 1536-37 Dugd vi

Cokewald(') 1242-43 Fees, 1254 ValNor, lHy3 *NCot*, 1275, 1276 RH, 1281 QW, 1288 Ipm, 1305 Pat, 1316 FA, 1332 *SR et passim* to 1431 FA, *-walde* 1276 Cl, 1276 Ipm, 1327 *SR*, 1428 FA, *-waud* 1242-43 Fees, *Kokewald(')* 1244 ib, 1303 FA, *Cokewold* 1291 Tax, 1304, 1340 Ipm, 1341 *Extent*, 1346 FA, 1347, 1375 Cl, 1387 Ipm, a1567 LNQ v

Cokkewalde 1398 Cl

Cocouold (sic) 1350 Fine, 1350 Ipm, 1356 Fine

Cokwald 1428 FA, *-wold alias Cokeswolde alias Cokwawde* 1544 LP xix

Cokeswold 1519 DV, 1526 Sub, 1535 VE iv, 1610 Speed, *-wolde* 1577-80 *Terrier*, *Kokeswold* 1545 LP xx, 1554 PrState, *Cokeswowld* 1576 Saxton

Coxwold 1552 Pat, 1558 InstBen, 1576 LER, 1627 Hungate, *-woulde* 1601, *-would* 1612, 1625, 1679, 1686 all *Terrier*

Cuxwold 1706, 1718, 1788 all *Terrier et passim*

'Cuca's high woodland', from the OE pers.n. *Cuca* and **wald**. Dr Insley points out that OE **Cuca* is a short form of names in *Cwic-*, *v.* DEPN, s.n. Cuxham, and note also *on cuceles hylle* (in the bounds of Portisham Do) 1024 (contemp.) S 961, containing OE **Cucel*, **Cucol*, a diminutive of OE **Cuca* formed with the *-l-* suffix. ME *cokkōu*, *cuk(k)ou*, *cuk(k)u* etc. 'the European cuckoo (*Cuculus canorus*)' can be ruled out here, since it is only attested later (in surnames from 1191 and in independent use from 1300, *v.* MED s.v.). In any case, the normal word for the cuckoo in Lincolnshire would have been the Scandinavian loan-word *gouk* < ON *gaukr*. OE *cucu*, a side-form of OE *cwicu* 'live, living' (in place-names probably with the sense 'having taken root, growing', *v.* EPN, s.v. **cwicu**), can be excluded, since it is a specifically West Saxon form.

The original meaning of **wald** is 'forest', and no doubt the sense here is something like 'an area of woodland on higher ground', as suggested by Smith, PN Gl **4**, 8 n.4. The development to 'open high ground', as in the Lincolnshire Wolds, is later and cannot be reckoned with in early place-names. Forms in *-waud(')* show vocalization of *-l-* as a result of French influence (*v.* Jordan paragraph 252 Anm.). Early spellings with initial *Ch-* also reflect French influence. It is noteworthy that forms in *-es-* (whence the modern spelling) do not appear before the early 16th century.

Cuxwold is situated in a distinct saucer, surrounded by higher open land with patches of woodland and fed by a stream.

ASH HOLT, 1824 O, 1838 *TA*. BEECH HOLT (lost, approx. TA 166 021), 1828 Bry, 1838 *TA*, 1877 *MiscDon 466*; the **holt** is still there, but is not named on maps. THE BECK (local), *the Beck* 1612 *Terrier*, *The Becks* 1838 *TA*, *v.* **bekkr** 'a stream'. CABOURNE PLOTS (lost), *Cabourn Plots* 1828 Bry, named from the adjacent parish of Cabourne. It denoted an area near the parish boundary north of the track leading from the village to Badger Hills in Cabourne. COCKED HAT PLANTATION is so-named from its distictive shape. CUXWOLD HALL, 1877 *MiscDon 466*, *Hall* 1828 Bry, and cf. *iuxta terram aule de Kaburne* eHy2 (e13) *NCot*, *v.* **hall**. DOUBLE COTTAGE (local), 1877 *MiscDon 466*. THE RECTORY (lost), *the mansion howse* 1577-80, *the Parsonage-house* 1679, *A Parsonage house* 1686, *The Parsonage House* 1690, *One Parsonage house* 1697, *No buildings* *thereon* (sic) 1788, *The Rectory-House* 1864 all *Terrier.* The Rectory has recently been demolished and a house called Rowlands erected on the site. ROWLANDS, *Ruelandes* l12, c.1200 (e13) *NCot, Rowlands* 1838 *TA,* 1877 *MiscDon 466, v.* **rūh, land**. The name of the modern house replaced The Rectory and has itself been taken from the large open field in which it stands and which runs to the south to the Beck.

Field-Names

Principal forms in (a) are 1838 *TA.* Forms dated eHy2 (e13), l12 (e13), c.1200 (e13) are *NCot*; l12 (13), eHy3 (13) are *Alv*; 1577-80, 1601, 1612, 1625, 1654, 1662, 1674, 1686, 1690, 1788, 1864 are *Terrier*, 1877 are *MiscDon 466.*

(a) Acre Dykes 1838, - Dikes 1877 (*v.* **æcer, akr, dík** and PN L 2, 13); Far -, Nr Beelsby Walk 1838, 1877 (cf. *super uiam de belesby* l12 (e13), *v.* **walk** denoting land used for the pasture of animals, especially sheep, as elsewhere in this parish; it should be noted, however, that these closes are described as "arable"); Caistor Walk (cf. *Cast'gate* c.1200 (e13), *v.* **gata, walk** and cf. Beelsby Walk *supra*); Chaise House and Stables; Church and Church Yard; Church Fd 1838, - and Plantn 1877; Cover 1838, The - 1877 (*v.* **cover(t)**); Cow Cl, - Walk 1838, 1877 (*v.* **walk** and cf. Beelsby Walk *supra*); Dove Coat Cl 1788 (*v.* **douve-cot(e)**); Fold Yd, Buildings etc.; Glebe Pce 1877 (*v.* **glebe**); Halls Cl 1838, 1877; Holt (2x) (*v.* **holt**); the Home Cl 1788; Horse Walk 1838, 1877 (*v.* **walk** and cf. Beelsby Walk *supra*); Keeper's Lodge 1877; Lings Cl 1838, 1877 (*v.* **lyng** 'heather'); Bottom -, Top Long Cl 1838, 1877; Milking Yd; Orchard; Paddock 1877 (*v.* **paddok**); Park 1877 (*v.* **park**); Pig Yd; Pingle 1838, 1877 (*v.* **pingel**); Plantation (4x) 1838, 1877; Pond; Ringle Dales 1838, 1877, - Dales Cover 1838; Rookery 1877; the Road to Rothwell 1864; Sandy Bush 1838 (cf. *sondehou* eHy2 (e13), *v.* **sand, haugr**); School Orchard 1877; Shrubbery; the Road leading ... to Swallow 1788, the Road to Swallow 1864, Swallow Walk 1838, 1877 (*the high way going to Swallowe* 1601, *v.* **walk** and cf. Beelsby Walk *supra*); Thorn Tree Plot 1838, Thorn Treeplatt 1877 (*v.* **plat, plot**); Far -, Middle Warren 1838, 1877 (*v.* **wareine**); Well Walk 1838, 1877 (*v.* **wella, walk** and cf. Beelsby Walk *supra*); Wood.

(b) *iuxta terram Abbatis de Humberstan* c.1200 (e13); *toftum quod fuit Agmund* eHy2 (e13) ('the toft which Agmund owned', *v.* **toft**; *Agmund* is the ON pers.n. *Qgmundr*, OSwed *Aghmund*, a pers.n. common in L); *the common* *lane* 1612; *pastura ad decem oues In tota commun' pastura de Cukewald* c.1200 (e13) ('pasture for ten sheep on the entire common pasture of Cuxwould'), *ye Commons* 1686; *Cukewald heuedland* eHy3 (13) (*v.* **hēafod-land**); *dikefurlanges* eHy2 (e13), *dicfurlandes* (sic), *dicfurlanges* l12 (e13) (*v.* **dīk**, **furlang**); *campum de Cukewald* l12 (13), *the Feylde* 1625, *ye field* 1690, *Coxwould feild* 1654, 1674, *Coxwold* - 1662, *Coxwould field* 1686 (*v.* **feld**); *fiftenacres* l12 (e13), c.1200 (e13) (self-explanatory, *v.* **æcer**); *Haldemilnestede* l12 (e13), *haldemilne* c.1200 (e13) (('the site of) the old mill', *v.* **ald**, **myln**, **stede**); *iuxta terram hospital' Linc'* c.1200 (e13) (the reference is to St Katherine's Hospital in Lincoln, *v.* PN L **1** 124-25); *mideldale* eHy2 (e13) (*v.* **midel**, **dalr**); *iuxta terram moniallium* (sic) *de Bulington* c.1200 (e13) (*v.* **nunne**); *thoreslandes* eHy2 (e13) (*v.* **land**; the first el. is probably the ODan pers.n. *Thōri*, though ON *Þórir* or ODan *Thōrir* is a possible alternative); *þwerandes* (sic) l12 (e13), *Thwerlandes* c.1200 (e13), *werlandes* (sic) l12 (e13) (*v.* **þverr** 'athwart, lying across', **land**); *Tidlegate* (sic) eHy2 (e13) (*v.* **gata**; Dr John Insley comments that the first el. seems to be the OE pers.n. *Tīdwulf*); *Wartedale, Wartedalle* eHy2 (e13) (*v.* **þvert**, **deill** and cf. *Þwerandes supra*); *Wheitedale* c.1200 (e13) (*v.* **hveitr** 'wheat', **deill** 'a share of land', a Scand. compound).

Fulstow

FULSTOW

Fugelestou (5x) 1086 DB, 1183, 1184, 1185 P, *-stowe* 1180 ib, 1202 Ass (p), 1213 Abbr, 1213, 1219 Cur, *-stov* 1182 P, *-stow(a)* 1191 ib, *-stouwe* 1219 Ass, *Fugelstowe* eHy3 (1409) Gilb, *Fuglestoua* c.1115 LS, *-stowa* c.1115 ib, Hy2 (1314) Ch, *-stou* lHy2 *Holywell*, *-stau* 1160-70 *ib*

Fughelstuo (sic) c.1160 Dane, *Fughelestowe* 1212-19 *Holywell*, *-stou* 1314 Ch, *Fogholestow* (sic) 1272 *Ass*

Fulestou 1147 RA iii, 1185 Templar, lHy2 *Holywell*, 1238-41 Fees, *-stoue* John (1409) Gilb, 1202 FF, *-stoua* c.1200 (1409) Gilb, *-stov* 1166-67 *Holywell*, *-stowa* 1176 P, 1221 Welles, *-stow'* 1202 Ass, 1212 Cur, *-stowe* e13 *Holywell*, 1210-12 RBE, 1213 Cur, 1214 FF, 1220 Cur, 1242-43 Fees *et passim* to 1311 YearBk, 1524 *Anc*, *-stouwe* 1218 Ass, *-stouue* 1252 Cl, 1253 Ch, *-stouwe* 1277-92 *Holywell*

Foulestow Hy2 (1409) Gilb, 1302 *Holywell*, 1343 NI, 1346, ix *et passim* to 1524 *Anc*, *-stou* 1296 RSu, *-sthowe* 1426 Cl, *Foulstowe* 1297 Pat, 1303 FA, 1328 Banco, 1340 Pat, 1349 *Cor*, 1357 Cl, 1375 Peace, *-stow* 1303 FA, *Foullestowe* 1521 *Anc*

Fowelstowe 1281 Ipm, *Fowlestowe* 1428 FA, 1498 Ipm, *-stou* 1461 Pat, *Fowlstowe* 1483 *AD*, 1560 Pat, *Fowll Stowe* 1488 *LCCA*, *Fowlstoe* 1576 LER

Folestow eHy3 (1409) Gilb, *-stowe* 1285 RSu, *Folstowe* 1376 Pat

Fullestowe 1212 Fees, 1220 Cur, 1431 Fine, 1539 LP xiv, *Fullstow* 1579, 1601, 1674 *Terrier*

Fulstowe 1239 RRG, 1249 Ch, 1253, 1255, 1256 FF, 1259 Cl, 1272 *Ass*, 1281 QW, 1281 Ipm, 1289 *Ass*, 1292 Ipm, 1292 Cl, 1464 Pap *et passim*, *-stow* 1402 FA, 1579, 1587 *Holywell*, 1610 Speed *et passim*, *-stou* 1506 Cl, *-stoe* 1653 LMR

Foulestowe Harsyke 1427 *LMR*, *- Harsyk'* 1437 *Anc*, 1442, 1446 *LMR*, *- Harsik* 1446, 1447 *ib*, *-stow Arsyk* 1438, 1498 *Anc*, *Foulstowe -* 1461 *LMR*, *Foullestow arsyk* 1504 *Anc*, *Fulstowe Arsyk* 1452 LLD, *Fulstow -* 1506 *LMR*, 1508 *Anc*, *Fullestowe Arsyke* 1461 *Anc*, 1503 *LMR*, *Fullestow -* 1502 *Anc*, *Foullestow -* 1503 *LMR*, *Fulstow -* 1508, 1509 *Anc*, *- Arsykfee* 1510 *LMR*, *Foulstowe Arcyk* 1462 *Anc*, *Foulestowe -* 1462, 1464, 1465 *ib*, *- Arsik* 1474 *LMR*, 1469, 1479 *Anc*, *Fulstowe -* 1475 Pat, *Fullstowe Arsicke alias Fullstow Marshchapple* 1613 *Holywell*, *Fulstow Arswicke* (sic) *als Fulstowe Marsh Chappel als Fulstowe cum Marsh Chappell* 1694 *ib*

Fulstowebeek 1475 Pat, *Fulestow Beke* 1494 *LMR*, *Foullestow -* 1502 *ib*, *Fulstow -* 1505, 1506 *ib*, 1509 *Anc*, 1511, 1514 *LMR*, 1519 *Anc*, *Fulstowe -* 1507 *LMR*, *Fulestow Beck* 1498 *ib*, *Fulstowbek* 1534 LP vii, *Fullstowe Beake* 1613, 1620 *Holywell*, *Fulstow -* 1712 *Foster*

Perhaps 'Fugol's place, place of assembly' from the OE pers.n. *Fugol* and **stōw**, cf. Fulstone PN YW 2 239, for the same pers.n. However, EPN 2, 161 points out that compounds of **stōw** with a pers.n. are rare and when they do occur they are usually hundred-names. Fulstow is not a wapentake-name. So, it is probably better to take the first el. as being OE **fugol** 'a bird' in a general sense, hence 'the place where birds abound'.

The associations of the families *Arsic* and *Bec* with Fulstow are discussed in detail by Dorothy M. Williamson, "Some notes on the Medieval Manors of Fulstow", LAAS iv, 1-56.

BONSCAUPE, *Burnscalpe* 1615, 1617, 1618 *LMR*, *Born-* 1619, 1622 *ib*, *Burntscalpe* c.1638 *Holywell*, *-scalp* 1663 *ib*, cf. *Bornescalp close* 1725 *Foster*, *Bonscorp Close* (sic) 1819 *EnclA*. This is paralleled by the f.n. Burn Scalp PN WR **1**, 124 and **7**, 240 s.v. **scalp**, **scaup**. It is recorded late and indeed the name may well be a 17th-century formation since it does not occur on the 1595 *FMap* or in the *FSurv* of the same date. Bonscaupe appears to be a compound of *burn* and *scalp* 'the scalp, the crown, or top of the head' (from ME *scalp(e)*, ON *skálpr*), the latter in some transferred topographical sense. *Scalp* is recorded in EDD sb 4 from Yorkshire as 'a bare dry piece of stony ground' and from Lancashire as 'a bare place in a pasture field'. Neither of these seems topographically appropriate, and Dr John Insley suggests that Bonscaupe had the sense 'the area of land laid bare of vegetation by burning'. The modern form in *-scaupe* is due to the vocalisation of [l].

CHURCHTHORPE, *Kyrkthorp'* 1386 *Anc* (p), 1409, 1448 *LMR*, 1505 *ib* (p), *Kyrkethorp* 1396 *Anc* (p), *Kirkthorp'* 1404 *LMR* (p), 1514 *ib*, 1555 *Anc*, *Kerke -* 1517 *ib*, *churche Thorp* 1529 Wills ii, *Church Thorpe* 1828 Bry, cf. *at Kirk 1366 LMR* (p), 'the small hamlet around the church', *v*. **kirkja**, **þorp**, a Scand. compound and a late instance of the use of **þorp**. The change from *Kirk-* to *Church-* is noteworthy.

CONISHOLME CROSS (lost), *Conysyn crosse* 1578 *Anc*, *Conisome crose*, *Conisholme Crosse* 1585, 1587 *ib*, 1613, 1617 *LMR*, *le Connysome -* 1589 *Anc*, *Conesom -* 1690 *ib*, *Conysholme -* 1616 *LMR*. *- crosse* 1624 *ib*, *Conyson Crosse* 1595 *FMap*, *- crosse* 1595 *FSurv*, *Counessome Cross* 1828 Bry, cf. *loco ... vocat Conysome* 1588 *Holywell*, *Conyson* 1595 *FSurv*, *cunisholm* 1725 *Foster*, *conysholme hedge* 1615 *LMR*. *Conisholme -* 1620 *ib*,

Cunnisholme - 1657 *ib, Connissome crosse* - 1656 *ib,* cf. *Conyson furlonge* 1595 *FSurv, Conysonfur long* (sic) c.1638 *Holywell, cunisholme meadow* 1725 *Foster.* The cross was a cross-roads at the junction of the road forming the southern boundary of the parish and that from Fulstow to Covenham. *Conisholme* is recorded as the name of a place in 1588, 1595 and 1725. It appears, therefore, that that form is a rationalisation of an earlier name or the result of popular etymology, associating it with Conisholme LSR over five miles to the east. The earliest form so far noted for *Conisholme Cross* is *Conysyn crosse* which as was first proposed in LAAS iv, 44, suggests that it may well be a later reflex of *le Cunigeseng* eHy3 (1409) Gilb, *Cunnighenges* 1251 RRG, *Conyngsenges* 1347, 1399 *LMR, Conyng-* 1366, 1369 *ib, -eng* 1384 *ib, Conygesenge* 1407, 1427 *ib, le conyneseng* 1408 *ib, Conyngesenges* 1429, 1442 *ib,* 1452 *Anc, Conysynge* 1564, 1565 *ib, -hynge* 1564 *ib, -ynges* 1567 *ib,* presumably 'the rabbit meadow(s)', *v.* **con(n)ing, eng**. It will be noted that the latest date this name has been noted is 1567 and the earliest for *Conisholme Cross* is 1578. No certainty is possible.

GRIFF LANE (local), cf. *le grift* 1409 *LMR,* (*le*) *gryfte* 1425 *ib,* 1583 *Holywell, le Grift* 1438 *Anc,* - *Gryft* 1442 *LMR,* cf. *le gryfte dyke* 1543 *Anc, Griftdyk* 1562 *ib, le Griffe dike* 1623 *LMR, Gryft banke* 1545 *Anc, griftbanke* 1555 *LMR*; this is dial. *grift, v.* EDD s.v. where it is recorded only from north L in the sense 'a channel shaped out by water for itself, a runnel'. EDD compares *grift* with North Country dial. *griff* 'a small deep valley', itself derived from ON **gryfja** 'a hole, a pit'. Grift, itself, is probably derived from the same word, with dissimilation of *-ff* to *-ft.*

LAND DIKE, *Langedic* 1160-70 RA vii, 1314 Ch, 1408 *LMR, Langdik* 1310 *Holywell,* 1325 *Anc, -dyk* 1334, (*coēm Seweram vocata*) 1334 *ib,* 1410, 1416 *LMR, langdykgote* 1415 *ib,* 1438 *Anc, -dyke* 1342, 1526 *ib, longdyke* 1460, 1461, 1464 *ib, land dyk* 1438 *ib, -dyke* 1494 *LMR,* 1517 *Anc,* 1553 *LMR,* (*the grafte called*) 1595 *FSurv,* (*sewer voc'*) *land dyke* 1511 *LMR,* 1555 *Anc,* 1586 *Holywell,* (*le*) *landyk* 1415, 1505, 1508, 1510 *LMR,* 1556, 1562, 1567 *Anc, Landike* 1564, 1567, 1575, 1582, 1586, 1589 *Anc,* - *Sewer* 1595

FMap, Landick 1574 *Anc, -dicke* 1651 *LMR, le landike* 1615, 1618 *LMR, Land Dike Drain* 1819 *EnclA, Land Dyke* 1824 O, 'the long dyke' *v.* **lang**, **dík**, with **lang** replaced by **land** already in the 15th century, cf. Waterland Drain in Marsh Chapel *infra*. It is referred to as a *sewer*, a *gate*, a *graft* and in the 19th century as a *drain*; at least once it is *sewera vocat' langedyk bank* 1446 *LMR*, cf. *landykbanke* 1465 *Anc, -bank* 1491 *LMR*. Land Dike flows through Fulstow and Marsh Chapel, *infra*, where it joins Waterland Drain.

MOATED GRANGE is *Manor F.^m^* 1828 Bry and was *the maner howse called Westhall* 1595 *FSurv, Manor of Westhall* 1595 *FMap, Maner house of Fulstow ... called the West hall garth* 1615 *Holywell* (*v.* **garðr**), *the West Hall* 1725 *Foster, West Hall* 1842 White, self-explanatory and cf. *Westhallepastur* in f.ns. (b) *infra*. The moat is shown on *FMap*, and is still there today.

NEW DIKE, *Neudik'* 1310 *Holywell*, 1325 *Anc, le new dyk* 1409 *LMR, Newdyk* 1416, 1417 *ib, sewer voc' Nudyke* 1460 *Anc, le Nudike* 1590 *ib, Nudyk* 1494 *LMR, le Newdyke* 1510 *ib*, 1562 *Anc, Newdike* 1561, 1572, 1604 *ib*, 1622 *LMR, - Drain* 1819 *EnclA, -dicke* 1564 *Anc, leȝ Newe dyke* (sic) 1565 *ib, -ditch* 1785 *Foster, New Dyke* 1824 O, 1828 Bry, self-explanatory, *v.* **nīwe**, **dík**. New Dike forms the northern boundary of the parish with North Thoresby and North Coates and enters the sea near Horse Shoe Point.

THE RIDINGS (lost), 1828 Bry

Fulstow Redhenges lHy2 (13) *Alv, Redhenges* 1291 *Holywell, le Rede-* 1409 *LMR, Redheng* p1261 *Holywell*

Fulstowe Redenges l12 (13) *Alv, redenges* 1283 *Holywell, le Redenges* 1317 Ipm, 1438 *Anc, leȝ -* 1442 *LMR*, 1452 *Anc, Redenges* 1425, 1429 *LMR, -engs* 1366, 1369 *ib*, 1372 Ipm, *le -* 1399, 1408 *LMR, les -* 1407 *ib, -eng* eHy3 (1409) Gilb, *le Redenge* 1417 *LMR*

les Redynges 1342 *LMR, le -* 14, 1519, 1556 *Anc, leȝ -* 1505 *LMR, le redynges* 1588 *Holywell, leȝ Redinges* 1562 *Anc, le* - 1567, 1576, 1590 *ib*, 1618 *LMR*, *les* - 1622 *ib*, *le Redings* 1588 *Anc*, *les* - 1614 *LMR*, *the* - 1668 *Holywell*, *Ouerredinges* 1595 *FSurv* (*v.* **uferra** 'upper')

le Redeings 1405 *LMR*

Reddinges 1541 *LMR*, *Redde Inges* 1595 *FSurv*, *the Red-ynges* 1637 *Holywell*, *Red Inges* 1666 *ib*

les Rydynges 1522, 1542 *Anc*, *leȝ Rydinges* 1567 *ib*, *les* - 1567 *ib*

le Ryddynges 1543, 1545 *Anc*

Readinges 1560 Pat, *-ings* 1582 *Anc*, *la* - 1585 *ib*, *le* - 1574, 1587 *ib*, *y^e^* - 1588 *Holywell*, *les* - 1620 *LMR*, *the* - 1628 *ib*, *Fulstowe Readings* 1585 *Anc*, *Readings Drain* 1819 *EnclA*

le Reedings 1632 *LMR*, *the* - 1659 *Holywell*, *Broad* -, *Narrow* - 1819 *EnclA*, *Reedings Close* 1595 *FSurv*

All the forms quoted above refer to the same name, in spite of the varied later developments. It means 'the (outlying) meadows where reed grows', *v.* **hrēod**, **eng** in the pl., with occasional spellings in the sg. The name apparently denoted a fairly extensive outlying area in the west of the parish. *The Ridings* 1828 was in the extreme south-west corner of the parish with *Redde Inges* and *Reedings Close* 1595 in the same area and *Ouerredinges*, also 1595, a little to the north-east. *Readings Drain*, 1819, ran alongside Bull Bank, the southern boundary of the parish here. *Broad* and *Narrow Reedings* on the *EnclA* Plan 1819 were fields further north - north of the Fulstow-Ludborough road and along the boundary with Ludborough. The frequency in the recording of this name in medieval sources seems to indicate its local importance.

SOUTHFIELD FM, *in suth campo de Fulestowe* 1277-92 *Holywell*, *in campo australi de fulstow* 1277-92 *ib*, *in campo austr'* 1425 *LMR*, 1462 *Anc*, *in australi camp'* 1442 *LMR*, *in austr' campo* 1452 *Anc*, *in Austral' Camp'* 1543 *ib*, *in Campo Austral'* 1567 *ib*, *in Australi Campo* 1637 *Holywell*, *Suthe campis* 1291 *ib*, *in South campo* 1384 *LMR*, *Southe feld* 1425 *ib*, 1574 *Anc*, *Southfelde* 1514 *LMR*, *le southe feld'* 1522 *Anc*, *the South feld* 1610 *Holywell*, *the South fielde* 1636 *LMR*, *-field* 1637 *Holywell*, *ye South field* 1725 *Foster*, *the South Field* 1808 *HD*, 1819 *EnclA*, 1827, 1832 *HD*, self-explanatory, *v.* **sūð**, **feld**; it was one of the two great fields of the village, cf. the North Field in f.ns. (a) *infra*.

SUMMERHEAD (lost), *Summerheade* 1595 *FMap*, 1595 *FSurv*, *Someryde* 1613 *LMR*, *the Summer Head*, *- Eat Closes* 1819 *EnclA*; fields called *Summerhead* are found both in Fulstow and in Marsh Chapel, *infra*, as well as in North Coates, *v. Summereat Lane infra*. For forms of the name and a discussion of the etymology, *v. Summerhead* in Marsh Chapel *infra*. The fields here called *Summerhead* lie south of New Dike and north of the road running east from Churchthorpe, and east of The Moorings and west of the unnamed lane running north from the Churchthorpe road. They are at a distance from the fields of the same name in Marsh Chapel, but earlier may well have comprised a single pasture.

WAINGROVE HO, *Wayngraues* 1277-92 *Holywell*, 1407, 1408, 1430, 1442 *LMR*, *les* - 1622 *ib*, *Wayngraves* 1452 *Anc*, *les* - 1615 *LMR*, *-graue* 1366, 1369, 1384 *ib*, *Waingraue* 1595 *FSurv*, *-graves* 1583 *Holywell*, 1725 *Foster*, 1843 *RevesbyA*, probably 'the grove(s) or copse(s) where waggons are kept', *v.* **wægn**, **grāf**, though **grāf** is difficult to separate from **græfe**, a word of similar meaning. The consistent *-a-* spellings, however, point to **grāf**.

BULL BANK forms part of the boundary with Covenham St Bartholomew, where forms are given. COVIN'S LANE. DOUBLE TUNNEL BRIDGE. ENFIELD HO. FIRE BEACON, 1824 O, cf. Beacon Hill in Marsh Chapel *infra*. FULSTOW BRIDGE (lost), *atte brigge* ?1277 *Anc* (p), *infra pontem* 1325 *ib*, *ad Pontem* 1327 *SR* (p), *atte Brygg'* 1332 *ib* (p), 1421 *LMR* (p), *at Brig de Foulestowe* 1407 *Holywell* (p), *Brig'* 1415 *LMR* (p), *at Brigg'* 1334 *Anc* (p), *att* - 1397 *ib* (p), 1407 *LMR* (p), *del* - 1340 *Anc* (p), *at Brigge* 1461 *ib* (p), *v.* **brycg** in a Scandinavianized form; there is no evidence to indicate to which bridge the forms relate. FULSTOW GRANGE, HIGH GRANGE FM, *in grangia* 1325 *Anc*, *atte graunge* 1331 *ib* (p), *le lytill graunge* 1535-37 LDRH, cf. *Grange yate* 1411 *LMR* (*v.* **geat** 'a gate'), *v.* **grange**; the 1535-37 reference is to a grange of Louth Park Abbey.

FULSTOW HALL, perhaps cf. *atte Halle* 1331 *Anc* (p). FULSTOW TOP. FULSTOW WINDMILL, *molendino de foulestowe* 1366, 1372, *molend' de Foulestowe* 1369, 1384, *mol'd' ventrit'* - 1399, 1405, 1442 all *LMR*, *molend' ventr' ... in Foulestowe* 1452 *Anc*, *molendini ventritici in Fulstow* 1514 *LMR*, *Fulstow Mill* 1824 O, self-explanatory. GLEBE FM is *Pars.ᵉ F.ᵐ* 1828 Bry. GRANGE FM is close to the southern boundary of the parish and is probably a late use of **grange**, common in L, denoting a homestead, small mansion or farm-house, especially one standing by itself remote from others. HARNESS FM, cf. *Harneis Close* 1841 *MC*, named from the *Harness* family, cf. John *Harnis* 1587 *Anc*, - *Harneyes* 1595 *FMap*; the farm buildings are now in ruins. THE HAWTHORNS. HEELGATE FM, cf. *Hellgate* 1563 *Anc*, *Hel-* 1586 *Holywell*, 1595 *FSurv*, *Hellgates* 1586, 1663 *Holywell*, *Hel-* 1595 *FMap*, 1595 *FSurv*, cf. *hell gates close* 1725 *Foster* and *littel Hellecroft* 1412 *LMR*, *Hellecroft* 1438 *Anc*, *Helcroft* 1425, 1510 *LMR*, *pastur' voc' Hellecrofte* 1437 *Anc*. This is probably derived from **gata** 'a road', later 'a right of pasturage, pasturage' and the surn. *Hell* noted a number of times in the parish, cf. Roger *Helle* 1334 *Anc*. The continuation of the road in Marsh Chapel is called Ellgate Lane *infra*, north of which are the f.ns. *le gret hell*, *lyttell Hell*, etc. (quoted under Ellgate Lane) and this may affect the more obvious etymology suggested above. *Helgates* is shown on *FMap* as a field on the boundary between Fulstow and Marsh Chapel, midway between Heelgate Fm and New Dike. LORD NELSON HO, *The Lord Nelson* 1828 Bry, *Lord Nelson* 1842 White. The former inn is now a dwelling house, but the inn name survives on the street side wall. MAIN ST, *the streete* 1595 *FSurv*. MANOR HO, *the Maner howse* 1595 *ib*, *yᵉ Manor house* c.1638 *Holywell*, *The Manor House* 1843 *RevesbyA*; it was the site of *Manerium de North hall* 1595 *FMap*, *the Maner of* - 1595 *FSurv*, cf. *Northall garthes* 1595 *ib*. THE MOORINGS. PEAR TREE LANE (local), 1828 Bry; it is probably named from the family of Henry *Pertre* 1522 *Anc*, common in 16th century documents. VICARAGE (lost), *the vicaredge howse* 1579 *Terrier*, *the site of the vicarige* 1595 *FSurv*, *yᵉ Rectory* c.1638 *Holywell*, *the vicarige* 1662, *One Vicaridge house* 1664, 1703, *Vickridg* - 1674, *A Vicarage* - 1724, *Vicaradge* - 1822, *The Old Vicarage* 1864 all *Terrier*. In 1822 it is said to be *totally unfit for the residence of a Clergyman* and in 1864 *in the tenure of the sexton*.

Field-Names

The principal forms in (a) are 1843 *RevesbyA*. Spellings dated 1160-70 are RA vii; lHy2 (13), l12 (13) *Alv*; Hy2 (1314), 1314 Ch; Hy2 (1632), lHy2 (1632), eHy3 (1632) *Dods*; *eHy3* (1409) Gilb; p1261, 1277-92, 1282, 1283, 1291, 1330, 1407, 1579, 1583, 1586, 1588, 1597, 1609, 1610, 1611, 1624, 1631, 1633, 1637, c.1638, 1656, 1659, 1663, 1666, 1668 *Holywell*; 1272 *Ass*, 1317, 1373 Ipm; 1327, 1332 *SR*; 1388 Peace; 1451-53, 1496-98, 1523-24, 1646-47 *MinAcct*; 1529 Wills ii; a1567 LNQ v; 1579, 1601, 1668, 1671, 1822, 1864 *Terrier*, 1595[1] *FMap*, 1595[2] *FSurv*; 1725, 1785, 1786 *Foster*, 1808[1], 1827 *HD*, 1808[2] *BRA 838*; 1818 *Hill*; 1819 *EnclA*. Forms with a date followed by +, e.g. 1311+, are *Anc* and those dates followed by *, e.g. 1339*, are *LMR*. In some cases it is difficult to determine whether the field is in Fulstow or Marsh Chapel. Doubtful examples are normally included in Fulstow f.ns.

(a) Bank; Bottoms (*v.* **botm**); Caporn Cl (probably to be identified with *Capen Close* 1725 and cf. *Capon Crofte* 1567+, - *crofte* 1595[1], *-crofte* 1595[2], *Capon(s)wonge* 1595[2], *Capenwong* c.1638; this is probably from the surn. *Capon, v.* Reaney s.n., with **clos(e)**, **croft** and **vangr** 'a garden, an in-field', common in this parish. Alternatively it could be from ME *capoun* 'a castrated cock', the source of the surn. itself); Common 1818, the East - the West Common 1819, Common Piece 1843 (*y[e] Commons* 1588, *the commons, the common of Fulstowe* 1595[2], *Fulstowe Common* 1595[1], - *Comon* 1595[2], and cf. *les communes pastures* 1282); Cornham (1595[2], *Cornholm(')* 1407*, 1430*, *-holme* 1442*, 1580*, *Corne-* 1452+, 1514*, 1545+, *Cornam* 1507*, *Corn-holme* 1637, *Corn Holme* 1659, presumably from **corn** 'corn, grain' and **holmr** 'raised land in marshy ground', as elsewhere in this parish; cf. also *Corncroft*, *Corneheads* and *the Cornfeildes* in f.ns. (b) *infra*); Far -, 1st -, 2nd Cottager's Plat, Third -, Fourth -, Fifth -, Sixth Cottager's Plot (*v.* **plat**[2] 'a small piece of ground', **plot**); Court Garth (*a close called Cotegarth* 1595[2], c.1638, *v.* **cot** 'a cottage, a hut', **garðr** 'an enclosure, a small piece of ground'. as elsewhere in this parish); (The) Cow Cl; Cow Croft (*cowecroft* 1425*, *Cow-* 1438+, 1442*, 1595[1], c.1638, 1725, *-crofte* 1595[2], *Cowcroft graunge* 1553* (*v.* **grange**) (self-explanatory); the Cow Dikes 1808[1]; Crossey Cole (sic) 1786 (*the sewer called Crossecole* (sic) 1595[2], *Crosse colr.* (sic) c.1638, *crossek hole* 1725, named from the family of Thomas *Crossok'* 1289 and **hol**[1] 'a hollow'); The first -, Second -, Third eight acres; the 18 Acres; the Five Acres; the Four Acres; the fourteen Acres; Grimsby Rd 1819 (cf. *Grymsbie gate* 1583+, *the feildwaie called Grimsbye* - 1595[2], *Grimsby* - c.1638, self-explanatory, *v.* **gata** 'a road, a way', as frequently in this parish); Hag Hill (cf. *le hag* 1366*, - hagge 1409*, - *hagg* 1430*, - *Hagg*

1442*, 1450+, *the Hagge* 1595[1], 1595[2], *y^e* - c.1638, cf. *le hagyate* 1366*, *Hagfurlonge* 1595[2], *-furlong, ye Hag hedge* c.1638, from ON **hǫgg** 'a felling of trees' dial. *hag* denoting a place where trees were felled; *v.* also **geat**, **furlang**, **hecg**); the Harp 1785, The Harps 1843 (*le harp(')* 1399+, 1441+, 1450+, *- harpe* 1409*, 1452+, *the Harpe* 1595[1], 1595[2], *a close called y^e* - c.1638, cf. *Harpe close* 1725; this was a piece of land shaped like a *harp*; the same name referring to a different field occurs in Marsh Chapel f.ns. (b) *infra*); (the) High Holme 1819, 1843 (1610, *Hegholm* 1366*, 1369*, 1407*, *Heg-* 1384*, 1399*, *Hegh-* 1408*, *Heholme* 1498*, *Highholme* 1595[1], *- holme* 1595[2], *Hyholme* 1618, cf. *Heghholmleys* 1384*, *Hegholmleys* 1408*, *Hygholm-* 1430*, *Higholm-* 1442*, *Highholmleis* 1450+, *Hyholme leise* 1521, *Heyholm leys* 1542+, *heigholme* - 1556+, *Higholme Leyes* 1595[1], *High-holme Lees* 1595[2], *- leas* c.1638, *high holme Lease* 1725, 'the high dry land in marshy ground', *v.* **hēah**, **holmr**, with **lea** (OE **lēah**) 'meadow, pasture' in the pl.; all the variant spellings of the latter are found as appellatives in north L. High Holme was situated near the parish boundary north of Bull Bank at approximately TF 339 964; the same name referring to a different piece of land occurs in Marsh Chapel f.ns. (a) *infra*); Hill Cls (cf. *Hille* 1277-92, *at Hill* 1399+ (p), *del* - 1461+ (p), *- Hille* 1463 (p), *v.* **hyll**); Hockins (sic) 1808[1], Hockerin 1808[2], the Hockering 1813 (*Hockeringe* 1573+, 1595[2], *Hockeringe* 1595[1], *Hockerings* 1610, cf. *Hockering Slackes* 1595[2], *- slakes* c.1638 (the forms are late, but the first el. may be OE **hocer** 'a hump', with **ing**[2] denoting 'the place with a hump'. We may compare this with *Hockeryll* 1517*, identical with Hockerill, PN Hrt 202-3, 'the humped hill', *v.* **hocer**, **hyll**. There is a distinct rise towards the southern edge of the field called Hockering. *Slackes, slakes* are from **slakki** 'a shallow valley', 'a hollow in the ground', an OWScand word rare in the East Midlands, but for which several examples have now been noted in north L, e.g. *v.* PN L **2**, 27, 132); Home Cl (a note in the document states *The Parish Pound containing 3 Perches stands in this Field*); Incrofts (c.1638, 1725, *yncrofte* 1544+, *Incroftes* 1545+, *the Incrofte* 1595[1], *- Incroftes* 1595[2], *le Incrofts* 1636* ('the inner croft(s)', *v.* **in**, **croft**); Ingcrofts 1808[1] (*Engcroftes* 1317, (*le*) *Engcroft* 1342*, 1399*, 1407*, 1430*, 1438+, 1442*, 1452+, 1514*, (*le*) *Engecroft* 1409*, 1425*, 1452+, *les ingcroftes* 1562+, and *Estengcroft* 1366*, 1384*, 1407*, 1408*, 1430*, 1442*, *mydil-* 1366*, *midil-* 1369*, *medel-* 1407*, *medil-* 1430*, *midel-* 1442*, 1450+ (*v.* **eng** 'meadow, pasture', **croft** with **ēast**, **middel**, and cf. the foll. f.n.; the forms in *medel-* and *medil-* are Scandinavianizations of OE **middel**); Ings 1818, 1819, 1843 (*at Enges* 1347* (p), 1409* (p), *Enges* 1410* (p), *Inthehenges* 1422* (p), *le Inges* 1579+, 1588+, *les* - 1586+, 1616*, *the* - 1595[2], 1613*, *- Ings* 1725, *- ynges* 1616*, *ye Inges* c.1638, cf. *ye Ings meadow* 1725 ('the meadows, pastures', *v.* **eng** in the pl., as frequently in this parish); Lawson's

Garth 1808[1] (*Lausongarth, Lawson-garth* 1595[2], named from the family of Stephen *Lowson* 1386+ and **garðr**); The far -, The First -, Middle Low Close; Louth Rd 1819; Ludborough Rd 1819 (cf. *Lugborough Gappe* (sic) 1595[1], *Ludborough Gap* 1595[2], *le gappe* 1578+ and *ludbrough hedge* 1619*, 1623*; the *gap* is where the road from Fulstow to Ludborough leaves Fulstow); The Far -, The first -, The second middle pasture; Mill Cl (*Milclose* 1595[1], *Mill close* 1725); The Far -, - first 19 acres; the North Field 1808[1], 1818, 1819 (1725, *campo boriali de Fulstow* 1277-92, *campo boreal'* 1277-92, 1430*, 1442*, 1588, - *borial'* 1277-92, 1452+, 1544+, *campos bor'* 1566+, 1578+, *borial' campo de Fulstow* 1597*, *borealis Campis* 1553+, *Boreali Campo* 1637, *North campo* 1277-92, 1384*, 1399*, - *campis* 1291, - *Camp'* 1369*, *Northfeld* 1429*, *le northe feld'* 1542+, *the north feld* 1583, *y[e]* - 1588, *the northfield* 1637, - *North feild* 1659, one of the two great fields of the village, *v.* **norð**, **feld** and cf. Southfield Fm *supra*); the North Garth 1819 (*v.* **garðr**); North Hurdles; Oliver's Garths (from the surn. *Oliver* and **garðr**); Paddock; The Parks 1818, Parks 1843 (*le Park* 1342*, - *park* 1425*, 1505*, - *Parke* 1438+, 1520+, *y[e]* - 1545+, *the park'* 1567+, *leʒ parke* (sic) 1564+, *le Parke* 1585+, 1587+, 1636*, *the* - 1583, 1595[1], 1595[2], 1611, 1632*, 1637, 1663, *y[e]* - c.1638, *le parkes* 1575+, 1577+, cf. - *parke banke* 1573+, - *clowte* 1586, *Parkende* 1399*, 1442*, 1450+, *le parke pasture* 1604+, *the* - 1725, *le park syke* 1342*, from ME **park** in the sense 'a small enclosure, a paddock, a field', *v.* also **banke, clote, ende**[1], **sík**); the parsons Cl 1822 (*le Parsons Close* 1585+, *parsons close* 1587+. *Le parsons closse* 1589+, *Parsons* - 1590+, *parson Close* 1604+, *Parsons Close* 1616*, *le Person close* 1617*, *Person close* 1623, and cf. *parsons crosse* 1613*, self-explanatory); Far -, First Piece; Pingle(s) (*v.* **pingel** 'a small enclosure'); Pottery; The Royalty Piece (the same name occurs as Great & Little Royalty PN L **1**, 202 and as the Royalties *ib,* 220, where it is discussed in some detail, as well as PN Ch **5** 1:ii, s.v. **roilte**. It denotes a piece of land for which a payment is made to the owner(s) by the lessee); Rush Cl (*the Rush close* 1725); Rush Fen (*Rush fenne* 1595[1], 1595[2], *-fenne* 1663, *the Rush fenn close* 1725 (self-explanatory, *v.* **risc**, **fenn**; it was situated close to New Dike at approximately TF 329 991); the Seven Acres; the Seventeen Acres; Sink Pasture (from dial. *sink* 'a gutter, drain, sewer' and *v.* further Sinks Covert, PN L **2**, 199-200, but note *There are several springs in this field* 1843); The Six Acres; South Garth (cf. North Garth *supra*); Stack Yard (cf. *le Stakgarthyate, portam de Stakgarth* 1366*, *porta de* - 1372* (*v.* **stakgarth** (ON **stakkgarðr**) and **geat** 'a gate'; the apparent replacement of Stackgarth by Stack Yard is noteworthy); Storr's House and Garden, Storrs Pingle (cf. *unum toftum ... vocat Henry Storre thinge* 1578+, *v.* **þing** 'property, premises'; for the same surn. *v.* Willowtree Lane in Marsh Chapel *infra*); the Sykes 1819 (*Le Syk* p1261, 1369*, *le Sik* 1317, 1399*, - *Syk* 1366*, 1372, 1407*, 1417*, - *Syke* 1405*, 1428*, 1442*, 1452+, 1542+, 1633*, *y*[e] *Sike* 1514*, c.1638, *le* - 1575+, *The* - 1595[2], *the* - 1637, *Foghelstou syke* 1451-53, *Foghelstowe* - 1496-98, *Fulstowe* - 1523-24, 1546-47, *le Sikes* 1322*, *les* - 1553+, 1585+, 1615*, - *Sykes* 1366*, cf. *Sykeclose* 1595[1], 1595[2], c.1638, *the sewer called* - 1595[2], *Sike close* 1615*, *Sykecrosse* 1613*. *Sike dyke* 1508*, *Syke dyke* 1541*, *Sike dike* 1564+, *le Sikedike* 1590+, - *Sike head* 1603+, *v.* **sík** 'a ditch' as elsewhere in this parish; note it is once referred to as a *sewer*, *v.* also **clos(e)**, **cros**, **dík** and **hēafod**); Far -, First -, Second -, Third 10 Acres; Thorpe Cl (- *close* 1725, cf. *terr' Thome Thorp'* 1577+, named from the *Thorpe* family, cf. Christopher *Thorp* 1408*, and **clos(e)**); the three Acres; Top Cl (perhaps from Fulstow Top *supra*); Town End Gate; Tranmere Cl 1819 (*Tranmar'* 1384*, *-mare* 1425*, *-meare* 1595[2], c.1638, *fur: called Tranmear* c.1638, cf. *Tranmereclose* 1595[1], 1595[2]; the close was situated north of the road from the village to Ludborough, between the Moated Grange and Waingrove Ho. The meaning may perhaps be 'the marsh, fen where cranes are found', *v.* **trani**, **marr**[1], a Scand. compound, but the fields are not marshy today and the second el. could well be **(ge)mǣre** 'a boundary, land on a boundary'); Twelve Acres.

(b) *abitoft* 1464*, *tofti voc' Aby toft* 1514* (named from the family of Thomas *de Aby* 1332*, William - 1396+ and **toft** 'a messuage, a curtilage' as frequently in this parish); *Southabbott Croft* 1547*, *Sowthabbotcrofte* 1576+, *south abbot croft* 1577+, *South Abbotes* (sic) 1595[1], *a pasture ... called South Abbot* 1595[2], *Northabbot croft* 1417*, *-abbotcroft* 1553*, - *Abbotes* (sic) 1595[1], *a pasture ... called North Abbottes* 1595[2], *North Abbey* (sic) 1604+ (there is no indication which *abbot* is referred to, but it could well be the Abbot of Louth Park Abbey, which held land in Fulstow, cf. *y*[e] *2 former peeces voc abbutte* in Marsh Chapel f.ns. (b) *infra*); *Ackeholm* lHy2 (1632) (*v.* **āc**, **holmr**); *Acrheudes* 1342* (*v.* **æcer** 'a plot of arable or cultivated land', **hēafod** 'a strip of land left unploughed for the plough to turn on' in the pl., as elsewhere in this parish; note the appellative use of *heudes* in *xii heudes* 1384*); *Aicdales* 1160-70 (13), *Akedail* 1442*, *-daill'* 1452+ (perhaps from OE **āc** 'an oak-tree' and **deill** in the pl. in the first form; for the first el. cf. *Akebrige* in Marsh Chapel f.ns. (b) *infra*); *le Akerdyke* 1509+, *fossa voc acre-* 1510+, *acardyk'* 1517+, *le acre dyke* 1543+, *Acerdyk'* 1545+, *le acerdicke* 1575+, *le Akerdike* 1665*, cf. *leʒ acre dike hedge* 1567+ (*v.* **æcer**, **akr**, **dík** and cf. *y*[e] *acredikes* PN L 2, 13); *Alesbydaille* 1283 (no doubt from the surn. *Aylesby* and **deill** 'a share, a portion of land' as elsewhere in this parish); *Halohowe* 1442*, *Allohowe* 1443*, 1447*, *le aloo* 1523+, 1553+, *allowe* 1561+, *North Aller* 1595[1], *a pasture ... called* - 1595[2], *Northhallowe* 1618*, *North Aller* c.1638, *Esthallowe* 1465+, *South Allowe*

1567; the first el. is uncertain, the second is **haugr** 'a mound'); *partoni ... voc Appleton* 1567+, *Appletondale* 1595[1], 1595[2] (named from the holdings of the Cistercian Priory of Nun Appleton (*v.* LAAS iv, 28-29) and **deill**; the same name referring to a different piece of land occurs in Marsh Chapel f.ns. (b) *infra*); *archercroft* 1461*, 1505*, *unum toftum vocat Archercroft* 1553+ (named from the family of Henry *archar* 1396+ and **croft**; it is worth noting that it is described as a *toft* in 1553); *Arcykgarthe* 1465+ (*v.* **garðr** and for the *Arcyks v.* Fulstow *supra*); *Arkelmare* 1277-92 (named from an ancestor of Robert *arkill* 1369* and **(ge)mǣre** 'a boundary', 'land on or forming a boundary'); *Askew garth* 1725 (named from the *Askew* family, cf. Robert *Askew* c.1638 and **garðr**); *Bailey toft* 1514* (presumably from the surn. *Bailey* and **toft**); *Beamond thinge* 1566+ (from the surn. *Beamond, Beaumond* and **þing** 'property, premises'); *le bek* 1366*, 1399*, 1408*, - *Bek* 1399*, - *bekke* 1442*, - *Becke* 1452+, 1514*, cf. *Bekcroft* 1421, *Long Becklands* c.1638 (*v.* **bekkr** 'a stream, a beck'); *Beueregestoft* 1415* (named from the family of William *Bevereg'* 1303+ and **toft**); *Blakesheadlande, Blacksheadland* 1595[2] (from the surn. *Blake, Black* and **hēafod-land** 'the head of a strip left for turning the plough' as elsewhere in this parish); *Blinde lane* 1595[2] (a common name for a cul-de-sac); *Blindemeares* 1595[2], *-mears* c.1638 (from **blind** and **(ge)mǣre**, probably denoting a boundary or land on a boundary hidden by vegetation); *Bondmanscroft* 1334+ (from ME **bond(e)-man** 'a customary tenant, an unfree villager or farmer, a husbandman' (MED s.v.) and **croft**, thought it may alternatively be from a surn. formed from *bond(e)-man*); *Bordeland(e)* 1409*, 1442*, *bordland, borde-* 1412*, 1438+, -*land* 1542, *demeane landes called bourd land* 1556+ (from ME **bordland** 'land held by the lord of the manor to produce food for his table' (MED s.v.) and cf. *bourde close* in Marsh Chapel f.ns. *infra*); *Bothams close* 1725 (presumably from the surn. *Botham* and **clos(e)**); *Brakandale* eHy3 (1409) (*v.* **brakni** 'bracken', **deill**); *the Branchams, Longe -, Short Bransham* 1595[2], *Longbransham* c.1638 (obscure); *Brian Knoll* 1595[2], -*knoll* c.1638 (named from the family of Walter *Brian* 1287+, 1325+ and **cnoll** 'a hillock' and cf. *Brianholme* in Marsh Chapel f.ns. (b) *infra); brod land, - medow* 1553+ (*v.* **brād**, **land**, **mǣdwe** and cf. *the Broade land* in Marsh Chapel f.ns. (b) *infra); Brotherheadland* 1415*, 1417*, -*hedland* 1438+, 1514*, *-heuedland* 1425*, *-hedeland* 1442*, *headlande* 1595[1], 1595[2] (*v.* **hēafod-land**; the sense of *Brother-* here is uncertain); *brusse toft* 1553+ (the first el. is probably a surn, though none has been noted in the sources searched); *Bulbekhalle* 1430*, 1442*, *Bulbeck-* 1452+, *tofti voc Bobeck hall* 1514*, *Bullebeck' Hall* 1566+, *a garth called Bulbeckhall*

1595[2], - *hall* c.1628, *Bulbeke hall* 1595[1] (it was the hall of the *Bulbeck* family, on which *v.* LAAS iv, 21-25; in 1566* it is described as *Toftum vastum*); *Butgreene* 1595[2] (probably 'the green, the grassy place where the archery butts are situated', *v.* **butt**, **grēne**[2]); *Burnham Garth* 1595[1], - *garth* 1595[2] (presumably from the surn. *Burnham* and **garðr**); *Cadwalls meadow* 1663 (probably from the surn. *Cadwall*); *Calerothelone* (sic) 1508*, *Cawthrop brigg* 1538, *Calthorp Garthes* 1595[2], *Calethorpgarths* c.1638, *Cawthorpe hedge* 1614+, *Cauthorpe* - 1637*, *Calthrop Waye* 1595[2] (the lane, bridge, garth, hedge and way were all named from the lost *Cawthorpe* in Covenham St. Bartholomew *supra*); *Calfgarth* 1595[1] (*v.* **calf**, **garðr**); *le calf gates* 1572+, *a little ... pasture called Calues gate* 1595[2], *ye Calfe gates* 1663 (*v.* **calf**, **gata** (*calf-gate*) in the sense 'a right of pasturage'; this is to be compared with the common *sheep-gate* 'pasturage or the right of pasturage for a sheep' found frequently in L; it is the first example of *calf-gate* so far noted in this Survey; the word occurs also as an appellative in *1 calf gate, 4 Caluegates* 1595[2]); *Cappam croft* 1580*; *Caredaill* 1452+, *Caredyk* 1416* (the first el. is uncertain but may well be the ON pers.n. *Kári* with **deill** and **dík**; for the pers.n. cf. Carholme, PN L **1**, 20, while *Caredyk* seems to be identical with Car Dyke in Kesteven and Car Dike PN Nth 5); *Castell Croft* 1556+ (named from the family of William *Castel* 1430* and **croft**); *Castel(l)er* 1160-70 (checked from MS) (perhaps a scribal error for ME *castelet, chast(e)let* 'a small castle, a small tower, a turret'); *Catmerefurlong* 1595[2], c.1638, *-mearheadland* 1595[2] (these are on the boundary with Ludborough and *Catmere* may well be 'the boundary, the land on a boundary where (wild-)cats are found', *v.* **cat(t)**, **(ge)mǣre**, with **furlang** and **hēafod-land**); *Cauk hill, Cauke-* 1595[2], *Cauk-* c.1638 (*v.* **calc** 'chalk', **hyll**, with *-l-* vocalised to *-u-* [w], cf. the local pronunciation of Calke PN Db 626-27); *Certiercroft* 1411* (the first el. is obscure); *the Church-path, - church streete* 1595[2]; *Collingwood thinge* 1575+ (named from the family of James *Collingwood* 1562 *BT* and **þing**, cf. *Collingwood Gate* in Marsh Chapel f.ns. (b) *infra*); *Cony Crofte* 1604+ (*v.* **coni** 'a rabbit', **croft**); *Corncroft* 1553+, c.1638, *-crofte* 1595[1], *Corne-* 1579+, *-crofte* 1595[2] (self-explanatory, *v.* **corn** 'corn, grain', **croft**); *Corneheads* 1567+, *leȝ* - 1581+, *les* - 1582+, *le Corne Heades* 1575+, *les* - 1615, *Corneheades* 1583+, 1595[2], *les Corneheads* 1617*, *-heades* 1619*, *Cornheads* c.1638 (*v.* **corn**, **hēafod** in the pl. and cf. *y[e] corne hades* in Croxby f.ns. (b) PN L **3**, 28); *the Corne feild* 1613*, - *Cornfeildes* 1615*, - *Cornefield* 1636*, *-feild* 1638*, 1655*, *Fulstow Corne field* 1632*; *Crookteheadlande* 1595[2], *Crooktheadland* 1595[1], - *head-land* c.1638 ('the crooked headland', *v.* **croked**, **hēafod-land**); *at Crosse* 1407, *Crosse* 1410*, 1415*, *atte* - 1414* all (p) (*v.* **cros**); *Crosse at enges* 1410* (*v.* **cros** and Ings in f.ns. (a) *supra*); *y[e] Crossegreene* 1595[2] (*v.* **cros**, **grene**[2]); *duas acras .... voc Cullyettes* 1543+ (presumably

Cullyett is a surn.); *Deadecroft* 1465* (*v.* **dēad**, **croft**, denoting disused or worn-out land, cf. Field s.n. Dead Acres); *the meadowes called the Dockes* 1595², c.1638, *le dockes* 1580*, *the* - 1725 (*Dockes* may well be from **docce** 'a dock', referring to a place where docks grow); *the Dolles* c.1638; *Doubay toft* 1407*, 1408* (from the family of Roger *Doubay* 1339*, 1407* and **toft**); *le dreyn* 1522+ (self-explanatory, *v.* **drein(e)**); *le Dyke* 1291 (*v.* **dík**; it was in the North Field); *Easteygarth* 1595¹, 1595², c.1638, *Easie garth* (sic) 1725; *eastmill* 1595², *Eastmillhill* 1595¹, 1595², *Eastmillgrene* 1595², *Eastmilfurlonge, -waye, eastmillane* 1595², *Eastmill-furlong, East-millane* c.1638 (self-explanatory, cf. *yᵉ West miln infra*); *Emme Whitefurlonge* 1595², *Emmewhite fur.* c.1638, *-wonge* 1595², *Inne Whitewongs* (sic) 1595¹ (these might well be 'Emma White's furlong' and 'garden, in-field', *v.* **furlang** and **garðr** and cf. *Anne White garth* 1514*, which is presumably to be associated with them); *le Endyke* (sic) 1462+, - *Engdyke* 1463+, - *Hyng'dyke* 1509+ (*v.* **eng**, **dík** and cf. Ings in f.ns. (a) *supra*); *Eshgarth* 1595² (*v.* **garðr**); *Estegarth, Eastgarth* 1595² (*v.* **ēast**, **garðr**); *sewer voc' Eastfled* 1498* ('the east rivulet', *v.* **ēast**, **flēot**); *Estdail* 1438+ (*v.* **ēast**, **deill**); *Esthorp* 1461+, a1567 (*v.* **ēast**, **þorp** 'a dependent outlying farmstead, etc.'; there is no indication of its situation); *Estonne* a1567 (*v.* **ēast**, **tūn**; the exact significance of this is not clear; associated with it may be *Easton'holme* 1556+, *Eastone Holme* 1585+, *Easten holme* 1595¹, *-holme* 1595², *v.* **holmr**); *esturdails* 1342*, *Esturdayll'* 1441*, *-dale* 1514*, *Esterdaills* 1425* ('the more easterly share(s) of land', *v.* **ēasterra**, **deill**); *leȝ fendike* (sic) 1564+, *le* - 1575+ (*v.* **fenn**, **dík**); *les Fenn Heads* 1618* (*v.* **hēafod**); *Fenhou* 1277-92 (*v.* **fenn**, **haugr** 'a mound, a hill'), *campis de Fuglestowa* eHy2 (1314), - *de Foulestoue* Hy2 (1632), - *de Fulstow* 1510+, 1555*, - *de Foulstowe* 1528+, *campo de Fulestowe* 1277-92, *the common feld* 1579, *the field* 1601, *Fulstow feild* 1668, - *Field* 1671 (*v.* **feld** and cf. The North Field in f.ns. (a) *supra* and Southfield Fm *supra*); *les Firres* 1425*, *leȝ Fyrreȝ* 1438+, *les Firreȝ*, - *Fyrreȝ* 1441+, *lez firres* 1452 (from **fyrs** 'furze', denoting places where furze grows, and cf. *the Dockes supra*); *Fiuelandfurlonge* 1595², *the fivelands furlong* 1637, *Fiuelandfur:* c.1638 ('the five selions or strips', *v.* **fīf**, **land** in the pl. with **furlang**, a reference to a consolidation of five strips in the common field); *Foxolles* 1399*, *-holes* 1407*, 1442*, *les* - 1425*, *leȝ foxeholes* 1438+, *les Foxholes* 1452+ ('the foxes' earths', *v.* **fox-hol**); *Frogghole* 1595², *Frog-* c.1638 (*v.* **frogga**, **hol¹**; the reference may be ironic, referring to boggy land, rather than literal, *v.* Field s.n. Frog Hall); *Furre lee* 1595² (probably 'the meadow, pasture where furze grows', *v.* **fyrs**, **lea** (OE **lēah**) in the later sense 'meadow, pasture'); *leȝ furthes* 1564+ (cf. *Neufriht infra*); *toft' voc' Garetcroft* 1412* (named from the family of Bernard *Garratt* 1586+, 1591 *BT*; the description of the *croft* as a *toft* is noteworthy); *Garnercroft* 1443 (from the surn. *Garner* and **croft**); *fossat' vocat the Garth* 1633*, *y*[e] - c.1638 (*v.* **garðr**); *le Gatedayll'* 1425, *Gatedaill'* 1442*, *gatedail* 1438+ (*v.* **gata, deill**); *gateland* 1415* (*v.* **gata, land**); *Gatherum dyke, gatherome Dyke* 1588 (obscure); *Germthorpecroft* 1410* (named from the adjacent parish of Grainthorpe LSR and **croft**); *Golden-wonge* 1595[2], - *Wonge* c.1638 ('the garden, in-field where golden flowers grow', *v.* **gylden, vangr**); *Goosedales* 1595[2], 1613*, *-dalls* 1613* (*v.* **gōs, deill** in the pl.); *le gott* 1507*, *leȝ Gooite* (sic) 1565+, *le Gote* 1588+ (*v.* **gotu** in the sense 'a sluice', *v.* PN L **3** xvii, cf. also *leȝ Gootes* in Marsh Chapel f.ns. (b) *infra*); *the Grafte, the graft dyke* 1595[2], *the* -, *y*[e] *Graft* c.1638 (from ME **graft** 'a ditch', recorded as an appellative in *the grafte* 1595[2]); *Grass lees* 1595[1] (*v.* **gærs, lea** (OE **lēah**) in the pl.); *an acre called great acre* 1595[2] (*v.* **grēat, æcer**); *le Greitcroft* (sic) 1522+, (*the*) *great* - 1553+, 1582+, c.1683, *Great Crofte* 1595[2], *gret croft dyke* 1508 (*v.* **croft, dík**; the first el. is ME *gret*, from OE **grēot** 'gravel', ON **grjót** 'stones', which was replaced by the common **grēat** in the course of the 16th century; it is described as *unam pastur' voc great croft cont' vj acr'* in 1577+); *les grene gates* 1587+, *Greengates* c.1638, *-gateway* 1595[1], *grene gate way* 1595[2], *North -, South Greengates* 1595[2], *Southgreenegates* c.1638 (*v.* **grene**[1], **gata**, which as Mr John Field suggests may denote a grassy road or a green lane, an occupation way); *le grippe* 1580* (*v.* **grype** 'a ditch, a drain'); *Ten'ti voc' Gyldhows* 1514* (self-explanatory, *v.* **gildi-hús**); *Gyrdikes* 1517+, *le Gyrdike* 1575+ ('the muddy, the marshy dike', *v.* **gyr, dík**); *Gyrsholm* 1448* (*v.* **holmr**; the first el. is obscure); *Habbedale* 1277-92; *le Hallegarthes* 1447*, *West hallgarthes* 1595[2] (*v.* **hall, garðr**, perhaps cf. Fulstow Hall *supra*); *le hals* 1342*, 1399*, - *Hals* 1407*, 1408*, 1430*, 1442*, 1450+, - *Halse* 1542+, - *halsse* 1553+ (*v.* **hals** 'a neck' in a transferred topographical sense such as 'a narrow neck of land'); *1 daill ... voc' Handax* 1407*, *i acre i rod prat' voc* - 1408*, *1 acr' 1 rod' ... voc* - 1430*, 1442*, 1452+, *loco vocat Handax* 1553+ (this is presumably named from the shape of the piece of land, from ME **hond(e)axe** 'a battle-axe', *v.* MED s.v.); *le headland* 1575+, *y*[e] - c.1638 (*v.* **hēafod-land**); *leȝ Heddinges* 1553+, 1555+, *le headinges* 1583+ (*headings* is found elsewhere in north L both as a f.n. and as an appellative, *v.* PN L **2**, 14; it must have had much the same sense as *headland supra*); *le hed dyke* 1509+ (*v.* **hēafod, dík**); *Helyer toft* 1514* (from the surn. *Helyer* and **toft**, though Helyer has not been noted in the sources searched); *le hempgarth* 1408* (self-explanatory, *v.* **hænep, garðr**); *in y*[e] *here* 1410*, 1414*, *del Here* 1447*, 1451+, 1461*, 1462+, *Here* 1464+ all (p) (obscure); *le Heuedale* eHy3 (1632), - *heued dail'* 1438+, - *hevedaill'* 1442* (*v.* **hēafod, deill** and note its appellative use in *a peece of meadow ... called a head-dale* 1637); *Hobecke* 1595[2], c.1638, - *furlonge, Hoe beck furlonge* 1595[2], *Hobecke fur:* c.1638 (earlier forms are needed to suggest an etymology of the first el.; the second is

bekkr); *Hobidike* 1277-92, *hooby-* 1595[2], *-dicke* c.1638 (presumably from the surn *Hoby* and **dík**, though such a surn. has not been noted in the sources searched); *Holebec* 1160-70 ('the stream running in a hollow', *v.* **hol**[1], **bekkr**, cf. Holbeck PN Nt 83); *Holmare* 1160-70, *Hollmarehille* 1283 (perhaps 'the boundary, boundary land lying in a hollow', *v.* **hol**[1], **(ge)mǣre**); *le Holm* 1317, 1372, *- holm* 1505*, *- Holme* 1514*, 1553+, and *Holme Lees* 1565+, *- Leas* 1583 (*v.* **holmr** 'raised land in marshy ground'; *v.* also **lea** (OE **lēah**) in the later sense 'meadow, pasture'); *les Holmes* 1366*, 1369*, 1384*, 1399*, *leȝ -* 1407*, *le Holmes* 1505*, 1542+ (*v.* **holmr** in the pl.; this refers to a different field from the prec.); *East-*, *Westhousams* 1595[2], *Easthousam, Middle -, West housham* c.1638 (if the name is old *Hous(h)am* probably means 'at the houses', from the dative pl. of **hūs**, ON **hús**); *Humerston Lees* 1595[2], *Humberstone leas* 1619* (named from the family of Robert *de Humberstan* ?1277, John *de Humberstan'* 1332 and **lea** (OE **lēah**) in the pl., cf. Humberstone Croft in Marsh Chapel f.ns. (a) *infra*); *East -*, *Westhumbrel, Middle Humbrell* 1595[2], *East humbrill, Middle humbrell, West-Humbrell* c.1638 (obscure); *le huppecott* 1311+ ('the upper cottage, shed', *v.* **up**, **cot**); *Hurst close* 1618* (named from the family of Lucia *Hurst* 1635* and **clos(e)**); *Hush close* (sic) 1725; *the hyeway* 1579, *- hye waye* 1601, *the high waye that partes the 2 feildes* 1595[2] (cf. *del Way* 1369 (p) and Main St *supra*); *le Hyrne* 1272, 1277-92, 1327, 1452+, *in the hirne* 1366*, 1438+, *del hyrne* 1461*, 1462+, *at Hyrn'* 1519+, 1522+, *in Angulo* 1304+, *- angulo* 1340+ all (p) ('the angle, the corner of land', *v.* **hyrne**); *the Joysepastures* 1553+, *le Joicepasture* 1554+, *the Joice pastures* 1610 (named from the *Joyce* family, cf. John *Joyes* 1615*, and **pasture**); *Judhous* 1334+ (probably from the pers.n. or surn. *Judd*, a pet-form of *Jordan*, and **hūs** 'house', and cf. *Judcroft* in Marsh Chapel f.ns. (b) *infra*); *Kampster Toft* 1446*, *Camster tofte* 1514* (*v.* **toft**; the first el. is no doubt an occupational name or a surn. derived from it - ME *kembestere, kempstere, Kemster* etc. 'one who combs wool or flax, especially a female comber'); *Keeldail* 1430*, *-daill'* 1452+, *Keeledayll'* 1442* (named from the surn. *Keele*, cf. John *Kele* 1452+, and **deill**); *Kettlecroft* 1595[2] (named from the family of Robert *Ketill'* 1289+ and **croft**); *Kynyardholme* 1366*, *-holm(')* 1369*, 1384*, 1407*, 1430*, 1442*, *Kenyardholm* 1399*, *Kyniardholm'* 1408*, *Kyneardholme* 1452 (from the surn. *Kynyard*, derived from the OE pers.n. *Cynegard*, also noted in Kingerby PN L 2 47f, and **holmr**; no instances of the surn. have been noted in the sources searched); *le kyrkcausey* 1555+ (*v.* **kirkja**, **caucie** 'an embankment or dam, a raised way across marshy ground or along a dike'); *loco vocat Ladystaffe* 1603+ (obscure); *Ladyesclose* 1595[1], *Ladies close* 1595[2] (since the **clos(e)** was next to the Vicarage, the first el. probably refers to 'Our Lady', *v.* **hlǣfdige**); *Lagonland* 1334+ (named from the surn. *Lagon*, cf. Alan *Lagon(n)*

1334+, mentioned in the same document, and **land** 'a selion'); *Landmaresyk'* 1366*, 1369*, *-marsyk'* 1407 ('the boundary ditch, trench', *v.* **land-(ge)mǣre, sík**); *Langcroft* 1366*, *Medelongcroft* 1408* (*v.* **lang, croft**; *Medel-* is from ON **meðal** 'middle'); *North langhals* 1399*, *-langhals* 1384*, 1407*, 1430*, 1442*, 1452+, *Northlonghalse* 1514* (for *langhals*, cf. *le hals supra*; the meaning is something like 'the long narrow neck of land', with the prefix **norð**); *langmaresyk* 1430*, *langmarsyke* 1442*, *langmer-* 1452+ (perhaps 'the long boundary', *v.* **lang, (ge)mǣre** with **sík**); *le lea hyrne* 1586+ (probably from **lea** (OE **lēah**) 'meadow, pasture', with **hyrne** 'a nook, a corner'); *le Leyholme* 1553+ (probably 'the fallow holme', *v.* **lǣge, holmr**); *litelholmes* 1311+, *Little holmes, Little holme lees* 1595[2] ('the little raised piece of ground in marsh', cf. **lytel, holmr** with **lea** in the pl.); *Long-, Shortlocklands* c.1638 (perhaps 'the selions, strips that could be locked', *v.* **loc, land**); *long forlandes* 1583, *long furlands* 1587+, *Longefurlong(e)* 1595[2], *Longfurlong* c.1638 (*v.* **lang, furlang**; *forland* and *furland* are fairly common variants of *furlong* in north L); *Longheades* 1595[2], c.1638 (*v.* **lang, hēafod** in the pl.); *longlands* 1595[2] (*v.* **lang, land** 'a selion, a strip' in the pl.); *leȝ lottes* 1416*, *les -* 1582+ (*v.* **hlot** 'a lot, a share' in the pl.); *loucausy* 1416* ('the low causeway', *v.* **caucie**); *le Louth Liddes* 1575+, *Louthlydes, - lidesgreene* 1595[2] (*Liddes*, etc. is perhaps from **hlid** 'a slope', for the field slopes slightly towards boundary with Covenham St. Bartholomew; *Louth* here is probably from Louth Park Abbey which held land in Fulstow); *Ludmer(e)dale* 1595[2], *ludmore dale* 1620*, *le ludmeare dale* 1626* (the forms are too varied to suggest an etymology); *malle toft* 1412* (the first el. is the pers.n. or surn. *Malle*, from *Mary*, with **toft**); *Markby holme* 1553+ (from the surn. *Markby*, cf. Gilbert *de Markeby* 1289+, 1330+, and **holmr**); *the Marsh pingle* 1727 (*v.* **pingel** 'a small enclosure'); *medildyke* 1409*, *le myddle dike* 1577+ (self-explanatory; *medil* is from ON **meðal** 'middle'); *le mendaile* 1342*, *Meondaille* (sic) 1366*, *Meendale* 1369*, 1408*, *-daill'* 1399*, 1452+, *meendaille* 1384*, *-dayle, -daills* 1407*, *-daile* 1430*, *-dail* 1442* ('the communally-held share of land', *v.* **(ge)mǣne, deill** and cf. *leȝ Meneholme* in Marsh Chapel f.ns. (b) *infra*); *the mid-dle streete* 1595[2]; *Milncroft* 1430*, *Milne-* 1442*, *mylne-* 1452+, *- Croft* 1543 (cf. Mill Cl in f.ns. (a) *supra*); *(le) milndam* 1366*, 1369*, 1408*, *Myln-* 1384*, *myln-* 1407*, 1430*, *Milne-* 1442*, *mylnedame* 1452+ (*v.* **myln, damme** (ON **dammr**) 'a dam, a pond'); *milneholme* 1565+ (*v.* **myln, holmr**); *del more* 1340+ (p) (*v.* **mōr** 'marsh'); *mumbye close* 1567+, *Mumbymeregrene* 1595[2], *- greene* c.1638, *Mumby Garth* 1725 (from the surn. *Mumby*, cf. William *Mumby* 1429*, Thomas - 1451+, with **clos(e), (ge)mǣre, grene**[2] and **garðr**;

Mumbymeregrene was situated on the Ludborough boundary; cf. *Thomas Mumby's Garth* in Marsh Chapel f.ns. (b) *infra*); *Mutton Wonge* 1595[2], *Mooton wonge* 1595[1] (the significance of *mutton*, ME *mouton*, is uncertain, but it could be a nickname or a term for a loose woman); *myredale* Hy2 (1632), *Mire-* lHy2 (1632), (*v.* **mýrr** 'a mire, a bog'; the meaning of *dale* here is not clear); *Nablecunbecke* 1595[2], *-cunbecke, -cumbeck* c.1638 (obscure); *Newcroft* 1314, 1317, 1399*, 1407*, 1408*, 1442*, 1452+, *Nieu-* 1366*. 1369*, *Neu-* 1384*, *newe-* 1430* (self-explanatory, *v.* **nīwe, croft**); *le new close end* 1579*, 1580*; *Newellegripp'* 1438+, *grype vocat' newelgryp'* 1517+, *Newell grypp* 1541+ (the sense of *newelle* here is uncertain but may well be 'the new spring', *v.* **nīwe, wella**, with OE **grype**, dial., *grip* 'a ditch, a drain'); *new goat Botham* 1725 (*v.* **nīwe, gotu, boðm** 'bottom'); "grange of" *Neufriht, Newfrith* 1314, *Neu-* 1322* (p), 1340 (p) (from **nīwe** and **fyrhð** 'fenland overgrown with brushwood', in ME 'a park, a woodland meadow', 'an enclosure'); *Newtomholm'* (sic) 1388 (cf. *terram Rogeri Newtom* in the same document, and **holmr**); *Nordale* 1277-92, *Northdaill'* 1369*, 1399*, 1425*, 1452+, *-daille* 1384*, 1407*, 1442*, *-dall'* 1408*, *-dailles* 1430*, *nordale pyt* 1583, *Nordelbeck* 1595[2] (*v.* **norð, deill**, with **pytt** and **bekkr**); *Oakdales* 1595[2] (*v.* **āc** 'an oak-tree', **deill** in the pl.; this *may* be a later form of *Aicdales supra*); *ye onset* 1597, *the Onsett* 1631 (*v.* **onset** NED sb[2] 'a farm-house with its outhouses, a farmstead', and cf. Onset in Marsh Chapel f.ns. (a) *infra*); (*les*) *Outengs* 1366*, 1369*, (*le*) *outeng* 1384*, 1415*, *le Outengs* 1399*, (*le*) *Outenges* 1406*, 1412*, 1438+, 1452+, *leȝ* - 1430*, - *Outengeȝ* 1441*, - *Owtenges* 1452+, *Outynges* 1514* ('the outer meadows, pastures', *v.* **ūt, eng** in the pl.); *oxcroft* 1417*, *Ox-* 1425*, 1464+, 1514*, 1521+, 1587+, 1595[1], c.1638, 1663, *Oxe-* 1438+, 1595[2] (self-explanatory, *v.* **oxa, croft**); *le Ox daile* 1342* (*v.* **oxa, deill**); *ye oxe pasture* 1586; *Overlark hill* 1595[2], *ouerlark(e)hill* c.1638 (this is 'the upper *Larkhill*', but it is uncertain whether *Larkhill* means 'the hill where larks abound', *v.* **hyll** or whether *Lark* is a surn. as in Nicholas *Larke* 1503*); *Paddayle* 1282, 1330, *-dall'* 1555+ (probably from **padde** 'a toad' and **deill**); *Padwell* 1595[2] (*v.* **padde, wella**); *the Patch* 1595[2] (self-explanatory); *Paintermere* 1595[2], *-meare* c.1638 (named from the family of Ralph *Paintour* 1322* and **(ge)mǣre** 'a boundary, land on or forming a boundary'); *parcell prati voc' pache koke* 1543+ (obscure, but note *the Patch supra*); *le Pepper Holme* 1523+, 1586+ (*Pepper* is probably a surn. here with **holmr**, though again none has been noted in this parish); *percy dale* 1542+, 1556+ (presumably from the surn. *Percy*, but none has been noted in the sources searched); *Toftum ... voc Pettie thinge* 1576+ (named from the family of Thomas

Petty 1566 *BT* and **þing** 'property'); *Pikson Close* 1586+ (*Pikson* is no doubt a surn., with **clos(e)**); *Pinder deale* 1595[2], *-dele* (sic) 1595[1] (*v.* **deill**), *pyndergates* 1462+ (*v.* **gata**), *Pindergrene* 1595[1], *-greene* 1595[2] (*v.* **grēne**), *Pynder House* 1529, *- mare* 1582+, *Pinder-meare, -mearefurlonge* 1595[2], *-mearefur.* c.1638 (*v.* **(ge)mǣre, furlang**), *unum messuagium voc' pynder oxgan'* 1508 (*v.* **oxgang** 'a measure of land' ten to thirty acres in extent) (this group of f.ns. is probably named from the village *pinder* (OE **pyndere**) though the surn. *Pinder* is very common in this parish. The reference to *Pinder greene* 1595[2] states *the Pinder hath by custome the feeds therof*; cf. Pinder Holme in Marsh Chapel f.ns. (a) *infra*); *Tofti voc ponyhows* 1514* (*pony* may well be the same surn. as *Punny* in *punnyland infra, v.* also **hūs** 'a house'); *viam voc' pohenheyelane* 1517* (obscure); *the Pooke* (sic) 1595[1]; *Portas thinge* 1575+ (named from the family of John *Portas* 1562 *BT* and **þing**, and cf. Porcas Garth (sic) in Marsh Chapel f.ns. (a) *infra*); *Prestholm'* 1277-92 (*v.* **prēost** 'a priest', **holmr**); *punnyland, unam nouam grang' apud punnyplace* 1430+, *Punnypatch* 1595[1], c.1638, *- patch* 1595[2] (named from the *Punny* family, cf. Ralph *Punny* 1277-92, John - 1289+, 1325+ with **land, place** and **patch**); *Richardson thinge* 1577+ (from the family of George and Philip *Richardson* 1577+ and **þing**); *Rinnendefures* 1277-92, *Running Furlonge* 1595[2], *-fur.* c.1638 (this is 'the running furlong', *v.* **furh**, but the significance is uncertain); *Ristalmare* 1366*, 1399*, 1407*, *-mar* 1384*, 1430*, *Ristallemare* 1369*, 1384*, *Ristal-* 1399*, *Ristilmares* 1408*, *Rystallmar'* 1442*, *Rystalmare* 1452+, *Rustlemerefurlonge, -grene* 1595[2], *-merfur.* c.1638 (perhaps *Ristal(l)* etc. are from OE **ryge** 'rye' and **stall** 'a place', denoting a place where rye grows, but this is quite uncertain); *Row(e)thyng* 1505* (probably from the surn. *Rowe*, cf. perhaps William *Roe* 1577 *BT*, and **þing**; *Toftum vocat Rose thinge* 1579+ very likely belongs here too); *Rush pastur* 1595[1], *-pasture* 1595[2], c.1638, *Rish -* 1575+ (*v.* **risc, pasture**; it was on the boundary with Marsh Chapel; cf. Rush Fen in (a) *supra*); *Rylay garthe* 1575+ (from the surn. *Rylay* and **garðr**); *sewer apud Saxgote* 1374+ (this is perhaps 'Saxi's sluice', from the ON pers.n. *Saxi* and **gotu**); *Schepyncroft* 1408* (from **scypen** 'a cow-shed' and **croft**); *Schortholm* 1317, 1372, *Skortholm(')* 1342*, 1425*, 1519+, *-holme* 1442*, 1502*, 1556+, 1583+, 1595[2], *Scortholm* 1438+, 1542+, *-holme* 1521+, 1595[2], 1610, c.1638, *Schort-* 1553+, *Estshortholm, Midil-, Westschortholm(e)* 1366*, *Est-, Midil-, West schortholm* 1384*, *Est-, Medil-, Westscortholm'* 1408*, *Est-, Middil-, Westschortholme* 1514*, *South Shortholme* 1589+ (*v.* **sceort, holmr**, with *sc-, sk-* spellings Scandinavianized); *Scortorne* 1583 (apparently 'the short thorn-bush' *v.* **sceort, þorn**); *Scotholm* 14+,

-lee 1595[2], *-les* 1595[1], *-lea* c.1638 (the 1595[2] reference adds *in the ten' of Scott* and cf. William *Skotte* 1331+, *v.* **holmr** and **lea** (OE **lēah**) 'meadow, pasture'); *Sewer voc Segdyke* 1514* ('the dike where sedge grows', *v.* **secg**, **dík**, with *Seg-* a Scandinavianized form); *Shepcotegarth* 1408* (*v.* **shep-cote**, **garðr**); *the short dales* 1583, *Shortedailes* 1595[2], *-dales* c.1638 (*v.* **sceort**, **deill** in the pl.); *Skeldaill(')* 1400*, 1408*, 1430*, *-dall* 1514*, *-dale* 1556+, *Skilledail'* 1442*, *Skyldaill* 1452+ (perhaps from ON **skial** 'a boundary' and **deill**); *Skriddle-hill* 1595[2] (obscure); *le Slede* 1411* (cf. Slead pce in Utterby f.ns. (a) *supra*); *Sleghdaille* 1366*, 1384* (probably from the ME surn. *Slegh* and **deill**); *Smaldykcrose* 1460+ ('the narrow dike', *v.* **smæl**, **dík**, with **cros**); *Smalthornleys* 1407*, 1430*, 1442, 1514, *-lays* 1408*, *-leis* 1452+ (*v.* **smæl** 'narrow, thin', **þorn**, with the pl. of **lea** (OE **lēah**); *smallthorn* is frequently found in minor names and may be a term for some unusual type of thorn-bush, but this does not seem to be recorded as such in dictionaries); *Southaabanke* 1465+ ('the south stream', *v.* **sūð**, ON **á**, with **banke**); *le South dyk* 1415*, *-dyk* 1416*, *Southdyk bank* 1446* (*v.* **sūð**, **dík**, with **banke**); *Southgreene* c.1638 (*v.* **sūð**, **grene**[2] 'a green, a grassy place'); *Spittelhirne nooke* 1553+, *Spittlehyrne* 1595[2], *-hyrne* c.1638, *-hornes* (sic) 1619*, *-thornes* (sic) 1626* (*v.* **hyrne** 'a nook, a corner of land'; the Prior of the Hospital of St. John of Jerusalem held land in Fulstow, *v.* LAAS iv, 27-28, *v.* **spitel**. The forms dated 1619 and 1626 presumably refer to the same piece of land and reflect some kind of popular etymology or are simply errors); *del Stable* 1366* (p) (self-explanatory); *le Standhale* 1366* (*v.* **halh**); *Stanecroft* 1498+ (*v.* **stān**, **croft** and cf. *At Stanes* 1366*, *le Stones* 1585+); *Stangfurres* 1595[2], c.1638 (probably from ON **stǫng** 'a pole' and **furh** 'a furrow' in the pl.); (*le*) *Stirkpastur'* 1342*, 1390+ (*v.* **stirc** 'a young bull' and **pasture**); *Stopewonge* 1595[2], *-wongs* 1595[1] (probably from ON **stólpi** 'a post, a stake' and **vangr**); *Sudmeardale* c.1638; *Sutton hospitall* 1640*, *Suttons* - 1651*, 1656*, *-hospital* 1655* (the history of this name has not been traced, but the *Sutton* family is well-represented in the parish, cf. *Richard Sutton mil.* 1637*); *Swinecotmeare* 1595[2], *-coatmeare* c.1638 (*v.* **swīn-cot** 'a pigsty' with **(ge)mǣre** and cf. the following f.n.; it was on the southern boundary of the parish); *Swynstalmare* 1366*, 1399*, 1407*, 1452+, *-mar* 1430*, *-stallmar'* 1408*, *Swynstallemar'* 1369*, 1384*, 1442* (identical in meaning with the last, from **swīn** 'a swine, a pig' and **stall** 'place, etc.,' with **(ge)mǣre**; the two may, of course, refer to the same pigsty); *Sydeslippe* 1595[2], *Side-* c.1638 (in NED *side-slip* sb.1 is explained as ?'a slope or rise', with a reference from L; there is a marked slope here to one corner of the field); *le Sydick* 1575+, *Sydykbanke* 1506*,

Syddyke banke 1583 (this is apparently 'the broad dike', *v.* **sīd, dīk**); *Thoresbie crosse* 1582+ (a cross on the boundary with the neighbouring parish of North Thoresby); *Thyselstowe* 1566+ (from **þistel** and **stōw**, presumably in the sense 'the place where thistles grow'); *le trebrigges* 1342* (perhaps a bridge marked by a tree or made of trees, *v.* **trēow, brycg**, the latter in a Scandinavianized form); *Northe Thurdales* 1277-92, *Northturdayles* 1505*, *the north Tyrdales* 1583, *Northturffdales* 1564+, *North durdales* 1619* (the forms are too varied for any certainty); *the Updyke* 1588 ('the upper dike'. *v.* **upp, dīk**); *Utterby lane* 1617* (the lane to the adjacent parish of Utterby); *Wadecroft* 1438+, 1595[1], *-crofte* 1595[2], *Waid croft* 1575+ (named from the *Wade* family, cf. Gilbert *Wade* 1277-92, and **croft**; it is possible that *Watecroft* 1465+ belongs here); *Walkerley thinge* 1567+ (the property, *v.* **þing**, was held by Henry *Walkerley*); *Watpasture* 1595[1], 1595[2] (probably from ME *Wat*, a pet-form of *Walter*, and **pasture**); *at Welle* 1366* (p) (*v.* **wella** 'a spring'); *Welledayle* 1283 ('a share of land with a spring', *v.* **wella, deill**); *Welthorn* 1442*, 1452+, 1588, *-thorne* 1452+, 1595[2], c.1638 ('the thorn-bush by the spring', *v.* **wella, þorn**); *west croft* 1545+; *Westerpasture* 1587 ('the more westerly pasture', *v.* **westerra, pasture**); *Westhallepastur'* 1366*, 1369*, 1442*, *-pasture* 1384*, 1408*, 1430*, *-hallpasture* 1407*, *-pastur'* 1452+, *Westall pasture* 1582+, *a great pasture called Westhall pasture* 1595[2], *West Hall pasture* c.1638 (the pasture itself is situated north of the road from Churchthorpe to Harness Fm and south of New Dike; even so it may well have belonged to West Hall (for which *v.* Moated Grange *supra*) though this is some distance away; however a single example of *Esthalpastur'* 1442+ has been noted; there is also a *westhall croft* in Marsh Chapel f.ns. (b) *infra*); *Westmikelmare* 1277-92, *-mykilmare* 1366*, *-mykelmare* 1384*, 1452+, *-mar'* 1369*, *-mekilmare* 1379*, 1429*, 1441*, *-mekelmare* 1407*, *-meklmare* 1408* ('the big boundary, land on or forming a boundary', *v.* **mikill, (ge)mǣre**, with **west** prefixed; no contrasting *East* has been noted); *ye West miln* 1579, *Westmill* 1595[2], *West millane* 1595[1], 1595[2], *westmilfurlonge, -grene* 1595[2], *Westmill fur.*, *-greene* c.1638 (self-explanatory, *v.* **west, myln**, with **lane, furlang** and **grene**[2]; it is named in contrast to *eastmill supra*); *West pingles* 1725 (*v.* **pingel**); *le west yate* 1623*, *portam vocat' the West yate* 1629+ (*v.* **west, geat** 'a gate'); *Whimerowe, Whym-merowe* 1595[2], *Whim(e)rowe, Whinne row* (sic) c.1638 (obscure); *messuag' voc Amy Whitehouse* 1613* (self-explanatory); *Wildgooseheadlande* 1595[2] (self-explanatory, *v.* **hēafod-land**); *Wilughmare* 1366+, 1399*, 1407*, 1430*, *-mar'* 1369*, 1384*, *Wylughmare* 1408*, 1441*, 1452+, *Willowmearheadlande* 1595[1], *-merheadlande* 1595[2], *Willowmergrene.*

-merefurlonge 1595[2] (*v.* **hēafod-land**, **grēne**[2], **furlong**) (Dr John Insley points out that the *-gh-* spellings in the 14th and 15th centuries speak against OE **wilig** 'a willow' as first el. and suggests that we are rather concerned with the ON pers.n. *Vīglaugr* or a surn. derived from it; *-mare* is probably derived from **(ge)mǣre** 'a boundary'. The field is just east and north of Waingrove Ho and the f.n. Tranmere (in (a) *supra*) and is marked by a row of trees); *a garth called Witherwickes* 1595[2] (named from the family of Richard *Wytherwicke* 1562+ and **garðr**); *Witton close* 1580* (named from the family of Ralph *Wytton* 1501+ and **clos(e)**); *Woodcraft* (sic) c.1638 (*v.* **wudu**, **croft**; *craft* is an occasional variant spelling of *croft* in L); *Woorleby* -, *Woorliby garth* 1595[2] (no doubt from the surn. *Worlaby* and **garðr**, though no member of the family has been noted in the sources searched); *a well called Wrangwell* 1595[1] (from **wrang**, **vrangr** 'crooked, twisted' and **wella** 'a spring', though a meaning crooked or twisted hardly goes well with *spring*. EPNE ii, 278, s.v. **wrang**, notes that the cognate *wrangh* in Middle Low German means 'sour, bitter', while NED s.v. *wrong* notes that in Dutch *wrang* means 'acid, tart'. Some such figurative sense would fit well here, but there is no independent evidence to support it in English).

Grainsby

GRAINSBY

Grenesbi 1086 DB, 1146 RA i (p), c.1150 Dane (p), 1156-62 (l13) YCh iv (p), Hy2 Dane (p), 1197 P (p), 1198 Cur (p), 1198 CurR, l12 *HarlCh* (p), 1202 Cur, 1202 Ass, 1202 FF (p), 1207 P, 1208 ChancR, *-bia* 1136-45 YCh iv (p), *-by* 1207 OblR, 1225 Cur, 1251 Ch

Grenebi 1178 (p), 1197, 1193 (p), 1198 all P

Greinesbi c.1115 LS, 1150-60 Dane (p), p1150 *HarlCh*, 1156-58 *ib*, 1170-98 Revesby (p), l12 Dane (p), 1202 Ass (p), 1205, 1210 P (p), 1218 Ass, *-by* 1235-47 RA i (p), Hy2 (1409) Gilb (p), 1202 Ass (p), *Greynesby* 1242-43 Fees, 1254 ValNor, 1281 Ipm, 1290, 1296 RSu, 1297 CoramR, 1303 FA, 1315 Orig, 1316 Pat, 1332 *SR*, 1352 Ipm, 1428 FA, 1483 Pat, 1503 Ipm

Grainesbi 1147-53 Dane (p), c.1156 (13) *Kirkst* (p), 1166 RBE (p), Hy2 LN (p), l12 (1409) Gilb, *-bia* 1212 Fees, *-b'* 1238-41 ib, *-bie* a1567 LNQ v, 1576 LER, 1589 NCWills,

-bye 1613 *BT, -by* 1672 *ib, Graynesby* a1155 (e13) *NCot*, 1245 FF (p). 1276 RH, 1295 RSu, 1297 Pat, 1315 Ipm, 1315 Cl, 1316 FA, 1316 Pat *et passim* to 1588 *BT, -bi* 1333 Pap, *-bie* c.1577 *Terrier*, 1586, 1591, 1597 *BT, -bye* 1623 *Hill*, *Graynysby* 1475 Pat

Granesby 1390, 1393 Pap, 1427, 1461 Pat, 1526 Sub, 1530 Wills ii, 1535 VE iv, 1554 Pat, *-bye* 1576 Saxton, 1610 Speed, *Granysby* 1428 FA, 1509 Ipm, *-be* 1562 *BT*

Cranesbi (sic) 1165 RBE (p)

Graynsby 1556 *Mad*, 1591, 1665 *BT*, 1668 *Terrier, -bye* 1563 *BT*, 1662 *ib, Grainsbye* 1562 *ib*, 1601 *LCS, -be* 1570, 1597, 1601, 1608 *BT, -bie* 1594, 1597 *ib*, 1601, 1611, 1628 *Terrier*, 1632 *BT, Grainsby* 1633 *ib*, 1638, 1679 *Terrier*, 1682 *BT*, 1690 *Haigh*, 1692 *BT et freq*

'Grein's farm, village', *v.* **bȳ**, as suggested by Ekwall, DEPN s.n. ON *Grein*, OEScand *Grēn* is a byname belonging to ON *grein*, ODan *gren* 'a branch' and is discussed by Insley, SPNNf 142. Gillian Fellows-Jensen, SSNEM 50, suggests that it may rather be the appellative ON *grein* 'a fork (of a river)', with a secondary gen. in *-es*. This word survives in dialect as 'a small valley forking off from another' but there is nothing in the topography of Grainsby which would support this sense.

BEGGARS PARK PLANTATION, cf. *the Beggars Park* 1793 *Haigh*, perhaps here a name for worthless land, *v.* Field 17-18. BOWLINGS PARK. BURNHAM'S VILLA, named from the *Burnham* family, cf. William *Burnam* 1623 *Inv* and note *Here is a Wesleyan chapel erected by Mrs Sands and the late Francis Burnham, Esq., in the year 1860* 1868 Kelly. FAR PLEAD PLANTATION, cf. *the plade, Plade furlonge* c.1577 *Terrier, Far -, Near Plead* 1840 *TA*, obscure. GLEBE FM, cf. *Glebe close* 1840 *ib.* GRAINSBY GRANGE, presumably a late dial. example of **grange** 'a homestead, a small mansion or farm-house, esp. one standing by itself remote from others'. GRAINSBY HALL, 1828 Bry, 1830 Gre, 1842 White, *Grainsby House* 1824 O. GRAINSBY HEALING, 1840 TA, *Heeling* 1745 *Terrier, Healing* 1762 *ib*, *- otherwise Heeling* 1797 *Haigh, Grainsby Heeling* 1824 O, 1828 Bry;

early forms are needed to suggest an etymology of Healing. GRAINSBY HOLME, 1824 O, 1828 Bry, *the Holme* c.1577, *- holme* 1601, 1664, *ye Holm* 1697, *- holme* 1715, 1724 all *Terrier, Grainsby Home* (sic) 1668 *PR*, *- holme* m17 *Haigh*, *- Holmes* 1788 *ib*, cf. *the Holme furres, ye Holme pasture* c.1577 *Terrier, Mr Nelthorps Holm* 1703 *ib*, *v.* **holmr** 'a water-meadow, raised land in marsh'. GRAINSBY LANE, 1723, 1821, 1826 *Haigh*, 1824 O, *Grainsby-lane* 1636 *Terrier.* GRAINSBY MOTOR HALT is on the disused railway. NEW PARK PLANTATION. OLD FLEET DRAIN, *ye Narrow fleet* 1697, *- Fleet* 1703, *a ditch called the Fleet* 1864 all *Terrier, Grainsby Beck coms thro Thoresby, which together with the vast number of Blow Wells forms the River called the Fleet* 1774 *Hill*; the same name is recorded from North Coates and North Thoresby *infra.* THE RECTORY, *the -* 1668, 1671, *y^{e} -* 1668, 1671, *ye -* 1703 all *Terrier, one dwelling House called the Rectory* 1864 *ib*, *ye parsonage* c.1577, 1724, *- parsonage-house* 1638, *One Parsonage hous* 1706 all *ib*, *Pars^{n}* 1828 Bry, cf. *Grainesbie parsonage plott* 1628 *Terrier.* ROSE COTTAGES. VALLEY FM. WINGFIELD HO.

Field-Names

Principal forms in (a) are 1840 *TA*; forms dated 1332 are *SR*; c.1577, 1577, 1601, 1611, 1628, 1638, 1662, 1664, 1668[1], 1671, 1679, 1697, 1703, 1706, 1709, 1715, 1724, 1822[1], 1864[1] are *Terrier*, 1659 *BRA 833*; 1668[2], 1672, c.1692 *PR*; 1675 *AS*; 1690, 1691, 1698, 1699, 1707, 1712, 1723, 1788, 1789, 1793, 1796, 1797, 1798, 1799, 1807, 1812, 1814, 1821, 1822[2], 1852, 1853, 1855, 1858, 1863, 1864[2] *Haigh*; 1730 *Td'E.*

(a) Barn Walk (*v.* **walk**); Beck Cl (*v.* Turf-Close *infra*); Bottom, Far Bottoms (*v.* **botm**); Bowlands Cl 1789, 1812 (*Bowlands* 1699, named from the *Bowland* family, cf. *Mr Bowlandes* 1611 *Terrier*); Brokenback Wong 1840 (*v.* **vangr**), Broken Back - 1858 (*Broken backe* c.1577; the sense is 'hunchback', for which cf. Brokenback PN L **3** 115, the name of a round barrow. However, the field in question is flat and there are no signs of a former barrow, now levelled. Local enquiry indicates that the land has poor drainage and in this case the name may be simply indicative of a field difficult to work. With this may perhaps be compared Broken Back PN Ch **1** 317, where it is suggested that it denotes land hard to till); Burtons Cl (Miles *Burton* is named in the document); Buttock Cl; Gt -, Lt - Calf Cl (*Calfe Close* 1691, *the* - 1698); Church Cl & House, Church Fd, - Yd (cf. (*atte*) *Kirkeyate* 1332 (p), *v.* **kirkja**, **geat**); Cooks Cl (named from the *Cook* family, cf. Edward *Cooke* 1729 *BT*, John *Cook* 1840 *TA*); (Bottom -, Top) Cow Cl, Cow Walk; Down Cl; the East Cl 1793, 1864[2]; the East Fd 1788 (*the East feild* c.1577, *the East field* 1699); the east platt of grainsby 1822[1] (*ye East Platts* 1703, *ye East plat* 1724, *the east & west Platts* 1706, *v.* **plat**[2] 'a small piece of ground', as elsewhere in the parish); the Eighteen Acres Cl 1821, Part of the 18 Acres 1840; Far Fd 1858; the Farrow Cl 1793; the Great Fenn Cl 1788, the Syer -, the Well Fen Cl 1793 (*the fenend, the fenne, the fenne furlond* c.1577 (*v.* **furlang**), *the great Fenn-Close, the little Fenn Close* 1699, *v.* **fenn**); Firr Cl 1789, 1812; First Fd 1858; Foot Bridge otherwise Brigg Cl 1788, Foot bridge - 1799; Part of the 4 acres (2x), The 4 acres 1840, the four - 1840, 1864; Fourteen Acres 1840, the - 1864[2] (*the fourteen Acres or fourteen acres close* 1723); (Low) Garth (*v.* **garðr** 'an enclosure', as elsewhere in the parish); Grainsby Cl 1840, - Dales 1793, - Fd 1840 (*Grainsbye field* 1577, *Grainsby feld* 1611, *v.* **feld**); Grassthorpe 1788 (*grass-Thorps* 1699, *v.* **gærs** and cf. The Land Thorpes and The Gt Thorpe Cl *infra*); Gt Walk or the Gt Sheepwalk 1796 (*the great Walke or the great Sheepe Walke* 1675, *Great Walk* c.1692, *the Great Walk or the Great Sheep* - 1712, *v.* **walk**, **shepe-walk**); the Green Cl 1793; the High Fd 1796 (*the High feild* 1659, *the high feild* 1675, *High Field* 1712, 1719); the Hitch Bullock Cl 1793 (*This last Parsonage Close is called Hitch Bullock* 1671, *Hitchbullock* 1703); House and Long Cl; the Gt -, the Lt -, the Long -, the Square Hunhams, the Hinhams 1796, North Long Hummums, (North -, South) Low - 1840 (*Hunnian, Hunniam furres* (sic) c.1577, *Six Severall closes of pasture ... called ... Hunhams* 1659, *those Sixe Closes of pasture heretofore one parcell called or known by the name of Hunnhams* 1675, *Hunnum* c.1692, *ye Hunnums* 1697, *one parcell Called Hunhams* 1712, obscure); Kettlewell Pits Cl 1793 (*Tho: Kettlewells house & Pitts* c.1692, named from the *Kettlewell* family, cf. Thomas *Kettlewell* a1710 *PR*, John *Kettlewell* 1721 *BT*); Kings House & Garth (named from the *King* family, cf. Thomas *King* 1796 *BT*, with **garðr**); the Land Thorps 1788 (*the Land-Thorps* 1699, *v.* **land** and cf. Grassthorpe *supra* and the Gt Thorp Cl *infra*); Lane Pingle (cf. *Lane close* c.1692, *v.* **pingel**); the Great -, The Little Lee Cl 1796, Bottom -, Top - 1840 (*v.* **lea** 'grassland, pasture' (OE **lēah**)); the Lt Walk or the Lt Sheep walk (divided into 17) 1796 (*the Little walke or the little sheepe walke* 1675, *Little Walk or Little Sheep Walk* 1712, *v.* **walk**, **shepe-walk** and cf. Gt Walk or the Gt Sheepwalk *supra*); Long Cl; the Lowns Cl 1793 (perhaps from **lundr** 'a glade'); Mansion & Homestead; Meadow Cl. - Pce; Needles Yd (possibly from the surn. *Needler*, cf. *Needler house* c.1692); Norlands Cl 1798; North Dales 1788, Nordells 1840 (*Nordale* c.1577,

Nordales 1699, *v.* **norð**, **deill** 'a share of land' in the pl.); North Yd; Odlins Cl (named from the family of John *Odline* 1631 *PR*); the Onset 1793 (*v.* Onset Yd in the f.ns (a) of North Coates *infra*); Ostlers Cl 1793, Bottom -, Top Ostler Cl 1840 (perhaps from the surn. *Ostler*); Ozier Holmes; Paddock; The Pingle 1797, Pingle 1840 (*v.* **pingel**); Pitts Cl 1788, Bottom -, Top Pitts Cl 1840 (*ye pitte, the pittes* c.1577, *the Pitts* 1690, *Pitts* 1691, *Pitts Close* 1699, *v.* **pytt**); Plantation (3); Pottages Cl 1863; The Gt -, the Lt Rape Walk 1796, Gt -, Lt Rape Walk 1840; Robinson's Eleven -, Three Acres 1863 (named from the *Robinson* family, cf. Richard *Robinson* 1754 *BT*); Rush Cl (*v.* **rysc**); the Rye Garth 1793 (*v.* **ryge**, **garðr**); the Far -, the Middle -, the Near Sand Hills Cl 1793, (Gt -, Lt -, Top) Sand Hills; Sands Plot 1863 (perhaps from the surn. *Sands*); the Far -, the Near Scallow Cl 1793, Far -, First Scallow (*Skallowe furlound* c.1577 (*v.* **furlang**; perhaps 'the mound, hill with a temporary hut', *v.* **skáli**, **haugr**)); The Great -, the Litlle (sic) Scrub Cl 1796, (Bottom -, Top) Scrub Cl 1840; the East -, the West Segham Cl 1793, Seghams (*Seggam furlonge* c.1577, *Segame* 1601; perhaps the second el. is **holmr** 'island of land etc.' which frequently has later forms in -(*h*)am in north L; the first el. is **secg**, in a Scandinavianized form); Shop Cl, Shop and Rush Cl; Smiths Fm 1855 (named from the *Smith* family, cf. Thomas *Smith* 1634 *BT*, Allen *Smith* 1855); the South Fd 1793, South fd 1840 (*the South Feild* 1698, *South Field Close* 1730); the Stagworth Walk 1796, Stagworth - 1797; the Street Cl 1796 (*the Street Close* 1659, *the streete* - 1675, *Street close* c.1692, *the Street Close* 1712 and cf. *Litle streete gate* c.1577, the reference presumably being to Barton Street); (the Gt -, The Lt) Sugar Cl 1796, Bottom -, Top - 1840 (*Sugar Close* 1659, 1675, 1712, *Compensation* -, *Tyth sugar close* c.1692, *ye nar Sugar* - 1697, no doubt a complimentary name for sweet land, *v.* Field 222); the Tetney lane 1864[1] (*Tetney Lane* 1703); The Thoroughfare Walk, - Cl 1796, Low -, Top Thorofare Cl 1840 (the reference is to Barton Street); the Gt -, the Lt Thorp Cl 1798, Thorpes 1840, a site of ground called the "Thorpes" (sic) 1853 (cf. Grassthorpe and The Land Thorps *supra*, respectively grassland and arable, *v.* **þorp**); Top Fd; the (Gt -, the Lt) Town Cl 1796, Great -, Little Towns Cl 1840, Little Town's Cl 1852 (*the Towne Close* 1659, *the towne Close* 1675, *Townes close* c.1692, *the Town close* 1712); Turf-Close 1788, the Turff Cl ... but now called Beck Cl 1797, Turf Cl ... now called Beck Cl 1799, Turf Cl or Beck Cl 1814 (*Turf Close* 1699, *v.* **turf** 'turf, greensward', **bekkr**); the twelve acres cl 1822[2]; the Upper Cl 1793; Walk 1793 (2) (*v.* **walk**); the Well Cl 1793 (*v.* **wella**); West Cl 1793, the West Cl 1864 (*the West*

Close 1698); the West Fd 1788, 1814, Far -, Near West Fd 1840 (*ye west feild* c.1577, *West Feild* 1690, *the west field* 1691, *the West Field* 1699, one of the open fields of the village); the Wray Cl 1793, the Wray and Hiche Buttock (sic) 1807, Wray Cl 1840 (*wreyfurland* c.1577 (*v.* **furlang**), *Wraie* 1601, *Wraye* 1611, *One close of pasture ... called the wray* 1662, *One close (of pasture) called Wray* 1668, *Wray Close pasture* 1679, *ye Wray* 1703, *- wray* 1715, 1724, *v.* **vrá** 'a corner of land', in dial. 'a nook, a cattle shelter').

(b) *Boddamhilhole, Bottham hill* c.1577 (*v.* **botm, hyll**); *Boothbie west mares* c.1577 (cf. *East -, west westmares infra*; *John Boothbie* is named in the document); *a close of pasture known by ye name of ... Boulinge* 1671; *Boyntons house, - Pingle* c.1692 (*v.* **pingel**; ... *Boynton* (no forename) is referred to in the document); *bradendes* c.1577, *Bradinge gate, Bradine nabbe* (sic) c.1577 (presumably from **brād** 'broad' and **eng** 'meadow, pasture'); *Bullockemaire* c.1577; *Buriinges* c.1577 (the reading is doubtful, *v.* **eng**); *burt acre, burt acre grene, - headland, Burt acerwonge* c.1577 (perhaps from the surn. *Burt* and **æcer**, with **grēne**^{2}, **hēafod-land, vangr**); *Clarks south field* c.1692 (Mathew *Clark* is named in the document); *Cotcher close* c.1692 (*cotcher* is the frequent dial. form for 'cottager' found in North L); *Dawe lane* 1611, *Dawbank* 1703 (probably from the surn. *Daw(e)*, *v.* Reaney s.n. *Daw*); *ye dike* 1628; *dockdailes* c.1577 (*v.* **docce, deill**); *ye eastermore plat* 1697, *Grainsby eastermore plat* 1703, *ye East plat belonginge of Grainsby glebe* 1709, *ye Eastermost platt at Grainsby* 1715, *- Platt at Grainsby* 1724 ('the more easterly/most easterly plot', *v.* **plat**^{2}, with obsolete *eastermost* (recorded first in NED in 1555) and *eastermore* (not recorded in dictionaries) formed analogically for the comparative form, *v.* **easterra** and cf. *ye Westplattes infra*); *est grenne* c.1577 (*v.* **ēast, grēne**^{2} 'a green, a grassy spot'); *ye farr plott* 1662; *Fenbie hedge* c.1577, *the Hedge of Fenbie* 1601, *Fenby Closes* 1703 (from Fenby in Ashby cum Fenby parish); *gosse mare* c.1577 (*v.* **(ge)mǣre**; *gosse* may be for 'gorse', *v.* **gorst**, or the surn. *Gosse*, *v.* Reaney s.n. *Goss*); *Grainsby uper grounds* 1672; *Hambie headeland* 1601 (*v.* **hēafod-land**; the first el. is presumably a surn.); *Tho: Harrisons walk* c.1692 (*v.* **walk**); *Harwoods segum* (sic) 1703 (named from the *Harwood* family, cf. William *Harwood* 1693 *BT* and Segham in (a) *supra*); *ye hether plott* 1662 (i.e. *hither*), *hither & far platts* 1668[2] (*v.* **plat**^{2}, **plot** and cf. *farr plott supra*); *hie hole, the hole grene, one land at howle fowrs* c.1577 (*v.* **hēah**, with perhaps **hulu** 'a shed, a hovel', **furh** 'a furrow'); *line landes* c.1577 (*v.* **līn** 'flax', **land**); *the longe grene* c.1577 (*v.* **grēne**^{2} and cf. *est grenne supra*); *longmare* c.1577, *Langmare* 1611, *Langmore Hil* 1638 (*v.* **hyll**), *Langmore* 1703 ('the long boundary, boundary land', *v.* **lang, (ge)mǣre**, the second el. being replaced by **mōr** in later forms);

Mirie hole c.1577 (Dr Insley suggests that this is 'the swampy hollow', from ME **mīrī** 'swampy, boggy, marshy' and **hol**^{1}); *the Narrowfleite, the Narrowfleyte* c.1577 ('the narrow stream', *v.* **nearu, flēot**); *the newedicke end* c.1577 (*v.* **niwe, dīc, dīk**); *Normare, Normare gate, normareside* c.1577 (*v.* **norð, (ge)mǣre** 'a boundary, land on a boundary'); *North fielde* 1601 (*v.* **norð, feld**, one of the open fields of the village); *the north grenne* c.1577 (*v.* **norð, grēne**^{2} and cf. *est grenne supra*); y^e *Parsonageplats* 1706 (*v.* **plat**), y^e *Parsons Wray* 1706 (*v.* **persoun, vrá**); *two closes called the platts* 1664, *Two closes ... called Platts* 1668, *plats* 1679 (*v.* **plat**^{2}); *one land called S. Nycholas acre* c.1577; *Sandall tree* c.1577; *a litlle close called Segmire* (sic) 1611 (*v.* **secg** in a Scandinavianized form, **mýrr**); *Sharpe thorne furlonge* c.1577, *Sharpthorne* 1638, *sharpe thorngate* 1703 (*v.* **þorn**; the first el. is perhaps from the *Sharpe* family, cf. Anthony *Sharpe* 1615 *BT*); *the sheep Close* 1703; *Shift-Close*, 1699 (probably alluding to *shifts* in a crop rotation, as discussed s.n. *a shifte Acre* in the f.ns. of South Ferriby PN L 2 116, cf. Shift cls in Immingham f.ns. (a) ib 169); *Skergatefurlond* c.1577 (*v.* **gata, furlang**; the first el. in this and the following f.n. may be ME *sker(re), scār(re)* 'rocky cliff, crag, jagged outcrop' from ON **sker**); *Skermer, Skermermowthe* c.1577, *Skirmer* 1699, *little Skirmarr* 1707; *Snaw gaires, snaw garres* c.1577 (*v.* **geiri**); *the sowth furlong* c.1577; *South lane* 1601; *Swathes* c.1577 (*v.* **swæð** 'a strip of grassland'); *Amos Thompsons Walke* 1690, 1691, - *Thompson Walke* 1698, *v.* **walk**; the land was described as "*formerly in tenure of Amos Thompson*" 1690); *Thoresbie closes* 1628, *thoresby lane* 1697, 1703 (from the adjacent parish of North Thoresby); *Thorne fairlond* c.1577 (*fairlond* is presumably another variant form of *furlong*); y^e *towne end furlonge* c.1577; *the waie headinge from Wathe to Fenbie* 1611 (two adjacent places); *the west end of the towne* c.1577; *East -, west westmares* c.1577 (*v.* **west, (ge)mǣre**); y^e *Westplatts* 1697, y^e *West Platts* 1703, y^e *west plat* 1724 (*v.* **plat**^{2}); *Weyth meare* c.1577 ('the boundary of Waithe (an adjacent parish)'. *v.* **(ge)mǣre**); *Whelpsdales Farm* c.1692, *Farme ... called Wetherhoggs als Whelpdales Farm* 1698 (described in 1698 as "formerly in tenure of Edward *Wetherhogg*, afterwards John *Whelpdale*"; for the respective family names cf. Edward *Wetherhogg* 1641 LPR, John *Wheldale* (sic) 1670 *BT*); *williamfurlound* c.1577 (*v.* **furlang**); *Mr Welfits walk* c.1692 (*v.* **walk**); *Mr Wrights Pitte* c.1692 (*v.* **pytt**).

Hatcliffe

HATCLIFFE

Hadeclive 1086 DB, 1226-9 Fees, 1228 Welles, 1231 Cl, 1231

Ch, 1242-43 Fees, 1247 RRG, 1252 Cl, *-cliva* c.1115 LS, *-cliue* 1204 P, 1206 Ass, 1206 P (p), 1271 *Ass, -clyue* c.1240 IB, 1284 *HarlCh, -clif* 1220-40 *Foster*, 1238-41 Fees, 1271 FF (p), *-clyf* 1327 *SR*

Haddecliue c.1184 (15) Templar, c.1200 RA iv, 1230 Cl (p), *-cliva* 1219 Welles, *-clive* 1286, 1289 RSu, 1294 ib (p), *-clif* 1275 RH, 1316 FA, *-clyff'* 1332 *SR, -clyf* 1347 *Cor*, 1399 Pat, *Addecliue* 1196 ChancR, 1196 P

Hadcliff 1309 Inqaqd, *-clif* 1312 Pat, 1364 Cl, *-clyve* 1313 Orig, 1428 FA, *-clyf* 1437 AD, *-clyfe* 1510 LP i, *-cleve* 1397 Pat

Hateclive 1328 Ipm, *-clife* 1596 *BT, -cliffe* 1635 *ib*

Hatteclif 1364 Cl, 1383, 1392, 1393, 1397 Pat, 1586, 1592, 1597 *BT, -clyf* 1374, 1380, 1384 Pat, 1388 Fine, 1427 Pat, 1431 FA, *-clyff(e)* 1513 LP i, 1560, 1562, 1604, 1608 *BT, -cliff(e)* 1562, 1566, 1586 *et freq* to 1632 *ib*

Hatclyf 1338 Misc, 1362 Ipm, 1368 Orig, 1368 Cl, 1368 Fine, 1375 Peace, 1434 Pat, *-clyfe* 1380 AASR iv, *-clif* 1368 Ipm, 1382 Cl, 1576 LER, 1588, 1594 *BT, - alias Hadclif* 1402 Pat, *-clife* 1589 *BT, -clyffe* 1437 Fine, *-clyff* 1529 Wills ii, 1535 VE iv, 1553 Pat, *-cliff* 1526 Sub, 1598, 1603 *et passim* to 1757 *BT, -cliffe* 1600 *BT*, 1601 *Terrier*, 1623, 1666 *BT et passim*

Hautecleue 1202 HarlCh, 1202 Dugd iv

Hakclyff 1576 Saxton, *-cliff* 1610 Speed

'Hadda's cliff, slope', *v.* **clif**, the first el. being the OE pers.n. *Hadda, Hædda*, a well attested short form of names in *Haþu-*. The village itself lies in a hollow straddling Hatcliffe Beck, with fairly steeply rising ground on each side. For a discussion of the topographical meanings of **clif**, *v.* PNITL 130-36.

GUNNERBY

Gunresbi 1086 DB, c.1115 LS

Gunreby a1182 (13) *Alv*, 1252 Cl, 1281 QW, 1299 Cl, *-bi* 1196 ChancR

Gunerb' 1238-41 Fees, *-by* 1553, 1554, 1561 Pat

Gunnerby 1242-43 Fees, 1311 Ipm, 1311 Pat, 1312 Fine, 1327, 1332 *SR*, 1334 Cl, 1349 Fine, 1353 Ipm, 1361 Cl *et passim*

Goṇnerby 1290 Abbr, 1312, 1548 Pat

Gonerby 1364 Cl, 1431 FA, 1698 *MiscDon 400*
Goneyerby 1529 Wills ii
Gunaby 1828 Bry

'Gunnar's farm, village', *v.* **bȳ** the first el. being the ODan pers.n. *Gunnar*, recorded a number of times in DB, but not in L.

FARFIELD PLANTATION, cf. *The Farr field* 1762 *Monson*, *Far Field* 1839 *TA*. GUNNERBY COVER (lost), 1824 O. HATCLIFFE MILL, 1828 Bry, *Mill* 1824 O, 1839 *TA*, cf. *Bredemilnecroft* 1220-40 *Foster*, perhaps 'the mill made of planks', *v.* **bred**, **myln**, with **croft**. In the charter it is said to be the site of a mill. HATCLIFFE PLANTATION. HATCLIFFE TOP, 1824 O. HOME WALK PLANTATION, cf. *Home Walk* 1829 *BH*, 1839 *TA*, *v.* **walk** probably a sheep-walk, a range of pasture for sheep. OAK PLANTATION is *Plantation* 1829 *BH*. OLD FM is *Manor House* 1824 O. THE OLD RECTORY, *ye Parsonage* 1606, *the* - 1662, *ye parsonage* 1697, *a parsonage house* 1703, 1712, 1715, *the Parsonage House* 1822, 1834 all *Terrier*, *Pars.^e* 1828 Bry, *the Rectorie* 1638, *ye rectorie* 1671, - *Rectory* 1690, *the* - 1703, *the Rectory House* 1822 all *Terrier*, *a new Rectory House was built in 1840* 1842 White, cf. *the parsonage yate* 1601 *Terrier*. ROUND HILL PLANTATION, cf. *Round Hill* 1839 *TA*, self-explanatory. ROUND PLANTATION, self-explanatory. SCRUB CLOSE PLANTATION, cf. *Scrubb Close* 1762 *Monson*.

Field-Names

The principal forms in (a) are 1839 *TA*. Spellings dated a1182 (13) are *Alv*; 1327, 1332 *SR*; 1347 *Cor*; 1529 Wills ii; 1601, 1638, 1662, 1671, 1679, 1690, 1712, 1715, 1822, 1834 *Terrier*; 1756 *BRA 641*; 1762 *Monson*; 1829 *BH*.

(a) The Ash Cl 1762 (*v.* **æsc**); Beckfield 1762, Beck Fd 1829, 1839, Little Beck Fd 1839 (*v.* **bekkr**); Best Fd; The Bottom, Hatcliffe Btm 1762, Bottoms 1829 (*v.* **botm** 'a valley bottom', as elsewhere in the parish); Chalk Pit Cl (*v.* **pytt**); The Church Cl 1762, Church Cl, - Yd 1839; The Clay Pit Cl 1762 (*v.* **pytt**); The Corne Sheep Walk 1762 (*v.* **shepe-walk**); Cow Btm (3x) (*v.* **botm**), - Cl (2x); Crew Yd (2x) (from dial. *crew* 'a shed'); Mr Cunningham's Ings 1834 (*v.* **eng**); Deep Dales (*v.* **dēop**, **dalr**); Dalton Cl 1762 (named from the *Dalton* family, cf. Thomas *Dalton* 1759 *BT*); The Ewe Cl 1762; Far Ings 1839 (*v.* **eng**), - Walk 1829, 1839 (*v.* **walk**); Mr Fauldings Ings 1822 (*v.* **eng**); Flag Garth 1829 (*v.* **flagge** 'a marsh plant, an iris' or 'a reed, a rush', **garðr** 'an enclosure'); Fox Cover Cl; Gravel Pit Cl; Great Fd (cf. Little Fd *infra*); Hay Yd; Gt -, Lt High Fd 1829, 1839; The Hogfield 1762, Far -, Near Hog Fd 1839; Home Cl 1762, 1839 (3x), Home Cl and Fish Pond 1829; Horne Walk (named from the *Horne* family, cf. Robert *Horne* 1585 *BT, v.* **walk** 'land used for the pasture of animals, especially sheep', as elsewhere in the parish); Horse Cl (2x); The Gt -, The Lt How Cl 1762, How Cl, Lt Hows 1839 (*v.* **haugr** 'a mound, a hill'); Hunters Paddock; The Ings Mdw 1762, Ings 1829, 1839 (*the Great Ings* 1638, *the litle Ings* 1662, *a Close calld the Ings* 1712, *the meadow called the Inggs* 1715, *v.* **eng** 'meadow, pasture', as elsewhere in the parish); James' Garth 1829, James - 1839 (probably named from Andrew *James*, Curate of Hatcliffe 1753-79 *BT, v.* **garðr**); The Little Fd 1762, Little - 1839 (cf. Great Fd *supra*); The Long Fd 1762, Long - 1839; Low Btm (*v.* **botm**); The Lycence Cl 1762, Gt -, Lt Licence 1829 (on the parish boundary with East Ravendale); The Lyme Pitt Field 1762, Lime Pit Field 1839 (*v.* **pytt**, cf. *the linekill feild* (sic) 1601, *the lime-kilne feild* 1638, *lime kilne feild* 1662, *lime kilne feeld by ye hovell side* 1671); Thomas Marsdin's Cl 1822; The Marsh 1762, Marsh 1829, 1839 (*v.* **mersc**); Meadow fd; Methodist Chapel; The Middle Fd, - Ings 1762, Middle Field, - Ings 1839 (*v.* **eng**), Middle Walk 1829, 1839 (*v.* **walk**); Mill Cl 1839 (cf. Hatcliffe Mill *supra*); The Out Sheep Walk 1762 (*v.* **shepe-walk**); Orchard (2x), Orchard and Garden; Paddock; Pig Yd; The Pinfold Cl 1762 (*v.* **pynd-fald**); Three Pingles 1762 (*the pingles* 1662, *v.* **pingel**); Pond and Plantn; Pond Cl; Quarry 1829; Far -, Great -, Middle Sand Fd; Seed Walk; Senob Cl; Seven Acres 1829; The Gt -, The Lt Snicks (sic) 1762, Far -, Grass Sinks 1839, Gt -, Lt Sinks 1829, 1839 (presumably dial. *sink* 'a gutter, drain, sewer', recorded from north L, cf. Sinks Cover PN L **2**, 199-200); South Dale Mdw 1762; South Walk 1829, 1839 (*v.* **walk**); Stack Yard (Cl); The Strait Peice 1762, Streight pce 1839 (cf. *in Fulstow there are Brick Tunnells called streights* 1774 *Hill* 22/1); The two Street Cls, Streetfield 1762, First -, Second -, Third Street Fd 1839 (the reference is to Barton Street, *v.* **strǣt**); Tare Cl; Thorganby Cl 1839, The Thorganby Ings 1762 (*v.* **eng**) (from the adjacent parish of Thorganby); The Thorne Cl (Pasture & Pingle) 1762,

Thorn Cl 1829, 1839 (*v.* **þorn**); Three Cornered Walk 1829, Cornered Walk 1839 (named from its triangular shape); The Warren Walk 1762 (*v.* **wareine**, **walk**); Watergrist Mill & Kilne 1756, Water Grist Mill & Kilne 1762 (a water-mill for grinding grain); The Well Cl 1762; Willow Holt 1829 (*v.* **wilig**, **holt**); The Wood Cl 1762 (*v.* **wudu**); The Zacherly Cl 1762, Zakerley 1839.

(b) *Banys Thyng* 1524 (a house, *v.* **þing** 'premises, property'; *Banys* is probably the surn. *Baines*); *One glebe close* 1690, *the Glebe Close* 1712, 1715; *Gonnerby gate* 1601 ('the road to Gunnerby', *v.* **gata**); *ye Hall Ings* 1690 (*v.* **eng**); *in valle de Gunreby* a1182 (13) ('in the valley of Gunnerby'); *Hattecleffe feild* (sic) 1601 (*v.* **feld**); *Jacob Thyng* 1534 (from the pers.n. or surn. *Jacob* with **þing** 'premises, property'); *the little Close* 1712, *the little Closes* 1715; *the Parsonage close* 1662, *Parsonage yard or garth* 1679 (cf. The Old Rectory *supra*); *the spring-garth* 1638 (*v.* **spring**, **garðr**); *Atte yate* 1327, *ad portam* 1332 both (p) (*v.* **geat**).

Hawerby cum Beesby

HAWERBY CUM BEESBY, 1679, 1726 *BT*, 1822 *Terrier et passim*, - *cum Beesbye* 1576 LER, *Hawreby cum Beasby* 1577 *Terrier*, *Haurebie & Beesbie* 1586, *Hawerbie cum Beesbie* 1591, 1594, 1595, 1615, 1616 all *BT*, 1724 *Terrier*, *Hawerbye cum Besbye* 1602, - *cum Beesbye* 1605, 1606, - *cum Beasbye* 1611, *Hawerby cum Beasby* 1620, 1625, 1639 all *BT*, 1639 Brasses, - *cum Beasby* 1674 *Terrier*, - *with Beasby* 1671 *BT*, - *with Beesby* 1762 *Terrier*, *Hawarby cum Beesby* 1683, 1698 *BT*, 1686, 1697, 1703 *Terrier*, *Beesby cum Hawerby* 1732, 1740 *Yarb*.

HAWERBY

Hawardebi 1086 DB, 1196 ChancR, 1202 *HarlCh*, 1202 Dugd vi, *Hawardabi* c.1115 LS, *Hawardeb'* 1238-41 Fees, *-by* 1244 RRG, 1254 ValNor, 1261, 1271 FF, 1275, 1276 RH, 1281 QW, 1291 Tax, 1295 *Ass*, 1295 Ipm, 1299, 1300 Cl *et freq* to 1431 FA, *Hawardiby* 1241 RRG, *Hawordeby* Hy3 *HarlCh*, 1311 Pat, 1311 Ipm, *Hawerdeby* 1428 FA

Hauwardeby 1204 *AddCh*, 1312 Fine, *Houwerdeby* 1312 Pat, *Hawrth'bi* 1204 P

Hawardb' 1238-41 Fees, *-by* 1292 RSu, 1299, 1349 Pat, 1356 *FF*, 1370 Pat, 1373, 1375 Peace, 1385 Pat, 1395 AD, 1438 Pat *et passim* to 1610 Speed
Hawarby 1526 Sub, 1561 Pat
Howerby 1535 VE iv, *-bie* a1567 LNQ v
Hawerby 1553, 1554 Pat

For 16th-18th century variants, *v.* Hawerby cum Beesby *supra*, and Orby Rd in North Thoresby f.ns. (a) *infra*.

'Hawarth's farm, village', from the ODan pers.n. *Hāwarth*, ON *Hávarðr* and **bȳ**. Presumably the same man gave his name to both the village and the wapentake in which it is situated, *v.* Haverstoe Wapentake *supra*.

BEESBY
Basebi 1086 DB, *-by* 1320 Orig
Besebi 1086 DB, 1180, 1181, 1182 P all (p), Hy2 (1314) Ch, Hy2 Dane (p), a1184 (1409) Gilb, 1196 ChancR, 1202 *HarlCh*, 1204 P, *Beseby* lHy2 (13) *Alv*, e13 RA ii (p), 1202 Dugd vi, 1204 *AddCh*, 1208 Cur (p), 1214 RA iv, 1219 Welles, 1225 Cur (p), 1242-43 Fees, 1249 Pat, 1254 ValNor, 1259, 1260 Ch, 1260 Cl, 1275, 1276 RH, 1291 Tax, 1295 *Ass*, 1295 Ipm, 1299 Pat, 1299 Cl, 1300 Orig, 1311 Pat, 1311 Ipm *et freq* to 1431 FA, - *alias Beysbye alias Bleysbye* 1554, 1561 Pat, *Besebye* 1576 Saxton, 1610 Speed
Besabi c.1115 LS
Beisebi 1162, 1163 P (p), *Beyseby* 1249 Pat, 1249, 1260 Cl
Besyby eHy3 (1409) Gilb
Bexseby (sic) 1259 Cl
Besseby 1275 RH, 1340 Pat
Besby 1294 *Ass*, 1316 Ipm, 1331 Cl, 1359 *Cor*, 1370, 1408 Pat, 1483 *AD*
Beysby 1500 VisitN, 1553-5 EPC, *Beisbye* 1560 Pat
Beasby 1548 Pat
Beesbie a1567 LNQ v, *Beesby* 1765 *Yarb et passim*

For 16th-18th century variants, *v.* Hawerby cum Beesby

supra.

'Besi's farm, village', *v.* **bȳ**. The pers.n. *Besi* is recorded in DB from L and is considered to have been certainly Scandinavian, *v.* Feilitzen 201, where a later example of the name, also from L, is given. The etymology of Danelaw *Besi* is difficult, but it would seem most plausible to link it with ODan *Bøsi*, OSwed *Bøse. Besi* also occurs in Beesby in the Marsh LSR and Fellows-Jensen prefers to take the first el. of both as being from OE **bēos** 'bent-grass', *v.* SSNEM 35-36. However, p.ns. certainly from **bēos** have medieval forms in *Bes-*, not in *Bese-*, *v.* e.g. Beeston PN BdHu 107-8, PN Nt 139 and PN YW **3**, 217. Beesby is now depopulated and is today represented by Beesby Fm and Beesby Hall. For the latter, *v. ad Aulam de Beseby* in f.ns. (b).

BARTON STREET, 1762 *Terrier*, 1786 *Yarb*, cf. *the hie Strete* 1577, *the streete* 1626, - *Streete* 1638, *the streete Furlong* 1626, - *furlong* 1636 all *Terrier, Street Field* 1832 *Yarb*, the name of the pre-Roman trackway from Louth to Barton upon Humber, found in other parishes in this wapentake. BEESBY TOP. BEESBY WOOD, 1828 Bry, 1838 *TA*. HARDING'S PLANTATION, cf. *Hard Ings* 1786 *Yarb*, 'the meadows hard to till', *v.* **heard, eng** in the pl, the same as Hard Ings in f.ns. (a). HAWERBY HALL is *House* 1828 Bry. THE OLD RECTORY, *the parsonage* 1626, 1664, *the parsonidge howse* 1638, *Parsonage of Hawerby cum Beesby* 1674, *The Parsonage of Hawarby cum Beesby* 1686, *the Parsonage house* 1697, - *House*, 1724, 1762, *the Rectory house* 1762 all *Terrier, Parsonage* 18 *MiscDep 16* (Plan). PIT CLUMP (lost), 1828 Bry, the name of a ploughed-out tumulus, which is probably the site of the meeting place of Haverstoe Wapentake *supra.*

Field-Names

Forms dated Hy2 (1314) are Ch; those dated lHy2 (13), l12 (13), eHy3 (13), Hy3 (13) are *Alv*; 1260-70, 1312, 1318, 1319, 1359[1] *Foster*, 1276 RH; 1294, 1295, 1329 *Ass*; 1327, 1332 *SR*; 1353 *Cor*; 1355, 1356 *FF*; 1359[2] Cl; 1369 *Holywell*; 1378 Fine; 1387 Peace; 1577, 1625, 1626, 1638, 1664, 1674, 1679, 1686, 1697, 1703, 1706, 1709, 1724, 1762, 1822, 1864 *Terrier*; 18 *Misc Dep 16*; 1772, 1786,

1810, 1832, c.1832 *Yarb*; 1838 *TA*.

(a) Barn Pce 1832, 1838; Beacon Fd 18, Gt -, Lt Beacon Field 1838 (*Horby beacon* 1703, *the Beacon field* 1709, *the Beacon* (*field*), y^e *Beacon* (*Field*) 1724, *v.* **(ge)bēacen**; there is a tumulus (round barrow) in this field, now ploughed out, which was no doubt the meeting place of the Wapentake, *v.* Haverstoe Wapentake *supra*); Brick Kiln 1832, Brick Kiln Cl 1838; Cadeby First Pce 1832, 1838, - 2nd Pce 1832, - Second Pce 1838, - 3rd Pce 1832, - Third Pce 1838; Calk-Pit-Pce 18, Calk Pit (Plantn) 1838, Chalk Pitt Fd 1786, - pit Fd 1810 (*v.* **calc**, **pytt**); Cheesemans Cl 1786, 1810 (named from the *Cheeseman* family, cf. Thomas *Cheeseman* 1748 *BT*); Church Cl 1832, 1838 (cf. *atte Kirke de Besby* 1294, *ad ecclesiam* 1319, 1327, *atte Kirk'* 1332 all (p)); the Churchyard at Beesby 1762, Church Yd 1786, One Piece of Land in Beesby called the Church Yard 1822 (*the Gleabe* w^c*h is now visible in Beesby is onely the Church yard* 1674, *One little close called* y^e *Church yard in Beesby* 1679, *the Old Church yard att Beesby* 1686, *The Church yard att Beesby* 1697, - *in Beesby* 1703, *The church yard in Beasby* 1706, *The Church Yard of Bessebie* 1709); Claybourns 1786, Clay bourns 1810, Clay Btm 1838; High Cottage 18 (the next field to a cottage); Cow-Cl 18, Cow Cl 1832, 1838; Deep Btm 1832, 1838 (*v.* **botm**); The fifteen Acres 1832, Fifteen - 1838; Fold 1786, 1810, Fold Yd Cottage etc 1838; Furr Cl 18 (*the fowres* 1577, *Furr close* 1625, *the* - 1626, *the furr close* 1638, 1686, *The Firr Close* 1697, *v.* **furh** or perhaps cf. the following f.n.); Furze Cl 1838 (*v.* **fyrs**); Gravel Pit Pce 1832, 1838; Green 1786, 1810; Hardhill Plantn 1838; Hard Ings 1786, 1810 (*a fourlong called the heardinges* 1577, *v.* **heard**, **eng**); Hawerby Fd 1772, Orby - c.1832 (*Horby field* 1697, 1703); High Ings 18, 1838 (*v.* **eng**, cf. *the Einges* 1577, (*the*) *Inges* 1625, *the* - 1638, 1686, cf. also Low Ings *infra*); Hills & Valleys 1832, - and Valleys 1838 (alluding to undulating land); Home Cl 1838, - Wd 1786, 1810; Horse Cl 1832, 1838; House Stable and Home Cl 1838; Ings Hole 1838 (*v.* **eng**); Laith Pce 1786, - pce 1810 (probably from **hlaða** 'a barn'); "the Len" cl (sic) 1864; Low Cottage Cl 18, 1838 (a cottage is marked in the field); Low Fd 1786, 1832, 1838, Lowfield 1810; Low Ings 18, 1838 (*v.* **eng** and cf. High Ings *supra*); Meadow Cl 1832, - Pce 1838; Mill Fd 1786, 1810, 1832, 1838 (cf. *Miln Gate* 1724); New Cl 18 (*the New close* 1724); Orchard 1786, 1810, 1838; Paradise 18; Parsonage-Close 18, Parsonage (Cl) 1838, - cl 1864, Parson's Paddock, - Cl 1822 (y^e *Parsons Close* 1664, 1674, - *parsons close* 1679, *the* - 1703, 1706); Pin Fold 1786, Pinfold 1810 (*v.* **pynd-fald**); Plantation 1832, 1838; Home cl adjoining to the Rectory house 1762; Sancfoin Pce (sic) 1786, Sainfoin pce 1810 (*v.* **sainfoin**); Sand Pit Fd 1786, 1810, 1832, 1838, - pit Fd 1810 (*v.* **sand**, **pytt**); First Scallows 1832, 1838, 2nd - 1832, Second - 1838 (perhaps 'the mound, the hill with a temporary hut', **skáli**, **haugr**, cf. the Far -, the Near Scallow Cl in Grainsby f.ns. (a) *supra*); Scrub Cl 1786, 1810, - Ings 1786, 1810 (*v.* **eng**); Upper Seed Pce 1786, Ripper - (sic) 1810; Six Acres 1786, 1810, 1832, 1838; Sixteen Acres 1832, 1838; Standings 1832, 1838; (Top) Street Fd 1838; Sue Rennard Garth 1786, Sus: - 1810 (*v.* **garðr** 'an enclosure, a small plot of ground' as elsewhere in the parish); Syke 1786, 1810 (*v.* **sík**); Bottom -, Top 10 Acres 1832, 1838, Farr ten Acre 1786, Far ten Acres 1810, Home ten Acre 1786, - ten Acres 1810, Ten Acres 1832, 1838; Thorough-Fare 18, Thoroughfare 1838 (the field bounds on Barton Street); Tims Cls 1786, - Cl 1810; Top Fd 1832, 1838; Twelve Acres 1786, 1810; Twenty Acres 1832, 1838; The Wold or Walk 1810, Walk 1786, 1832, 1838, Far - 18, Far Walk, East Side, - West Side 1838, First -, Second Walk 18, 1838 (cf. *the sheepwalk Bottom, ye Sheep walk Bottom* 1724, *v.* **shepe-walk**); Well Cl 1832, 1838; White-Hills 18, White Hills 1838; Farr Wood 1786, Far - 1810, Wood Cl 1832, 1838, - Hill 1786, 1810, Wood Nook Fd 1832, 1838 (cf. *woddail fourlong* 1577, *woodaile* 1625, *Wooddale furlong* 1626, *the woodaile Furlong* 1638, *Wood dale Bottom* 1709, - *Bottem* (sic) 1724, *v.* **wudu**, **deill**, **furlang**, **botm**).

(b) *a fourlong called the acares* 1577, (*the*) *Akers* 1625, *the Akers* 1626, *the Ackers* 1638 (*v.* **æcer**); *Alstanegate, alstangate* eHy3 (13) (*v.* **gata**; the first el. is the OE pers.n. *Alstān*, from *Aldstān*, *Ælfstān* or *Æðelstān*); *Aslacwang* eHy3 (13) (from the ODan pers.n. *Aslāk* (ON *Áslákr*) and **vangr** 'a garden, an in-field'); *de Ballio* 1327, 1332 both (p) (*v.* **bailie**, but this may not be a local name); *in Brert* (sic) *inter terram p'dc' nemus* eHy3 (13); *buschauwang* eHy3 (13) (presumably 'the mound, hill with a bush' *v.* **buskr**, **haugr**, a Scand. compound, with **vangr**); *Castergate* 1626, *castergate* 1638 ('the road to Caistor', *v.* **gata**); *the Cherry garth* 1664, *ye Cherrye garth* 1674, *ye Cherry Garth* 1679, *the Cherry garth* 1686, *a little garth called the Cherry garth* 1703, - *cherry garth* 1706 (*v.* **garðr** and cf. *the onset infra*); *cotcher lane* 1626, 1638 (*cotcher* means 'cottager' as freq. in L); *in the croftis de eodem* [i.e. *Beasby*] 1294 (*v.* **croft**); *of the Dale de Beseby* 1353 (p) (*v.* **dalr**); *a Close Called dalling garths* 1577, *dawling garthe* 1626, *dawlin garth* 1638 (*v.* **garðr**; the first el. is obscure unless it is a surn. from Dalling (Nf)); *the draw well* 1638; *Ensedich, Enskedic* eHy3 (13), *Ensedikes* Hy3 (13) (Dr Insley suggests, if the form *Enske-* represents the original form, it may be ON *enskr* 'English'); *in campis de Besebi* Hy2 (1314), *ad campum de Beseby* lHy2 (13), *campum de Beseby* 1276 (*v.* **feld**); *Fenby gapp* 1625 (alluding to the neighbouring parish of Fenby, *v.* **gap**); *ad Aulam de Beseby* 1312, *ad aulam* 1318, *ate halle de Beseby* 1295, *atte Halle de Beseby* 1329, 1387, *atte halle de* - 1355, *attehalle de* - 1359[1], *at Halle de Beasebi* 1369, *atte Halle of Beseby* 1378 all (p) (*v.* **hall**); *hastangat* 1260-70 (the first el. is the

ODan pers.n. *Hasten* (ON *Hásteinn*), partially anglicised, with **gata**); *a pite Called inggrum pit* 1577, *Ingeram pitt* 1626, *Ingram pitt* 1638 (from the surn. *Ingram* with **pytt**); *langlandes* eHy3 (13) (*v.* **lang, land**); *the Lea close* (described as meadow or pasture) 1664, *ye Lea Close* 1674, *ye lea close* 1679, *lee close* 1686, *the lea close* 1703, *- Lea Close* 1706, *v.* **lea** (OE **lēah**), **clos(e)**); *lingdale* eHy3 (13) (*v.* **lyng, deill**); *the Little Acer Close* 1709, *Little Acres Close* 1724; *Atemare* 1327, *atte Mare* 1332. *atte Mare de Hawardby* 1356, *atte Mare of Hawardeby* 1359[2] all (p) (*v.* **(ge)mǣre** 'a boundary, land on a boundary'); *le marefure* eHy3 (13), Hy3 (13), *le merefure* (sic) eHy3 (13) (*v.* **marfur** 'a boundary furrow'); *a gate calld neuton gate, neuton gates* 1577 (*v.* **gata**), *Newton Hedge* 1724 (referring to Wold Newton, *v.* **hecg**); *in nort campo de Beseby* eHy3 (13), *the north feild* 1577 (*v.* **norð, feld**); *the Northfurlong, ye North Furlong, - furlong* 1724 (*v.* **norð, furlang**); *the Onsett* 1625, *the onset or foreyard* 1674, *The Onset -* 1679, *The Onset* 1686, *The Onset Commonly Called the Cherry gart* (sic) 1697 (*v.* **onset** and cf. *the Cherry garth supra*); *partrichil* 1260-70 ('partridge hill', from ME *partriche* 'a partridge', with **hyll**); *a great Pit* 1664, *a great pitt* 1679, 1703, *- pit* 1706 (the same as *inggrum pit supra*); *Randall hedge* 1625 (the hedge with East Ravendale); *a fourlong Called Long rusdickes* 1577, *Rusdyke* 1625, *Rusdikes* 1626, 1638 (*v.* **risc, dík**); *Shortakers hedge* 1626 (from **sceort, æcer** with **hecg**); *ad spinam de Beseby* l12 (13), eHy3 (13); *in campis de su de Beseby, in su campo de Beseby* (sic) eHy3 (13) (*v.* **sūð, feld**); *the south furlong* 1724 (*v.* **sūð. furlang**); *a fourlong against the towne* 1577; *tuahoes* eHy3 (13) ('the two mounds', *v.* **twā (twēgen), haugr**); *the upper Fourlong* 1625 (*v.* **furlang**); *the west feild* 1577 (*v.* **west, feld**, i.e. of Hawerby); *What fourlong* 1577 (*v.* **vátr** 'wet', **furlang**); *the Great Whin-Close* 1709 (*v.* **hvin** 'gorse'); *white hill* 1625, *the -* 1626, *- Hill* 1638; *yedericdale* eHy3 (13) (probably 'Edric's share of land', *v.* **deill**, the first el. being the OE pers.n. *Eadrīc* with prosthetic *y*).

Marsh Chapel

MARSH CHAPEL

Fullestowe merske, Folestow - e13 *Holywell, Foulestowemerske* 1329 *Ass, Fulestowmersk* 1277-92 *Holywell, Fulstow-* 1278-90 *ib, Fule stowe -* (sic) 1294 *ib, Foulestow-* 1302 *ib,* 1386 Peace

marisco de Fulestowe c.1270, 1277 *Holywell, - Fulstowe* 1566 *Anc*

Foulestowemers 1355 *Cor, Foulestowemersh(')* 1358 *FF, Foulestow-* 1420 WillsCal, 1522 *Anc, Fullestowe-* 1528 *ib,*

Foulestowmershe 1367 Cor, 1432 Cl, *Fullestowe-* 1519 *Anc, Fulstow* - 1522, 1576 *ib, Foulstowemerssh*(') 1375 Peace, *Foulestowe-* 1381 *FF,* 1422, 1439 Pat, *Foulstowemersshe* 1411 ib, *Fowlesto-* 1496-98 *MinAcct, Fulstou-* 1523-24 *ib, Fullestow-* 1546-47 *ib, Fulstowemerche* 1374 Pat, *Foulestowmersch'* 1396 Peace

Fulstowe Marshe 1503 Ipm. 1530 Wills ii, *Foulstomarshe* 1528 ib, *Fulstow marshe* 1586 *Holywell, - Marshe* 1587 *ib, Fullstowe* - 1620 *ib, Foullestowmarsh* 1504 *LMR, Fulstoue* - 1551 *AD, Fulstowe March* 1519 DV

Mersch Chapel 1347 Pat, *Merchchapelle* 1462 Pap, *Mershe Chaple* 1609 *Anc, le Merschapell'* 1381 Peace, *Mersschapell* 1464 Pap

Marshchapell 1457 *Harm,* 1509 Wills i, 1510 *Anc,* 1530 Wills ii, 1535 VE iv, 1545, 1555 *Anc,* 1559 *LMR, - Chappell by northe Cottes* 1587 *Yarb, -chappell* (*als Fulstow Marsh*) 1595 *FSurv,* 1606 *LCS, -chapel* a1567 LNQ v, - *Chaple* 1610 Speed, - *Chapell* 1626 *BRA 513, -chappel* (*alias Fulstow marsh*) 1632 *LMR, -chaple* 1652 WillsPCC, - *Chappell* 1653 *Foster,* 1666 VL

Marsschapell' 1466 Pap, 1517 *Anc, Marschapell* 1508 Wills i, 1528 ib ii, 1545 Pat, *Marshe-* 1529 Wills ii, 1569 Admin, *-chaple* 1546 *Elwes, - chapple* 1576 Saxton

Marchappelle 1536 Dugd vi, *-chapell* 1550 *Goulding, March Chaple* 1538 *AOMB 409,* - *Chapell* 1571 Pat, - *Chappel* 1594 SP iii, *Marche Chapell* 1539 LP xiv

Chapell Marshe 1503 Ipm, *Chappel Marsh* 1695 Morden

'The marsh belonging to Fulstow', *v.* **mersc**. The earliest forms in *mersk*(*e*) are Scandinavianizations. The later development is from the **chapel(e)** there, and note Adam *capellano de Capelle* c.1270 *Holywell, v.* **capel**.

BEACON HILL, *le Fyre bombe* 1416 *LMR, le firebeacon* 1556 *Anc, Firebeaconhill* 1595 *FMap, Fier beacon hill by Warholme waie* 1595 *FSurv, Fire Beacon hill* 1653 *Foster,* from ME *fir-bome,* for which *v.* MED s.v. *fir* n. 7 (b). There, a reference *Beekne or fyrebome,* dated 1440 is given. The present form predates this and perhaps we ought to consider a ME spelling *fir-bombe.* The history of *bomb* itself is uncertain and is not recorded in NED before 1588. In the present name, *bombe* has been replaced by *beacon* (OE **(ge)bēacon**) and the meaning is the same. Cf. Fire Beacon on the boundary of Marsh Chapel and Fulstow, *supra*. Firebeacon has been noted in Devon, *v.* PN D 78 and 545, to which Mr John Field adds Higher -, Lower Firebeacon in Beaford. Beacon Hill is recorded from the West Riding of Yorkshire, *v.* PN YW **1** 127, **3** 59, 90, **4** 205.

ELLGATE LANE, *Hellgates, Helegate* 1595 *FSurv, hell gaits lane* 1657 *LMR, Hell Gate Lane* 1712 *Foster*, 1828 Bry, called simply Bridle Rd today. It is the continuation of a road in Fulstow on which Heelgate Fm is situated and north of which is a field *Helgates* shown on *FMap*. However, north from Ellgate Lane as far as New Dike, which forms the boundary with North Coates, are four fields called *Hell*. These are *le gret hell* 1505 *LMR, gret Hell* 1553 *Anc, le great Hell* 1567, 1581 *ib, great Hell* 1595 *FSurv*, 1659 *Holywell, Great hell* c.1638 *ib, - Hell* 1712 *Foster, - Ell* 1839 *TA, the North great hell* 1663 *Holywell*; *lyttell Hell* 1510 *LMR, Little -* 1564 *Anc*, 1595 *FMap*, 1595 *FSurv, little -* 1616 *LMR*, 1803 *Hill, litle hell* 1626 *LMR, - hells* 1627 *Dudding, Little-ell* 1847 *Padley, Little Ell* 1848 *EnclA*; *Inhell pitt* (sic) 1595 *FSurv, Inhel pitte* (sic) 1595 *FMap, Inhellpit Close* c.1638 *Holywell, Hell Pits* 1712 *Foster, Ell Pit* 1839 *TA*, 1841 *MC*, 1847 *Padley*; *norton Hell* 1564 *Anc, Norton helles* 1563 *ib, le Norton Helles* 1567 *ib, Norton Hells* 1572 *ib*, 1581 *ib, Nortonhell* 1595 *FMap, - hells* 1595 *FSurv, - Hells* c.1638 *Holywell*, 1803 *Hill, - hills* 1637 *LMR*, 1803 *Hill, - Hill* 1821 *AH, - Ell* 1839 *TA*, 1847 *Padley* (presumably from the surn. *Norton*, though none has been noted in the sources searched). Under Heelgate Fm in Fulstow *supra* it is suggested that the first el. is the surn. *Hell*, recorded several times in Fulstow documents. It would appear that Heelgate and Ellgate are modern forms of the same name. The occurrence of f.ns. called *Hell*, north of Ellgate, however, suggest that association with a surn. can hardly be correct. OE **hell** 'hell' seems to occur occasionally in p.ns. "as a term of contempt", while Field, s.n. Hell Carr, accepts that *hell* may have a derogatory reference in some f.ns. There can be no connexion with an L-shaped field here, which is possible in some names, nor can *hell* be a form of

OE **hyll** in north L. We are left, therefore, with the possibility that the first el. of Ellgate Lane and Heelgate Fm is indeed **hell**, though it should be noted that today there is nothing in the topography of these fields to support a derogatory meaning.

ESKHAM, *in Ascholmo* eHy3 (1409) Gilb, *Eskeholm* 1314 Ch, 1339 *LMR*, 1353 Misc, *-holme* 1327 *SR* (p), *Eskholme* 1390, 1396 *Anc*, *Eshholm* 1325 *ib*, *Escholm'* 1332 *SR* (p), 1464 *Anc*, *Esholm'* 1355 *Cor*, *Escolm'* 1449 *LMR*, 1452 *Anc*, *Escome* 1554 *ib*, *Escham* 1595 *FMap*, *Eskam* 1650 *LMR*, *- Cherry howse* 1652 *ib*, *This pte of the Towne is called Eastham* 1595 *FSurv*, *East Holme* 1824 O, cf. *Eskholmegote* 1374 *Anc*, *Eschamgote* 1404 *LMR*, *gurgit' voc' Eschamgote* 1505 *ib*, (*v.* **gotu** 'a sluice'), *Escombryge* 1507, 1508 *ib* (*v.* **brycg**), *Escham pasture* 1595 *FMap*, *- Past* c.1638 *Holywell*, *Eastham pasture* 1595 *FSurv*, *West Eastham* 1595 *FSurv*, *Eskham Field* 1839 *TA*; 'the raised land in marsh where ash-trees grow', *v.* **askr**, **eski**, **holmr**. The earliest form suggests **askr**, the later ones in *E-* point to **eski**. The interchange between *-holme* and *-ham* is very common in north L. For a parallel *v.* Eskin Beck, earlier *Escomebecke*, in Keswick, PN Cu 303.

FIRE BEACON LANE (local), *the Firebeacon or Margate Lane* 1813 *HD*, *Fire Beacon Road* 1819 *EnclA*, 1864 *Terrier*, *Fire-Beacon Lane* 1822 *ib*. The earlier name is *le Margate* 1415, 1510 *LMR*, *the -* 1595 *FSurv*, *Margate* 1785 *Foster*, *Margayt* 1506 *LMR*, *margate* 1547 *ib*, *le Marrgate* 1510 *ib*, *Camplyn Marr gate* 1647 *Holywell* (from the family of William *Camplin* 1585 *Anc*), *Marsh Chapel Ings or Maregate Lane* 1828 Bry and cf. *Southmargate* 1415, 1442 *LMR*, 1575 *Anc*, *-mergate* 1452 *ib*, *north margat* 1583 *Holywell*, *Northmargates* 1595 *FSurv*, c.1638 *Holywell*, *the west margat* 1583 *ib*, *West Mar gate* 1595 *FSurv*, 'the boundary road', *v.* **(ge)mǣre**, **gata**, a common name in north L. It ran from Beacon Hill to Fire Beacon in Fulstow, and formed the boundary with Grainthorpe.

THE FITTIES, 1839 *TA*, 1847 *Padley*, *Fitties* 1567 *Anc*, 1841 *MC*, *the fittees* 1595 *FSurv*, 1814 *Hill*, *ye Fitties* 1595 *FSurv*, *the -* 1613

MinAcct, The Salt Marshes called the Fittyes which are at Spring tydes overflowene 1595 *FMap*, cf. *ye Fettie ground, a peece of Fittie grounde* 1595 *FSurv*. This is a common name in north L coastal parishes meaning 'the outer marsh', dial. *fitty, fitties* 'the outermarsh or land lying between the sea or Humber and the bank, generally intersected by numerous reticulating creeks', *v.* E. Peacock *A glossary of words used in ... Manley and Corringham* (EDS) 1899, 206; it is a derivative of ON **fit** 'grassland on the bank of a river'.

KEDWICKS (lost), 1846 *EnclA, Kirkedic* 1314 Ch, *-dikis* 1324 *Anc, Kirkdikes* 1325 *ib*, 1631 *LMR, les -* 1638 *ib, sewera de Kyrkedykes* 1347 *ib, Kyrkdykes* 1417 *ib, Kirkedykes* 1595 *FSurv, Common called the Kirkedykes* 1595 *FMap, Kyrdykes* 1447 *LMR, Kirdike* 1583 *Anc*, 1628 *LMR*, c.1638 *Holywell, -dyke* 1595 *FSurv, the common called Kirdykes* 1595 *ib, Kerdickes* 1633 *LMR*, 1654 *ib, ye kirdix* 1725 *Foster, Kirksdike Common* 1808 *BRA 838*, cf. *Kirdykbank* 1446, *Kyrdyk bank* 1448, *Kirdicke banke* 1651 all *LMR*; 'the church ditch', *v.* **kirkja**, **dík**, no doubt a Scand. compound. It is described at least once as a *sewer*. The significance of *church* here is not clear. It is worthy of note that it is referred to as a "common" in the late 16th century and again in the early 19th.

KEYHOLME FM, *Kaholm'* 1415 *LMR, duo le Holmes voc west keyholme* 1578 *Anc, Eastkeieholme, Westkeyholme* 1595 *FMap, East key holme, West -* c.1638 *Holywell, Key Holme* 1712 *Foster*, 1847 *Padley, -holme* 1839 *TA*, apparently named from the family of Walter *Kaa* 1338 *Anc, - Caa* 1348 *ib* and **holmr** 'higher ground amidst marsh', a word very frequently found in this parish, *often* denoting a saltern or a salt hill. Its appellative use in the 1578 reference is noteworthy. KEYHOLME LANE, *Caime Lane, Kaime -* 1595 *FSurv, Kamelane* 1595 *FMap, Kettle Holme Lane* 1828 Bry.

SEADYKE WAY (local), *le Sedike* c.1270 *Holywell, -dick* 1383 *Anc, - Seedyk'* 1338 *ib*, 1384 *LMR*, 1390, 1396 *Anc, the way called the Seadyke* 1595 *FSurv, Seadykeway* 1595 *FMap, the Street or high way called the Seadike* 1651 *MiscDon 38, Seadike Road* 1821 *AH*, cf. *Sedykebanke* 1555 *Anc.* Note also *ex orientali parte fossat' maris* a1274 *Holywell, extra fossatum maris* 1294 *ib, super littus Maris* 1383 *Anc, super fossat' maris* 1409 *LMR.* Self-explanatory, *v.* **sǣ**, **dīk**. It is the name of the main road through the village, the modern A 1031.

SUMMERHEAD (lost), 1595 *FMap*, 1624 *Holywell*, 1808 *HD, - Close* 1839 *TA, Great -, Little -* 1847 *Padley*, 1848 *EnclA, Sumerette* 1277-92 *Holywell, Le sumerette de marisco de Fulestowe* 1310 *ib, Sumerhet* 1283 *ib, Somereth* 1317 Ipm, 1330 *Holywell, le -* 1342, 1613 *LMR, Someret* 1282 *Holywell*, 1372 Ipm, 1399 *LMR, Pastur' voc' -* 1408, 1430, 1442 *ib*, 1452 *Anc, Someret* 1545 *ib, -ett* 1522, 1553 *ib, le Sommeret* 1414 *LMR*, (*le*) *Somered* 1347 *ib*, 1604 *Anc*, 1612, 1638 *LMR, Marsshechappell' Somered* 1622 *ib, les -eds* 1615, 1616, 1620 *ib, le -edd* 1632 *ib, Le somerred* 1636 *ib*, (*Le*) *Sommerid* 1589 *Anc*, 1668 *LMR, Somerhed* 1557, 1580 *Anc, leȝ -* 1561 *ib, le -* 1576 *ib, -hede* 1575 *ib*, (*le*) *-head* 1577, 1579 *ib*, 1579 *Terrier*, 1584 *Anc*, 1663 *Holywell, -heade* 1567 *Anc, Sommerhead* 1579 *LMR*, 1588 *Anc*, c.1638 *Holywell*, 1667 *LMR, le Somereates* 1631 *ib, le Somridd* 1637 *ib, the Sumered* 1664 *Terrier, le Summered* 1625 *LMR, the -* 1654 *ib, le Sumeredd* 1663 *ib, Sumerhed* 17 *Holywell, ye Sumerid* 1725 *Foster, - Summeridge* 1703 *Terrier, the Summerings* 1822 *Terrier, Summer Ings* (sic) 1828 Bry. 'The summer pasture', *v.* **sumor**, **ete**, a name found also in Fulstow *supra* and as *Summereat Lane* over the parish boundary in North Coates, *infra.* It is perhaps likely that all three originally comprised a single extensive pasture. In both *FMap* and *EnclA* the names in Marsh Chapel denote the same area, covering a large field at approximately TF 353 986, as well as other fields north of Ellgate Lane and the parish boundary. The name is recorded so often in medieval sources that the land so-called must have been of considerable local importance.

WATERLAND DRAIN, 1848 *EnclA, le Waterlade* 1399, 1425 *LMR, - waterlayd* 1506 *ib, the waterlaid dike* 1579 *Terrier, fossam voc the Water laide* (sic) 1593 *Anc, Waterlad* 1595 *FSurv, - Sewer* 1595 *FMap, Water Lade Drain* 1819 *EnclA, Water Landik* 1595

FSurv, le waterland 1571 *Anc, Water Land* 1622 *LMR, ye Water Lands* 1712 *Foster, Water Lands* 1839 *TA, Waterlands* 1841 *MC*, 'the water channel, open drain', *v.* **wæter, lād**, and for a discussion of OE **lād** in p.ns. PNITL 23-25, where it is pointed out that the word is found in fenland areas of Hu and more so in C in minor names and f.ns. It has not, however, occurred so far in the survey of north L, though Marsh Chapel is the first marsh parish to have been researched in detail. By the late 16th century, **lād** was being replaced by **land**, cf. Land Dike in Fulstow *supra*.

BELLE VUE COTTAGE. CLYDE HO. CAWTHERNSOME LANE (lost), 1828 Bry, *Cauter holme Lane* 1595 *FSurv*, 1595 *FMap*, c.1638 *Holywell*, cf. *Cauterholme* 1595 *FMap*, 1595 *FSurv*, *v.* **holmr** 'raised land in marsh, etc.', *Cauter* is obscure. Most of the names in *-holme* in Marsh Chapel east of Seadyke Way are those of salterns or salt-hills, also called *maures, mawres*. On *FMap* it is said *The round groundes at the end of Marshchappell are called mavres and are first formed by layinge together of quantities of moulde for the making of Salte.* Note also *5 pastures or holmes called Mavres, Six holmes or Mavres, a little rounde Mavre, A Mavre wth 2 Saltcoates vpon itt, a Mavre more east being arrable grounde* all 1595 *FSurv*. The etymology of *mawre, maure* is not clear, but the word is once described as *A great Maure or salt hill* 1657 *Anc*. CHURCH LANE (local), *the narrow Church lane, the Church way* 1595 *FSurv, the Church Way* 1595 (18) *Foster*. DUCKTHORPE LANE (local), *Duckthorp Lane* 1595 *FSurv, Duck Thorpe Way* 1595 (18) *Foster*, cf. *Duck thorpe* 1595 (18), *-thorpe* 1712, *-thorp* 1737 all *ib*, self-explanatory. This is apparently a late use of OEScand **þorp** in some such sense as 'the outlying part of a village', in this instance where ducks were kept. DUNHAM LANE (lost), 1595 *FSurv, - lane* 1595 *FMap, Dunholm Lane* 1828 Bry, cf. *Dun hams* 1712 *Foster, - Holmes* 1808 *BRA 838, High Dunholme* 1839 *TA* and *Dunham pasture* 1595 *FSurv*, 1595 *FMap, - Past.* c.1638 *Holywell, a close caled Donams* 1737 *Foster*, named from the surn. *Dunham*, well-represented in the parish in the late 16th century, cf. George *Donnam* 1588 *BT*, Richard *Dunham* 1590 *Anc*. It is the unnamed cul-de-sac at the opening of which is situated Belle Vue Cottage. HARPHAM RD (local), cf. *Walter Harphams pasture* 1595 *FSurv*;

it is named from the *Harpham* family well-evidenced in the parish, cf. Bernard *Harpham* 1555 *LMR*, - *Harppam* 1561 *Inv*. LAND DIKE, *v*. Land Dike in Fulstow *supra*. LITTLEFIELD LANE (local) is *Plumlane* 1595 *FMap*, probably named from the *Plum* family, cf. Thomas *Plome* 1592 *Inv*; for the later name cf. *Litle feilde* 1595 *FSurv, the litle feilde* 1627 *FLDudd, litlefeild* 1628 *LMR*, self-explanatory. LOW GATE (local), *le lowe gate* 1581 *Anc, Low gate* 1785 *Foster, Low gate Lane* 1813 *HD*, cf. *Lowgate Pingle* 1712 *Foster*, 1821 *AH, Low Gate Pingle* 1839 *TA* (*v*. **pingel** 'a small enclosure'), self-explanatory, *v*. **gata**. MARSH CHAPEL HALL, *a Cappitall Messuage ... called the Hall* 1687 *Em*, cf. *Hall F.m* 1828 Bry, *v*. **hall**. MARSH CHAPEL INGS, 1824 O, *les Inges* 1587 *Anc, Inges* 1595 *FMap, the Inges* 1595 *FSurv*, c.1638 *Holywell*, 1665 *LMR, Marsh Chappell Ings* 1725 *Foster, v*. **eng** 'meadow, pasture' in the pl., as frequently in this parish. MILL LANE (local), *Mil Lane* 1595 *FMap, Mill Lane, Millane* 1595 *FSurv, le mill lane* 1626 *LMR*, cf. *ubi situm est molend' ventrit'* a1274 *Holywell, cum molendino ventritic', vnum molend' ventrit'* 1294 *Holywell, molend' de foulestowemerske* 1384 *LMR, mol'd' ventrit' de Foulestowmerssh'* 1399 *ib, molend ventrit' de Foulestouemerssh* 1406 *ib, molend' ventrit' de Foulestowmersh* 1408 *ib, molend' ventri' ... in le marsh* 1452 *Anc, Great Mill pasture with ye winde Mill at the west end* 1595 *FSurv, wind corn mill* 1831 *Deeds*, self-explanatory. NORMAN COTAGE is presumably so-named from its neo-Norman architectural features. NORTH CHURCH FIELD (lost), 1595 (18), 1712, 1779, 1785 *Foster*, 1839 *TA*, 1846 *EnclA*, - *Feild* 1687 *Em, the churche northe feilde* 1627 *FLDudd, le North Churchfeild* 1628 *LMR, North Church Feild* 1687 *Em, N. Church Field* 1821 *AH*, 1824 O, cf. *North Church field lane* 1822 *Terrier* and *le Kyrkfeld* 1509 *Anc*, - *Kirkfeld* 1561 *ib, Kirkfeilde* 1595 *FSurv, -feildes* 1657 *Holywell, Marsh chappil kirke fields* 1663 *ib, in Campo ecclesiastico* 1564 *Anc, the Church feild* 1595 *FSurv, le Churchfeild* 1617, 1619 *LMR*, - *feild* 1622, 1637 *ib*, - *Feild* 1665 *ib*, - *field* 1638 *ib*, and note *South -, West Church Field* 1779, 1785 *Foster, the South* - 1813 *MC, South Church field* 1813 *ib*, - *Field* 1848 *EnclA, South Church field Lane* 1822 *Terrier*, self-explanatory, *v*. **kirkja**, **cirice**, **feld**. The change from Kirk to Church is noteworthy. NORTH LANE (local), 1828 Bry, *Northlane* 1348 *LMR*, (*venell' voc le*) 1563 *Anc*, 1595 *FMap, le North lane, north layne* 1567 *Anc, northlane, north Lane* 1595

FSurv, self-explanatory. SALTER'S LANE (local), *Saltergate* 1331, 1337, 1338 *Anc,* 1555, 1556 *LMR, v.* **saltere, gata**; it forms part of the south boundary of the parish with Grainthorpe. SHIP INN, *The Ship* 1828 Bry. VICARAGE, *the Vicaridge* 1635, 1674, 1706, cf. *the vicardge close* (sic) 1674, *the viccars* - 1635 all *Terrier.* WEST END, 1824 O, 1839 *TA, le West ende* 1554 *Anc,* cf. *west end' dyke* 1518 *ib,* self-explanatory. WHITE HORSE INN, *White Horse* 1842 White. WILLOW TREE HO is *Easthouse* 1595 *FMap,* 1657 *Holywell.* WILLOWTREE LANE is *Storre Lane* 1595 *FMap, a Comon Lane called Storr Lane* 1651 *MiscDon 38,* which is named from the *Storre* family, cf. Thomas *Storre* 1561 *Anc.* There was another Willowtree Lane in Marsh Chapel running from approximately TF 343 987 to TF 353 991 and recorded as *Willowtre layne* 1574, 1575 *Anc, -lane* 1595 *FMap, the Willow Tree Laine* 1687 *Em,* self-explanatory.

Field Names

The principal forms in (a) are 1839 *TA.* Those dated e13, 1277, 1407, 1610, c.1638, 1657, 1659, 1663, 1666 are *Holywell*; 1314 Ch; 1317 Ipm; 1396 Peace; 1530 Wills ii; 1538 *AOMB 409*; 1559 LAAS viii; a1567 LNQ v; 1579, 1601, 1635, 1662, 1674, 1706, 1822 *Terrier*; 1584 *BRA 513*; 1595^1 *FMap*; 1595^2 *FSurv*; 1595 (18), 1637, 1686, 1712^1, 1727, 1779, 1785, 1795 *Foster*; 1613 *MinAcct*; 1627 *FLDudd*; 1687 *Em*; 1712^2, 1821, 1877 *AH*; 1717, 1810, 1813 *HD*; 1796, 1841 *MC*; 1808 *BRA 838*; 1847 *Padley* and 1848 *EnclA.* Forms with a date followed by +, e.g. 1287+ are *Anc* and those dates followed by *, e.g. 1366* are *LMR.*

(a) Acre Garth (*v.* **garðr** 'an enclosure', as frequently in this parish); Allotment (several); Atkinsons Cl 1808, Atkinson's Cl 1837, 1839, Atkinson Cl 1841 (named from the family of Richard *Atkinson* 1839); Long -, North Bank; Banks Land 1839, - Lands 1841; Barn Cl; Brackley Garth (1712^1, named from the family of Thomas *Brakley* 1657 *PR* and **garðr**); Bradley-field lane 1822, Bradley Fld 1841, 1848; Bratts 1839, 1841, The Bratts Rd 1848 (*Brattes* 1595^1, *ye Bratts* 1595^2, *a pasture called* - c.1638, *the brates* 1610, (*v.* **brot** 'a small piece (of land)'; the form Brat(t) is common in north L); Brick Cl 1808, 1839); Burnt Hill 1821, 1839, 1847 (*Burnthill* 1595^1, 1595^2, *Brunthill* 1595^2, c.1638, *Burnt Hill* 1712^1, self-explanatory); Burton Cl (named from the *Burton* family, cf. William *Burton* 1511*); Calf Cl; 1 Ley called Canaway Ley 1785; Chapel; Charter house Cl, - Land 1785 (cf. *An Act to Enable the Governors of* *the Hospital of King James, founded in Charter-House, to sell ... divers lands ... in Marsh, Chapel* (sic) 1796); Chequer (*Checkqr* (sic) 1595[1], *a square pasture called Checker* 1595[2], *the Checkqz* (sic) c.1638, *close called the Checquer* 1712, *v.* **cheker**; this is described as *a square pasture* and Field, s.n. Checker Meadow, explains the name as "Alternative patches of light and darker soil gave the bare earth the appearance of a chess board"); Cherry Pasture 1808, 1839 (*Cherypasture* 1595[1], *Cherrie pasture* 1595[2], cf. *Cheregarth* 1546+; both the pasture and the garth were presumably named from the family of William *Chery* 1446+ and John *chery* 1461+); Church Cl (*Churchclose* 1595[1], *-close* 1595[2]); Church Yard; Clever some (a f.n. of the nickname type); Close (several); Clover Cl 1841; Coat Holme 1808 (1712[1], *v.* **cot** 'a cottage, a shed', **holmr** 'raised land in marsh', both common elements in this parish); Cow Cl (cf. *Cow pasture* 1595[2]); Cream Poke (a complimentary nickname for a field giving rich pasture); The Crews 1808 (from dial. **crew** 'a shed'); Croft (several); Cross Ings (Cl) 1839, 1841 (*v.* **eng**); Crowson's Intake 1839, Crowsons - 1841 (named from the family of Bernard *Crowson* 1712[1] and **inntak** 'land taken in or enclosed'); Croston's Intake 1839, 1847 (from the family of Bernard *Crowstone* 1587+ and **inntak**); Cullow bean 1839, -bean 1841 (*parcella terre vocat Collenbeane* 1584, *Colubine* 1595[1], *a pasture called Collubine* 1595[2], *one close called Cullye beane* 1656*, obscure, unless it is from a surn., cf. Henry *Columbeyn* 1517+); Dawsons Cl 1808, Dawson's Cottage 1821 (from the family of James *Dawson* 1595[2]); Low Dreuholme (sic); Duncan Hill 1839, 1847 (named from the family of Henry *Dunkan* 1287+, 1325+); East Marsh 1821 (*Eastmarsh* 1595[1], c.1638, *- marsh* 1595[2], *- Marsh* 1712, cf. West Marsh *infra*); East Yard; Eighteen Acres 1839, 1847; the Eleven Acres; Eskham Rd 1848 (*Eastham gaite* 1595[2], *v.* **gata** and Eskham *supra*); Far Lands 1839, 1847, -lands 1841; Far Yard 1841; Fields Walk 1808 (*v.* **walk**), Field - 1821, 1839 (cf. *campis de Marsh chapell* 1518+, - *Marschappell* 1625* and *ye Feild Lane* 1595[1], *v.* **feld**); the Fifteen acres 1813; 50 Acres 2nd -, 4th, -5th Division (sic) 1839, Fifty Acres 1847 (*ye 50 Acres* 1712[1]); Five Acres 1841; Flat Ley 1785 (*v.* **lea** (OE **lēah**) 'meadow, pasture'); Fold Piece (cf. *Foldholme* 1595[1], 1595[2], *v.* **fald**, **holmr** 'raised land in marsh'; this is shown on 1595[1] as a salt-hill or saltern, on which *v. Cawthersome Lane supra*); Fore Lands; Fore Marsh; Four Acres 1808, 1821, 1839, The - 1848 (*the 4 acres* 1712[1]); Garth (several) (*v.* **garðr**); Glover Holme 1821, 1847 (1712[1], *Gloverholme* 1595[1], *a Mavre called Glover Holme* 1595[2], *a Mawre called Glover holme* c.1638, cf. *John Glover thinge* 1573 (*v.* **þing** 'property, premises' as elsewhere in this parish) (named from the *Glover* family, cf. also John *Glover* 1514, and **holmr**, in this case described as a *mavre* or *mawre*, for which *v. Cawthernsome Lane supra*; it is shown as a saltern on 1595[1]); Gowth holm 1839, Gowtholme 1841,

Goatholme Walk 1847 (*v.* **holmr**); Gowt Intake (*v.* **inntak**); the Gowt Piece 1821, 1841, Gowt Piece Hill 1838 (with this and the preceding two f.ns. cf. *le Gote* 1337+, *le gotte* 1557+, *le Gootes* 1561+, *le Goot(e)* 1563+, *v.* **gotu** in the sense 'a sluice' and cf. *le gott* in Fulstow f.ns. (b)); Grainthorpe Rd 1848 (leading to Grainthorpe LSR); Far -, Middle Grange (cf. *pontem magn' grang'* 1450+, *le gret Graunge* 1522+, - *great Graunge* 1553+, *Great Grange* 1595[2], *Greate* - 1595[1], *lyttil Grange* 1547*, *litill grange dyke* 1553*, *Lowgrange or Litle grange* 1595[2], *Highgrange* 1547*, *le high graunge dyke* 1553*, *High -, Lowe Graunge* 1595[1], *High Grange* 1595[2], *v.* **grange**, the bridge was over Land Dike and the fields called Great Grange were to the south, and west of West End. No evidence has been found to identify the house owning them; High and Low Grange were to the west bordering on Louth Navigation); Great Cl 1808, 1839 (1712[1]); Great Holme 1808 (*v.* **holmr**); Green Tail 1821, 1839, Evison's - 1849 (named from the family of Thomas *Evison* 1819; presumably Green Tail denotes a narrow strip of grassland, *v.* **tægl**); Gunny Lands 1808, 1839, 1841 (named from the family of Robert *Gunny* 1505+, William *Gunney* 1506+); Harlow Garth (*Harlow* is probably a local surn. here, *v.* **garðr**); 3 Leys called the Harp 1785 (*le Harpe* 1430*, 1505*, *The* - 1595[2], *y^e* - c.1638, so named from its shape, cf. the Harp in Fulstow f.ns. (a)); Harrold's Marsh 1839, Harrolds Marshes 1841 (named from the family of William *Harrold* 1839); Hedge Cl (1595[2], *-close* 1595[1]); Hewison's Intake 1839, Hewsons - 1841 (named from the family of Elizabeth *Hewson* 1839); High Grainings (cf. *le Graininges* PN L **2**, 132); High Holme 1839, 1841 (1595[2], *-holme* 1595[1], c.1638, 1663, -*holme* 1657, 1712[1] (*v.* **hēah**, **holmr**; this is the name of a saltern and for the same name with reference to a different field, *v.* (the) High Holme in Fulstow f.ns. (a) *supra*); Hill and Bottom 1839, 1841; The Hills 1808, 1839, 1877; Hinds Intake (named from the family of Joseph *Hind* 1839 and **inntak**); Home Cl (several); Humberstone Croft 1839, Humberston - 1841 (*Humberstoncrofte* 1595[1], - *stone croft* 1595[2], named from a family long-established in the district, cf. Robert *de Humberstan* 1321+, Walter *de* - 1331+, and croft and cf. *Humerston Lees* in Fulstow f.ns. (b) *supra*); (the) Ings Cl 1785, 1808, 1839, Ing Cl 1847 (*Ings Close* 1712[1], cf. Marsh Chapel Ings *supra*); Ings Land Cl; Gt -, Little Intake 1808, (the) Intake 1813, 1821, 1839, 1849 (*v.* **inntak**); Ivory Cl; Jack Holme 1847 (1712[1], **holmr**); Jennys Cl 1808 (perhaps cf. *the Jene wren garth infra* in f.ns. (b)); Jerry Lands 1839, 1847, - Cl 1841; Ketterapt (sic) 1841 (obscure); Keydike Cl 1839, Keydikes - 1841; Kiln Cl 1841; King's Garth (presumably *King* is a surn. here, *v.* **garðr**); Lady Land 1779, - Lands 1785, 1808, 1821, 1839, 1848 (*Lady lande,* - *landes* 1595[2], 1627, *-lands* c.1638, - *Lands Field* 1712[1], *the Lady lands* 1737 (probably selions dedicated to "Our Lady", *v.* **hlǣfdige**, **land** and cf. *Ladyesclose* in Fulstow f.ns. (b) *supra*); Laking

Garth (Both Mr J. Field and Dr John Insley suggest that this denotes 'an enclosure or small plot of ground where games are played', *v.* **garðr**. The first el. is ModE *laking*, NED s.v. 'playing, amusement', ME *leiking* 'diversion, amusement, playing'. This word survives as northern dial., including L, *v.* EDD s.v. *laking*.); Lamb House Walk 1808, 1839 (*v.* **walk**, denoting land used for the pasture of animals); Great -. Little Lamb Ring 1839, - Lambring 1841; (The) Lands 1808, 1821, 1839, 1847, Lands Bottom 1839 (cf. *the lands with the Pingle* 1712[1] and Pingle *infra*); Leyton Garth 1808 (probably *Leyton* is a surn. here, but none has been noted in the sources searched); Lilbourn 1839, 1841 (*Lilborne* 1595[1], *a pasture called Lilburne* 1595[2]; the forms are too late to suggest a plausible etymology); Lilly Croft (*Lillycrofte* 1595[1], *a pasture called Lilly Croft* 1595[2]; *Lilly* is probably an old Marsh Chapel family name, cf. *Thom' fil' Lilie* 1325+); Line Dike Hill 1839, 1841; Line Holme 1808, 1839, 1847 (1712[1], *Lineholme* 1595[1], 1595[2], *a Mawre called* - c.1638 (the first el. is probably **līn** 'flax', the second is **holmr**. It is described as a *Mawre* and is shown as a saltern on 1595[1]); Little Croft (*litlecroft* 1580+, self-explanatory); Little Pingle (*v.* **pingel**); Long Bank 1839, 1841; three Acres, ye Long - 1785; Longwald 1808; Low Homestead; Low Piece 1808, 1839; Low Pingle (*v.* **pingel**); Marsh, Second - (*a pasture ... called The Marsh* 1595[2]); Marsh Cl 1810; Meadow; Middle Cl; Middle Pasture (Bottom); Middle Rows 1808, - Row 1839 (*Middle Rows* 1712[1]); Mill Cl 1808, 1839, 1847 (*mylne close* 1583+, *the Mill Close* 1717); Mill Marsh 1821 (1712[1], *Myln mershe* 1521+, *milnemarshe* 1553+, *Millmarsh*, *milne-marsh* 1595[2], c.1638, selfexplanatory and cf. Mill Lane *supra*); Mill Yard; Mitchells Onset 1821 (cf. *Mitchells Pingle* 1712[1] and Thomas *Michell* 1653*, *v.* Onset *infra*); Moss Cl; Mosscroft 1822; Mownholme 1839, Moun- 1841 (*Mowenholme* 1595[1], *ye mavre called Mowen holme* 1595[2], *a Maure called* - c.1638, *Mown Holmes* 1712[1]; this is presumably 'the mown raised land in marsh', *v.* **holmr** and as two of the references show it was a saltern or salt-hill and is marked as such on 1595[1]); Mussendine Garth 1838, 1841, Messendine - 1847 (*Christopher Mussendines Garth* 1712[1], self-explanatory, *v.* **garðr**; for an earlier reference to the family note John *Mussendine* 1647 *PR*); Mustard Hills 1839, 1841; Nettle hills 1839, 1841; Newholme Cow Cl (*Newholme* 1595[2], *v.* **nīwe**, **holmr** and cf. Cow Cl *supra*); Noble Cl 1839, Noble's Cl 1847 (no doubt from the surn. *Noble*, but none has been noted in the sources searched); North Bank 1839, 1847, Nor Bank 1841; North Coates side (cf. *North coates mill close in Marsh chappel* 1666; North Coates is the adjacent parish to the north); (the) North Ings 1779, 1785 *et freq* to 1848 (*Northinges* 1557+, *-ings* 1595[1], *the north Inges* 1595[2], *les North Inges* 1614*, *-ynges* 1615*, *-ynges* 1616*, 1617*, - *North Inges* 1624*, *North Ings* 1712[1], *le Northynges de Marshchappell* 1615*, 'the north pastures, meadows', *v.* **norð**, **eng** in the pl. and cf. South Ings *infra*); North Side Fd; North Walk 1821, 1839, 1847, Nor Walk 1841 (cf. *North Walk hills* 1712[1], *v.* **norð**, **walk**); Onset 1808, Onsett 1839 (*le Onsett* 1626*, cf. *the Onsett* in Fulstow f.ns. (b) *supra* and *v.* Onset Yard in North Coates f.ns. (a) *infra*); Orchard; paddison's cl 1839, Paddison's - 1847, - Hill 1839 (named from the family of John *Paddison* 1785 and *v. William Habbergeons Close* in (b) *infra*); Paddock (several); parish pound; the Parson Cl 1822 (cf. the parson Cl in Fulstow f.ns. (a) *supra*); Pinder Holme 1847 (*Pinderholme* 1595[1], - *holme* 1595[2], *a Mawre called Pinderholme* c.1638, *Pinder Holme* 1712[1], named from the village *pinder* or the derived surn. which is common in Fulstow and Marsh Chapel and **holmr**; it is described as a *Mawre*; cf. also *pynder oxgan'* in Fulstow f.ns. (b) *supra*); Pinfold Cl (*v.* **pynd-fald**); Pingle 1808, 1839, 1847, - Bottom 1839 (*Pingle* 1712[1], and *v.* (the) Lands *supra*, *v.* **pingel** 'a small enclosure'); Plantation (several); the Poor cl 1822, Poor Cl 1839, 1841 (a close the rent of which went to the support of the village poor; it is still let today on a five-yearly lease); Porcas Garth 1839, 1847, porcas Intake 1839 (named from the *Porcas* family with **garð** and **inntak**; the family name was originally *Portas*, as in Henry *Portas* 1514* but changes to *Porcas, Porcus* certainly in 1727 with Charles *Porcus*, but note Joseph *Portus* and David *Porcus* both recorded 1776 *PR*); Quartersome Cl; Rape Lands 1839, - Land 1877; Reed Lands 1777, 1808, 1848, Reedlands Rd 1848, Red Lands 1785 (*le Schortrede landes* 1508*, *litle redelandes* 1554+, *Redlandes* 1595[2], *Redlandes heading* 1595[2], *Furlong called Redland* 1595 (18), *Readlandes* 1627, *-lands, Rede-* c.1638, *Reed Lands* 1712[1] ('selions where reeds grow', *v.* **hrēod**, **land** in the pl.); River Cl; Rush Cl 1808, 1821, 1839, 1847 (1712[1], cf. *Risschcroft* and *Rush Common infra*); Rush 9 acres; Sanderson's Cl 1839, Sanderson - 1841 (no doubt named from the surn. *Sanderson*, though no such references have been noted in the sources searched); Sand Piece; The Sands (- *Sandes* 1595[1], and cf. *le Sand head* 1573+, *Sandy groundes* 1595[2]); School House; Sea Cl; the Sea Intake (*v.* **inntak**); Seed Piece 1808, 1839; Seven Acres 1839, 1841; Sharp Holmes 1839, - Holme 1847 (*Scharpholme* 1553+, *Sharp(e) Holme* 1595[1], 1712[1], - *holme* 1595[2], 1663, *a Mawre called Skarpholme* (sic) c.1638 (named from a long-established family here, cf. Nicholas *Scharp* 1277-62, John *Scharpe* 1289+, and **holmr**; this was also a saltern or salt-hill); Sheep Walk (*v.* **shepe-walk**); Side Piece; Six Acres 1839, 1841, the six acres 1847; Skin Garth (*v.* **garðr**); Sluice Piece 1808, 1839; South Croft 1839, 1841, 1847 (1712[1]); (the) South Field 1779, 1785 *et freq* to 1848 (*in Australi campo* 1564+, *in australi* - 1627, *the south feilde* 1595[2], *le Southfeild* 1612*,

1613*, 1628*. *les* - 1619*, *Southfeild* 1650*, *ye South feild* 1652*, *le South field* 1623*, *the South Field* 1712[1], self-explanatory, *v.* **sūð, feld,** one of the open fields of the village); South Holme 1821 (1712[1], *Southholme* 1595[1], *-holme* 1595[2], *v.* **sūð, holmr,** also a saltern); South Ings 1779, 1785, 1821, 1848 (*South enges* 1425+, *le Southinges* 1561+, *-ynges* 1628*, *leȝ Sowthinges* 1561+, 1567+, *les* - 1564+, - *Southynges* 1619*, *South Inges* 1595[1], 1619*, *le* - 1623*, *the medowes of Marshchappell called the south Inges* 1595[2], 'the south meadows, pastures', *v.* **sūð, eng** in the pl. It is part of what is today called Marsh Chapel Ings *supra*); Stanland 3 acres 1839, - Acres 1841; Stephen's Garth 1839, 1841, 1877 (perhaps from the surn. *Stephen* noted in *Joh' fil' Stephen* 1399+ and **garðr**); Stothards Intake (from the *Stothard* family, cf. Thomas *Stothard* 1839, and **inntak**); Suck Croft 1839, 1841; Tackholme; Templeholme 1795 (1686, *Templeholm* 1595[1], - *holme* 1595[2]; the Knights Templar had considerable holdings in Fulstow in 1185, *v.* Templar 105, but *Temple* has also been noted as a local surn., cf. William *Temple* 1615*; *v.* **holmr.** Templeholme is shown as a saltern or salt-hill on *FMap*); Ten Acres 1808, 1821, 1839, The - 1849 (*the 10 acres* 1717[1]); Thirty Acres 1821 (*ye 30 Acres* 1712[1]); Thistleho 1808, Thistelow 1839, 1841 (*Thistlehowe* 1561+, *North -, South Thistleho* 1595[1], *north Thistle* (sic), *South Thistle hoe* 1595[2], probably 'the mound where thistles grow', *v.* **þistel, haugr;** the two fields lay on the eastern boundary of the parish between Land Dike and New Dike, the boundary with North Coates); The Three Acres; Thorey Cl (probably from the surn. *Thorey*, cf. Tristram *Torey* (sic) 1613 *PR*); Top Cl; Twenty Acres 1821; Two Acres (*the 2 Acres* 1712[1]); Uphills; Close ... called the Walk 1813, (The) Walk 1839, 1841 (*Walk, The Low Walk* 1712[1], *v.* **walk** which is common in the parish and denoted land used for the pasture of animals, especially sheep, hence the common *Sheepwalk);* Webster Cl (named from an old established local family, cf. Alan *Webster* 1396+); Welholme 1839, 1847, Wilholme 1841, Little Willom 1808 (*Welleholme* 1404*, *Welholme* 1623*, *Welham (pastur)* 1595[1], *Wel(l)ham* 1595[2], *Pastur called Welham* c.1638, *Close called Wellham* 1721[1], 'the raised land in marsh with a spring', *v.* **wella, holmr**); Welsh Walk (*v.* **walk**); West Garth 1808 (*v.* **garðr**); West Gate Holme 1839, 1841, -gate Holme 1847, West Gate Walk 1839 (*v.* **west, gata** 'a road' with **holmr** and **walk**); the West-lane 1822, West Lane Pingle 1839, 1841 (*v.* **pingel**); West Marsh 1821 (*Westmersk* 1347+, *Westmarsh* a1567, c.1638, - *Marsh* 1595[2], *Westemarsh* 1595[1], *Westmarsh pasture* 1595[1], 1595[2], self-explanatory, *v.* **west, mersc,** with *-mersk* a Scandinavianized form. West Marsh was to the east of Seadyke Way, with East Marsh, *supra*, further to the east); Westmoor Cl 1808, - more Cl 1839, -more Cl 1841; Westmoreland Ings 1839, 1841 (named from the family of Christopher *Westmoreland* 1839 and **eng** in the pl.); West Yard; Wether Walk Bottom

1839, - Hill 1841 (this was pasture for wether sheep, *v.* **weðer, walk**, and *v.* (The) Walk *supra*); Wilkinsons Garth 1808 (named from the family of Richard *Wylkynson* 1506* and **garðr**); Wingarth 1808 (*v.* **wīn, garðr** 'a vineyard'); Woofles 1839, 1841 (*un' pastur' vocat Woofull* 1561+, *Wooffle* 1595[1], *a pasture in-closed called Woofles* 1595[2], *Woffles* 1712[1], *Woofols* 1737, a derogatory nickname, from ME *wāful, wōful* 'woeful', no doubt denoting land hard to work); Yard 1841.

(b) *ye 2 former peeces voc abbutte* 1595[2] (this is different from *Southabbott Croft* in Fulstow f.ns. (b), but it was probably similarly named from the Abbot of Louth Park Abbey); *Akebryge* 1507* (perhaps 'the bridge by an oak-tree', *v.* **eik, brycg**, with *-bryge* in a Scandinavianized form, cf. *Aicdales* in Fulstow f.ns. (b). The first el., however, may well be OE **āc** 'an oak-tree' rather than its Scand. cognate **eik**. In this case it would, as Dr John Insley points out, show the normal development of OE **āc** in Northern dialects of ME); *Appletondal* 1595[1], *10 ac' called Appletondale* 1595[2], the same name but referring to a different **deill** from *Appletondale* in Fulstow f.ns. (b)); *Askhill* 1595[1], c.1638, *Ask(e)-* 1712[2] (*v.* **askr** 'an ash-tree', **hyll**); *Barnesdale* 1595[2], *Barmes-* c.1638 (*v.* **deill**); *berwardbryg* 1464* ('the bridge of the bear-keeper', *v.* **bera-ward**, (ME *ber(e)-warde*), **brycg**); *the close is called y[e] bottome* 1595[2] (*v.* **botm**); *bourde close* 1554*, *- closse* 1586* (denoting a close held by the lord of the manor to produce food for his table, *v.* *Bordeland(e)* in Fulstow f.ns. (b)); *Break backe* 1595[1], *an acr' called Broak backe* 1595[2], *Broak backe* c.1638 (a derogatory nickname for a piece of land difficult to work); *Brianholme* 1595[1], *a pasture called Bryan holme* 1595[2] (named from the family of Walter *Brian* 1347* and **holmr**; it was a saltern or salt-hill, but the second reference suggests it had become pasture land); *quondam pontem apud Foulestowe mersk* 1311+, *Brygg'* 1404* (p) (*v.* **brycg**; some of the forms given under *Fulstow Bridge supra* may belong here); *brigholm* 1415* (*v.* **brycg** (in a Scandinavianized form), **holmr**); *the Broade lane* 1595[2]; *Brocklebanks Cottage* 1712[2] (named from the family of Christopher *Brockelbanke* 1656*); *Brovdale* 1595[2], *Broudale* c.1638 (Dr Insley suggests that is 'the share of land at the brow of a hill', the first el. being ME **broue** (OE **brū**) 'an eyebrow; a brow of a hill', the second **deill**); *Byardes Lee* 1595[2] (presumably from the surn. *Byard* (Reaney s.n.) and **lea** (OE **lēah**) 'meadow, pasture'); *Caldusholme* 1538 (*Caldus* is probably 'the house in a bleak, exposed situation', *v.* **cald, hūs**, to which was added **holmr** 'a piece of raised land in marsh'); *Calfholme* 1595[1], *Calfe-, the Calue -* 1595[2] (*v.* **calf, holmr**; this is shown as a saltern or salt-hill on 1595[1]); *Capeldale* 1595[1], *Capell-* 1595[2], *Capull Hill* 1553* (the first el. in these names may be **capel** 'a chapel', referring to land held by the Chapel here); *Car's Farme* 1712[1]

(Richard *Car* is named in the same document); *The Cockle Sands* 1595[1] (self-explanatory; it was in the east of the parish by the sea); *Collingwood gate* 1727 (*v.* **gata**; Nathaniel Collingwood is named in the same document); *ye commens* 1601, *the towne-Comon* 1635, *les commons* 1638*, *ye Comon of ye towne, the Comon feild* 1662 (self-explanatory); *le Cote* 1337* (*v.* **cot** 'a cottage, a shed'); *le Cotes* 1578+ (*v.* prec.); *Cowpasture* 1595[1], *- pasture* 1595[2], *the -* 1610 (self-explanatory); *Cranecroft* 1595[2] (*v.* **cran** 'a crane, a heron', or the derived surn., and **croft**); *le crosse bryge* 1461*, 1505* ('the bridge by the cross', *v.* **cros**, **brycg**, with the second el. in a Scandinavianized form; it went over Land Dike); *Crosse Close* 1657 (*v.* **cros**, **clos(e)**); *Crosshille* 1595[1], *-hill* 1595[2] (*v.* **cros**, **hyll**); *dearbought* 1610 (a derogatory nickname for land difficult to work); *Dikeholme* 1595[1], *a pasture called Dykeholme* 1595[2] ('the holme by the dyke', *v.* **dīk**, **holmr**; this was a saltern or salt-hill, but the second form indicates that it had become pasture); *Dogcrofte* 1595[1], *Dogge Croft* 1595[2], *Dog -* 1659 (*v.* **dogga**, **croft**); *le Dovecote garth* 1619* (*v.* **garðr**); *Eastclose* 1595[1], *a long pasture ... called East close* 1595[2]; *Easthilles* 1595[1], *a pasture ... called East hilles* 1595[2] (this was a saltern or salt-hill, but the second forms suggests that it was no longer in use as such); *East holme* 1595[2] (*v.* **holmr**, also a saltern); *Eastley holme* 1595[2] (*v.* **ēast**, **lea** (OE **lēah**), **holmr** and cf. *Westley holme infra*); *le Eddishe* 1667* (*v.* **edisc** 'an enclosure', in dial. 'aftermath, stubble'); *the estcotte holmes* 1559 (*v.* **ēast**, **cot** with **holmr**); *Eylmer croft* 1325+, *Aylmercroft* 1366*, 1408*, *Ailmers toft* 1595[2] (named from the family of *Aylmero filio Sywardi* e13, *Walter' fil' Hugonis fil' Ailmer* ?1277+, William *Ailmer* 1303+ and **croft**, with **croft** apparently later replaced by **toft** 'a messuage, a curtilage'; the ME pers.n. *Ailmer* goes back to OE *Ǽgelmǣr*, as Dr Insley points out); *Fells Garth* 1712[1] (named from the family of Robert *Fell* 1636* and **garðr**); *Frecrofte* 1595[1], *Free-croft* 1595[2], *free -* c.1638 (no doubt denoting a croft free from rent, *v.* **frēo**, **croft**); *gangeholm* (sic) ?1277+ (most probably from OE, ON **gang** 'a path, a track', later 'a cattle-walk' and **holmr** 'raised land in marsh', though the exact sense seems uncertain); le ȝ *Gappestedes* 1557+, *le gapsted in le Sedick* 1583+ ('the site of a gap', *v.* **gap**, **stede**, a compound not noted in Sandred; it is described as being a gap in Seadyke Way); *the garthes* 1595[2] (*v.* **garðr** 'an enclosure (near a house)' in the pl.); *le Gowle* 1554* (from ME **goule** 'a watercourse, a ditch, a channel'); *Grace hill* 1595[2], *-hill* c.1638 (the significance of *Grace* is not clear); *Graunt thinge* 1573+ ('Graunt's property, premises', *v.* **þing**; Richard *Graunt* is mentioned in the same document); *le greves* 1583+ (cf. *marsh called the Groves or Greaves* PN L **2**, 155, where it is stated that *grove* is the dial. term for sites where digging (for turf) takes place. *Greave* is apparently an alternative form; it was on Seadyke Way); *Grythbanke* 1507* (obscure); *William*

Habbergeons Close, - *late Paddison West Close* 1712[1] (cf. paddison's cl in (a) *supra*); *le halke* 1563+ (*v.* **halc**, ME *halke* 'nook, corner' and PN C 328); *Hallington thinge* 1557+, 1580* (from the surn. *Hallington*, cf. Peter *Hallington* 1520+, and **þing**; in 1557 it is described as *unum Toftum*); *Hawise Lane*, *Houyslane* 1325+ (the first el. is the ME (OFr) pers.n. *Haueis*, itself derived from Frankish *Hadwîdis*); *le Hode Dyke* (sic) 1510* (*Hode* is perhaps an error form *Hede*, but the sense is doubtful); *le Holm* 1505*, - *Holme* 1521+, *holme waye* 1595[2] (*v.* **holmr**); *leȝ Holmes* 1452+, *les* - 1553+, *le* - 1561+, 1567+, 1572+ (*v.* **holmr** 'raised land in marsh' in the pl.); *Horne daile* 1595[2], *Horndale* c.1638 (*v.* **deill**; the first el. is perhaps **horn** denoting 'a share of land shaped like a horn'); *Horsebridge waie* 1595[1], - *brigge way* 1595[2] (self-explanatory); *the Horse Close* 1687; *Hubcrofte* 1595[1], - *Croft* 1595[2], *-croft* c.1638 (the first el. is ME *Hub*, a short form of ME *Hubbold* (OFr *Hubaut* from Frankish *Hugibald*), *v.* Reaney s.n. *Hubling*, used as a surn.); *Huppecote* ?1277+ (probably 'the upper cottage, shed', *v.* **upp**, **cot**); *Inge croftes* 1623*, *Inge pasture* 1595[2] (named from Marsh Chapel Ings *supra*); *the Jene wren garth* 1579 (*v.* *jenny wren* NED s.v. 1 'a popular, and esp. nursery, name for the wren', first recorded there in 1648. It was presumably a fanciful name for a very small field, *v.* **garðr**); *Judcroft* 1595[1] (for the first el. *v.* *Judhous* in Fulstow f.ns. (b) *supra*); *Kirke thinge* 1573+ (from the family name *Kirk* and **þing**; Thomas *Kyrke* is mentioned in the same document); *Kitchencrofte* 1595[1], *Kitchinhill* 1595[2] (both names are probably derived from a local family, cf. George *Kytchin* 1592 *PR*, *v.* also **croft** and **hyll**); *lady Croft* 1570* (it no doubt has the same connotation as Lady Land in f.ns. (a) *supra*); *lamcroft* 1366*, 1439*, *Lamb-* 1369*, 1384*, 1407*, 1408*, 1442*, *lambe-* 1442*, *Litillamcroft* 1505*, *Lytle Lamcroft* 1561+, *Little lambe Croft* 1595[1], - *Lambcroft* 1595[2], - *Lambecroft* c.1638 (self-explanatory, *v.* **lamb**, **croft**); *lambholme* 1282, *lamholme* 1507*, *Lamb-* 1595[2], *Lambe Holme* 1595[1] (*v.* **lamb**, **holmr**); *Lampland* 1595[1], *Lamp(e)rigge* 1595[2] (*v.* **land**, **hryggr**, a selion and a ridge the proceeds of which went to the upkeep of a lamp in the village church); *Landsic* 1314 (*v.* **land**, **sík**); *Leson toftes* 1581+ (from the *Leson* family, cf. John *leson'* 1451+, and **toft** in the pl.); *Lisons thinge* 1573+ (from the surn. *Lison* and **þing**; Robert *Lison* is named in the same document); *Litelhill'* 1461+, *Litlehill* 1595[1], *a Mawre called Little hill* 1595[2], *little hill* c.1638 (self-explanatory; it was a saltern or salt-hill); *littelholmes* 1331+ (*v.* **lȳtel**, **holmr**); *Little marsh* 1595[2]; *lobh[a]m* (sic) 1547* (obscure); *Mr Loft Land* 1712[1] (named from the *Loft* family, but the earliest reference so far noted is to John *Loft* 1822); *Long Close* 1712; *Longwonge* 1595[1], - *wonge* 1595[2], *-wongs* 1650*, - *wange* 1652*, *the Long wong* 1712[1] (*v.* **lang**, **vangr** 'a garden, an in-field'); *Loue wongs* 1650* (*v.* **vangr**); *Lower close* 1712[1]; *the Lo: Willo:* (sic) 1595[2] (i.e. *the Low Willow*);

Maire & Foale 1595[2] (for the same *v.* PN L **2** 193 and 243; in the first it is referred to as *one broode* (i.e. broad) *land*, in the second as *ii lands*; for the first it was suggested the name denoted a foaling strip, for the second two adjoining strips of unequal sizes. There is nothing in the context here to indicate which of these suggestions is more likely); *Malton toft sometime belonging to Malton Abba* (sic) 1595[2] (the *Abba* is Malton Priory, Yorkshire, *v.* also **toft** 'a messuage, a curtilage', as elsewhere in this parish); *mancroft* 1650* (*v.* **croft**; the first el. may be **(ge)mǣne** denoting a croft communally held, but no certainty is possible; cf. *leȝ Meneholme infra*); *maraystoft* 1409* (named from the family of Alan *marays* 1289+ and **toft**); *Close called Marcroft* 1652; *mardykebanke* 1555* (probably 'the boundary dyke', *v.* **(ge)mǣre**, **dīk**, with **banke**); *Marsh common, ye north Marsh Common, the Southe* - 1595[2] (cf. *ye commens* in f.ns. (b) *supra*); *Maudcroft* 1595[1], *Maud(e) Croft* 1595[2] (from the ME fem. pers.n. or derived surn. *Maud*, derived from *Mahald*, a colloquial form of *Matilda*. This pers.n. is ultimately OGer *Mahthild*, OFr *Mahaut*); *Meare holme* 1627 (probably 'the boundary holme', *v.* **(ge)mǣre**, **holmr**); *leȝ Meneholme* (sic) 1564+, *Meane-* 1595[1], *a pasture called Mean-* 1595[2], *meane-* 1626* (probably 'the communally-held holme', *v.* **(ge)mǣne**, **holmr**; it was a saltern or salt-hill); *Middlecotholme* 1595[1], *-coate holme* 1595[2], *-cotholm* c.1638 'the middle cottage or shed', *v.* **middel**, **cot** with **holmr**; in 1595[2] it is described as being *wth 2 saltcoates vppon itt* and in c.1638 *wth 2 Salt coats*; it is shown as a saltern or salt-hill on 1595[1]; *Middle holme* 1595[1], *Midle holme* 1595[2], 1663 (self-explanatory); "two places (*placeis*) called" *Molfanges* 1314, *le moldfang* 1314+ (this name has been noted as *le Moldfanche* and *le Moldefang* in Habrough f.ns. (b) PN L **2**, 145-46, where a possible etymology is discussed. However, in PN L **3**, xix-xx Mr Arthur Owen draws attention to two articles by his wife (LAAS 4, 1-56 and LAAS 8, 76-84) where it is clear that this term is linked with saltmaking, especially in Fulstow Marsh. He further points out that Dr Kathleen Major in a note in RA v, 188 comments "A *moldfang* is apparently an alternative word for a sandpit or place where sand could be taken, *molde* being glossed as *sabulam* in the Anglo-Saxon period", attributing this interpretation to the late Sir Frank Stenton. As a result, it is suggested that, though the exact meaning of *moldefang* is uncertain, it may be 'a place where sand is taken'. A further instance of the appellative use of *molde* has been noted in a French document of 1356, AASR xxiii, 276, *une mese di' bou' de terre une Saltcote en le more pur salt molde*); *le More Inge Lane* 1637* (*v.* **mōr** 'a marsh', **eng**); *terr' vocat Mottye ground* 1584, *grounds ... called by the names of mottyns* 1613 (obscure; neither form appears to be recorded in dictionaries); *Moyne(s) more* 1595[2] (from the family of Alexander *Moyne* 1520+ and **mōr** 'a marsh'); *Thomas Mumbys Garth*

1712[1] (self-explanatory; the *Mumby* family is recorded earlier as in William *Mumby* 1574 Admin); *Muncheholm* 1314 ('the monks' saltern', *v.* **munuc**, **holmr**, described as such in the text; there is no indication which abbey they served, but it is probable that it was Louth Park); *mylne hyll* 1508* (self-explanatory, *v.* **myln**, **hyll**); *Milhilpasture* 1595[1], *Millhill pasture* 1595[2] (different from *Litle Millpasture* 1595[1], *Little Mill pasture* 1595[2], for which *v.* Mill Lane *supra*); *le new cawsey* 1557+ (*v.* **caucie** 'a raised way across marshy ground, etc.'); *Newerkcroft* 1409*, 1415+, *Newerkland* 1399*, 1407*, 1408*, 1442*, *Newark land* 1430*, 1452+. 1512+ (named from the family of John *de Newerk* 1340+ with **croft** and **land**); *New Ground* 1712[1]; *Norholm* 1509+, *Northolme* 1595[1], *North holme* 1595[2] (self-explanatory; it was a saltern or salt-hill); *North Hill* 1595[1], *-hill* 1595[2], *a Holme called North hills* c.1638 (self-explanatory; it is shown as a saltern on 1595[1]); *le north marshes* 1553+, *the North Marshes* 1610, *ye north Marsh Common* 1595[2] (self-explanatory); *Northorp* 1447*, a1567, *-thorpe* 1464+, *via voc' Northorp Way* 1508* ('the north outlying farmstead, hamlet', *v.* **norð**, **þorp**; unfortunately no real indication has been found of its site); *North pasture* 1595[1], 1595[2]; *le north sike* 1561+ (*v.* **norð**, **sík** 'a ditch, a trench'); *old Goat piece* 1712[1] (*Goat* is no doubt from **gotu** in the sense 'sluice'); *Outgat* 1325+ ('the way out', *v.* **ūt**, **gata**, perhaps to the open fields); *Outholme* 1595[1], *Out* - 1595[2], *a Mawre called Outholme* c.1638 (*v.* **ūt**, **holmr**; it was north of North Lane towards Poplar Grove and was a saltern or salt-hill); *Oxholme* 1595[1], *Ox Holme* 1595[2], *a Mawre called Oxholme* c.1638 (*v.* **oxa**, **holmr**; it is shown as a saltern on 1595[1]); *atte Oxhusse* 1331+ (p) ('the building for oxen', *v.* **oxa**, **hūs**); *Palmerholme* 1595[1], 1663, - *Holme* 1595[2], *a Mawre called Palmer(s) holme* c.1638 (from the surn. *Palmer*, cf. Walter *Palmer* ?1277+, Anne *Palmer* 1325+, and **holmr**, here 'a saltern, a salt-hill'); *Panmerdale* 1595[2] (perhaps an error for *Paumer*, i.e. *Palmer*, with **deill** and cf. the prec.); *le pan pece* 1563+ (*pan* is probably from **panne**, here a salt-pan); *pastur dicke* 1575+ (self-explanatory); *Peal Garth* (sic) 1712[1] (perhaps an error for the foll.); *Peat(e)garth* 1595[2], *Peat-* c.1638 (perhaps 'the enclosure, small plot of ground where peat is obtained', *v.* **pete**, **garðr**, though the first el. could well be a surn.); *Pennecroft* 1595[2] (*v.* **penn**[2] 'an enclosure for animals', ME *pen(e)*, **croft**); *Philcuphill* 1595[1], *Philcaphill* 1595[2], *a Holme called Filcup hill* c.1638 (this is shown on 1595[1] as a saltern or salt-hill; it is a complimentary nickname *Fillcup*); *Plan Lane, Planlain, y[e] Plain lane* 1595[2], *Plan Lane* 1595 (18); *plomtre Tofte* 1564+ (*v.* **toft**; the first el. is presumably the tree-name, though with **toft** it might well be a surn., though none has been noted in the sources searched); *The Plough'd Ground* 1712[1]; *Porecroft* 1595[1], 1595[2] (perhaps comparable with the Poor Cl in f.ns. (a) *supra*, a **croft** the rent of which was used for charitable purposes; *Purcrofte* 1538 may possibly belong here);

Primecrofte 1595[1], *- croft* 1595[2], *-croft* c.1638 (the meaning of *Prime* here is unclear); *le Readfeild* 1628* (perhaps 'the field where reeds grow', *v.* **hrēod, feld**); *Risschcroft* 1480+, *Rysh-* 1522+, *Risch-* 1567+, *Rush-* 1595[1], 1595[2], c.1638, *- Croft* 1712[1] (self-explanatory, *v.* **risc, croft**, cf. Rush Cl in (a) *supra* and *Rush Common infra*); *Robinson Croft* 1561+, 1595[2], *- Crofte* 1595[1], *Robinsons -* 1637+ and *Robynson thinge* 1566+ (the **croft** and **þing** 'property, premises' were named from the *Robinson* family, cf. John *Robynson* 1414*); *Rush Common* 1595[2] (cf. Rush Cl in f.ns. (a) and *Risschcroft* in (b) *supra*); *Salcotes* 1447*, *le Saltcotes* 1461*, *Salt cotes* 1553+, *Salte coates, - coate holmes* 1613 (*v.* **salt, cot** with **holmr** and cf. *duas Salinas voc' too Salte Cootes* (sic) 1545+, *una bercaria vocat a Saltcote* 1553+); *Saltholm, le Salt Holm* 1325+, *leȝ Saltholmes* 1561+, 1581+, *Saltholmes* 1567+ (*v.* **salt, holmr**; this was presumably a saltern or salt-hill); *Saltmersk'* 1348* (p), *the salt marshes* 1610 (*v.* **salt, mersc**, *-mersk'* being a Scandinavianized form); *duas Salinas vocat' Salt pannes* 1545+ (*v.* **salt, panne** and cf. *le pan pece supra*); *Saltwellyng'* 1396*, *-welles* 1556+ (*v.* **salt, wella** with **eng**); *Scamblesbie marsh* 1595[1], *Scamblebyes Marsh* 1595[2], *Scamelsby -* 1657*, *Scamblesby Marsh* 1712[1] (named from the family of Walter *Scamelsby* 1446*, *- de Scamulesby* 1463+ and **mersc**); *Schefeld croft* 1411* (named from an ancestor of Philip *Sheffeld* 1574+ and **croft**); *le Sheipoole* (sic) 1523+ (probably 'the sheep pool', *v.* **scēap, pōl**); *le Shittle gote* 1578+, *Shittle Goat Close* 1712[1] (the first el. may be OE **scyt(t)els** 'a bolt, a bar', which loses its *-s* and survives as dial. *shuttle* 'the horizontal bar of a gate, a flood-gate', with **gotu** in the sense 'sluice'); *Short Furlong* 1595[2], *-furlong, -furs* c.1638, *South Short Furlong* 1595 (18); *Shypcoteclose* 1530, *Shipcotholme* 1595[1], *a great Mavre called Sheepcote holme* (self-explanatory, *v.* **scēap, cot, holmr**; it is shown as a saltern on 1595[1]); *Small pits* 1631*; *Smitholme* 1595[1], *a pasture called Smith-holme* 1595[2], *pasture ... vocat Smythe-landes* 1627 (named from the *Smith* family, cf. Robert *Smyth* 1348+, Richard *Smyth* 1507* with **holmr** and **land**; this was a saltern or salt-hill which was already pasture in 1595); *stany pasture* 1564+ (*v.* **stānig** 'stony', **pasture**); *the ston cawseye* 1579 (*v.* **caucie**); *le Stothes* (sic) 1563+ (uncertain); *Stowland* 1407 (perhaps from the surn. *Stow* and land); *le Stubble Feld* 1561+, *- feild* 1631*, *- Stuble Field* 1585+ (self-explanatory); *Swetemilke holme* 1595[2], *a mawre called Sweetmilkholme* c.1638 (a complimentary nickname for a productive *holme* or salt-hill); *duas acras pasture vocat' tethering ground* 1619*; *Thorndale* 1595[1] (*v.* **þorn, deill** 'a share, a portion of land'); *Thorne Close* 1595[2] (it is described as being *by East holme*); *Three Crofts* 1637*; *throcroft* (sic) 1561+; *le tresyke* 1561+ (presumably a ditch marked by a tree, *v.* **trēow, sík**); *le tythelathe* 1563 ('the tithe barn', *v.* **tēoða**, ON **hlaða** 'a barn'); *Upper Close* 1712[1]; *a Mavre called Walde holme* 1595[2], *a Mawre called Woldholme* c.1638 (*v.* **holmr**, here a saltern or salt-hill, but the significance of

wald 'wold' is not clear since the site was east of Seadyke Way in the fens); *War(e)holme Waye* 1595[2] (the way to Wragholme situated over the southern boundary of Marsh Chapel); *War holme Sewer* 1595[2]; *fossat voc' Warlottes* 1563+ (this name has now been noted at least seven times in north L, *v.* PN L **2** 97-98, ib **3**, 43, 71, 123, 147, 188. For a full discussion *v.* PN L **2** 97-98 under Waterhill Wood. It appears to have been a piece of land or the like assessed to a specifically defined payment of geld); *Waterhouse pasture* 1959[1], 1595[2], *Waterhouse-Pasture* c.1638 (named from the family of Richard *Waterhouse* 1564+ and **pasture**); *Wellecrik* 1314, *Wel-* 1340 (*v.* **wella**, **crike** (ON **kriki**), the first reference being to a saltern in *Wellecrik*); *West Cote* 1447*, *the weste cote holmes* 1559, *Westcotholme* 1595[1], *a mavry* (sic) ... *called Westcote holme* 1595[2] (originally 'the west cottage, shed', *v.* **west**, **cot**, to which was added **holmr**; it is shown as a saltern or salt-hill on 1595[1]); *westhall croft* 1553+, *West hall croft* 1595[2], *Westhal Croft* 1595[1], cf. *Westhallepastur'* in Fulstow f.ns. (b) *supra*); *Westholme* 1595[1], 1595[2], *a Mawre called Westholme* c.1638 (*v.* **west**, **holmr**; it was a saltern or salt-hill to the west of *Northolme supra*); *Westley holme* 1595[2] (cf. *Eastley holme supra*); *westmarsh pasture* 1595[2] (it was to the *west* of East Marsh, in f.ns. (a) *supra*, between North Lane and the parish boundary with North Coates); *le Westwaies* 1579* (self-explanatory, *v.* **west**, **weg**); *Whitepeaferm* (reading uncertain) 1595[1], *Whitt pease Rigg* 1595[2] (*white* in this context is explained in NED s.v. 11 (b) as 'in names of plants distinguished by white flowers, or other parts ... as ... white.. peas'. Mr John Field draws attention to several references to *whitpeas* in Thomas Tusser, *Fiue Hundred Pointes of Good Husbandrie* (edited from the edition of 1580 collated with those of 1573, 1577) English Dialect Society, 21 1878. There *whitepeas* are distinguished from *Greene peason or hastings* and from *Graie peason or runciuals*, p. 56., and from the 1577 edition Tusser says:

> White peason, both good for the pot and the purse,
> by sowing too timelie, prooue often the wurse.
> Bicause they be tender and hateth the cold,
> prooue March er ye sowe them, for being too bold. (p. 97)

Mr Field points out that it is certainly worth noting that this f.n. "is a rare example of a variety being named, references to vegetables etc. being in general terms"); *a Mavre by Wild holme* 1595[2] (self-explanatory); *Willo way lane* 1595[2] (self-explanatory; it is not connected with Willowtree Lane *supra*); *Wybaldholm* 1314 (the first el. is from the ContGerm pers.n. *Wibald* (rather than the etymologically identical OE *Wigbald*) or a surn. derived from it; the second is **holmr**, probably denoting a saltern or salt-hill).

Wold Newton

WOLD NEWTON

Neutone 1086 DB, *-tun* 1170-85 *Holywell, -tona* 1175, 1182, 1245 (13) *Alv, -ton(')* 1204 P, 1213 Cur, 1235 Dugd vi, 1238-41, 1242-43 Fees, 1252 Cl, 1254 ValNor, 1275 RH, 1281 QW *et passim* to 1431 FA

Newtuna c.1115 LS, *-ton(')* 1176 P, 1196 ChancR, 1220 Cur, 1303 FA, 1314 Ch

Niwetuna c.1150 *DuDCCh, -ton(')* 1193 P

Newenton' 1220 Cur

Neuuton 1303 FA

Nuton 1428 FA

Newtona l12 (1409) Gilb, *-ton* 1428 FA, 1526 Sub, 1535 VE iv, 1557 Pat, 1566 *BT, -tonne* a1567 LNQ v

Wald neuton eHy2 (13) *Alv, - Neutone* 1278 RRGr, *- Neuton* 1308 Cl, 1308, 1367 Pat, 1375, 1376 Peace, *Waldneuton(')* 1238 RRG, 1307, 1311 Pap, 1317 Ipm, 1320 Pap, 1327 Banco, 1332 *SR*, 1361 Cl, 1361 Ipm, 1373 Peace, 1431 FA, *Waldeneuton(')* 1277 *DuDCCh*, 1298 RSu, 1310 *FF*, 1311 Pat, 1311 Ipm, 1318 Pap, 1319 ChancW, 1329 Ass *et passim* to 1445 *MiD, Walde Neuton(')* 1305 Ass, 1316 FA, 1327 *SR*, 1368 Cl, 1370 Pat

Woldneuton 1248 RRG, 1297 *HarlCh, Wold Neuton* 1295 Ipm, *Wolde -* 1299 Pat, 1300 Orig, 1406 RRep

Waldeneweton(') 1202, 1206 Ass, 1214 FF, 1236 RRG, 1272 *Ass*, 1272 FF, 1388, 1392 Pat, *Walde Neweton* 1235 FF, *Waldeneweton* 1318 Pat, 1319 ChancW, 1323, 1411 Pat

Waldnewton 1329 Pap, 1387 Peace, 1510 *Anc*, 1510 LP i, *Wald -* 1297 *HarlCh, Waldenewton* 1417 Fine, 1476 LAAS vii

Wand (*n* = *u*) *Niuueton'* 1213 Cur

Wandniweton (*n* = *u*) 1213 Abbr

Walde Newenton' 1281 *FF*

Wald Nieuton 1372 Ipm

Woldnewton(') 1466 *LCCA*, 1483 *AD*, 1530 Wills iii, 1553 Pat, 1614, 1618 *BT*, 1671 *Terrier*, 1688, 1701 *BT*, 1703 *Terrier, Wold Newton* 1557 InstBen, 1570, 1589 *BT*, 1603

Foster, 1608 *Anc*, 1622, 1674 *BT*, 1736 *Yarb et passim*, *Wolde* - 1500 *MiD*, 1602 *Foster*, *Woldenewton* 1510 LP i
Would Newton 1591, 1593 *BT*, 1599 *MiD*, 1603, 1605, 1607 *BT*, 1620 *LCS*, 1630 *BT*, 1631 VisitN, 1638 *LCS*, 1648 *MiD et passim* to 1734 *Yarb*, *Wouldnewton* 1610 Speed, 1687 *Yarb*
Wholdnewton 1574 *Foster*
Wowldnewton 1576 Saxton
Wooldnewton 1580 *Terrier*, 1586 *BT*, *Woold Newton* 1724 *Terrier*
Oldenewton 1507 Pat, *-newtonne* 1558 Admin
Vetera Neuton' 1386 Peace

'The new farmstead, village', *v.* **nīwe**, **tūn**. The affix is from the situation of the village in a dip in the Wolds, *v.* **wald**. Forms with the loss of initial *W-* are paralleled by those for Old Weston in Huntingdonshire (PN BdHu 250). They must have been current in the 14th century since in 1386 Peace the affix was interpreted as 'old'.

THE GRANGE, *clausuram grangie ... de Neutona* 1175 (13), *super grangiam* 112 (13), *Grangiam de Neutona* 1245, 1254-61 (13), *Grangiam quam habetis in uilla que dicitur Neuton'* a1251 (13) all *Alv*, *a grange in Woldenewton* 1560 Pat, *the Grange Farm* 1696 *Yarb*, cf. *uersus West grangie sue de Waldneut'* eHy3 (13) *Alv*, *Grange garth stones* 1668, 1671, 1679 *Terrier*, *-Stone* 1697 *ib*, *grange garth Stone* 1703 *ib*, *Grange Garth Stone* 1834 *ib*, *Grange Garth* 1772, 1810 *Yarb* (*v.* **garðr**). It is called *Newton Green* 1828 Bry. This was a **grange** of Alvingham Priory as is clearly indicated by the form dated a1251. THE LANGMORE (local), *Langmore* 1834 *Terrier*, cf. *Long Moor* 1772 *Yarb*, *Long Moor Willowe* 1810 *ib*. NORTH FM, *North Hall* 1604, 1629 *MiD*, - *hall* 1605 ib; it is north in the village and it may be purely coincidental that a family called *North* is well-represented in early documents, cf. *terram Ade North* Hy3 (13) *Alv*, Peter *North* 1327, 1332 *SR*, Peter *North* of *Waldeneuton* 1349 Fine, and cf. South Fm *infra*. PETTERHILLS FOX COVERT, cf. *Peterill* 1810 *Yarb*, *Far* -, *First Pettlehill* 1843 *TA*; Petterhills is in East Ravendale parish *infra.* RECTORY, *ye parsonage* 1580, 1679, - *house* 1668, 1671, *Parsonage-house* 1834 all *Terrier.* SOUTH FM, situated to the south of the village, but cf. the surn. *South* recorded in early documents, William *South'* 1332 *SR.* STOCK FURLONG, cf. *a fourlong called Stockfourlonges* 1577, *Stockfurlonges* 1638, *stok furlonges* 1626 all *Terrier, Far -, Great Stock Furlongs, High -, Little Stock Furl^gs^* 18 *MiscDep* 16, *ye Stock furlonge* 1703, *the Stockfurlong* 1709, *ye Stock Furlong* 1724, *the upper Stockfurlong* 1724 all *Terrier, Stock furlong Close* 1772, - *Furlong* 1786, 1810 all *Yarb, Stocks Furlong Cover* 1824 O, *Stoke Furlong Cover* 1828 Bry, presumably 'the furlong marked by a tree-trunk or stump', *v.* **stocc**, **furlang**. It is on the boundary with Hawerby cum Beesby parish and many of the references are in fact from Hawerby documents. WOLD NEWTON COVERT, - *Cover* 1824 O, *The Cover* 1828 Bry; it is on the boundary with Binbrook.

Field-Names

Spellings dated eHy2 (13), lHy2 (13), c.1175 (13), 1175 (13), a1182 (13), l12 (13), eHy3 (13), a1227 (13), 1276 are *Alv*; 13 *Holywell*; 1310 *FF*; 1300, 1312 *Foster*; 1314 Ch; 1327, 1332 *SR*; 1328 Banco; 1329 *Ass*; 1338, 1399, 1608 *Anc*; 1444 *LMR*; 1445, 1461, 1466, 1500, 1502, 1512, 1523, 1547, 1573, 1599, 1608, 1648, 1688, 1703 *MiD*; 1482-83 *AD*; 1531 Wills iii; 1560 Pat; 1580, 1606[1], 1611, 1625, 1626, 1638, 1668, 1671, 1679, 1697, 1703, 1709, 1724, 1762, 1834 *Terrier*; 1620 *LCS*; 1606[2], 1625, 1665, 1687, 1696, 1772, 1810, c.1832 *Yarb*; 1712 *NW*; 1842 *MiscDep 118*; 1843 *TA*.

(a) Ackers (sic) c.1832, 1843 (*v.* **æcer**, **akr**); Ash Cl 1772, 1810, c.1832 (*v.* **æsc**); Great -, Little Autby Fd c.1832, 1843 (named from Autby in North Thoresby parish *infra*); Beesby Style 1834 (1697, *Beesby Stile* 1703, 1724, cf. *uiam de Beseby* a1182 (13), *uiam de -, viam de Beseby* eHy3 (13)), Beesby Walk c.1832, 1843 (from Beesby in Hawerby cum Beesby parish *supra*); Binbrook Gate 1834 (1724, *Binbrocgate, binbrokegate, uiam de Binbroc* eHy3 (13), *vie de Binnebrock'* Hy3 (13), *binbrook gate* 1697, 'the road to Binbrook' *v.* **gata**); Far -, Middle Bottom Cl 1772, 1810, First bottom Cl 1772, Near Bottom - 1810, Far -, First -, Middle Bottom c.1832, 1843 (*v.* **botm**); Bowdale 1834 (*boidale, boydale (furlanges), Boydale, Boydalefurlang* eHy3 (13), *1 furlong called* *budell* 1580, *a furlong called Boodale* 1668, *Bowdale* 1671, 1697, 1703, *Budel Hill, Budale Bottom* 1724; the first el. is OE **boi(a)**, ME *boie* a boy, a servant', the second **deill** 'a share of land'. The sense of **Boi(a)** in p.ns. has always been considered to be uncertain. However, Dr Insley draws attention to a comparable f.n. in Nf, *Bondesboydale* 1214-29 (SPNNf 98), in which the first el. is the ODan pers.n. *Bondi.* Here *-dole* is from OE **dāl**, the cognate of ON **deill**. He suggests that perhaps both names *boidale* and *-boydale* denote a share or portion of land appropriate to a boy, but not to a man); Brame Hills 1834 (*Brame hills* 1668, 1697, *Braim hills* 1671, *- hils* 1703, *Bramehills* 1679); the Brats Corner 1834 (*brate furlonge* 1580, *Bratts furlong* 1668, 1671, 1679, *- Corner* 1697, *y^e^ -* 1703, *- Bratts Nook* 1724, *v.* **brot** 'a small piece (of land)'); Brick Kiln Pce c.1832; Brintle 1834 (1697, 1703, *ye upper Brintle* 1668, 1671, 1679 (probably 'the burnt hill', as suggested by Dr Insley, *brint* being a variant of *burnt*); Bull Bank 1834 (*bulbank* 1703, *ye Bull bank* 1724); Bunting Cl 1772, 1810; Cabbage Gdn 1843; (Far) Church Fd, - Plat c.1832, 1843, - Yd 1843 (cf. *Kirke Wang* 13, *v.* **vangr** 'a garden, an in-field'); Clay pitt Hill 1772, - pit hill 1810; Coney Hills 1772, - hills 1810 (*v.* **coni**); North -, South Corn pce 1772, 1810; First Cottom Cl 1772 (if the name is old, this is perhaps 'at the cottages', *v.* **cot** (dat.pl. *cotum*)); Cow Cl 1772, Cow Pasture c.1832, (Far) - 1843, Cow Walk c.1832, 1843, Cowleares or Eastward Gate 1834 (*Cowlares* 1697, 1703, *Cowlayers* 1724. Mr John Field suggests that the second el. is ModE *layer* 'a field of grass or clover' and draws attention to a further example in Cow Layer in the f.ns. of Billesdon Lei. This sense of *lay* v. is discussed in NED s.v. *layer* sb 3c, where it is suggested that it is "perhaps a special development of *lair* sb[1] 5, influenced by association with *layer.*" The ultimate source is OE *leger* 'a burial place', later 'a lair'. Cf. Summer Layers in Cabourne f.ns. (a) *supra*); East Fd 1772, 1810, the East Fd 1834 (*ye East feild* 1668, 1671, *- Feild* 1679, *- field* 1697, *- Field* 1724, *- east Feild* 1703, *v.* **ēast**, **feld**, one of the open fields of the village, cf. West Fd *infra*); Eddy Pce c.1832, 1843 (probably from the surn. *Eddy*); 18 Acres c.1832, Eighteen Acres 1843; Far Cover Pce c.1832; Far -, Near Fd c.1832 (*v.* **feld**); Far Pasture c.1832; Farrow Yard 1772, - Garth 1810 (next to Church Yard, named from the *Farrow* family, cf. Thomas *Farra* (sic) 1713 *BT*, Thomas *Farrow* 1742 *ib*, with **geard** and **garðr**); Fifty Acres c.1832, 1843; Fox Cover 1772, 1810, c.1832 (2x), Fox Cover 1772 (on the south boundary), Fox Cover (Pce) 1843; Furz Hill (sic) 1772, Furze hill 1810, the Furze Hill 1834 (*v.* **fyrs**); Garth (3x) (cf. *Greate Garth* 1573, *v.* **garðr** 'an enclosure, a small plot of ground', as elsewhere in the parish); Gig Ho c.1832, Gig House etc. 1843 (perhaps a building for a light two-wheeled one-horse carriage, *v.* NED s.v. *gig* sb[2], 1, where it is first recorded in 1791); Gravel Pit

Pce c.1832, 1843; Green Cliffe 1834 (*greneclife* 1580, *green cliffe* 1668, 1697, *Grenecliffe* 1671, *Greencliffe* 1679, 1703, *v.* **grēne**[1], **clif**); Green Paddock c.1832, 1843, Green Paddock and Buildings 1843; the Heaninge, - Hegninge 1843 (*le heynninghe, heynsdickes* eHy3 (13), *y*[e] *heyninge* 1580, *y*[e] *Heanings* 1668, 1671, 1679, 1703, *y*[e] *Heaninge* 1697, *v.* ON **hegning** 'enclosed land'); Great -, Little High Cl 1772, 1810, the High close corner 1834 (*y*[e] *hy close* 1697, *y*[e] *hy Close Corner* 1703); Hill Cl 1772, 1810, c.1832, 1843 (*at Hill'* 1399 (p)); Home Cl 1843; House Farm Buildings Stack Yd and Pleasure Grds 1843; Houseing & Fold 1810; 100 Acres c.1832, Hundred Acres 1843 (area: 98a. 2r. 3p. in c.1832); Lane 1810; Lings 1772, 1810 (cf. *lingwang* a1182 (13), eHy3 (13), *v.* **lyng**, **vangr** 'a garden, an in-field'); Long Plat c.1832 (*v.* **plat**[2]); Long Walk 1843 (*v.* **walk**); Micklemoor Fds 1772, Mickemoor (sic) c.1832, Mickamoor 1843, Pond called Mickle moor Well 1772 (*Mickle-more* 1724, *v.* **mikill**, **mōr**); New Cl 1772 (*y*[e] *New Close* 1724); Newton Feild 1762 (*in campis de Neutun* a.1182 (13), *in campis de neutun* 112 (13), *super campus de Neutun* eHy3 (13), *in brueria & in campis de neutun* 112 (13) ('in the waste and in the fields of Newton'), *in brueria* 112 (13), Hy3 (13), *pasturam que uocatur brueria de Neutun* eHy3 (13), *brueriam de Neuton* 1276 (13), *campum de Neutun* Hy3 (13), *in campo de Neuton'* 1338, *in campis de Newton* 1444, *campis de Walneuton* 1445, *campis de Wolde Newton* 1500, *Newton-feild* 1625, *newton field*, - *Felde* 1626, - *feeld* 1638, *y*[e] *fyldes of Wooldnewton* 1580, *Would Newton feilde* 1606[1], *the feild of Would Newton* 1611, *Wold-Newton feild* 1665, *v.* **feld**); Old Pasture 1772, 1810; Old Sainfoin Cl c.1832, Old Sanfoine - 1843 (*v.* **sainfoin**); Orby Fd c.1832, 1843 (i.e. Hawerby Fd); Ostler Cl 1772, 1810 (named from the *Ostler* family, cf. Robert *Ostler* 1567 *Inv*); Ozier Holt c.1832; Paddock 1810, 1843; Parson Paddock c.1832, Parsons - 1843 (if not self-explanatory, perhaps named from the *Parsons* family, cf. Robert *Parsons* 1732 *BT*); Parsonage Yd 1772, - Garth 1834 (*v.* **geard**, **garðr**); Plantation c.1832, 1843; Pond called Side Dike 1772 (*v.* **sīd** 'large, long', **dīk**); the Pond 1810, Pond c.1832; Ralph Garths 1772, Ralphe Garth 1810 (*v.* **garðr**); Rape Garth c.1832, 1842, 1843 (*v.* **garðr**; *rape* alludes to the crop grown for oil-seed and fodder); Ravendale Pce 1772, Near - c.1832, 1843 (from East Ravendale *infra*, referring to the same field); Sandhole 1834 (*Sandholes* 13, *Sande holes* 1580, *sandhole* 1668, 1679, *Sand hole* 1671, 1703, *Sandhole* 1697, *v.* **sand**, **hol**[1]); Scotgate 1834 (*scotegate* 1580, *Scotgate* 1668, 1671, 1697, *Scotgate or Shepherd hill* 1679. There are at least five examples of this name in the Wapentakes of Walshcroft and Yarborough, two of which may well have been named from the surn. *Scot*. *Scotgate* is discussed in some detail in PN L **2** 103-4, where it is interpreted in three instances as 'the road of the Scots', *v.* **Scot(t)**, **gata**. This may well be the meaning here, though, of course, a surn. is possible, as well as perhaps **scot** 'a tax, a payment'); Seven Acres c.1832, 1843; Shepherd Hills 1772, - hills 1810, Sheepheard Hill 1834 (*Shepherdhill* 1668, *Shepheard hill* 1671, 1697, *Shepherdv* - 1703, - *Hill* 1724, *v.* **hyll** and 1679 form of Scotgate *supra*); Slater Cliff c.1832, 1843, - Cliffe 1834 (*slaþercliue* (2x) eHy3 (13), *Slaterclif* 1580, *Slater-cliff* 1668, *Slater clyfe* 1671, - *cliffe* 1697, *Slatercliffe* 1679, *slater Cliffe* 1703, *Sclater Cliff* 1724; Dr John Insley suggests that this is 'the hill where animals were slaughtered', from ME *slaghter* 'slaughter' and **clif**, though the first el. is uncertain); Stack Yard Cl c.1832, - Pce 1843; Stoned Horse Paddock c.1832 ('grass enclosure for a stallion'); Summer Hills 1834 (*Somer hill* 1580, *Sommer-hill* 1668, *Sommer hills* 1671, 1697, *Somer hills* 1679, 'hill(s) used in summer', *v.* **sumor**, **hyll**); Swinhope Btm 1834 (*Swinhop bottom* 1697, 1703, *Swinnope* -, *Swinhope Bottom* 1724, *svyneopedale* eHy3 (13), *Swynope dalle* 1580, *Swinehop dale* 1668, *Swin hop* - 1671, *Swinhop* - 1679, *v.* **botm**, **dalr**; *Swinhop bottom* seems to be a later name of *svyneopedale*), Swinhop Walk c.1832, 1843 (*v.* **walk**) (alluding to the neighbouring parish of Swinhope); Thorganby Saintfoin pce 1772 (*v.* **sainfoin**), Thorganby Walk 1772, 1810, c.1832 (1703, *Thorganby Nook* 1724, *v.* **nōk**), Thorganby Walk Buildings etc. 1843 (*v.* **walk**, alluding to the neighbouring parish of Thorganby); Tranmore c.1832, Tranmoor 1843 (perhaps to be identified with *Stranmore* (sic) 1668, 1671, 1679; Tranmore seems to be 'the crane marsh', *v.* **trani**, **mōr**^{1}); 28 Acres c.1832, Twenty Eight Acres 1843; Victim Flg (sic) 1834; West Fd 1772, 1810, the - 1834, (Near -, Top) West Fd 1843 (*in campo occidentali* 13, Hy3 (13), *ad campum occidentalem* 1461, - *occidentale* (sic) 1466, *the westfeeld* 1573, *West filde* 1580, - *feild* 1679, *ye west feild* 1668, 1703, - *Feild* 1671, - *West field* 1697, - *Field* 1724, *Newton west feild* 1625, *v.* **west**, **feld**, one of the open fields of the village, cf. East Fd *supra*); Yard (2x) 1772.

(b) *barfe* 1580, *Barffe* 1668, 1671, 1679 (from dial. *barf* (OE **beorg**) 'a hill'); *Barnehoudale* eHy3 (13) (from the Scand. pers.n. *Barni* and **haugr** 'a (burial) mound, a hill', a Scand. compound, with **deill**); *Byornesgaire* eHy3 (13), *Boirnesgaire* (sic) 112 (13), *Beornisgaire* lHy2 (13) (the first el. is the Scand. pers.n. *Bjǫrn*, the second being **geiri** 'a triangular piece of land', a Scand. compound); *Bond enghes* 1314 (probably from **bondi** 'a peasant landowner' and the pl. of **eng** 'meadow, pasture', a further Scand. compound); *Brakenhou* lHy2 (13), 112 (13), *brakenhou* a1182 (13), *brakenhou(wang)* 112 (13) ('the bracken covered mound, hill', *v.* **brakni**, **haugr**, with **vangr**, a fourth Scand. compound); *at Bryg* 1444 (p) (*v.* **brycg** in a Scandinavianized form); *Burnham Post furlong* 1709, 1724, *Burnam* - 1724 (*v.* **furlang**; *Burnham* is probably a surn. and *Post* presumably alludes to a boundary marker); *Caldecliue* eHy3 (13) (*v.* **cald, clif**); *castor gate* 1580, *Caster gate* 1668, 1671, 1697, *Castergate* 1679 ('the road to Caistor', *v.* **gata**); *Chubesgarthe* 1531 (from the surn. *Chubb*, with **garðr**); *Clifshaw Farm* 1696 (*Clifshaw* is probably a surn.); *Colewang* eHy3 (13) (Dr Insley suggested that this is 'Koli's garden, in-field', from the Scand. pers.n. *Koli* and **vangr**, though the first el. could formally be the OE pers.n. *Cola*); *Crakehou stigtes* 13 (*v.* **kráka** 'a crow, a raven', **haugr**, with **stīg** 'a path'; *Crakehou* is a Scand. compound); *Crane daile* 1606[1], *Crane Daile* 1606[2], *a Daile there called Crayne daile end* 1611 (*v.* **cran** 'a crane', **deill** 'a share, a portion of land', as elsewhere in the parish, cf. Tranmore *supra*); *Croft* 112 (13) (*v.* **croft**); *at Crosse* 1399 (p), *Crosse Lane* 1573 (*v.* **cros**); *Cuuedale* (2x) eHy3 (13) (obscure); *daulandes* (sic) eHy3 (13), *dedelandes, le dedelond* eHy3 (13) (It is most likely that *Daulandes* and *dedelandes* refer to the same selions. It is remarkable that here we have a second example of the interchange of ON **dauð** and its OE cognate **dēad**, the sense probably being 'the barren, uncultivated selions'. Cf. *dedlandes* and Douthlandes in West Rasen f.ns. (b), PN L 3 120); *Dunfant thinge* 1620 (probably from a surn. and **þing** 'property, premises', and cf. *Grundie thinge infra*); *Egecroft* eHy2 (13) (perhaps *v.* **ecg, croft**, but Dr Insley suggests that the first el. is rather the OE pers.n. *Ecga* and this is probably more likely); *enschedik* a1182 (13), *ensdikes* (sic) eHy3 (13), *Ensedikes* Hy3 (13) (the first el. is obscure); *etischedic* a1182 (13) (*v.* **etisc** 'a plot of land', probably pasture land, **dīk**); *euendelandes* a1182 (13) (Dr Insley notes that the first el. "belongs to the past.part. of the ME verb *evenen* 'to make level or smooth; to level off or smooth out, etc.', cf. MED s.v. The name therefore would denote strips of land (*v.* **land**) which had been levelled out"); *viam de Fenby, fenbigate* eHy3 (13) ('the road to Fenby (in Ashby cum Fenby)', *v.* **gata**); *floẙbẙfurlanges* (sic), *flopberpfurlanges* (sic) Hy3 (13) (Dr Insley suggests that "the first component of the first el. *floẙbẙ-*, *flopberp-* must be ODan *flōth* 'flooded land' and that the second component is uncertain". He compares *flōth* with OIcel *floábarð* 'the edge of a fen'); *frebyland* Hy3 (13) (Dr Insley comments "the first el. is comparable with that of the medieval Norwegian p.n. *Frøland*, which Magnus Olsen took to be ONorw **frøy-* used in connection with the suitability of the land for sowing as arable, cf. also ON *frær, frjór* 'fertile', and for further discussion, *Norsk stadnamnleksion*, ed. J. Sandnes and O. Stemshaug, Oslo 1976, snn. *Frøgn, Heggen og Frøland*. The L *frebyland* then denotes 'fertile land, land suitable for sowing as arable belonging to the village', *v.* **bȳ, land**"); *the Gathering Furlong* 1709, *- gathering furlong* 1724 (*v.* **furlang**; Mr Field draws attention to the fact that "Adams 89 refers to several terms relating to ridge-and-furrow ploughing which include *gathering*, e.g. *twice* -, *thrice gathering*, but does not give clear references for further information". He adds that "it is certainly possible that *gathering* in this f.n. refers to ridge-and-furrow ploughing"); *le grift* eHy2 (13) (from dial. *grift*, recorded in EDD only from north L with the meaning 'a channel shaped out by water for itself, a runnel', cf. Griff Lane in Fulstow *supra*); *Grundie thinge* 1620 (from the surn. *Grundy* and **þing** 'property, possessions'); *uiam de Gunerby* eHy3 (13) ('the road to Gunnerby (in Hatcliffe parish)'); *ad aulam* eHy3 (13), *Aulam de Wald Neuton'* 1300, *Attehalle de Waldeneuton'* 1310, *atte Halle* "of" *Newton* 1328, *atte halle de Waldeneuton'* 1329, *ad Aulam* 1327, - *aulam* 1332 all (p) (*v.* **hall**); *hanckeland* (sic) c.1175 (13) (the first el. may well be the AScand pers.n. *Anki*, a short form of names in *Arn-*, with **land**); *Hannow dale* 1668, *hanna Dale* 1671, *Hanna* - 1679 (obscure); *uiam de Hawardeby* a1182 (13), *vias de auwordeby* eHy3 (13), *uias de Hauwordeby* eHy3 (13), *Hawerby Gate* 1724 ('the road to Hawerby (a neighbouring village)', *v.* **gata**); *Hawerbie short Butts* 1709, *Hawerby Short* - 1724 (*v.* **butte**); *a furlonge caled Hye furres* 1580, *high furres* 1668, - *furrs* 1671, - *Furres* 1679, *hy furrs* 1703 (*v.* **furh** in the pl.; *ye furr hill* 1687 refers to the same field); *holegate* eHy3 (13) ('the road running in the hollow, the sunken road', *v.* **hol**[2], **gata**, a common name); *Irfordhows* 1502, *Irffod hows* (sic) 1512, *Tofte ... vocat Irfford thyng* 1547 (*v.* **hūs**, **þing** 'property, premises'; *Irford* is presumably a surn. from Orford PN L **3** 125-7); *landemere, Langemerehau* (sic) l12 (13), *landemarehov* Hy3 (13) ('the boundary', *v.* **land-(ge)mǣre** with **haugr**; *Langemere-* is presumably an error); *langfurlanges* eHy2 (13), eHy3 (13), *Langfurlanges* l12 (13) (*v.* **lang**, **furlang**); *langhousslede* y3 (13) (**lang**, **haugr** 'a mound, a hill', with **slæd** 'a valley'); *linfurlanges* eHy3 (13) (*v.* **līn** 'flax', **furlang**); *Lingerdale* Hy3 (13); *ye litle Acre Close* 1724; *the lowe Farm* 1696; *ad uiride fossatum uie de Lude* lHy2 (13) ('to the green ditch of the road to Louth'), *super viam de Luda, viam que tendit uersus ludam* eHy3 (13) ('the Louth road, the road which runs towards Louth', though which road this denotes is not clear; it cannot be Barton Street, which does not run through the parish); *Luthedale* eHy3 (13) (this appears to mean literally 'Louth valley', *v.* **dalr**; there is no indication of its situation, however); *the mannor howse* 1611; *Lamare* (sic), *terram Ric' alamare* eHy3 (13), *ad Maram de Woldeneuton* 1312, *Atte Mare* 1327, *atte mare* 1332 all (p) (*v.* **(ge)mǣre** 'a boundary'); *le marefure* Hy3 (13) (*v.* **marfur** 'a boundary furrow'); *Mikelwang* Hy2 (13), a1182 (13), *the litle mickle wonge* 1599,

Mickle wonge 1608, *Mickell Wonge* 1648, *Michellwong hedge* 1668, *mickell wong* - 1671, *michell* - 1679 (*v.* **mikill**, **vangr**); *ye mill gates* 1703, *the Millgate furlong* 1709, 1724, *Millgate Furlong* 1724 (*v.* **myln**, **gata**); *Nettelakeres* eHy3 (13) (*v.* **netel**, **æcer**); *Neutunclif* l12 (13), a1227 (13) (*v.* **clif**), *Neutundic* l12 (13) (*v.* **dīk**); *Newdale* Hy3 (13) (*v.* **nīwe**, **deill** 'a share of land'); *Northlanges* eHy3 (13) (*v.* **norð**, **lang**[2] 'a long piece of land'); *ye Onsett* 1697 (cf. Onset Yard in North Coates f.ns. (a) *infra*); *Orgaie* 1560 (apparently a p.n. near Wold Newton and completely obscure); *the Oxgang* 1482-83 (*v.* **oxgang**); *Ringaldehou* a1182 (13) (*v.* **haugr**; the first el. may be the OE pers.n. **Hringwald*, adduced for *hringwoldes beorh* 938 (12) BCS 729 (S 440)); *Ringhov* Hy3 (13) ('the circular mound, hill', *v.* **hring**, **haugr**); *Scamlandis* eHy3 (13) (*v.* **skammr** 'short', **land**); *le scortbuttes* eHy3 (13) (*v.* **sceort**, **butte** with the first el. in a Scandinavianized form); *les sikes* Hy3 (13) (*v.* **sīk**); *ad publicam uiam que tendit per mediam uillam* lHy2 (13) ('to the public way which runs through the middle of the vill'), *the commen streate* 1573, *The Towne street* 1688 (*v.* **strǣt**); *a fossato australi* lHy2 (13) ('from the south ditch'); *ad stroume*, *stroumes* (lit. *strouemes*, with *e* deleted), *stroumes* eHy3 (13) (probably from ON **straumr** 'a stream'); *viam de Swyneop*, *svineope(e)gate* eHy3 (13) (*v.* **gata**), *Swynhop dala* a1182 (13), *Svineopdale* eHy3 (13) (*v.* **dalr**), *Svynopheuedland* (*v.* **hēafod-land**) eHy3 (13) (alluding to the adjacent parish of Swinhope); *ad thoawes* (sic) eHy3 (13) (obscure); *thorgrambigate*, *uiam de Thorgramby* eHy3 (13) ('the road to Thorganby', an adjacent parish, *v.* PN L **3** 157-8, and cf. Thorganby Sanfoin Piece *supra*); *thornedale* 13, *thorindale* (sic) eHy3 (13), *Thorndale* 1724 (*v.* **þorn**, **dalr**); *ye towne furlonge* 1580, - *towne-furlong* 1668, - *Town furlong* 1671, - *town furlong* 1679 (*v.* **tūn**, **furlang**); *t^u^aemare* (sic) Hy3 (13) (probably 'the two boundaries', *v.* **twā (twēgen)**, **(ge)mǣre**, cf. *too mares* in Covenham St Mary f.ns. (b) *supra*); *vrchin furlong* 1697, *Urchin furlong* 1703 ('hedgehog furlong', from **furlang**, with ME *urchen* 'a hedgehog'); *Walterwang* eHy3 (13) (from the ME pers.n. *Walter*, with **vangr**); *Watelandes* 1679 (*v.* **land** 'a selion' in the plural; earlier forms are needed to explain the first el.); *Wellecroft* l12 (13), *Well Close* 1573 (*v.* **wella**, **croft**, **clos(e)**); *a fossate occidentali* lHy2 (13) ('from the west ditch'); *landes ... called or known by the name of Willoughbies Lands sold by Pergrine Lord Willoughbye of Earsby* 1608, *that Farme called Willoughby Farme* 1687, *Willoughby Farm* 1696, *Willoughby Closes* 1687 (self-explanatory); *Wimundehou* a1182 (13) ('Wimund's mound', from **haugr** with the pers.n. *Wimund*, probably a reflex of ON *Vígmundr*); *a furlonge caled Windinges* 1580, *windinges* 1668, 1679, *ye windings* 1671 (for a discussion of *windings*, *v. wynedyngs* PN L 2 173); *Wodedale* eHy2 (13), *Wdedale* 112 (13), *Woodedalle cote* 1580, *wood-dale* 1668, *Wood-dail* 1671, 1679, *Wood dale Bottom* 1709, 1724, *Wooddale* - 1724 (*v.* **wudu**, **dalr** (later confused with **deill**) with **cot** and **botm**).

North Coates

NORTH COATES

Nordcotis c.1115 LS

Northcotes 1202 Ass (p), 1242-43 Fees, c.1250 (13) *Alv* (p), 1253 FF, 1254 ValNor, 1275, 1276 RH, 1291 Tax, 1295 Ipm, 1300 Cl, 1309 Pat, 1311 *Anc*, 1311 Ipm, 1312 Fine, 1316 FA, 1317 Ipm, 1331 Cl, 1332 *SR et freq* to 1781 *BT*, *- Cotes* 1294 Ipm, 1299 Pat, 1300 Orig, 1428 FA, 1610 Speed, 1690 *Terrier*, 1769, 1776 *BT*, 1789 *Foster*, *-cots* 1535 VE iv, a1567 LNQ v, 1664 *Terrier*, *- Coots* 1536-37 Dugd vi, *-cootes* 1626 *BT*, 1634 VisitN, *- cotes* 1577, 1625 *Terrier*, *-cotis* 1353 Misc

Northecotes 1226-28 Fees, 1327 *SR*, 1360, 1361 Pat, 1524 *MinAcct*, 1562 *BT*

Northcote 1276 RH, 1303 FA

Norcotes 1212 Fees, 1256 FF, 1375 Works, 1389 Cl, 1705 *NW*, *-kotes* 1275 RH. *-cotts* 1526 Sub, *-cottes* 1553, 1554 Pat

Norhtcotes (sic) 1238-41 Fees

Nortcotes 1242-43 Fees, 1275 RH

Northcoates 1616 *BT*, 1658, 1661 *Foster*, 1679 *Terrier*, 1685 *BT*, *- Coats* 1686 *ib*, 1729 *Foster*, *- Coates* 1695, 1688, 1692 *Em et passim*

Coates Borealis 1723 SDL

'The cottages, the huts to the north', *v.* **norð**, **cot**. There is no contrasting South Coates; it is likely, therefore, that North Coates was named in relation to Fulstow, the village to the south.

HAVEN, 1842 *TA*, *portum de Nortcotes* 1275, 1276 RH, *del Hauen* 1303 *Anc* (p), *atte* - 1311 ib (p), 1323 *LMR* (p), *le hauen* 1312 *Anc*, *Le Hauen* 1327 *SR* (p), *la -*, *atte Hafne* 1332 *ib* (p), *at*

Hauen 1338, 1348 *Anc* both (p), *the Haven* 1692 *Em, the Old Haven* 1702 *ib*, 1710 *Foster, v.* **hafn** 'a haven, a harbour'. An alternative name seems to have been *clootam vocat abgristgote* 1411 (*v.* **gotu** 'a sluice' and ME **clote** described in PN C 315-16 as "a fenland term, apparently something to do with draining and barring waters. Its history is obscure"), *coēm sewer voc' abgrift* 1416, *Waterladd vocat' abgrist* 1415 all *LMR* (for *Waterladd, v.* Waterland Drain in Marsh Chapel *supra*), *sewer apud Habgrift* 1438 *Anc, in portu ... voc' abgriste apud North'cotes* 1451-53, *in portu voc' Agrest* 1496-98, - *Halgriste* 1523-24, *port' vocat' Halligriste* 1608 all *MinAcct, Haggrest hauen, Haggriste Crike* 1609 *DuLaMB* (*v.* **crike** (ON **kriki**)). It is very difficult often to distinguish between *s* and *f* in medieval documents and the forms in *MinAcct* and *DuLaMB* have all been read as *s*, though it should be pointed out that five of the six spellings from these sources appear to be corrupt. At least two of the four 15th century forms from *Anc* and *LMR* certainly read *-grift* and there can be little doubt that this is the "correct" form. It is derived from dial. **grift**, a word recorded in EDD s.v. only from north L and said there to mean 'a channel shaped out by water for itself, a runnel', for which *v.* Griff Lane in Fulstow *supra*, where forms from the early 15th century are given. Though *Abgrift* is recorded late, it may be suggested that the first el. is the OE pers.n. *Abba* or ODan *Abbi* (Feilitzen 140, s.n. *Abba*). An *Abo* whose name must be derived from one of these is recorded in DB TRE in Osgodby PN L **3**, 52-53.

CHERRY PARK (local). A modern name given to the estate outside the disused airfield here. THE GRANGE (2x), late example of the use of **grange** in the dial. sense 'a homestead, a small mansion or farm-house, esp. one standing by itself remote from others', recorded in EDD from L. THE HUNDRED ACRES (lost), 1828 Bry; the name of the area on the coast south of the disused airfield. HORSESHOE POINT, self-explanatory. INGS FM, cf. *the Inges* 1577, 1635 *Terrier*, 1659 *Foster*, 1697 *Em, - Ings* 1609 *DuLaMB*, 1689, 1700 *Em, - Inggs* 1695 *ib, Close of pasture called Ings* 1710 *Foster, Mr Boultons Ings* 1710 *ib* (Anthony *Boulton* is named in the same document), *Ings* 1842 *TA, v.* **eng** 'meadow, pasture'. INGS LANE (local), *the Ings Lane* 1692, 1693,

1702 *Em, Ings Road* 1842 *TA.* NORTH BANK (lost), 1710 *Foster,* 1828 Bry, *- banks* 1609 *DuLaMB, the North Banke* 1702 *Em*; it formed the northern boundary with Tetney. NORTH COATES FITTIES, *le Fitz* (sic) 1452-53 *MinAcct, le Fites* 1496-98 *ib, the said Fyttesse or salt marsh* 1609 *DuLaMB, the Fittes* 1692 *Sib, - Fittys* 1789 *Foster, North Coates Fittys* 1775 *Yarb,* cf. *North Fyttes, - Fittize* 1609 *DuLaMB, the North fitties* 1659, 1661 *Foster, North Fyttes, - Fittys* 1775 *Yarb, South Fytts, - Fyttize* 1609 *DuLaMB, the South fitties* 1659 *Foster, - Fitty Lane* 1692, 1693 *Em, Fittes Close* 1842 *TA*; this is a common name in L coastal parishes meaning 'the outlying marsh', on which *v.* PN L 2, 153. OLD FLEET DRAIN, *the Fleet* 1692 *Em, v.* **flēot** in the sense 'a rivulet, a stream' and further the same name in North Thoresby parish *infra.* SEA LANE (local) is *Shore Lane* 1822 *Terrier,* 1842 *TA* and *Sewer Lane* 1828 Bry. SHEEPMARSH LANE (local), *the sheep marsh lane* 1692 *Em, sheepmarsh Lane* 1693 *ib, Sheep Marsh Lane* 1824 O, 1828 Bry, 1842 *TA,* cf. *the Sheep marsh* 1695, 1697, 1700 *Em, Sheep Marsh* 1842 *TA,* self-explanatory. SUMMEREAT LANE (lost), 1842 *TA,* cf. *the someryt* 1609 *DuLaMB, Sumereate* 1697 *Em, Sumer Eate* 1700 *ib, the Sumered* 1625 *Terrier, ye Comon pasture called Summered* 1635 *ib, Far -, First -, Fold Summereat* 1842 *TA, the Lowe Summer head* 1700, *- low Somereate* 1695, *- Summerhead* 1689, *the Summerhead Close* 1688, *- Summer head close* 1700, *Somered Close* 1689, 1692, 1693 all *Em,* 'the summer pasture', *v.* **sumor**, **ete** and cf. *Outdwellers pay 8 p Ac' Tith for* y^e *bad low Grounds* w^n *they summer-eat 'em* 1745, *Outdwellers pay eight Pence per Acre for the bad Low Grounds when they Summeat them* 1762 both *Terrier.* EDD records *summer-eat* as a verb 'to use land as summer pasture', cf. Summer-eaten Marsh in Habrough f.ns. (a) PN L 2, 142-43 and Kirk Summer eater Carr in Bonby f.ns. (a) PN L 2, 59. *Summereat Lane* was the name of the road from Thoresby Bridge towards the village and *Summereat* the area east of Louth Navigation and south of the lane. The same name occurs as *Summerhead* in Marsh Chapel *supra,* where earlier forms are given. THORESBY BRIDGE, on the boundary with North Thoresby *infra.* TUTTLE DRAIN, *Tuttle Crike* 1775 *Yarb* and cf. *Tuttyll haven* 1609 *DuLaMB, v.* **crike**, ON **kriki** and **hafn**. It is tempting to take *Tuttle* as a common shortened form of *Toothill,* 'look-out hill', *v.* **tōt-hyll**, cf. Tottle Brook PN Nt 9. Early forms are needed, of course, to confirm this suggestion. The site of the hill is not evident.

Field-Names

Principal forms in (a) are 1842 *TA*. Forms dated 1256 are FF; 1276 RH; 1311, 1312, 1338, 1348 *Anc*; 1321 Pat; 1352 AASR xxiii; 1451-3, 1475-7, 1496-8, 1523-4, 1535-46, 1546-7, 1576-7, 1597-8, 1608-9, 1613-15 *MinAcct*; 1529 Wills ii; 1577, 1625, 1635, 1664, 1679, 1686, 1690, 1697, 1745, 1762[1], 1822 *Terrier*; 1609 *DuLaMB*; c.1651 *LindDep 35*; 1659, 1661, 1671, 1710, 1729, 1760, 1762[2], 1771, 1789 *Foster*; 1685, 1688, 1689, 1692, 1693, 1695, 1697, 1700, 1702 *Em*; 1719 *NW*; 1765, 1766, 1769, 1774, 1796 *Yarb*.

(a) Barn Cl 1796, 1842; Brick Yd; Brown Cl 1796, 1842 (named from the *Brown(e)* family, cf. William *Brun* 1312 *Anc*, Robert *Brown* 1332 *SR*, William *Brown* 1561 *BT*); Bullen Hill 1770, 1796, Great and Little Bulling Hill 1842; Church Road 1822; Coble Cl (cf. *Cobblecoates* 1693, *Cobblecoats, Cobblecoat Hill* 1695, *Cobblecoate hill* 1697, *Cobblecoat*, *Cobble coat Hill* 1700, *v*. **cot** 'a cottage, a shed'; *Cobble* is perhaps *cobble* 'a small stone', denoting a shed or sheds built of small stones); Coney Hill ('rabbit hill', *v*. **coni**, **hyll**, cf. *that holme called Conygarth* 1659, 1661, *v*. **coni**, **garðr**); Corn Cl (cf. *the corne holmes* 1577, *Corneholmhill* 1609 (*v*. **corn**, **holmr**, with **hyll**), *the Corne feild* 1609, *the Corne field* 1625, *v*. **corn**, **feld**); Cow Cl (3x) (*the Cow close* 1700); Daniel Holme (*Daniell-holme* 1719, from the pers.n. or surn. *Daniel* and **holmr**); Downs; East Yd; Eatage Cl ('land which may be grazed after the hay has been cut'); Eleven Acres 1789, - 1842 (several); five Closes called Etts's 1762[1], two closes of Pasture called Etches 1789, (Far -, First) Etts (*the Ette pasture* 1577, *the long Ett* 1659; *Etts* is no doubt from OE **ete** 'pasture' as in *Summereat Lane supra*); Far Cl 1796, - 1842 (several); Field Cl 1760, 1762[2], 1842 (*the field* 1659, *the feild* 1661, *y[e] feild* 1664, *the Feild Close* 1689, *the Field Close* 1695, 1700, *the field close* 1697, *Feild Close* 1710, *v*. **feld**, **clos(e)**); Fifteen Acres (*the Fifteen Acres* 1671); Fittes Cl; Fittie Cl (cf. *M[r] Dales fitty Land* 1692, - *Fitty Land* 1693, *the Fitty Land* 1695, - *Lands* 1697, (*Close of pasture called*) *the Fitty Lands* 1700, 1702, cf. North Coates Fitties *supra*); Five Acres (several); Fold Cl 1770, 1796, Far -, First fold 1842; Fore Cl 1765, 1760, 1769, 1774 (*v*. **fore** 'in front', **clos(e)**); First -, Far -, River Foth (*the Fyrth* 1577, *the Forth* 1609, 1609, 1695, 1697, 1700, *a pastur called Fyrth* 1625, *the Furth* 1635, *a Close called the forth* 1680, *the Forths* (sic) 1702, 1725, *Close of pasture* ...

called ... a Firth 1710; this is from ME *frith* (from OE **fyhrðe**) here probably 'a park, a woodland meadow', *v.* MED s.v. *frith* (2) or 'a wood, plantation, coppice', 'unused pastureland', *v.* EDD s.v. *firth.* Cf. Little Firth in Cabourne f.ns. (a) *supra*); Four Acres (several); Fourteen Acres (2x); Glebe; Gout Holme (*the Goat home Close, - home bottome* 1680, *- Home Bottom* 1700, *Goateholme* 1695, *Goate Holme* 1697, *Goat -* 1700, *v.* **gotu** 'a sluice', **holmr**, with **botm** in some forms); Great Hill; Gursby Hill; Half Acre; Haven Eight Acres, Haven Ings (*v.* **eng** and cf. *le hauenmotes* (sic) 1311 and *Haven supra*; *-motes* is the pl. of ME *mōte* (OFr *mote*, MLat *mota* 'a natural or man-made mound; a defensive ditch, moat, fosse; boundary ditch; drainage ditch')); Hedge Acres, - Cl; Hill and Bottom (*v.* **botm**), Hills (*the Hill* 1702, *v.* **hyll** and cf. Little Hill *infra*); Holme (*Le Holme* 1311, *the Holme* 1695, *v.* **holmr** 'an island of land, raised land in marsh' as elsewhere in the parish, and cf. its use as an appellative in *unum Holme* 1336); Home Cl, - Six Acres (*the Great home Close* 1689); the Homestead 1789; Horsestep Cl 1765, 1766, 1769, 1774, Horse Step Cl 1796, 1842 (alluding to the small platform used in mounting a horse); House Cl; Intake (*the Intake* 1700, *- Intack* 1710), Intake Common (*v.* **inntak**; this is on the boundary with Tetney); Itlings (*Lyttyll Etlyng* 1529, *the great -, the litle Etlin* 1659, *ye eatlin* 1695, *Ittling* 1702, *All that close of pasture ... called Ickling* 1710); Ivory Hill (cf. *Ibray holme* (sic) 1609, *the Iveryholme* 1695, *Ivery Holme* 1700, named from the family of John *Ibrey* 1658 *BT* and **holmr**); Lane Cl 1771 (*le Lain Close* 1729); Levy Cl; Little Garth (*v.* **garðr**); Little Hill (*the little Hill Close* 1710); Long Haines; Low Cl; Meadow Cl; Mill Cl (Bank) (*the Mill banke* 1692, *the mill -* 1693, cf. *le Mylnehill'* 1546-7, *v.* **myln, hyll**); Gt & Lt Nabs (*v.* **nabbi**); close of pasture called the new Inclosed Ground 1760, the New Inclosed Ground 1762[2]; Newton Holts (presumably named from the family of Anthony *Newton* 1596 *BT* and **holt**); Nine Acres; North Coates Bank 1775 (cf. *ripa de Northcote* 1276, *the old sea bancke* 1609, *the Sea banke* 1702, *- Banke* 1710), North Coates Clow 1775 (*v.* **clōh** 'a clough'), North Coates -, North Cotes Marsh 1796, Marsh 1842 (cf. *Marisco* 1312 (p), *in marisco, in maresco* 1338, *Marsh Garth* 1700, *v.* **mersc, garðr**); North Cotes Sands 1767 LNQ ii (*sabulum Regis de Northcotes* 1451-53, *Sabulum' R' de North-cotes* 1496-98, *ȝabulum Regis in Northcotes, ȝabulum ... in Northcotes* 1546-47, 'the king's sand in North Coates', *v.* **sand**); Oldcroft 1760, 1762[2], old Crofts 1789, Far -, First Old Croft 1842 (*the old Crofts* 1609, *oldcroft close* 1697, *Old Croft Close* 1700, *Oldecroft* 1710, *v.* **ald, croft**); Onhill (it is next to Hill(s)) (*the one Hill* 1695, *- hill* 1697, *- One Hill* 1700, *v.* **ān** 'single', **hyll**); Onset Yard, Back Onset (*the yarde or onsett* 1625, *the Onsett* 1659, 1679, 1690, *The -* 1697, from dial. *onset* 'the dwelling house and outbuildings' (NED), some quotations also suggesting an approximate equivalence to 'home close' or 'in-field' as well, cf.

Adams 155); Open Salt Marsh (now part of the disused airfield); paddison Cl 1760, Paddison - 1762[1] (*Paddisons garth* 1710, named from the *Paddison* family, cf. Thomas *Paddyson* 1631 *BT*); Parsonage Cl 1842, The Parsonage House or rather one Cottage 1762, one thatched Dwelling House 1822 (*the parsonidg howse* 1635, *ye parsonage house* 1664, *the Rectorie house* 1679, *One Parsonage house* 1686, 1690, *The Parsonage house* 1697, *No Parsonage House save one small Cottage* 1745); Parson's Holm 1762[1], - Holme 1822 (*the Parsonage Holme* 1690, 1697, 1710, - *holme* 1702, *Parson's Holm* 1745, *v.* **persoun**, **holmr**); Pinfold Pitts (*v.* **pynd-fald**, **pytt**); Pingle (several) (*the pingle* 1671, 1695, - *Pingle* 1685, *Close of pasture commonly called a Pingle* 1710, *v.* **pingel**); Pits (*the pytts* 1609, *the Common called Pitts* 1710, *v.* **pytt**); Pudding Polk ('land with soft, sticky soil', cf. Pudding Poke, PN Db 297, 757 and Pudding Poke Nooking, in Tealby f.ns. (a), PN L **3** 145); Quaker Cl 1770; Rector's Garth, the Rector's Cl 1822 (cf. Parsonage Cl *supra*); Sallow Ings (*v.* **eng**; the first el. is ME *salou(e)* 'a tree or shrub of the genus *salix* 'a willow", from OE **salh**); Sea Cl; Seed Pce; Seventeen Acres; First of Seventy Acres; Six Acres (*a Six acre Close* 1710); Sixteen Acres (*the Sixteen acres feild close* 1702, *Sixteen acres Close* 1710); Small Drain Bottom (*v.* **botm**); Smiths Hills (named from the *Smith* family, cf. Thomas *Smythe* 1565 *BT*, Christopher *Smyth* 1658 *Foster*); Stephen Croft (*Stephencroft* 1695, 1697, from the pers.n. or surn. *Stephen*, with **croft**); Suckcroft (1700, *south Crofte, South Crafts* 1609, *the Southcroft* 1659, *two Suckcroft Closes* 1692, *Suckcroft Close* 1693, *the Snekcroft* (sic) 1695, *Soecroft* (sic) 1695, 1697, *Soecroft als Suckcroft* 1700, *v.* **sūð, croft**); Summerings (*v.* **sumor, eng**); Suttle Nooking (cf. *Southull'* 1475-7, *v.* **sūð**, **hyll** and for the development, cf. Tuttle Drain *supra*); Swans Nest Cl 1770; (Little) Ten Acres; Three Acres (several) (cf. *three acre hill close* 1689, *the three Acres Hill* 1695, - *acres hill* 1697, (*The*) *Three Acres Hill*, - *Acre hill Close* 1700); Twelve Acres; Twenty Acres; Two Acres; Waggon Yd; Walk (3x) (*v.* **walk**); Waltham Lane (*Wattams lane* 1710, leading to Waltham *infra*); Wash Dyke Pits; G^t^ Welsh Cl 1796, Welsh Cl 1842; West Crews (dial. *crew* 'a hut, a shed, a cabin').

(b) *Askough holme* 1659, 1661 (named from the *Ayscough* family, who held land here 1685, *v. NW* 1/9/5, with **holmr**); *Bailey Grasse Close of pasture* 1692, *Bayly Grasse* 1695, *Bayly* - 1697, - *grasse* 1700, *Baylisse grasse* (sic) 1702, *Close of pasture called Bayly Grasse* 1710 (from **baillie** 'a bailiff, a steward' or the derived surn., with **gærs**); *lands called Bottoms* 1609 (*v.* **botm**); *Boyers Farm & Late Hinds* 1671 (from surnames not noted in the sources searched); *the Bradercroft* 1695, *Brather Croft* 1702, *Brather Croft* 1710 (from the surn. *Brather* with **croft**; the surn. is common in the parish; William *Brather* is named in the

1710 document and cf. Thomas *Brather* 1562 *BT*); *the Brickhouse Farme* 1688, *the Bricke house* - 1695, *the Brick house* - 1700 (self-explanatory); *Catholme* 1523-4, *Cattelholme* (sic) 1546-7 (*v.* **catt**, **holmr**); *the church gren* (sic) 1577 (*v.* **grēne**[2]); *Clerk Garth* 1689, *Clerkes Garth* 1700, *Clarkes garth* 1702, *Clarke* - 1710 (from the surn. *Clarke*, cf. Thomas *clarke* 1570 *BT*, with **garðr**); *pasture ... voc' Close* 1609 (*v.* **clos(e)**); *Cokhill* 1321; *the Cow hill Close* 1689; *Cracroft Hills* 1700 (named from the family of William *Cracroft* 1663 *BT*); *Danceholme Barrs* c.1651 (may be in North Thoresby); *Danma'r'ke Creike* 1609; *the Eight acres Ings* 1702, 1710 (*v.* **eng**); *the feild lane* 1679, *ye Field lane* 1745, *the feild Laneyate* 1692, *the Feild Lane gate* 1693 (*v.* **feld** and cf. Field Cl in (a) *supra*); *Fisshe Holme* 1523-4, *Fissheholme* 1546-7 (*v.* **holmr**; *Fisshe* is presumably a surn.); *the five acres Ings* 1710 (*v.* **eng**, cf. Ings Fm *supra*); *Forlang* 1348 (*v.* **furlang**); *Forth'garth* 1451-3, 1496-8, *Forthgarth* 1523-4, *Frothergarth* (sic) 1609 (*v.* **garðr** and cf. First Foth in (a) *supra*); *the fourteen acres Ings* 1710 (*v.* **eng**); *terra Co'i de ... vasto vocat' le Grene* 1523-4 (*v.* **grēne**[2]); *Grissell Close* 1692, - *close* 1693, *Greizelyholme* (sic) 1695, 1697, *Grizley Holme* 1700 (*v.* **holmr**); *Harneis pasture* 1659 (presumably from a surn., though no such has been noted in the sources searched); *messuagii voc' Hemynglande* 1535-6, *messuag' ... vocat' Heninglande in Northcotes* 1576-7, *mes' ... voc' Hemingland'* 1597-8, *mes' voc' ... Heningland* 1613-15 (probably from the surn. *Heming* and **land**); *the horne* 1659 (*v.* **horn**); *Ingam well* 1625, *little Ingam well* 1635, *Ingham well* c.1651 (presumably from the surn. *Ingham*); *Ioneyhouse* (sic) 1695; *Jeckylls Three Acre Close* 1710 (named from the *Jekyll* family, cf. Samuel *Jekill* 1657 *BT*, Clement *Gikell* 1660 *ib*); *Kiddalls garth* 1710 (named from the *Kiddall* family, cf. William *Kiddall* 1672 *BT*, 1689 *Em*); *terr' voc' Kirkby* 1608-9; *Kirmond Holme* 1702, *Kirkman Holme or Kirkmond Holme* 1710 (probably from the surn. *Kirmond* with **holmr**); *close called Kytchen Chose* (sic) 1609; *Locking garth* 1659 (named from the *Locking* family, cf. John *Locking* 1561 *BT*, with **garðr**); *the two low Hills* 1695; *the Lowe Walk* 1700 (*v.* **walk**); *Marshall Garths* 1692, - *Garthes* 1693, - *garth* 1697, 1702, *Marshall garth* 1710 (named from the *Marshall* family, cf. William *Marshall* 1640 *BT*, with **garðr**); *Martin Pingle* 1659, 1661 (named from the *Martin* family, cf. John *Martin* 1609 *BT*, with **pingel**); *mate hole* 1659; *the Mottams* 1695, 1697, 1700, *Mottoms* 1702 (obscure); *New dike* 1692, *the Newdike* 1693 (self-explanatory); *Northegarthe al' dict' le Halegarthe* 1546-7 (*v.* **norð**, **garðr**); *North marsh* 1609; *Outsandes* 1451-3, 1523-4, *Outescordes* (sic) 1475-7, *Outesandes* 1496-8 (*v.* **ūt**, **sand** and cf. North Cotes Sands in (a) *supra*); *Oxholme* 1609 (*v.* **oxa**, **holmr**); *the Platch* 1609 (obscure, though it may be connected with (Scots) dial. *platch* 'to splash, to besmear'); *the Rushings* 1695 (*v.* **rysc**, **eng**); *uno Saltcot* 1338, *une Saltcote en le more* (sic) 1352, *the Salt coates* 1609, *a Salt Coate holme* 1609 (from **sealt**, **cot**, with **holmr**; this is no doubt the name of a saltern or salt-hill, discussed in detail under *Cawthernsome Lane* in Marsh Chapel *supra*. It is certainly possible too that other names in *-holme* in this parish denoted salterns, though there is no documentary evidence so far noted to confirm it); *the salt marshe* 1659, *-Marshe* 1661 (cf. North Coates Marsh in f.ns. (a) *supra*); *Sandhull* 1451-3, 1496-8, *Sandehyl'* 1523-4 (*v.* **sand**, **hyll**); *the seavenacres* 1693; *le sedikes* 1311 (*v.* **dīc**); *the seven acres Ings* 1710 (*v.* **eng**); *Seuenestang* 1256 (*v.* **seofon**, **stǫng** 'a pole, a measurement of land'); *Seven Croft* 1700 (*v.* **croft**); *Shedys marsh* 1625, 1635 (the first el. is probably a surn.); *the sheepes Common* 1609; *shepe Coate holme* 1609 (*v.* **scēap**, **cot**, with **holmr**); *Shepenmersshe* 1546-7 (from ME *shipen(e)*, *shepen(n)* 'a cattle shed, a shelter or shed for sheep' and **mersc** 'a marsh'); *Sisholme* 1451-3, 1475-7, 1496-8 (Dr J. Insley suggests that the first el. is probably ME *sīche* (OE **sīc**) 'a stream, usually a small one; a ditch, trench', with *s* for *ch*, perhaps the result of French influence; the second is **holmr**); *Six acres Ings* 1710 (*v.* **eng**); *smale dale end* 1609, 1635, *the Smal dayle end* 1625, *Northcotes small Dale* c.1651 (*v.* **smæl** 'narrow', **deill**); *the South holmes* 1609 (*v.* **sūð**, **holmr**); *Styward holm* 1256 (*v.* **holmr**); *the thirteen Acres close* 1695; *Thirteen acres Ings, the Thirteen acres Inns* (sic) 1710 (*v.* **eng**); *Thirty acres Ings* 1710 (*v.* **eng**); *the litle three leas* 1659 (*v.* **lea** 'meadow, pasture' (OE **lēah**)); *the Upholme* 1695 (*v.* **up(p)** 'higher up', **holmr**); *Wast Holme* 1700 (*v.* **weste**, **holmr**); *Mr Welfitts Rush Ickling* 1710 (cf. Ittlings in (a) *supra*); *Westcroft* 1702, 1710 (*v.* **west**, **croft**); *one Wyndmyll* 1609.

East Ravendale

RAVENDALE

Ravenedal (2x), *-dale* 1086 DB, *Rauendal* 1086 ib, "the other" *Ravenedale* 1086 ib

Ravendale 1086 DB, 1202 (1342) Pat, 1210-12 RBE, 1212, 1242-43 Fees, 1275 Pat, 1276 RH, 1281 QW, 1310 Cl, 1314 Ch *et passim* to 1610 Speed, *-dala* c.1115 LS, 1314 Ch, *Rauendala* 1185 Templar, 1202 *HarlCh*, 1204 *AddCh*, 1374, 1375, 1395 Peace, 1439 *Cragg*, 1576 Saxton, *-dal(')* 1235 IB, 1246 RRG, 1257 FF

Rauenesdal' 1196 ChancR, *-dale* 1295 Pat, *Ravensdal* 1249 RRG, *-dale* 1340 Cl

Raffenesdal' 1196 Cur

Rauuedall' 1382 Peace

Randall 1535 VE iv, 1539-40 Dugd iv

Raindall 1675 Ogilby

Forms without affixes have been collected together for convenience.

This is almost certainly a Scand. compound of **hrafn** and **dalr** 'ravens' valley', though the first el. could formally be the cognate OE **hræfn**. A local pronunciation, still sometimes heard, is reflected in the form *Randall*, noted from the early 16th century.

EAST RAVENDALE

Est Ravendale 1238-41 Fees, 1303, 1316, 1346 FA, 1275 RH, 1428 FA, - *Ravendal* 1276 RH, 1303 FA, - *Rauendale* 1374 Peace, - *Ravendall* 1402 FA, *Estravendale* 1242-43 Fees, 1291 Tax, 1347 Cl, 1365 Pat, *-ravendal'* 1254 ValNor, *-rauendale* 1272 *Ass*, 1327, 1332 *SR*

Est Randall 1519 DV i, *East* - 1652 *Rad*, 1653 WillsPCC, 1679 *Terrier*, - *Randal* 1723 SDL, - *Randale* 1697, 1703, 1706 *Terrier*

Estrandell 1526 Sub, *-randall* 1530 Wills iii, 1535 VE iv, a1567 LNQ v, 1576 LER

Estwandall alias Estrendalle LP xiv, - *alias Estrendall* 1569 Pat

East Ravendale 1822 *Terrier*, - *otherwise Great Ravendale* 1842 *TA*

It is *East* in contrast to the adjoining parish of *West* Ravendale.

AVENUE PLANTATION. BARTON STREET, - *streete* 1652 *Rad*, as elsewhere in this Wapentake. BROWNLOW'S BOTTOM PLANTATION, named from the *Brownlow* family, cf. Charles *Brownlow* 1842 White. COLLEGE FM, - *F^m^* 1828 Bry, commemorating the holdings here of Trinity College, Cambridge. CORNER PLANTATION. EAST RAVENDALE HALL, *Hall* 1828 Bry. EAST RAVENDALE PARK, cf. *the parke close* 1630 *DC*, *the parks* 1758, - *Parks* 1773, *Parks* 1864 all *BPLeases*. HOME HILL (lost, approx. TF 235 996), 1828 Bry. LEG OF

MUTTON PLANTATION, so-named from its shape. MOUNT GATE PLANTATION. OLD BRATS PLANTATION. *Brat* is common in north L and is from ON **brot** 'a small piece of land'. PETTERHILLS, *Pettrill* 1772 *Yarb, Petters Hills* 1824 O, obscure. RAVENDALE FIELD PLANTATION, cf. *campum de Est Ravindal* 1276 RH, *Randall feeld* 1638 *Terrier* (Hawerby), *Ravendale Field* 1824 O. SANDPIT PLANTATION. There is a Sand Pit adjacent to the plantation. TARGET PLANTATION. VICARAGE.

Field-Names

Undated forms in (a) are 1842 *TA*; spellings dated 1276 are RH; 1327, 1332 *SR*; 1415, 1575-6, 1614 ChronLP; 1535-46, 1613-15 *MinAcct*; 1536-7 Dugd v; 1539 LP xiv, i, 1570 Pat, 1605 LNQ x; 1609 *Foster*, 1652 *Rad.*

(a) Allotment; Church & Church Yd (cf. *the Church Close* 1652); Kitchen Gdn; Plantation; Pleasure Grds; Pond; School and Gdn; Stack garth.

(b) *Badmore Ings* 1652 (*v.* **mōr, eng**); *the Cow Close* 1652; *The Croftis* 1327, *the Croftes* 1332 both (p) (*v.* **croft**); *the East feild of Randall* 1652 (*v.* **ēast, feld**); "the Grange of" *Louthepark in Estravendale* 1415, *Estwandell Grange* 1535-6, *Estwandall graunge* 1535-46, *Est Wandall - Firma grangiæ* 1536-7, *Estwandalle grange* (sic) 1539, *Estwandall Grange alias Estrandall Grange* 1570, *East Randall grange* 1605, *east Randall' als East Randall' Graunge, Eastwandall Grang' seu Estrondall Grang'* 1609, *Eastrandall Grange* 1613-15, *Estrandell* - 1614 (*v.* **grange**; East Ravendale Grange was formerly a grange of Louth Park Abbey); *warennam in Ravendale* 1276 (*v.* **wareine**); *the Longe Close* 1652; *Long Furlong* 1652 (*v.* **lang, furlang**); *Mill hill* 1652; *Newton bottom* 1652 (*v.* **botm**; *Newton* refers to Wold Newton, a neighbouring parish); *Peach hill Lees* 1652; *Randall-hill* 1652; *a place called Wooddall, Wooddall bottom* 1652 (*v.* **wudu, dalr** with **botm**).

West Ravendale

WEST RAVENDALE

West Rauendale 1202 *HarlCh*, 1299 *Cragg*, 1327 *SR*, *-dal* 1347 *Cor*, *- Ravendale* 1202 (1342) Pat, 1221 LAHW, 1238-41

Fees, 1241 RRG, 1291 Tax, 1303 AD, 1306 Pat, 1316 FA, 1349 Fine, 1374 Pat, 1428 FA *et passim*, *-dal'* 1276 RH, 1279 RRGr, *-dall* 1402 FA, *Westravendale* 1219 Welles, 1283, 1288, 1298 RSu, 1332 *SR*, 1361, 1364 Cl, *-dal'* a1221 Welles, 1254 ValNor, 1279 RRGr

West Rauenesdal' 1262 RRGr

Westrandale 1386 Peace

Westrandell 1526 Sub

Westrandall (*alias Prior Allyns Graunge*) 1553 Pat, 1561 ib, a1567 LNQ *v. West Randall* 1535 VE iv, 1548 Pat, 1743 *BPLeases*, (*alias West Ravendall*) 1744 *ib*, (*alias West Ravendale*) 1788 *et passim* to 1842 *ib*, *West Randal* 1723 SDL

It is *West* in contrast to the adjoining parish of East Ravendale.

BEACON HOLT, 1828 Bry and is *Bacon Holt* 1824 O. THE GREAT WALK (lost), 1828 Bry; it is the name of the area south of Ravendale Priory and east to the boundary with East Ravendale. RAVENDALE PRIORY, commemorating the Premonstratensian Priory here. RAVENDALE TOP is *Little Ravendale F.m* 1828 Bry. SHEPHERDS HO (lost, TF 226 989), 1828 ib. WEST RAVENDALE VALLEY.

Field-Names

Forms dated 1630 are *DC*; 1744, 1758, 1773, 1779, 1788, 1800, 1802, 1810, 1814. 1816, 1821, 1823, 1830, 1835, 1842, 1844, 1864 *BTLeases*.

(a) the Bottam Cl 1773, 1788, the Bottom - 1802, 1816, 1823, 1844, Bottom - 1864 (*the Bottom close* 1630, - *Close* 1744, *v.* **botm**); Bracken Hills 1779, 1800, 1814, 1821, 1835, 1842 (*Bracken hills* 1744, cf. *The Brachenhill close* (sic) 1630, *v.* **brakni**, **hyll**); Great -, Little Burlands 1779, Great -, Little - 1800, the Great -, the Little - 1814, 1821, 1835, 1842 (*The East -, The middle -, The west Burlands* 1630, *Great -, little Burlands* 1744); Calf Cl 1864 (*The greate -, the little calfe close* 1630); Chappell Cl 1773, 1788, 1802, Chapel - 1816, Chapell - 1823, 1844, Chappel Cl 1864 (*The Chappell close* 1630, *Chappel Close* 1744); Far Fd 1864; the Field Walk 1773, 1788, 1802, 1816, - field walk 1823, 1844 (*v.*

walk, denoting land used for the pasture of animals, especially sheep, hence the common *Sheepwalk*); Far -, Near Hatcliffe Walk 1864 (named from the neighbouring parish of Hatcliffe, *v.* **walk**); the Holm Hill 1773, 1802, the Holme - 1788, 1816, 1823, 1844, Holme - 1864 (*The home hill close* 1630, *the Holme Hill* 1744, *v.* **holmr**, confused with ModE *home* in 1630); Homestead Cl 1864; the Ings 1779, 1800, 1814, 1821, 1835, 1842 (*the Ings* 1744, cf. *The greate Ings close, The little Ings* (sic) 1630, *v.* **eng** 'meadow, pasture', in the pl.); Markitt Hill 1773, 1788, 1802, Market Hill 1816, 1823, 1844, 1864 (1744); that Mill Fd 1773, Mill Fd 1788, 1802, 1816, 1823, 1844 (*the Millne feild* 1630, *Mill Field* 1744); Far -, Middle -, Near Newlands 1864 (*v.* **niwe, land**); New Walk 1864 (*v.* **walk**); The Oat Cl 1773, 1788, 1802, 1816, 1823, Oat Cl 1864 (*The oate close* 1630, *the Oat Close* 1744), First -, Second Oat Walk 1864 (*v.* **walk**); Pear Tree Cl 1773, 1788, Peatreee - 1802, Pear tree - 1816, - Tree cl 1823, 1844 (*The Peare tree close* 1630, *Pear Tree Close* 1744); Pingles 1864 (*v.* **pingel**); the Plow'd Fd 1773, 1788, 1816, 1823, 1844 (*the Plow'd Field* 1744); Walk ... called Sandfields 1779, 1800, 1814, 1821, 1835, 1842 (*Walk ... called Sandfeilds* 1744, *v.* **sand, feld**); the Thorn Cl 1773, 1788, 1802, Thorn Cl 1816, 1823, 1844 (*The Thorne close* 1630, *Thorn Close* 1744); Tup Cl 1773, 1788, 1802, the - 1816, 1823, 1844 (*the Tup Close* 1744, *v.* **tup** 'a ram'); the two Pit fd 1773, - Two pit Fd 1788, - Two Pit Fd 1802, 1816, - Two pitt fd 1823, Two Pitt Fd 1844 (*The two pitt feild* (sic) 1630, *the Two pit Field* 1744, *v.* **pytt**); West Walk 1758, 1772, 1778, 1802, 1810, 1823, 1830, 1844 (*v.* **west, walk**).

(b) *Blueston feild* 1630 (*bluestone* is copper sulphate); *The midlefeild* 1630; *The reod feild* (sic) 1630; *The South feild* 1630 (*v.* **sūð, feld**, described as *an open Sheep pasture*); *The west feild* 1630 (*v.* **west, feld**).

Rothwell

ROTHWELL

Rodowelle (2x) 1086 DB (*Rodeuuelle, Rodewelle* 1086 *Domesday Abbrevatio* (PRO E36/284))

Rothewelle (4x) 1086 DB, c.1155 Dane, *-wella* (4x) LS, c.1150, 1160-66 Dane, Hy2 (1409) Gilb, lHy2 (m13) *NCot, -well* R1 (1318) Ch

Rodwell eHy2 Dugd vi, Hy2 (1409) Gilb, 1535 VE v, *-wella* 1187 (1409) Gilb

Rowella 1130 P (p), eHy2 Dane, eHy2, Hy2 ib (p), a1180 (e13) *NCot* (p), lHy2 Dane, 1186-1200 ib,

-wellia m12, l12 Dugd vi, *-wel* 1166 RBE (p), *-well(')* Hy2 LN (p), 1180, 1181, 1182 P all (p), 1184-89 RA iv, 1191-95 ib i (p), 1196-99 ib ii (p), 1197, 1198, 1199 P (p), 1201 Cur (p) *et passim* to 1261 Cl, - *iuxta Thuancastr'* 1289 *Ass*, *-welle* l12 Dane, c.1200 RA iv, 1202 FF (p), 1203-6 RA i, 1242-43 Fees, 1304 Ipm, *Rouuelle* l12 (15) Whit

Roeuuel 1157-63 Dane (p), *Rouhewell'* c.1170 (13) *Kirk*, *Rohewell'* lHy2 (e13) *NCot*, *Rouwell(')* 1212 Fees, 1272 Dugd vi, 1282 Ipm

Rothewella Hy2 (1409) Gilb, *-welle* 1297 Pat, 1304 Ch, 1312 Pat, 1316 FA, 1386 Peace, *-well(')* 1272 *Ass*, 1291 Tax, 1303 Pat, 1303 FA, 1304 Fine, 1304 Orig, 1305 Misc, 1327, 1332 *SR*, 1335 Pat *et freq* to 1576 LER, *-uel* 1350 Ipm, 1350 Fine

Rothwelle c.1250 (1409) Gilb, *-welle* 1540 Whit, 1547 *MinAcct*, *-well* 1428 FA, 1491 Ipm, 1526 Sub, 1535 VE iv, 1557 InstBen, a1567 LNQ v, 1581 *Dixon*, 1587 *Yarb et passim*

Routhewel 1275 RH, *Routhewell* 1276 ib, *Rowthwell* 1539 LP xiv

The forms above exactly parallel those for Rothwell, PN Nth 118-9, and Rothwell, PN YW 2 143-44. All three names mean 'the spring in or by the clearing', *v.* **rōð**, **wella**, as first suggested by Ekwall, DEPN s.n. Rothley. The beck which flows through the village rises from a spring to the south. The persistent early spellings in *Rowell* etc. show AN loss of the medial *-the-*, as pointed out in PN YW, and the persistent *Rothe-* forms indicate that the first element has *-ō-*, subsequently shortened. The spellings in *Routh(e)-*, also paralleled in both the Northamptonshire and West Riding names, are late and have no significance.

BECKSIDE (local), cf. *the becke* 1577, 1606, *ye Becke* 1721 all *Terrier*, *ye Beck* 1719 Hungate, *the* - 1767 *EnclA*, *Rothwell Beck* 1815 *Dixon*, *the Becke* 1864 *Terrier*, *the Beake* 1587 *Yarb*, *the beecks* 1611 *Terrier* and *Beck hyll* 1577, *Beckehill* 1606, *Beckhill* 1611, *Beckehill* 1625, *beckhil* 1638 all *ib*, *v.* **bekkr**; it is also referred to as *the common suer* 1611, *Common Suer* 1626, *comon Sure* 1638 all *Terrier*. HIGH STREET, *the heighe Strete* 1577, - *high streete* 1606, *the strete* 1611, *-streete* 1625, - *Street* 1638, - *street* 1679, *ye street* 1721 all *Terrier*; this is the name of the ancient ridgeway from Horncastle to Caistor, known as Middlegate Lane northwards from Caistor to South Ferriby. LINGS FM, cf. *Lynge Styght* 1577, *ling stigh* 1606, 1638, *-stigh* 1611, - *Stigh* 1625, *Linge street* 1721 all *Terrier*, *the Lings* 1767 *EnclA*, *The* - 1831 *Brad*; the earlier forms are from **lyng** 'heather' and **stīg**, **stígr** 'a path' and for forms in *Styght* cf. *Kyrk Styghe* in f.ns. (b) *infra*. NICKERSON ARMS (local), is *Horse Shoes* 1828 Bry and later *Blacksmiths' Arms* 1842 White. The modern name is from Sir Joseph *Nickerson*, founder of the Nickerson Group of Companies in Rothwell. THE OLD RECTORY (local), cf. *the parsonage house* 1606, - *Parsonage house, the Scite or Homestead of the Rectory* 1686, *The Parsonage house* 1679, 1690, 1721, *y^e^* - 1703 all *Terrier*, *Pars.^e^* 1828 Bry. ROTHWELL FM is *Rothwell Lodge* 1824 O and is now CHERRY VALLEY FM. ROTHWELL GRANGE, 1828 Bry; this appears to be a later example of **grange**, for which *v.* EDD s.v. 2 'a homestead, small mansion house, esp. one standing by itself remote from others', a sense quoted from L. ROTHWELL STACKGARTH, cf. *The Stackgarth Field* 1864 *Terrier*, *v.* **stakgarth** (ON **stakkr**, **garðr**) 'the stack-yard', on which *v.* NED s.v. *stack-garth*. It was earlier *Scarboroughs Top F.^m^* 1828 Bry, presumably from the surn. *Scarborough*. ROTHWELL COVER, cf. *Rothwell Top Cover* 1828 O.

Field-Names

Forms dated 112 (13) are *Alv*; c.1200 RA iv; 1332 *SR*; 1349 Ipm, 1386 Peace; 1465, 1815 *Dixon*; 1577, 1606, 1611, 1625, 1638, 1679, 1686, 1690, 1703, 1706, 1721, 1864 *Terrier*, 1587, 1805, c.1830, 1832 *Yarb*; 1636 *Rad*; 1680 *MiscDon 158*; 1767 *EnclA*; 1831 *Brad*.

(a) Barn Cl 1864; William Bells Cl Corner 1767; Blacklands c.1830, Black Lands 1832 (*v.* **blæc**, **land**); The Upr -, The Lr Bledgnall 1831 (cf. *great bleybur* 1577, *Blaybour* 1606, *Bleybor* 1611, *furlong called great Bley bour* 1625, *great bleyber* 1638, *Blegbrough* (sic) 1679, *Great Blegbrough* (sic) 1721, but both the connection and the sense are obscure); Cabourn Corner c.1830, 1832 (cf.

Caborne mear 1577, - *meare* 1606, 1611, *caborne* - 1625, *Caborn* - 1638, *Caburn Meere* 1721, *v.* **(ge)mǣre** 'a boundary, land on a boundary', as elsewhere in the parish), Cabourne Hill 1864 (*Caborne Hyll* 1577, *Caborne hill* 1606, 1625, *caborne* - 1611, *Caborn* - 1638, *Caborne Hill* 1721, *v.* **hyll**), the Cabourn Rd 1767 (referring to the neighbouring parish of Cabourne); the Caistor Rd 1767, Caistor Rd 1832 (*Cayster gate* (*furlonge*) 1577, *Castergate* (*furlong*) 1606, 1611, *castergate* (*furlonge*) 1625, *Castergate* (*furland*) 1638, *castor gate, Castorgate furlong* 1679, *Caster Gate* (*furlong*), *Castor Gate* 1721, 'the road to Caistor', from **gata** 'a road', with **furlang**), Castor Walk 1805, Caistor - c.1830, 1832, The First & Second Caister Walks 1831 (*v.* **walk**, denoting land used for the pasture of animals, especially sheep, as elsewhere in the parish); Church Hill Cl c.1830, 1832, The Church Hills 1831 (*Kyrk hyll* 1577, *Kirk hill* 1606, *Kirke* - 1611, 1679, *Kirkhil* 1638, *Kirkhill* 1721, *v.* **kirkja, hyll**), Rothwell Church yard 1767, the Church-yard 1864 (*the church yard side* 1606, *Church yard side* 1611, 1679, *the church yard* - 1625, *the Church yard Side* 1638, *The Church-Yard* 1706, *ye Churchyard* 1721); Clowson c.1830, 1832, the Clowston Walk, the Cowston - (sic) 1831 (*a dalle of Clouston xxx acres* 1587, *on Clawston* 1606, *Clauxton* 1611, *clauxton* 1625, *Clowston* 1638, possibly from the surn. *Clowston*); Cow Cl 1805, c.1830, 1832, the Cow Pasture 1831; Croxby Btm 1767 (*v.* **botm**), the Croxby Rd 1767, Far -, Near Croxby Walk 1832 (*v.* **walk**, and cf. *Croxbie meare* 1606 (*v.* **(ge)mǣre**), referring to the neighbouring parish of Croxby); Cuxwold Gate 1767 (1721, *Cuxwolde gate* 1577, *Coxewold* - 1606, *Couxwould* - 1611, *Coxwold* - 1625, *Coxwould* - 1638, *v.* **gata**), the Cuxwould Rd 1767 (referring to the neighbouring parish of Cuxwold); Drove pce c.1830, 1832 (*v.* **pece**); Far -, Near Eight Acres c.1830, 1832; The Father Walk (sic) 1831 (probably for 'the farther walk', *v.* **walk**); Fifty Acres c.1830, 1832 (area in 1832: 55.1.18); the Great -, The little Flatt 1831 (*v.* **flat**); Forty Acres c.1830, 1832; Fox Cover c.1830, 1832, Fox-Cover cl 1864; The Furze Cover 1831 (*v.* **fyrs**); Far -, Near Gt Walk c.1830, 1832 (*v.* **walk**); Hill side 1805, - Side c.1830, 1832; Holes Btm c.1830, 1832, Holes Btms 1831 (*v.* **hol**[1], **botm**); Horn Cl, - Walk c.1830, 1832 (perhaps *v.* **horn**, alluding to a horn-shaped piece of land); Horse Walk c.1830, 1832 (*v.* **walk**); House pce c.1830, - Pce 1832 (*v.* **pece**); Limekiln Cl c.1830, 1832; Lincoln Hill c.1830, 1832, The - 1831 (*lincolnhyll* 1577, *Lincolne hill* 1606, 1611, 1625, *Lingcolne hil* 1638, *Lincolne Hill* 1679, *Lincoln* - 1721); Long Cl c.1830, 1832; the Louth Rd 1767 (self-explanatory); Low Cl c.1830, 1832; Mare Pce c.1830, 1832 (*v.* **mere**[2], **pece**); Markham Cl c.1830, 1832 (*markam Dale* 1638, *Markeham dale* 1679, *Markham dale* 1721, from the surn. *Markham*, cf. Walker *Markham* 1585 *PR*, with **deill**); the North Fd 1767, a Field in Rothwell now or lately called the North Fd 1815 (cf. South Fd *infra*); The Orchard 1831; Paddock c.1830, 1832; Poor Houses c.1830, 1832; the Raisin Rd 1767, the Road leading ... to Raisin 1864 (*raisin gate* 1606, *Rason* - 1611, *rasen* - 1625, *rason* - 1638, *Rasin* - 1679, *Rasin Gate* 1721, 'the road to (Market) Rasen', *v.* **gata**); Far -, Near Rough Pce c.1830, 1832 (*v.* **pece**); Round Cl c.1830, 1832; San foin Cl c.1830, The two old Sant Foin Cls 1831, Saint-foin Pce 1832 (*v.* **sainfoin**); the Seedlands, the seed Plat 1831 (*v.* **plat**); Seventy Acres c.1830, 1832; South Fd 1767 (like North Field *supra* perhaps one of the open fields of the parish, cf. *the Easte Fyelde, the Weaste fyelde* in (b) *infra*); South Hill c.1830, 1832, the - 1831 (*v.* **sūð**, **hyll**); Stone Pit Pce c.1830, 1832; Street Flg c.1830, 1832 (*Strete furlonge* 1577, *streete furlonge* 1606, *strete furlong* 1611, *streete furlonge* 1625, *Streetfurland* 1638, *Street-furlong* 1679, *v.* **strǣt**, **furlang**; the reference is to High Street *supra*); the Swallow Rd 1767 (*Swallow gate* 1638, *Swallow Gate* 1721, *v.* **gata**; Swallow is NE of Rothwell); Thoresway Rd 1805, 1832 (*thorswey gate* 1577, *Thoreswaie* - 1606, *Thoresway* - 1611, 1625, 1638, - *Gate* 1721, *v.* **gata**); Thoresway Walk c.1830, 1832 (*v.* **walk**, cf. *thorswey meare* 1577, *Thoriswaie* - 1606, *Thoresway* - 1611, 1625, 1638, - *meere* 1679, - meer 1721, *v.* **(ge)mǣre**, referring to the neighbouring parish of Thoresway); Town-end Cl 1864 (cf. *i land above towne* 1606); Town Street 1832 (*town street* 1690); Warren House Pce c.1830, 1832 (*v.* **pece**, probably alluding to a warrener's lodge), The Old Warren 1832 (*v.* **wareine**); Willingham Rd 1832 (North Willingham is some miles to the south of Rothwell).

(b) *Arterwalles* 1577 (*v.* **wall**); *Awdgate* 1577, *old gate* 1606, *Oldgate, Ouldgate* 1611, *Old gate* 1625, *audgate* 1638, *Oudgate* 1721 ('the old road', *v.* **ald, gata**); *the common bancke* 1606 (*v.* **banke**); *bell lande* 1577 (William *Bell* is named in the document); *Benettoft* 1465 (from the pers.n. or surn. *Bennet(t)* with **toft**); *Beverbuske* 1577 (*v.* **buskr** 'a bush, a shrub'; the first el. is probably ME **bēver** (OE **beofer**, the name presumably denoting a beaver's den); *Mr Bowles headlande* 1577 (*v.* **hēafod-land**); *brattes furlonge* 1577, *Brats* 1606, *Bratts* 1611, *furlong called* - 1625, *brats* 1638, *ye Bratts* 1721 (*v.* **brot** 'a small piece (of land)'); *Brokylsdale* (sic) 1577, *brocklesdale* 1606, *brocklesdaile* 1611, *Brocklesdale* 1625, 1679, 1721, *Brockelsdale* 1638 (perhaps from a contraction of the surn. *Brocklesby*, cf. John *Brokelsbye* 1577, with **deill**; Dr Insley, however, suggests that the first component is probably a topographical term 'badger hill', *v.* **brocc**, **hyll**); *Burdalls* 1606, *burdall* 1638, *Burdyll Hyll 1577, burdall hill* 1611, *burdalhil* 1638, *Burdale Hill* 1679, *Burdale hill, Burdale-hil* 1721, *Byrdyll pytt* 1577, *burdaile-pitts* 1611, *burdall pitts* 1625, *burdale pits* 1638, 1679 (possibly 'the share of land attached to a cottage, dwelling house', from **būr**[1] (ME *bour*), **deill**, cf. *burdell* in the f.ns. (b) of Binbrook, PN L 3, 11), with **hyll** and **pytt** in the pl.); *Busshtoft* 1465 (from **busc** or the derived surn., with **toft** 'a building site, a curtilage, a messuage'); *caw daile* 1606, *cawdale hill* 1611,

Caw dale 1625, *Cowdale Hill* 1679, 1721 (Dr Insley suggests that *caw daile* etc. is from ME *kawe*, a varient of ME *chough(e)* 'chough, jackdaw, jay', *v.* MED s.v. *chough(e)* and **dalr** 'a valley'); *Church lane* 1686, *Churchgate* 1721 (cf. *Kyrk Styghe infra*); *Clapton hyll* 1577 (*v.* **hyll**; *Clapton* is presumably a surn.); *Clewsgate* 1577, *Cluese gate* 1606, *Cluesgate* 1606, 1625, 1721, *cluesgate, clousegate* 1611, *Clewes gate* 1638, *Clues-gate* 1679 (probably from the ME surn. *Clewe*, quoted by Reaney s.n. *Clough*, and **gata**); *the Common* 1686; *Cowe Styghe* 1577, *Cow stigh* 1606, *kowstigh* 1611, *kow steighe* 1625, *Cowstigh* 1638, *Cowstight* 1679 (*v.* **stīg**; for the - *stight* form cf. *Kyrke Styghe infra); deyhous* 1349 ('the dairy house', *v.* **dey, hūs**); *the dogg Hutt* 1577, *Dogge hutt* 1606, *doghutt* 1611, *Doghut* 1625, *the dogs hut* 1638, *Dog hutt* 1721 (self-explanatory); *Dove hyll* 1577, *dovehill* 1606, *douehill* 1611, *Doue hil* 1638, *Dovehill* 1721 (*v.* **dūfe, hyll**); *the Easte Fyelde* 1577, *the East feild of Rothwell* 1587, *East-side feild* 1611, *East feild* 1625, *the East feilde* 1638, *The East Field* 1686, *y^e^* - 1703, *ye Eastfield* 1721 (*v.* **ēast, feld**, one of the open fields of the parish but not named in the Enclosure Award, cf. *the Weaste fyelde infra*); *Eshecroft* 1577, *estcroft* (sic) 1606, *Escroft* 1625, *Eshcroft* 1721 (*v.* **esc** 'an ash-tree', **croft**); *campum de rothwel,* - *de Rowell* 112 (13), - *de Rowelle* c.1200, *Rothwell field* 1636 (*v.* **feld**); *Fold* 1721; *glewedale* (*furlonge*) 1577, *Glue dale* 1606, *glue dale* 1611, *Gleudale* 1625, *Glewdale* 1638, 1679, *Glew dale* 1721 (Dr Insley suggests that the first el. is perhaps the ME surn. *Gleu*, a hypocoristic form of such names as *Gleudain, Gleulouen, Gleumarocus*, for which *v.* Feilitzen 262 n.1 and Kenneth Jackson, *A Historical Phonology of Breton*, Dublin 1967, para. 335.1. Reaney, s.n. *Glew*, gives ME examples of *Gleu, Glew* as a pers.n. and byname, but wrongly regards them as a derivative of OE *glēaw* 'wise, prudent'. The second el. is probably **dalr** 'a valley' rather than **deill** 'a portion of land', but the situation of the f.n. is unknown); *atte Grene* 1332, *de Grene de Rothewelle* 1386 both (p) (*v.* **grene**^{2}); *the highe waye* 1577, *high waie* 1606; *Hungere Hyll* 1577, *hunger hill* 1606, 1611, *Hunnger hill* 1625, *hungerhil* 1638, *Hunger hill* 1679, *hungerhill* 1721 (a common derogatory name for infertile land, *v.* **hungor**); *ynges furlong* 1577, *one dall of Inges* 1587, *Ings* 1606, *a furlong called Inges* 1611, 1625, *inges* 1638, *Ings-furlong* 1679, *Inges furlong* 1721 (*v.* **eng** 'meadow, pasture', **furlang**); *Kylnhousegarth* 1465 (*v.* **garðr**); *Kyngesenges* 1349, 1465 (perhaps from the surn. *King*, with **eng** in the pl.); *Kyrk Styghe* 1577, *Kirke stigh* 1606, *Kirk* - 1611, *kirke stighe* 1625, *Kirkestight* 1679, *Kirkstight* 1721 ('the path to the church', *v.* **kirkja, stīg**; *-stight* is a local variant found elsewhere in north L; cf. *Church lane supra*); *lambe Dale* 1577, 1606, *a certaine furlong called lambedale* 1611, *Lamedale* 1625, *one dail called Lamdale* 1638, *Lamb-dale or Ings* 1679 (*v.* **lamb, deill**); *longe furlonges* 1577, *longfurlongs* 1606 (*v.* **lang, furlang**, cf.

shortfurlongs infra); *Myckyll Hyll* 1577, *mickle hill* 1606, *mickle hill* 1611, 1625, *mickelhill* 1638, *Mickle hill* 1679, *Micklehill* 1721 (*v.* **mikill, hyll**); *ye Mudfang, Sheffields Mudfang* 1721 (*Sheffields Mudfang* is the name of one of the bounds of a piece of land, *v.* **mudfang** and for a discussion of this north L dial. word, *v.* PN L **2** 146, A *M^r^. Sheffield* is named in the 1721 document and cf. also *Mr Sheffield Close* 1577); *the mylne* 1577; *nettledales* 1606, *nettlesdaile* 1611, *nettledales* 1625, *nitledales* 1638, *Netledales* 1679, *Nettledales* 1721 (*v.* **netel, deill**); *Ourdale* 1721 (the reading is uncertain); *the pits* 1606, 1638, *the pitts* 1679, *pits* 1721 (*v.* **pytt**); *Plowson furlong* 1721 (*v.* **furlang**; *Plowson* is presumably a surn.); *Rigges* 1577, *one dall of Rigges* 1587, *riggs* 1606, 1611, *Riggs furlong* 1721 (*v.* **hryggr, furlang**); *Sand furlonges* 1577, *the Sands* 1606, *the sands* 1611, 1625, 1638, *ye Sands* 1721 (*v.* **sand, furlang**); *shepcote* 1349 ('the sheep-cote', *v.* **scēap, cot**); *shortfurlongs* 1611, *shorte Furlongs* 1625, *Shortfurland* 1638, *Short furlongs* 1679, *Shortfurlong* 1721 (*v.* **sceort, furlang**, cf. *longe furlonges supra*); *the Slede* 1577, *the Slead* 1606, 1638, *the slead* 1611, 1625, *Slead* 1679, *ye Slead* 1721 (*v.* **slæd** 'a valley', perhaps in one of its dial. senses, like 'land in a (marshy) valley'); *Smithfeld* 1349, *Smythfeld'* 1465 (*v.* **feld**, the first el. is either the occup. n. **smið** or the derived surn., cf. foll. f.n.); *capitallum Messuagium vocat' Smythtoft* 1465 (from **toft** 'a messuage' with the occup. n. **smið** or the derived surn.); *Stonewall headland* 1680; *le Southdale* 1349 (*v.* **sūð, dalr**); *Sudlandes* 1577, *Sudlands* 1606 (possibly 'south selions', *v.* **sūð, land**); *swyncote* 1349 ('the pigsty', *v.* **swīn-cot**); *the towen side* 1577; *Walterpyndertoft* 1465 ('the curtilage of Walter Pinder', *v.* **toft**); *a furlonge called weake howe* 1577, *wakhoe* 1611, 1625, *wakehou* 1638, *Wacow* 1721 ('look-out mound', *v.* **wacu, haugr**); *the Weaste fyelde* 1577, *the west feild* 1587, 1625, *the westfeild* 1611, *the west fild* 1638, *the West feild* 1679, *- field* 1680, *The West Field* 1686, *y^e^ -* 1702, *the West field* 1721 (*v.* **west, feld**, one of the open fields of the parish, but not named in the Enclosure Award, cf. *the Easte Fyelde supra* and North Fd, South Fd in (a) *supra*); *well Hyll* 1577, *- hill* 1611, *wellhill* 1625, *well hil* 1638, *wellhil* 1679, *Wellhill* 1721, *well Hooles* 1577, *Wellholes* 1721 (*v.* **wella, hyll, hol**^{2}).

Swinhope

SWINHOPE

Suinhope (3x) 1086 DB, *-opa* c.1115 LS, *-hop* 1263 Ipm
Suinahopa c.1115 LS

Svyneop 1194 (13) *Alv*, *-hop* 1301 *ib*, *Swynehopp* 1242-43 Fees, *-hop* 1244 FF, 1272 *Ass*, 1576 Saxton, 1610 Speed, *-hope* 1428 FA, 1461 Pat, 1535 VE iv, 1551 de l'Isle, 1560 Pat, *-opp* 1519 DV i

Suinehop 1212 Fees, *Swineop* 1229 FF, *-hop* 1242-43 Fees, 1246 RRG, *-hoppe* 1307 Ipm, *-hopp* 1756 LER

Swinope 1185 RotDom (p), 1592, 1641 *BT*, *-hop* 1226 FF (p), 1234 ib, 1285 RRGr, 1690 *Terrier*, 1794 *BRA 1208*, 1824 O, 1828 Bry, 1842 *TA*, *-hoppe* 1593, 1598 *et passim* to 1693 *BT*, *-hopp* 1599 *BT*, 1601 *Terrier*, 1636 *Foster*, 1638 *Terrier*, *-hope* 1606, 1609, 1647, 1668 *BT*, 1671, 1679 *Terrier et passim*, *-opp* 1722, 1728 *BT*, *-op* 1799 Young

Swynhop 1254 ValNor, 1291 Tax, 1303 FA, 1314 Ch, 1322 Ipm, 1327 *SR*, 1354 Ipm, 1428 FA, 1483 *AD*, 1719 *BT*, *-hopp* 1349 Ipm, 1428, 1431 FA, 1526 Sub, 1625 *LindDep 82*, *-hoppe* 1623 *BT*, *-hope* 1310 Ipm, 1316 FA, 1322 Fine, 1322 Cl, 1359 *Cor*, 1375 Peace, 1384, 1416 Pat, 1426 Cl, 1453 Pat, 1453 *Tat*, *-op* 1275 RH, 1332 *SR*, 1392 Pat, *-ope* 1373 Peace, 1404 Pat, *-oppe* 1539 LP xiv, 1569, 1590 *BT*, *-opp* 1563 *ib*

Swynnop 1281 Ipm, 1566 Pat, *-ope* 1386 ib, 1575 HMCRep

'The secluded valley of the swine (where pigs are kept)', *v.* **swin**[1], **hop**. This is the only village-name in **hop** in the whole of Lindsey. OE **hop** 'secluded valley' is discussed by Margaret Gelling, PNITL 111-21, who comments "Swinhope occupies an embayment in a very long, curving stream-valley". It may be added that there is no village here today, though the church remains and is situated where the valley is broadest.

ASH HILL, 1842 *TA*, the name of a Long Barrow, cf. Hoe Hill *infra*. BISHOP'S LANE. BRATS LANE, *v.* Swinhope Brats *infra*. CLAY BOTTOM, 1842 *TA*. CLICKEM INN, 1824 O, *The Talbot or Clickum Inn* 1828 Bry, *Talbot Inn* 1842 *TA*, 1842 *White*. It may be pure coincidence but the *Talbot* family is recorded from the parish, cf. Robert *Talbott* 1604 *BT*. CLICKEM WOOD, cf. *Click'em plat* 1842 *TA*. COLD HARBOUR, a common name for a sheltered place in an exposed situation. GLEBE FM. HOE HILL, 1842 *TA*;

Hoe is probably from **haugr** 'a (burial) mound' since this is the site of a Long Barrow. HOE HILL FM, 1842 *TA*. THE HOLT. HOME WOOD, 1842 *ib.* PORT HILL, 1842 *ib.* POTTERY POND. THE RECTORY, cf. *the parsonage house* 1601, (*the*) *Parsonage Buildings* 1621 (1822), 1634, 1662, *the parsonage buildings* 1674, 1679, *ye Parsonage* 1671, 1706, *the Parsonage house* 1690, 1712, *Parsonage House* 1762 all *Terrier*. THE ROOKERY, 1842 *TA*. SWINHOPE BRATS, *le Broth de Svyneop* eHy3 (13) *Alv*, *brottes* 1276 *ib*, *Swinhop Bratts* 1802 *Tur*, 1828 Bry, - *Brats* 1824 O, cf. *Close called New Bratts* 1621 (1822), (*the*) *newbratclose* 1625, 1634, *the new bratt close* 1662, - *brat close* 1674, 1679, *ye new bratts* 1671, *a certain Close called new Bratts* 1762 all *Terrier*, from ON **brot** 'a small piece of land', in the pl. SWINHOPE HO (site of), 1842 *TAMap*, *Swinhop House* 1824 O. It is probably to be identified with *the Mannor howse of Swynhopp* 1625 *LindDep 82*, and cf. *The Hall garth* 1601, 1634, *ye hallgarth* 1638, - *Hallgarth* 1671 all *Terrier*, *v.* **hall**, **garðr** 'an enclosure'. SWINHOPE PARK, *Park* 1842 *TA*. SWINHOPE PLANTATION (lost), *Swinhop Plantation* 1828 Bry; it was in the triangular corner of the parish, just west of Ash Hill.

Field-Names

Principal forms in (a) are 1842 *TA*; spellings dated 112 (13), a1182 (13), 1194 (13), eHy3 (13), a1227 (13), 1245 (13), 1254-61 (13), 1276, 1291, 1301 are *Alv*; 1310, 1322 Ipm; 1327, 1332 *SR*; 1605, 1629 *Yarb*; 1601, 1621 (1822), 1625, 1634, 1638, 1662, 1671, 1674, 1679, 1690, 1697, 1703, 1706, 1712, 1762 *Terrier*.

(a) Betts Plantn (named from the *Betts* family, cf. John *Betts* 1842); Bynbrooke way 1762 (*vie que ducit de binbrok' uersus Neuton* 1276 (13), *binbrooke way* 1601, *Binbrook way* 1622 (1822), 1671, *Binbroke way* 1638, *the high way to Binbrooke* 1697, 'the road to Binbrook (an adjacent parish)'), Binbrook Walk 1842 (*v.* **walk**); A Furlong of Arable Ground call'd broken back 1762, Broken Back (Plantn) 1842 (*a parcel of Ground called Broken back* 1621 (1822), *a furlonge of arrable ground there called brokenbacke furlonge* 1634, *a wonge called Broken back* 1638, *a furlong of arrable ground called Brockenback* 1671; unlike Brokenback PN L 3 115, there is no sign whatever of a round barrow in the field, but its etymology must be the same, OE **brocen-bæc* 'broken back', in the sense 'humped back'. It is a humped field sloping away on all sides to the boundary hedges); Carpenters Cottage (named from the *Carpenter* family, cf. George *Carpenter* 1842); Chalk pit Plantn, - pit Hill, - Pit Hill plantn; Church close (plantn), Church Ings (*v.* **eng**), Church Yd; ye Corn Fd 1762; ye Cottager's Wong 1762 (*the Cochers wonge* 1601, *the Cottager's wong* 1621 (1822), *the Cottagers Wong* 1634, - *wonge* 1638, *Cottagers wong* 1671, *v.* **vangr**; *co(t)cher* for 'cottager' is regularly found in north L); ye Cow Pasture 1762 (*the Cowpasture* 1674, *the Common Cowpasture* 1690); Crow Holt (*v.* **crāwe**, **holt**) and Mill cl; Dove Coat Cl 1762 (*Dovecoat Close* 1621 (1822), *ye Dove coate close* 1671, *v.* **douve-cote**); ye East End Fm 1762 (*the East End Farm* 1621 (1822), *the east end farme* 1625, *the Eastend* - 1634, *ye eastend* - 1638, *the East end* - 1662, *ye Eastend* - 1671, *the* - 1674, 1679, *v.* **ēast**, **ende**); Eight acres; Eighteen Acres; Fish Pond; Five acres; Forty acres (2x), Forty acres close plantn, Forty acres North Plantn, - South Plantn, - South West Plantn; Four Acre Plantn, Four acres plantn, Four acres (4x); Fourteen acres; Gravel Hill plantn; Grimsby way 1762 (1621 (1822), 1671, *viam de Grimesby* 112 (13), *the way that gooeth from Swinhop to Grimsby* 1638, *Grimsby gate* 1697, *v.* **gata**); Hackforth's farm (named from the *Hackforth* family, cf. Edward *Hackforth* 1803 *BT*, 1842); (the) Hall Garth 1762; (cf. *ad aulam* 1327 (p), *v.* **hall**, **garðr**); High Farm (plantn); Home cl; Home Wd (and Pond); Hortons Plat, - plat Garden, - Plat Plantn, - plat plantn (named from the *Horton* family, cf. William Horton 1842); ye Ings 1762, The Ings, Ings plantn 1842 (*the Inges* 1601, - *Ings* 1621 (1822), 1662, 1674, 1679, *the ings* 1625, *the Inge* 1634, 1638, *ye Ings* 1671, *v.* **eng**); Irford Road Plantn (from Orford in Stainton le Vale, PN L **3** 125-6); Lady Betty's Cl; a certain Meadow called Lady Crookes 1762 (*Lady Crooks* 1621 (1822), *the Ladycrookes* 1625, *the Lady crookes* 1634, 1671, *ye lady crookes* 1638, *the meadow platt called Lady Crookes* 1662, *a medow plot called Lady crooks* 1674, *the meadow plot called* - 1679); Lodge Gdn; Low Ings (Rd) (*v.* **eng**); ye middle Farm 1762 (*the Middle Farm* 1621 (1822), *the middle farme* 1634, *the midell* - 1638, *the Middle* - 1671); Middle ings (Plantn) (*middle Ings* 1674, *v.* **eng**); Mill Cl (*v.* Crow Holt *supra*; cf. *molendinum in Svyneop* 112 (13), - *de Swinhop* 1245 (13), - *de Swynhop* 1254-61 (13), *Milnecroft* 1322, *v.* **myln**, **clos(e)**, **croft**); Nashoba (unexplained); ye New Cl taken out of ye Cow Pasture 1762; ye Northfield 1762 (*the North Field*, *the North field Hedge* 1621 (1822), *the North feild* 1634, 1638, 1671, - *Feild* 1690, *v.* **norð**, **feld**, one of the open fields of the parish, cf. South fd *infra*); Oat Cl, Oat close plantn; Paddock; Parsonage Wongs 1762 (*the Parsonage Wonge* 1621 (1822), *the parsonage* - 1625, *-wonges* 1638, *the Parsonage wonges* 1662, *ye Parsonage wongs* 1671, *the Parsonage* - 1674, *the parsonage* - 1679, *v.* **vangr**); Pingle (2x) (*v.* **pingel**); Pudding Poke; Regans Farm (from the family of Anne and James *Regan* 1825 *BT*); Rousselet (Dr J. Insley suggests that this may be a compound of ME *russel* (OFr *rossel, russel, roussel*) 'something red or reddish' and the diminutive suffix *-ett*(*e*), *v.* EPN **1** 161, s.v. **et**[5], the name probably denoting a small ruddy-coloured piece of land); Saintfoin btm, Saintfoin Bottom Plantn (*v.* **sainfoin**, **botm**); Seven acres; Six acres (plantn); South fd 1762 (*the South field* 1621 (1822), - *Southfeild* 1638, *the South feild* 1671, - *Feild* 1690, *v.* **sūð**, **feld**, one of the open fields of the parish, cf. ye Northfield *supra*); Stable plantn; Sykes (*v.* **sík**); Ten acres; Thirteen Acres, - acres; Thirty acres acres (4x), Thirty acres close North plantn, - South plantn; Thirty five acres; Thorganby Plantn, - Walk (plantn) (from the adjacent parish of Thorganby); Three acres (3x), - Plantn; Top Ings (*v.* **eng**); Towlers Cottage (named from the *Towler* family, cf. Edward *Towler* 1842); Townend Walk (*v.* **walk**); ye Townsway 1762 (*The Towns way* 1621 (1822), *the townes-way* 1671, i.e. the village street); Twelve acres; Twenty acres (3x), - plantn; Twenty five acres; Twenty four acres (2x), - Acres plantn, - acres plantn; Twenty seven acres (plantn); Two acres (plantn); Warren close Plantn (*v.* **wareine**); Willow Walk (North Plantn), (- South Plantn) (*v.* **walk**); Wold Newton side Plantn; Woodgate 1761 (*woodgate* 1601, *Woodgate* 1621 (1822), 1671, *woodgatte* 1638, *wodgate* 1690, *v.* **gata**).

(b) *Ardens farme* 1691 (named from the *Arden* family, cf. Anthony *Arden* 1636 *Foster*); (*a little pingle by*) *ye becke Side* 1697 (*v.* **bekkr**); *Blafot*(*e*)*wang* 112 (13) (*v.* **vangr**; the first el. is the ON byname *Bláfótr* 'blue-foot', for which *v.* LindB 28); *iuxta pontem* 112 (13) (*v.* **brycg**); *le Broth de Svyneop* eHy3 (13) (no doubt from ON **brot** 'a small piece of land'); *Cobbeminst', totam culturam Cobminster uocatam* 112 (13), *Cobminst'* a1227 (13) (obscure); *the East feild* 1697, 1706, - *feilde* 1703, - *Easte Feild* 1712 (*v.* **ēast**, **feld**); *in campis de svynop* 112 (13), *campi de Svyneop* 1194 (13), *in campis de Svynop* 1301, *Swinhop Field* 1621 (1822), *Swinhoppefeild hedge* 1625 (*v.* **feld**); *William Glew his Inges* 1601 (*v.* **eng**); *heuedland, euedland* 112 (13), *Euedland* a1227 (13) (*v.* **hēafod-land**); *culturam uocatam Hotie* (sic) 112 (13), *culturam uocatam Hortye cum bercharia* a1227 (13), *bercariam suam dicitur Orty* 1301 (Dr Insley suggests that *Hortye* etc. means 'the meeting-place at a muddy site' *v.* **horu, tīg**[2]; *lingwang* 112 (13), *Lingwang* a1227 (13) (*v.* **lyng** 'heather'. **vangr**); *vie de Luda* 112 (13) ('the road from Louth'); *ex north parte diuise inter campos de binbrok' & Svyneop que dicitur le maregate* 1276 (13) ('the boundary road', *v.* **(ge)mǣre, gata**); *in pratis de Svyneop* 112 (13) ('in the meadows of Swinhope'); *mikelwang* 112 (13), a1227 (13), *Mickle wonge* 1605, *the Little Mickle wonge* 1629 (*v.* **mikill, vangr** 'a garden, in-field', as elsewhere in this parish); *Middlewonges* 1625 (*v.* **middel, vangr**); *neutundic* 112 (13) (*v.* **dīk** and Wold Newton, an adjacent parish); *Or.guendam* (?) 1291; *Petemannescroft* 1310, *Pidmancroft* 1322 (doubtless alluding to a turf-cutter, *v.* **pete, mann, croft**); *rauþelandes* 112 (13), *Roudlandes* a1227 (13) ('red selions', *v.* **rauðr, land**); *Roluesdale* (2x), *rofwesdaile* (sic) 112 (13) ('Rolf's allotment or share of land', *v.* **deill**; the first el. is the Scand. pers.n. ON *Hrólfr*, ODan *Rolf*); *two wonges Called Sixteene* 1638 (*v.* **vangr**); *steinwang* 112 (13), *stainwang* a1227 (13) (*v.* **steinn, vangr**, a Scand. compound); *Swynhopdale* a1182 (13) (cf. *in orientali parte valle* 112 (13), *de La Dale* 1327, 1332 both (p), *v.* **dalr**); *thorne wonges* 1638 (*v.* **þorn, vangr**); *vndregarth* 1332 (p) ('the place-) under, below the enclosure', *v.* **garðr**); *Waterdailes, - dayles* 112 (13), *-deiles* a1227 (13) ('the wet shares of land', *v.* **wæter, deill**); *ye west feilde* 1697, *the West feild* 1703, 1706, *-Feild* 1712 (*v.* **west, feld**); *Wiþemundhou* (sic), *Wymundhou* 112 (13), *Wimundhou* a1227 (13) ('Wymund's mound', *v.* **haugr**; Dr Insley suggests that the first el. is the OE pers.n. **Wiðermund*, the first el. of Wormingford PN Ess 403-4 and von Feilitzen *Namn och Bygd* 33 (1945), 91. He points out that forms in *Wymund-, Wimund-* would then show association of the first el. with OE *Wīgmund* or ON *Vígmundr*); *Wrangedailes* 112 (13), *Wrangdeiles* a1227 (13) ('crooked allotments', *v.* **vrangr, deill**).

North Thoresby

NORTH THORESBY

Toresbi (6x) 1086 DB, c.1115 LS, Hy2 Dane, 1202, 1219 Ass, *-by* 1275 RH
Toresbi 1202 Ass (p)
Thorisbeia 1137-39 YCh iii, *-by* 1242-43 Fees, 1277 RRGr, 1280 RSu, 1292 Ch, *Thorysby* 1420 YD iii
Thoresbi 1202 FF (p), c1220 FP, *-by* 1226-28 Fees, 1240 Cl, 1242-43 Fees, 1254 ValNor, 1268 RRGr, 1275 RH, 1282

Cl, 1291 Tax, 1294 Fine, 1294 Orig, 1294 Ch, 1306, 1307 Pat, 1311 Fine, *et freq* to 1610 Speed, *-b'* 1238-41 Fees, *-bie* a1567 LNQ v, 1608 *Foster*, 1631 VisitN, 1642, 1646 *Goulding*, *- als Northoresbie* 1565 *Yarb*, *-bye* 1576 Saxton

Thuresby 1526 Sub, 1553-55 ECP

North Thoresby 1292 RSu, 1437 Pap, 1453 Fine, 1464 Pat, 1479 Pap *et passim*, *North'thoresby* 1369 *FF*, 1384 Peace, *Norththoresby* 1411 Pat, *- Thoresbye* 1557-58 Lanc, *-bie* 1625 *Terrier*, *- Thorisby* 1671 *ib*, *Norththorsby* 1382 Peace, *- Thorsby* 1601, 1611 *Terrier*, *Northoresby* 1380 Gaunt, *-bye* 1577 *Terrier*

'Þori's farmstead, village', *v.* **bȳ**, as is South Thoresby (LSR), from which it is distinguished as *North*. The pers.n. is ON *Þórir*, ODan *Thorir*, recorded from Lincolnshire independently as Thori and Tori in DB and frequently in the 12th and 13th centuries, *v.* Feilitzen 393-94 and SPNLY 307-9.

AUTBY

Aduluesbi 1086 DB

Aldulvebi 1086 DB

Alwoldesbi l086DB

Alwoldebi 1086 DB, 1204 P, *Aluoldebi*, *Aluoldabi* c.1115 LS, *Alwoldeb'* 1238-41 Fees, *-by* 1272 Ass, 1291 Tax, 1299 Pat, 1300 Orig, 1346, 1406, 1407 Pat, 1428 FA, *Alwoldby* 1295 Ipm, 1347, 1408, 1409 Pat, 1606 *Yarb*, *Alwodeby* 1300 Cl, *Alwodbie* a1567 LNQ v

Alwaldebi 1196 ChancR, 1196 P, 1219 Ass, *-by* 1266 RRGr, 1271 FF, 1272 *Ass*, 1274 RRGr, 1311 Pat, 1311 Ipm, 1316 FA, 1327 *SR*, 1334 Cl, 1349 Pat, 1353 Ipm, 1356, 1358 Pat, 1361 Ipm, 1361 Cl, 1384, 1390, 1411, 1414 Pat, *Halwaldeby* 1242-43 Fees, 1312 Fine, 1312 Orig, *Alewaldeby* 1254 ValNor, 1281 QW, *Alewaldby* 1275 RH, *Alwaldby* 1332 *SR*, 1345, 1358, 1404, 1412 Pat, *Alwalby* 1354 AD, 1358 *Cor* (p), 1406 *FF*, 1451-53, 1475-77, 1496-98, 1523-24 *MinAcct*

Alewardebi 1202 *HarlCh*, *-by* 1204 *AddCh*, *Alwardeby* 1225 Cur, 1342 Pat, *Alwardby* 1298 Ass

Athewaldeby 1272 *Ass* (p)
Aylewaldby 1272 *Ass*
Aldwoldeby 1295 Ipm
Awdeby 1553-55 ECP, 1608 *Foster, Awdby* 1601, 1611 *Terrier*
Aldeby 1553, 1554, 1561 Pat, - *als Aswholdby* (sic) *Yarb*
Audby 1617 Admin, 1638, 1671, 1709, 1724 *Terrier*, 1824 O, 1828 Bry
Autby hs. 1872 White

This is a difficult name. The second el. is ODan **bȳ** 'farmstead, village'. Ekwall, DEPN, s.v., interprets the name as '*Alfwald's* BY', and comments: "*Alfwald* is an ODan pers.n. Or the first el. may be OE *Ælfweald*'. In Denmark, *Alfwald* is only attested as a Lund moneyer's name of the period 1080-86, and the name is generally regarded as representing OE *Ælfw(e)ald* (*v.* DaGP, 29a, s.v. *Alfwald*). An 'ODan' *Alfwald* can thus be excluded as a possible etymon for the first el. of Autby.

The majority of the early forms would suggest that we are concerned here with ME *Alw(e)ald, -wold* from OE *Ælfw(e)ald* or *Æðelw(e)ald* (*v.* Feilitzen 154-155). The 1272 forms *Athelwaldeby* and *Aylewaldeby* are interesting. The usual reflex of OE *Æðel-* in Middle English is *Ayl-, Ail, v.* Feilitzen 103-106 and Ekwall, *Early London Personal Names,* Lund, 1947, 197. B. Seltén, *The Anglo-Saxon Heritage in Middle English Personal Names: East Anglia 1100-1399,* ii (Lund, 1979), 35-36, shows that a common form of OE *Æðelw(e)ald* in East Anglia in the Middle English period has initial *Athel-*, not *Ail-*. It might be conceivable that the 1272 form *Athelwaldeby* represents a more conservative variant beside the usual *Alwoldebi, Alwaldebi.* If this is the case, then we can take the first el. of Autby to be OE *Æðelw(e)ald.* Forms in *Alewardebi, Alward(e)by* show confusion with ME *Alw(e)ard.* The DB forms *Aduluesbi* and *Aldulvebi* could be taken to imply that the first el. is OE *Aldwulf,* which became confused with *Alwald, -wold* as a result of the Middle English weakening of medial syllables, but it is perhaps more likely that they reflect the influence of Audleby in Caistor (PN L 2, 88), for which the form *Aldulvebi* is in fact recorded. The form of 1295, *Aldwoldeby,* has intrusive -d- in the first syllable probably again due to association with Audleby.

On balance, therefore, it would seem best to take the first

el. of Autby to be the OE pers.n. *Æðelw(e)ald, -wald.*

It will be seen that there are only two forms with the OE gen.sg. *-es*, and they are from DB, while there are many with medial *-e-*, as in *Alwoldebi*, etc. Ekwall, *Selected Papers* 65-66 considers that spellings with medial *-e-*, such as *Aldulvebi* (for Audleby), presuppose an original Scand. gen.sg. in *-ar* and that such names were formed by Scandinavians, even when an English pers.n. occurs as first el. Cf. Audleby PN L 2 86. The modern spelling *Autby* has not been noted before 1872, but *Autbie hedge* occurs as a f.n. dated 1578 *Terrier* in Ludborough f.ns. (b) *supra.* Audby is a "lost" village, though traces of it are still visible in the north-west corner of Autby Park. The name is still used locally, and today is represented by *Autby Manor, Autby Park* and *Autby Wood.* The house has been demolished and has been replaced by a factory.

APPLEHOLME (lost), 1828 Bry, - *Holme* 1824 O, *Abelholme* 1451-53, *-holl'* 1475-77, *Ableholme* 1523-24, 1546-47 all *MinAcct, Hable holme* 1577 *Terrier, Abbleholme* 1609 *DuLaMB*; the forms are late but suggest 'Abel's raised land amid marsh', *v.* **holmr**, though no certainty is possible. Appleholme is a piece of land between Old Fleet Drain and Thoresby Dyke and the road to Tetney branching from the road to Thoresby Bridge. AUTBY HO, *Awdby house* 1601, 1611 *Terrier, Audby Hall* 1733 *Yarb*, 1745 *Em*; the house has recently been demolished and replaced by a Factory. AUTBY PARK. AUTBY WOOD. BARTON STREET, *ye street called Barton street* 1638, *the Barton Streete* 1664, *Barton Street* 1671, *the streete* 1577, 1601, *y^e* - 1611, - *street* 1638, 1697, 1703, 1709, 1724, *the Street* 1664, - *street* 1715, 1822 all *Terrier* and cf. *ye strete furlonge* 1577, *streete furlong* 1601, *Streetefurlong* 1611, *street-furlong* 1625, (*y^e*) *street furlong* 1638, 1697, 1703, 1709, 1822, *Streete Furlong* 1664, *the Street furlong* 1671 all *Terrier*, Barton Street forms the western boundary of the parish and is the name of a presumed pre-Roman trackway leading to Barton upon Humber. BEAN LAND RD, cf. *Bean Lands* 1839 *TA*, self-explanatory. BLACK LEG DRAIN. BLOW WELLS, 1774 *Hill.* BOND CROFT DRAIN, cf. *Bond Croft* 1839 *TA*; it was probably named from the *Bond* family, cf. Francis *Bond* 1822 *Terrier*, Jane *Bond* 1842 White. CAUDLE GREEN, 1786 *Yarb*,

Caldewalgrene, 1786 *Yarb. Caldewalgrene* 1451-53, 1475-77, 1496-96 *MinAcct, Caudewell grene furlonge* 1577, *Cawld well greene* 1601, *Cawdwell greene* 1611, *Cald well green* 1697, *Caldwell Green* 1703, 1709, *Caldwellgreene* 1715, *Cauldwell greene* 1724, *Cadel green* 1822 all *Terrier*, cf. *Coldewell'* 1451-53 *MinAcct, Cawdwell* 1625 *Terrier*. Caudle is 'the cold spring', *v.* **cald**, **wella**, to which was added **grēne**[2] 'a grassy spot'. *Caldegrene* 1523-24, 1546-47 *MinAcct* are clearly errors. COXWOLD ROW. EASTFIELD FM, cf. *ye Eastfeld* 1601 *Terrier, the East(e) feild* 1609 *DuLaMB, the Eastfeld* 1611, *Eastfeild* 1625, 1638, 1679, 1697, 1703, 1715, (*the*) *East Feild* 1664, 1724 all *Terrier, the East Field* 1745 *Em, East field* 1786 *Yarb*, one of the great fields of the village, *v.* **ēast**, **feld** and cf. Westfield Fm *infra*. It is also referred to as *the est syde of the towne* 1577, *ye east side* 1709 both *Terrier*. FEN LANE, *the fenn lane* 1609 *DuLaMB, the fenne gate* 1577, *fengate* 1638, *Fenn gate* 1664, *ye fenngate* 1671, *the Fen Road* 1864 all *Terrier*, cf. *Thoresby Fenn Drayne* 1710 *Foster, Thoresby Fen* 1824 O and *South fenne* 1451-53, 1475-77, 1496-98, 1523-24 *MinAcct*, 1557-58 Lanc, *Long South Fen* 1839 *TA*; 'the lane to the fen', *v.* **fenn**, **lanu**, **gata**. GLOUCESTER HO. THE GRANBY, 1828 Bry, *Granby Inn* 1824 O, 1842 White. HELL FURZE, 1824 O, 1828 Bry, 1830 Gre, *Hellefures, -furrse* 1625 *Terrier, Hell Furz* 1775 *EnclA* and cf. *Hell forlonge* 1578 *Terrier*, this is presumably a derogatory name for a place overgrown with furze, *v.* **fyrs**. HIGHFIELD HO. HOLMEFIELD. KETTLE CAUSEWAY (lost), 1824 O, 1828 Bry, - *causeway* 1786 *Yarb*; the sense of *Kettle* is unclear. It denoted the road from Eastfield Fm to Thoresby Bridge. MICKLEMORE, *Micchelemore, Michelemore* c.1200 RA iv, *Mikelmare* 1451-53 *MinAcct, Mikelmare* 1451-53 *ib, Mekelmare* 1475-77 *ib, Mikylmare* 1496-98 *ib, Micklemare* 1523-24 *ib, mykle meere* 1578 *Terrier, Mykelmore* 1593-94 Lanc, *mickell-* 1625, *Mickle-* 1703, 1724, *Micle-* 1706, *Mickle-more* 1745, *Micklemer* 1697 all *Terrier, Micklemire or Micklemoor* 1786 *Yarb*, 'the big marsh', *v.* **mikill**, **mōr**', though forms in *-mare, -meere* suggest **(ge)mǣre** 'a boundary, land on a boundary'. The farm is close to the southern boundary of the parish. MULBERRY HO. NEW DIKE. Forms are given in Fulstow parish *supra*. NEW INN, 1882 White. NORTH THORESBY SCREED. NORTH THORESBY WINDMILL, *the Wind milne of Thoresbye* 1623 *MiscDep 16*, - *winde milne* 1679, *the Mill* 1664 both *Terrier* and cf. *Milne grene*

1475-77, 1496-98, *Mylnegrene* 1523-24, 1546-47 all *MinAcct* (*v.* **grēne**[2]), *Mill Field* 1839 *TA*. In 1623 it is said to be *late in decay*. OLD FLEET DRAIN, *the Fleet draine* 1693 *Em*, *The Old Fleet* 1824 O, 1228 Bry, *the Fleet Drain* 1864 *Terrier*, *v.* **flēot** 'a rivulet, stream'. The same name is recorded from Grainsby and North Coates *supra*. RECTORY, *the Parsonage House* 1611, 1822 *Terrier*, *- parsonage House* 1709 *ib*, *Pars* 1828 Bry. SOUTHFIELD HO, cf. *Southfield* 1593-94 Lanc, *v.* **sūð**, **feld**. STANHOLME LANE, cf. *Stayneholme* 1451-53, 1546-47 *MinAcct*, *Stan-* 1609 *DuLaMB*, *the gate that comes from Stainholme* 1664 *Terrier*, *- Comes from Stanholme* 1671 *ib*, *Stannum* 1822 *ib*, *Stanholm lane* 1864 *Terrier*, 'the stony raised land in marsh', *v.* **steinn**, **holmr**, a Scand. compound, with **gata**. THORESBY BRIDGE, 1824 O, 1842 White, *- & Wharf* 1828 Bry, and cf. *ad pontem* 1327 *SR*, *ad Pontem* 1332 *ib* both (p). THORESBY FIELD (lost), 1822 *Terrier* (Fulstow), 1824 O, 1828 Bry, *campis de Toresbi* 1202 Ass, *campo de Norththorsby* 1382 Peace, *Thoresbiefeild* c.1577, *Thoresbie fielde* 1611, *Thorsby-feild* 1638 all *Terrier*, *Thorsbee Field* 1725 *Foster*, *v.* **feld**; on 1824 O it is the area in the west of the parish around Park Fm and Westfield Fm. THORESBY PRIM FEN (lost), 1824 O, *The Prim Fen* 1828 Bry, obscure. On 1824 O and 1828 Bry it is the area between Old Fleet Drain and New Dike, east of Gloucester Ho. WESTBROOK. WESTFIELD FM, cf. *Westfield* 1593-94 Lanc, *the west feld* 1601, *y^e^ -* 1611 both *Terrier*, *the west feld* 1609 *DuLaMB*, *- West feilde* 1638, *- Feild* 1664, *west feild* 1671, *West feild* 1679 all *Terrier*, *the West Field* 1745 *Em*, 1786 *Yarb*, one of the great fields of the village, *v.* **west**, **feld** and cf. Eastfield Fm *supra*. It is also referred to as *the west side of the Towne* 1577, *ye west side* 1709 both *Terrier*.

Field-Names

Forms dated 1272 are *Ass*; 1327, 1332 are *SR*; 1347 *LMR*; 1451-53, 1475-77, 1496-98, 1523-24, 1546-47 are *MinAcct*; 1557-58, 1589-90, 1590-91 Lanc; 1562 *Surv*; 1577, 1601, 1611, 1625, 1638, 1664, 1671, 1679, 1703, 1709, 1715, 1724, 1822, 1864 *Terrier*, 1608-9, 1609 *DuLaMB*; c.1651 *LD 35*; 1659 LNQ i; 1710 *Foster*, 1720 *MiscDep 42*; 1745 *Em*; 1758 *BRA 898;* 1774 *Hill*; 1776 *Webb*; 1786 *Yarb*; 1799 Young; 1793, 1852 *Haigh*; 1839 *TA*.

(a) Allotment 1839 (*freq*); Antient Lane 1839; Asgams (Hill) 1786 (*Asgarmare dike* 1601, *Asgarmare furlonge* 1611, *Asgarmares* 1611, 1625, *Agarmears furlong* (sic) 1638, *Asgarmeares* 1638, *Asgarmars* 1664, from the ON pers.n. *Ásgeirr* and **(ge)mǣre**, with **dík** and **furlang**); Ash Holt 1839 (*v.* **æsc**, **holt**); Back Paddock 1839 (cf. *Back Close* 1745); Barkworth's Pingle 1839 (named from the *Barkworth* family, cf. Thomas *Barkworth* 1822, and **pingel**); Beasby slead 1822 (*Beasby Sledd* 1601, 1611, *Beesbie sleed* 1625, *Beasby sleade* 1638, *Beesby Sleade* 1664, *Slead* 1679, 1697, 1703, *slead* 1709, *Beasby Slead* 1715, *ye slead* 1724, *v.* **slǣd**), Beesby Gate 1786 ('the road to Beesby', *v.* **gata**); north bleamons 1822 (*North Bleaninges* 1601, 1611, *North Breanings* (sic) 1638, - *Bleamings* 1664, 1679, 1715, 1724, - *bleamings* 1671, - *blemings* 1697, *north* - 1703, *North Blemings* 1709, *South Bleamings* 1679, obscure); Botlands 1786; Bottom Pce 1839 (*v.* **pece**); Bowlam green 1786, bowlam - 1822 (*Boalam greene* 1638, *Bowlam Green* 1679, 1703, 1709, - *green* 1697, - *greene* 1715, *Boulom green* 1724, there seems to have been some confusion between Bowlam green, in *Terriers*, and *Bownam* s.n. *Bownūn infra*; *Bowlam* is perhaps a surn. here, *v.* **grēne²**); Brick Yds 1839; Buildings and Fold Yd 1839; Buildings and Garth 1839 (*v.* **garðr** 'an enclosure, small plot of ground, especially near a house', as elsewhere in the parish); Bull bank 1786; Calf Garth 1839 (*v.* **garðr**); Chappel Cl 1786, the chapell yd 1822 (*Chappelgarth* 1601, *chappell* - 1611, - *Garth* 1638, *the Chappell garth* 1664, *Chappell gath* (sic) 1671, - *garth* 1703, *the Chappel* - 1709 (*v.* **garðr**), *ye Chapell close* 1697, *Chappell close* 1715, *Chappell* - 1724, *Chappel Close* 1745, the references are to the same piece of land and were in Autby); Charles green 1786 (from the pers.n. or surn. *Charles* and **grēne²**); Church and church Yd 1839 (cf. *ad eccl'iam de Adwaldeby* 1272, *ad ecclesiam* 1327, 1332 all (p)); clay pitts 1822 (*Clay pitt* 1679, *ye Clay pit* 1697, 1703, *clay* - 1709, *the* - 1715, *ye Clay pitt* 1724); dewnhams (sic) 1822; dockdale 1822 (*Dockdales* 1601, 1679, 1724, *Doc-* 1611, *Dockdale* 1638, *Dock* - 1664, *ye greene commonly called duke* - 1671, *Dock dales* 1703, *dock dale* 1709, *-dales* 1715, *v.* **docce** 'a dock (the plant)', **deill**); Far Cl 1839; feenfurs (sic) 1822 (*fen Furrs* 1609, - *firrs* 1697, *Fen* - 1703, 1709, *fenn furs* 1715, *ye Fen fors* (sic) 1724, 'the fen furrows', *v.* **fenn**, **furh**, cf. Fen Lane *supra*); Low -, Upr Flecklands, Upr Flecklands furlong 1786, fleck lands 1822, Low Fleck - 1852 (probably to be identified with *Flitlandes* 1625, *Flet-* 1638, *Pletlands* (sic) 1664, 1671, *Flet-* 1697, 1715, *Flettlandes* 1703, *Flet lands* 1709, *Lower Flet-* 1724 'land in dispute', *v.* **(ge)flit**, **land**); Fold yd, Buildings etc. 1839; Far -, Middle -, Nr Freemars 1786, the farr freemares (sic) 1822 (this is probably to be identified with *thremares* 1601, *Three-* 1611, 1625, 1724, *Three mares* 1638, 1709, *3* - 1697, *three* - 1703, 1715, 'the three boundaries', *v.* **þrēo**, **(ge)mǣre**, no doubt where three boundaries meet. The development of initial *Th-* to *F-* is well-established in p.ns., e.g. Freebirch PN Db 221 and is usually modern); furwell 1822 (*forwells* 1703, 1709, *fur-* 1715, 1724, v. **wella**); Far(r) -, Near Furze Cl 1786 (cf. *Great -, Little Fur Close* 1745), Gt -, Lt furze hill 1786, Gt Furze Hill 1839, Furze Hill Cl 1786 (*Audby Furhill* 1609, *Furhill closes* 1745, v. **fyrs, hyll**); Garsills 1786, garsill 1822 (*Garsill* 1577, 1638, 1664, 1679, 1697, 1703, 1709, 1724, *garsill* 1671, 1715, *garsell furlong* 1601, *Garsell* 1611, 'grass hill', v. **gærs, hyll**); Glebe Pce 1839; Goat Btm 1786 (v. **botm**; the first el. is probably **gotu** in L in the sense 'a sluice'); Gown Sleeves 1786 (doubtless a fanciful allusion to the shape of the field); Grainsby cl 1839 (*Graynsby close* 1638, *Grainsby Close* 1664, *grainsby Closes* 1671), Grainsby hedge flg (sic) 1786, Grainsby hedge 1822 (*Grainsby hedge* 1611, 1679, 1697, 1709, 1724, *- Hedge* 1625, *- hedg* 1703, *grainsby hedge* 1715, v. **hecg**); Grainsby lane end 1822 (*Graynsby lane end* 1638, *granesby lane end* 1671, *Grainsby -* 1697, 1703, 1709, 1724, *grainsby -* 1715, cf. *grainsby Laine* 1664, *Grainsby lane* 1679, alluding to Grainsby, the adjacent village to the west); the green (v. Thoresby green *infra*); Hacker dike 1786 (perhaps for *Acredike*, v. **æcer, dík**, common in north L, cf. PN L **2** 13); the hall clouts 1822 (*wast grounde called the hall clowt'* 1562, *Hall Clout* 1589-90, *Halle clowte* 1590-91, *Hall Clout* 1703, *ye Hall clout* 1709, *ye hall -* 1715, *Hall Cloote* 1724, v. **hall**; Dr Insley suggests that *clout* seems to be ME *clout* 'a clod' (OE *clūt* 'patch; cloth'), perhaps in the sense 'a patch of land'); Holmar Btm 1786 (v. **hol**^{2}, **(ge)mǣre**); Home Cl 1839; House, Maltkiln Yard etc. 1839; House Mill and Garden 1839; House Shop and Primitive Methodist chapel 1839; Houses, Methodist chapel Yard and Garden 1839; howks 1822 (*Howcasse* 1601, *Hocas* (sic) 1703, 1709, *Howcas* 1715, 1724, obscure); Hungry Hill 1786 (a common derogatory name for infertile land, v. **hungor**); (Far) Langmere Hill 1839, longmare 1822 (*Langmare* 1451-53, *lang-* 1475-77, 1496-98, *long-* 1451-53, 1523-24, 1546-47, *longemer* 1475-77, *longemare* 1546-47, *lang-* 1611, *Lang-* 1625, 1724, *long -* 1697, 1703, 1715, *- Mare* 1709, 'the long boundary', v. **lang, (ge)mǣre**; the two fields, so called in *TA*, are on the north boundary of the parish); Line Hills 1839, -Lds 1822 (v. **līn** 'flax', **hyll, land**); Long Cl 1839; Long Flg 1786; Long lds 1786 (*Long land* 1664, *- Lands* 1671, 'the long selions, strips', v. **land**); Longmoore 1822 (*longhmore* (sic) 1638, *Lange-* 1679, *Langmore mouth* 1697, 1709, 1724, *- Mouth* 1715, v. **lang, mōr**); maden hill 1822 (*Maiden hill* 1679, 1697, 1703, 1709, 1715, 1724, the sense of *maiden* here is uncertain); Margate flg 1786, the maregate 1822 (*the mare gate, ye mar -* 1577, *the Mar-* 1679, *Mar-* 1697, *y^e -* 1709, 1724, *ye margate furlonge* 1577, *Margate furlong* 1601, 1611, 'the boundary way', v. **(ge)mǣre, gata**); Meadow Btm 1839 (*ye medow* 1601, v. **mǣd, botm**); Mid Becks 1786 (probably '(place) between the streams', v. **mid, bekkr**, cf. *the becke* 1577, *y^e -* 1577, 1601, *Beckdale* 1697); the moore 1822 (*ye moore* 1577, *ye more* 1697, 1703, *- More*

1724, *morefurlong* 1601, *Morefurlong* 1611, *the More Foreland* 1679, *ye Moore furlong* 1715, *v.* **furlang**), Moregate end 1822 (*more gate* (*wonge*) 1577 (*v.* **ende**, **vangr**), *more-* 1601, 1611, *Moregate* 1638, 1671, *the* - 1664, *More* - 1697, 1703, *ye More* - 1709, *the Moore* - 1715, *ye more-* 1724, self-explanatory, *v.* **mōr** in the sense 'marshland', **gata**); North Nook 1786 (*ye nooke by Grainsby* 1625, *ye North Nooke* 1638, *the* - 1664, *the north nooke* 1671, *v.* **norð**, **nōk**, the references are to the same piece of land which adjoins Grainsby, to the north); Orby Rd 1786, hourby road 1822 (*Hawrebie gate* 1577, *Hawerby* - 1601, 1697, *Hawreby* - 1611, *horbie* - 1625, *Horby* - 1638, 1671, *Orby* - 1638, *haurby gaite* 1664, *Haurby gate* 1671, 1715, 1724, *Howerby* - 1703, *Howarby* - 1709 'the road to Hawerby (a neighbouring village)', *v.* **gata**. The variant spellings for Hawerby are noteworthy and have not been noted for the village name itself); Orchard 1786, 1839 (*ye Orchard close* 1638, *the orchard Close* 1664, 1671); Owl Moor Btm 1839 (*v.* **botm**); the Oxholme 1758 (*Oxholme* 1609, *v.* **oxa**, **holmr** 'higher ground in marshland etc.', as elsewhere in the parish); Oysier Cl, - Close dale 1786 (*Oysier Close* 1745, *v.* **oyser** 'an osier, a willow'); Paddock 1786, 1839 (*freq*); Pinfold Orchard 1839 (*v.* **pynd-fald**); Pingle (*freq*), Pingles 1839 (*v.* **pingel**); Plantn 1839 (*freq*); Poor Pce 1839 (perhaps 'a piece of endowed land to support the parish poor', but it may of course simply refer to the quality of the land); Quick Fenn 1786, quickfenn 1822, Quick Fen Cl 1839 (*Quicke fenne* (*gate*) 1577, *Quick Fen Nook* 1601, *Quickson* (sic) *Close* 1608-9, *Quickfen corner* 1611, *Quickfen* 1625, 1638, *quickfenn* 1671, *quick fen end* 1697, 1703, 1715, *Quick* - 1709, 1724, *v.* **fenn**, **ende**; *quick* probably has the sense 'mobile, shifting, readily yielding to pressure', NED s.v. *quick* A (10), cf. MED *quik-mire* 'quaking bog'); Ridal Bank 1786, rydale 1822 (*Ridale* 1451-53, 1496-8, 1638, *Ry-* 1475-77, 1523-24, 1546-47, 1679, *Ridall* 1577, 1601, 1611, 1638, 1664, *ridall, ridell* 1671, *Rydall* 1697, 1709, 1715, *Riedall* 1724, *Rydal furlong* 1601, *Ridall* (*furlonge*) 1611, from **ryge** and probably **deill** 'a share of land', with **furlang** and **banke**); Rochdale 1786 (*rochdale* 1671, perhaps as Dr Insley suggests from ME *rōche* 'a rock or boulder' and **dalr** 'a valley'); Rope Walk 1786; Round Cl 1839; Rye Cl 1786; Sand pitt hill 1786, Sand Hill 1839; scale pitts 1822 (*Skale pits* 1697, *Scale pits* 1703, 1709, *Skelpits* 1715, this is apparently a compound of **skáli**, 'a (temporary) hut or shed' and **pytt**; **skáli** is an OWScand word common in NW England and rare in the East Midlands, but several examples have now been noted in north L, *v.* also PN L **2** 69, 173 etc.); Segg green 1822 (*Segge grene furlonge* 1577, *seggreene* 1601, *Seggreene* 1611, 1664, *Seggholme greene* 1638, *Seggam greene* 1664, 1671, *Seggreene* 1679, *Seggegreene* 1697, *Segge Green* 1703, 1709, *Segg greene* 1715, - *Greene* 1724, *v.* **secg** 'sedge', **grēne**[2] 'a grassy spot'), segholms 1822, Segams Cl 1839 (*Seggum 5 stongs* 1625, *Seggham side* 1638, *Siggam side* 1664, 1724, *Siggam* 1671, *Segham*

Side 1697, *Seggam side* 1703, *Segam side* 1709, *Seggam fore land* 1679, *- furlong* 1715; as in the preceding f.n. the first el. is **secg** in a Scandinavianized form, the second el. here is uncertain); Shepherd Cl 1786, Shepherds - 1839 (named from the *Shepherd* family, cf. Christopher *Shepherd* 1841); Shop cl 1786, the shop cl 1822 (*ye shop close* 1697, *the* - 1703, *ye Shop* - 1709, *Shop* - 1715, *ye Shop Close* 1724, *the Shop Closes* 1745, *v.* **sc(e)oppa** 'a shed'); side lds 1822 (*Sidelandes* 1601, 1611, *Side lands* 1638, 1664, 1703, 1709, 1715, - *Lands* 1671, 1724, *Sidelands* 1697, 'the large, long selions, strips', *v.* **sīd, land**); South End Cl 1839; Long South Fen 1839 (*v.* **suð, fenn**); Stands Maize 1786; Stocks green 1786, Stocksgreen 1822 (probably to be identified with *Stokdalgrene* 1451-53, *Stokedale-* 1475-77, *Stokdale-* 1496-98, *Stockdale green* 1697, - *Green* 1703, 1709, - *greene* 1715, 1724, *ye Stockdalgreene willows* 1724, *Stocktgreene willow* (sic) 1601, *Stokes Daye greene* 1608-9, *Stock greene Willow* 1611, *Stockstay Greene Willows* 1625, *Stocksly Greene Willows* 1638, *Stocksey greene* 1664, *Stockes a green Willowes* 1671, *Stocksey green knowles* 1671, *Stondale green Snowles* (sic) 1679; unless the first el. *Stockdal(e)*, *Stokedale* is an original p.n. identical with Stockdale PN YW **6** 152, it is presumably the surn. *Stockdale* with **grēne**[2] 'a grassy spot', the later forms have been subject to considerable corruption); Stone Quarry 1786, stone quarry 1822 (*Stone squiere* (sic), - *furlonge, Stone squeriegoote* 1577, *Stones Querry furlonge* 1601, *Stonesquerry furlong* 1611, *Stonesquery* 1625, 1724, *stones quarry* 1638, *Stone querry* 1671, *Stonquarie* 1679, *Stone squary* 1697, *Stone Squary* 1703, *Stone Quarry* 1709, *v.* **stān, quarriere**, with prosthetic *S-* in some forms); Stothards Cl 1839 (named from the *Stothard* family, cf. Thomas *Stothard* 1812 *PR*); two closes in the Fen called Summer-head 1864 (*Close ... called the Somerytt* 1608-9, *Thoresby Sumerett* c.1651 *v.* **sumor, ete** 'grazing, pasture', for a detailed discussion of the name *v.* *Summerhead* in Marsh Chapel *supra*); sunwell or south well close 1776; Swaith headland dale 1786 (*v.* **swæð, hēafod-land**); Swandale 1786; swineshead hole (sic) 1822 (*Swinheard Hole* 1601, *Swinherd hole* 1611, *Swine head Hole* 1638, *Swinheard* - 1664, *Swinhearde hole* 1671, *Swineherd* - 1697, *Swine herd* - 1703, *Swinerd* - 1715, 1724, probably from the occupational name or derived surn. ME *Swineherd*, cf. *Jo Swinheard* 1606 *PR*, and **hol**[1] 'a hollow'); Thompsons Cl 1786 (*Willm Thompson Close* 1724, *Thompsons* - 1745, named from the *Thom(p)son* family, cf. Richard *Thomson* 1557 *PR*); Thoresby Green 1793, the green 1822 (*the grene* 1577, 1608-9, *the grenne* 1577, *ye greene* 1638, *the* - 1664, *the Green* 1709, 'the village green', *v.* **grēne**[2]; *the greene furlong* 1577, 1601, *y^e^* - 1611, *Greene* - 1638, *greene furlonge* 1671, - *Furlonge* 1664, *the Green furlong* 1679 may belong here, but are perhaps more likely to refer to a green furlong); Thoresby Holme 1774 (*v.* **holmr**), Thoresby Warren 1799 (*v.* **wareine**); John Tower's cl 1822; West Cl 1839; the willows 1822 (*the Willowes*

1679, *ye willows* 1697, *ye willowes* 1703, 1709); Wood 1839 (cf. *att Wodesende de Thoresby* 1347 (p), *v.* **wudu, ende**); wreenooke 1822 (*Wree nooke* 1697, *wrye* - 1703, *Wree Nooke* 1709, *Wreanooke* 1715, *Renooke* 1724, the first el. being ModE *wry* 'bent, twisted', the second **nōk** 'a nook', as Dr Insley suggests).

(b) *Acfordale* 1451-3, 1475-77, 1496-98, 1523-24 (*v.* **āc, ford** with **dalr**); *Audbye Closs* 1609, *Audby brattes* 1611 (cf. *ii bratt Leas at Audby* 1601, *v.* **brot**), *Audby greate feld* 1601, *Audby well* 1679 (alluding to Autby *supra*); *aughtange* 1451-53, *Aught'ank'* 1475-77, *Aughtange* 1496-98 (obscure); *Close ... called Azure Mouse* (sic) 1745; *atte Bele* 1332 (p) (for a discussion of this name, *v.* Utterby f.ns. (b) *supra*); *Benecrofte* 1451-53, 1475-76, 1496-97, 1523-24, 1546-47 (*v.* **bēan, croft**); *Bengedyke* 1451-53, *Bengidike* 1475-77, *Bengedike* 1496-98, *Byngdale* 1523-24, *Byndale* 1546-47 (the first el. is obscure); *Edward Bennitt close* 1715; *Bonecrofte* (sic in transcript) 1557-58, *Boone Crofte* 1608-9 (if not copying errors for *Benecroft* (*v.* Bean Land Cl in (a) *supra*) perhaps containing the surn. *Boon(e)*, *v.* **croft**); *Bownūn furlonge* 1577, *Bownān furlong* 1601, 1611, *Bownam* (sic) 1625, 1664, 1671, 1715, *Bowman* (sic) 1638, *bownam* 1709, *Bowram* (sic) 1724, *Bownam green(e)* 1664, 1697, cf. Bowlam Green in f.ns. (a) *supra*); *Brightleues* 1451-53, *Bright'leues* 1475-77, *Brightbenes* (sic) 1496-98, *Brigh'benes* 1523-24, *Bryghtbenes* 1546-47; *Richard Brownes Greene* 1638, *Brownes greene* 1664 (*v.* **grēne**[2]); *the Cath holme* 1608-9 (perhaps *v.* **catt, holmr**); *the church yarde* 1611; *Corneholme* 1451-53, 1475-77, 1496-98, *-hill* 1496-98, 1523-24, 1546-47 (*v.* **holmr, hyll**); *Corne lands* 1638, 1664, - *Lands* 1671 (*v.* **land**, the first el. of this and the prec. f.n. is ME **corn** 'corn, grain', cf. ME *cornescroft* 'the place where grain is grown (MED s.v.)); *Counteacr'* 1451-53, 1496-98, 1523-24, *Countesacre* 1475-77, 1546-47 (perhaps 'the countess's arable land', *v.* **countes, æcer**); *The Courte house* 1608-9; *Common called the Cowpasture* 1608-9; *Crackebeck* 1638, *Cracke* - 1664, *Crack* - 1671 (*v.* **kráka** 'a crow, a raven', **bekkr**); *dykefordale* 1546-47 (*v.* **dīk, fore, dalr**); *Ernesendale* (sic) 1451-53, *Arneson-* 1475-77, *Arnesen-* 1496-98, *Areston-* 1546-47 (*v.* **deill**; the first el. is a Cont Germ fem pers.n., with which Dr Insley compares West Frankish *Ermensinda*); *Estkirkepittes* 1451-53, 1496-98, *Kirkepyttes* 1523-24, *Krikepittes* (sic) 1546-47 (*v.* **kirkja, pytt**); *Eylefenne* 1451-53, *Gillesherne* 1475-77, *Gillefenne* 1496-98, *Erlesfenne* 1523-24, *Erlefenne* 1546-47 (the forms are too varied to suggest a convincing etymology); *Footebale Close* 1609; *Gallowell* 1638, *gallo-* 1664, *gallow* - 1671 (*v.* **galga, wella**); *Goldewell* 1546-47 (*v.* **gold** '(marsh) marigold', **wella**); *the greate feld* 1601, 1611, *Great and Little Field* 1745 (*v.* **feld**); *Grouthewich'* 1451-53, *Growith'* 1475-77, *Grouthwith'* 1496-98, *Grouthworth'* 1523-24, *Grouthworthe* 1546-47 (obscure); *Hakemare* 1451-53, 1496-98, *Hakmer* 1475-77, *Hokemare* 1523-24, 1546-47 (*v.* **haca** 'a hook', presumably in some topographical sense, **(ge)mǣre**); *Halce iuxta Foghelestouwe syke* 1451-53, *-iuxta Foghelestuwe* - 1496-98, *Cromeholmehalce iuxta Foghelstuwe* 1523-24, *Cromeholmehalce* (sic) 1546-47 (*v.* the Sykes in Fulstowe f.ns. (a) *supra*; Dr Insley suggests the first el. of *Cromeholmehalce* is ME *crumb, croum, crom(e)* (from OE **crumb**) 'bent, cracked, curved', the second **holmr**, hence 'a curve-shaped land in marsh, water-meadow', with **halh** 'a corner of land'); *halgrene* 1451-53, *Hallegrene* 1475-77, *Hal-* 1496-98, 1523-24, *Halle-* 1546-47 (*v.* **hall**, **grēne**[2], cf. *iuxta Claus' Manerii* 1496-98, 1523-24 - *claus' manerii* 1546-47); *halhill'* 1451-53, *Hallehull'* 1475-77, *Halhill'* 1496-98, 1523-24, *Halhill* 1546-47 (*v.* **hall**, **hyll**); *Hawerby Gapp* 1679, *Haurby gap* 1715, 1724, *v.* **gap**); *Hawreby knowles* 1601, *Hawrby* - 1611, *Horbie knolles* 1625, *Horby Knowles* 1638 (alluding to the neighbouring village of Hawerby, *v.* **gap**, **cnoll**); *One headland with the fellow* 1671 (presumably 'the headland with its counterpart', cf. the headland and his fellow in Barnetby le Wold f.ns. (a), PN L **2** 12, *headland & fellow* in Binbrook f.ns. (b), PN L **3** 10 and *Headland and fellow* in Ludborough f.ns. (b) *supra*); *Henningby oxgange* (sic) 1608-9 (*v.* **oxgang**); *herdebanks* 1451-53, *Hardebankes* 1475-77, 1496-98, *Harebankes* (sic) 1523-24, *Harebanke* 1546-47 (*v.* **banke**; the first el. being perhaps OE **heord** 'a herd, a flock', with later confusion with **hara** 'a hare'); *Haudetake* 1546-47; *ye hie gate* 1577 (*v.* **hēah**, **gata**), *ye high street close, ye low* - 1638; *Howcliffe* 1611 (*v.* **haugr**, **clif**); *Igelmarre* 1451-53, *Ingelmare* (sic) 1475-77, *Igel-* 1496-98, *Iglemere* 1523-24, *Inglemare* 1546-47 ('the leech fen', *v.* **ighli**, **marr**, and for **ighli**, *v. Higelmare* in North Ormsby f.ns. (b) *supra*); *Toft cald Jackhouse* 1609 (presumably this means 'Jack's house'); *Jew headland* 1601, *Jewheadland* 1611 (*v.* **hēafod-land**); *Lough gate, - gattes* 1577, *louth gates* 1601, *Loath gates hill* 1609, *Louth gates* 1611, 1724, - *gate* 1625, 1638, 1664, 1671, 1697, - *Gates* 1679, - *Gate* 1703, *Lowth gate* 1709, *Louth gates furlong* 1611 ('the road to Louth', *v.* **gata**); *lyuelond'* 1451-53, *lyfeland'* 1475-77, *lyvelande* (sic) 1496-98, *levydale* 1523-24, *legydale* (sic) 1546-47 (Dr Insley suggests that *lyuelond'* is from ME *lēf* (OE **lēof**) 'pleasant, prized' and **land**. The two later forms are clearly errors); *in the Mare* 1327, *en la mare* 1332 both (p) (*v.* **(ge)mǣre** 'a boundary, land on a boundary'); *the marfaire* 1664 (*v.* **marfur** 'a boundary furrow'); *Midby* 1327, *middeby* 1332 both (p) (for the same name, *v.* Ludborough f.ns. (b) *supra*); *Mikelgrene* 1451-53, *Milnegrene* (sic) 1475-77; *Mickleholme* 1638 (*v.* **mikill** 'big', **holmr**); *Moreseke* 1451-53, *Moresike* 1475-77, *Moresyke* 1496-98, 1523-24, 1546-47 (*v.* **mōr**, **sík**); *Murbanks* 1589-90; *ye narrow strete* 1577; *oxondale* 1451-53, *Oxendale* 1475-77, 1496-98, 1523-24, 1546-47 (*v.* **oxa**, **deill**); *on* (i.e. one) *Close at the streete called parson Crofte, ye parson croftes* 1601, *parson crofte* 1611 (*v.* **croft**), *ye parson wall nooke* 1557, *parson wall Nooke furlong* 1601, - *nooke furlong* 1611, *parsonage Wall nook* 1625, *v.* **persone**, **wall** with **nōk**, **furlang**);

pedydale 1451-53, *Pedy-* 1475-77, *pedi-* 1496-98, *Pety-* 1523-24, *Putty-* 1546-47 (from **deill**, with perhaps the surn. *Peddy* or *Petty*); *Pilkington Close* 1745 (from the surn. *Pilkington*); *the Pitts* 1659 (*v.* **pytt**); *the platts* 1664 (*v.* **platt**^{2} 'a small piece of land'); *ii locis ... qui dicuntur poyntes* 1451-53, *poyntes* 1475-77; *preist Croft* 1562, *Presteclose* 1601, *Prest Close* 1611, *ye Preist close* 1638, *the preist -* 1664, *ye preist -* 1671, *ye preyst grene* 1577, *one peece of Medow called preist -* 1601, *Prestgreene* 1611, *ye Preist Grene* 1638, *the preist greene* 1664, *prest greene* (*one litle greene*) 1671, *the Preist Greene* 1679 (*v.* **prēost**, **croft**, **clos(e)**, and **grene**^{2}); *ye Rundell* 1638 (*v.* **rynel** 'a small stream, a runnel'); *Skirpittes* 1451-53, 1475-77, 1496-98, *Skirpyttes* 1523-24, *Scarpittes* 1546-47, *Skir-* 1577, *Middelskir-* 1451-53 (*v.* **middel**), *Mikelskerpittes* 1475-77, *Mikilscar-* 1496-98, *Mikylcarpyttes* (sic) 1523-24, *Mikilcarpittes* 1546-47 (*v.* **mikill**), *Westkir-* 1451-53, *Westkirke-* 1496-98, *Westlerpyttes* (sic) 1523-24, *Westcar-* 1546-47 (*v.* **west**, **pytt**; the first el. is uncertain since the forms are so varied; the change from *Middel-* to *Mikel-*, *Mikil-* may be erroneous, as 'middle' is more likely to contrast with 'west'); *Skytermarre* 1451-53, *Sketmar langmar* (sic) 1475-77, *Skitermare* 1496-98 (the first el. is OE **scitere** 'a sewer, a stream used as an open sewer', as in Skitter Beck and Ulceby Skitter PN L **2** 292, with the initial *sc-* in a Scandinavianized form; the second el. is apparently **(ge)mǣre** 'a boundary, land on a boundary'); *Common called South Fleete and Howells* 1609; *Common called the stake* 1608-9; *Steuen Wath* 1611 (presumably from the pers.n. or surn. *Steven* and **vað** 'a ford'); *Stokmarre* 1451-53, *Stokmare* 1496-98, *Stoke-* 1523-24, *Stoke-* 1546-47; *stony hill* 1577; *the suer Streete Close* 1664, *ye suer streete* 1671 (*v.* **strǣt**, but there is insufficient evidence in the sources to tell whether this is a reference to Barton Street); *Tabusgrene* 1451-53, 1496-98, 1523-24, 1546-47 (*v.* **grēne**^{2}); *the Thackground* 1608-9 ('land from which thatching material was obtained', *v.* **þak**); *Thickings Close* 1608-9; *Turfe Fen* 1609 ('peat fen', *v.* **turf**, **fenn**); *Twetstange* 1451-53, *Twe-* 1475-77, *Twestang'* 1496-98, *Westange* 1523-24, *west-* 1546-47 (perhaps from **west** and **stǫng** 'a pole'; if so the prefixed *T* in some early forms is from the misdivision of *atte west*); *Two Mearbalks* 1590-91 (*v.* **(ge)mǣre**, **balca**); *ii pence grene* 1577 (alluding to a rent, *v.* **grēne**^{2}); *Tykyng* 1451-53, 1475-77, 1496-98, *Tygyng'* 1523-24, *Tygyne* 1546-47; *the garth of Jo Underwod* 1562; *Urchermore Furlonge* 1664, 1671 (perhaps from **urcheon** 'a hedgehog' and **mōr**, with **furlang**); *Vivorie Close* 1589-90 (the first el. is perhaps from **viver** 'a fish-pond'); *le Waire* 1451-53, *le Ware* 1475-77, *le Waraa* 1451-53, 1496-98, *Wraa* 1475-77, 1523-24, 1546-47 (perhaps *v.* **vrá**); *the House at Thorsby Commonly called the Worlds End House* 1720 (*World's End* is often used for a remote spot); *Wronge landes* 1577, *wrong-* 1601 ('twisted selions', *v.* **vrangr** 'crooked', **land**).

Waithe

WAITHE

Wade (4x) 1086 DB, 1194 CurP, 1213 Abbr, 1303 Cl, *Wada* (2x) c.1115 LS, 1212 Fees, *Uada* (2x) c.1115 LS

Wadde 1203 FF

Wadhe 1231 Ch, 1231 Cl

Waða 1177 P (p), *Waþe* e13 HarlCh (p)

Wathe 1196 ChancR, c.1200 (c.1330) *R*, 1203 Cur, 1210-12 RBE, 1229 Cl (p), 1238-41, 1242-43 Fees, 1254 ValNor, 1272 *Ass*, 1281 QW, 1282 *AD*, 1282 Cl, 1291 Tax, 1294 Ch, 1303, 1316 FA, 1320 Pat, 1320 Orig, 1327 *SR et freq* to 1681 *Haigh*, *Watha* 1275 RH, *Wath'* 1202 Ass, 1204 P, 1207 FF, 1349 *Cor*, 1375 Peace, *Wath* eHy3 (1409) Gilb, 1294 Fine, 1294 Orig, 1297 AD, 1309 Pat, 1322, 1325 Cl, 1338 Pat, 1362 Ipm *et freq* to 1716 *Haigh*, - *al Waith* 1723 SDL

Wayth 1406, 1408, 1415 Cl, 1526 Sub, 1555 Pat, 1638 *Terrier*, 1666 *Haigh et freq* to 1715 *ib*, *Waythe* 1529 LP xiv, 1745 *Terrier*, *Wayeth* 1673 *Haigh*, *Waith* p1561 *ib*, 1623 *Hill*, 1675 *Em*, 1679 *Terrier*

Wayte 1553 Pat, *Waite* 1653 *ParlSurv*

The earliest forms in *-d-* suggest that Waithe is derived from OE **(ge)wæd** 'a ford'. By the later 12th century the *-d-* had been replaced by *-th-*, either because of the Scandinavianization of *-d-* to *-th-*, as in Louth (LSR), earlier *Lude*, or by the replacement of **(ge)wæd** by the cognate ON **vað**. In either case the meaning of the name is 'at the ford', which must have been over Waithe Beck, where a minor road crosses the stream half a mile east of the church. Dr Insley points out that early forms with final *-e* indicate an oblique case with locative function. Early forms in *Waþe* etc. stand for a pronunciation [wa:ðə] from the latter part of the 12th century onwards due to open syllable lengthening in disyllabic words. The forms indicate loss of final [ə] in the 14th century at the latest, and this would have been accompanied by the devoicing of [ð]. Cf. also Wath PN NRY 52, 219, Wath upon Dearne PN WRY **1**, 118.

CROSS. NORMAN WELLS HO, on the boundary of Ashby cum Fenby parish in which the name is noted *supra*. VICARAGE (lost), *the vicaridge howse* 1602, 1692, *The Vicarage house* 1638, *Vickerage* 1668, *A vickridge house* 1679, *There has been lately no Vicaridge House* 1745, *one dwelling house called the Vicarage now divided into two cottages* 1864 all *Terrier*, cf. *the vicaridge garth* 1602 *ib*. WAITHE BECK, *the Becke* c.1650 *Haigh*, *- becke* 1656 *Haigh*, *Wayth beck* 1680 *ib*, *v*. **bekkr**. For additional forms, *v*. Beck Cl in Ashby cum Fenby f.ns. (a) *supra*. WAITHE GRANGE is apparently an example of the late use of **grange** in the dial. sense 'a homestead, small mansion or farm-house, especially one standing by itself remote from others', a meaning recorded in EDD from L. WAITHE HOUSE FM. WAITHE MILL (disused), 1824 O, *Waythe Mill* 1828 Bry, *A mill in the East part of the Parish* 1822 *Terrier*. WATHALL (lost). This was the name of a manor recorded as *Wathehalle* 1349 Ipm, *Wath Halle* 1416 Cl, *Wathall'* 1421-23, 1496-98, 1497-98, 1523-24, 1546-47, 1608-9 all *MinAcct*, 1608-9 *DuLaMB*, 1720 *Haigh*, *Wat'halle* 1451-53 *MinAcct*, *Wathehall'* 1477 *DC*, *Wathe Hall* 1491-92 Lanc, *the Lordship or Manor of Wathall with Houghton and Tetney* 1765 *TLE*, *Manor of Wathall* 1820 *GDC*, *the Manor or Lordship of Wathall cum Tetney and Houghton otherwise Wathall Tetney cum Holton* 1829 *BRA 641*.

Field-Names

Forms dated 1209-35 are LAHW 43; c.1221 Welles iii; 1327, 1332 *SR*; 1384, 1398, 1436, 1472 *AD*; 1386, 1395 Peace; 1477 *DC*; 1491-92 Lanc; 1497-98 *MinAcct*; 1537-38 *AOMB*; c.1577, 1601, 1602, 1611, 1612, 1638, c.1650, 1664, 1668[1], 1671, 1690, 1697, 1703, 1706, 1715[1], 1724, 1745, 1822, 1864 *Terrier*, 1608-9 *DuLaMB 119*; c.1650, 1656, 1666, 1668[2], 1679, 1680, 1683, 1685, 1687, 1702, 1705, 1710, 1715[2], 1717, 1720, 1723, 1725, 1807, 1860 *Haigh*; 1675 *Em*.

(a) Bay Green 1807 (perhaps to be identified with (*The*) *Bray greene* c.1650, *Bray* being from ME (Northern) *brā* (from ON *brá* 'an eye-lid') 'a bank (of a stream)' etc, cf. MED s.v. *brō*); Bullens Cl 1807 (probably from the surn. *Bullen*); the East Fen of Waith 1807 (cf. Waith West Fen *infra*); the East Fd of Waith 1807 (*the east field* 1656, *the East Field* 1666, 1668[2], *- East feild of Wayth* 1680, *- east feild* 1683, *- East Field* 1702, *- feild* 1717, *the East & West* *feilds* 1685, - *feildes* 1687, *Waith East-feild* 1723, *v.* **ēast**, **feld**, one of the open fields of the parish, cf. Waith West Fd *infra*); Far Ld 1807; Glebe Cl 1860, the glebe Cl 1864; Higher Nooking 1807 (from dial. *nooking* 'a nook', *v.* **nōk** and The Nookings PN L **3** 144); the Ings (Btm) 1807 (*Wath Inngs* 1608-9, *the Inges, the Inges gate, the Inges hedge(s)*, - *Ings hedg* c.1650, *the Ings* 1656, 1683, *the Inges* 1687, *Waith Ings* 1679, *Ings* 1723, *v.* **eng** 'meadow, pasture' as elsewhere in the parish); Marsh Btm 1807 (*v.* **botm**), Marsh Leys 1807; the North Ld, North Lds 1807 (*Norland gare* c.1650, *Norlands* 1725 (*v.* **geiri** 'a gore'), *the Northlandes* 1687, *Norlands* 1723, *v.* **norð**, **land**); the Paddock 1864; Peaseland Cl 1864 (*v.* **pise**, **land**); Waith Fen Side, Waith West Fen 1807 (*Weith fenne* c.1577, *the Fenn, the Fen boddom* c.1650 (*v.* **botm**), - *gate* (*v.* **gata**), *the Fenclose* c.1650 (*v.* **clos(e)**), *the Fen* 1683, *the Fenn* 1687, *Waith fen* 1710, - *Fenn* 1725, *v.* **fenn**); Waith West Fd 1807, the West Fd 1822 ("the West field" 1384, "the west field" 1436, *the West Feild of Waith*, - *of Wayth* c.1650, *the West feild* 1656, 1680, - *Field* 1666, *the west Field* 1668[2], - *feild* 1683, *the Westfeild* 1687, *Waith* -, *wath west Field* 1697, *the West Feild* 1705, - *feild* 1717, *v.* **west**, **feld**, one of the open fields of the parish, cf. the East Fd of Waith *supra*).

(b) *Ashby closes* c.1650, *ashby hedge* 1690 (from Ashby cum Fenby *supra*); *the banke* c.1650 (*v.* **banke**); *the Beck Side* 1723 (*v.* **bekkr**, the reference is to Waithe Beck *supra*); *ben* -, *bend gate* c.1650 (Dr Insley suggests that this is 'the gate fastened with a cord or chain', *v.* **geat**, the first el. being ME *bende* 'fetter, shackle, chain; a cord for tying or fastening', cf. MED s.v.); *Bryning mare* 1436, *Brian Maire* c.1650 (*v.* **(ge)mǣre**; Dr Insley suggests that the first el. is probably a ME surn. derived from the OE pers.n. *Bryning*, later being confused with the pers.n. or surn. *Brian*); *One stong ... called by the name of the Butcher* c.1650, *The First* -, *The Second Butcher* 1723 (*Butcher* is one of three terms for pieces of meadow in Waithe, not previously noted in the survey. They are recorded in *severall other parcells of Meadow called Butcher, Frank, and Isabell* (sic) c.1650. The meaning of *Butcher* is obscure and the word is not found in dictionaries, but it is recorded as an appellative in Waithe in *A Butcher* 1723. For *Frank* and *Isabell*, *v. infra*); *Childrens farm* 1723; *ad ecclesiam* 1327 (p), *atte Kirke* 1332 (p) (*v.* **kirkja**); *Common Close* 1537-38; *the corne* c.1650, *the Cornfield* (*of Wayth*) 1720 (*v.* **corn**, **feld**); *one land called ... the Cow* c.1650; *Crocked land* 1537-38 (*v.* **crōked**, **land**); *culture que vocatur Croft* 1209-35, *Crofft ex orientali parte ecclesie de Wathe* c.1221, *a forland called Croft gates* c.1650 (*v.* **croft**); *Daile sicke, dailesike gutter* (*v.* **goter**), *the dayle sike* - c.1650, *a forland called Dailesike hill* c.1650, *dalesike* 1656 (*v.* **deill**, **sík**, cf. *eastdaile sike, west dailesike gutter infra*); *eastdaile sike,*

East dailesike gutter c.1650 (*v.* **ēast**, **deill**, **goter**, and *Daile sicke supra*); *the Feild* (*v. Wathe Feild infra*); *Fenby daile* c.1650 (*v.* **deill**; from Fenby in Ashby cum Fenby parish); *The first -, The Second Frank* 1723 (*Frank* is recorded as an appellative in *A Frank, A Frank by dale* in the same document. It is defined in MED s.v. as "an enclosure; a pen for fattening domestic fowls" and in NED sb^2 as "an enclosure, esp. a place to feed hogs in". For *by dale*, cf. *the Is bell infra* and *Grafurthe Bydle* and *Vincent Bydale* in Waltham f.ns. (b) *infra*); *Grainsby closes* c.1650, *Grain(e)sby hedg* c.1650, *Grainesby hedge* 1656, *Graynesbygate* 1384 (*v.* **gata**, named from Grainsby); *green gate, South side greene gate forland* c.1650 (*v.* **gata**); *Grenethyng* 1472 (from **þing** 'property, premises', with probably the surn. *Green*, cf. *atte Grene* 1327, 1398, *of the Grene* 1332, *de Grene* 1386, *othe Grene* 1395, 1398 all (p)); *Hargholme dayll* 1537-38, *Hougham Dale* (sic) 1687, *Harthum, litle* - 1723, *little hath ham* c.1650 (obscure); *Hing hipp* c.1650 (unexplained); *Howlon Inge* 1656 (*v.* **eng**); *two Dales called Houlton Dales* 1675 (*v.* **deill**, referring to Holton le Clay); *hunnam Dyke* c.1650; *Iglemore* c.1650 (*v.* **ighli**, **mōr**^{1} and *v. Higelmare* in North Ormsby f.ns. (b)); *the impited middow* c.1650 (the sense of *impited* here is quite uncertain. It occurs as an appellative in 1723, descriptive, it appears, of sub-divisions of pieces of meadow, several of which are said to be *Impitt.* or *Impitted*); *the Is bell, The Third Isbell, the Isbel Bydale* 1723 (*Isbel* is recorded as an appellative in *An Is bell, An Is bel bidale* in the same document, but its meaning is obscure and the word is not found in dictionaries. For *Bydale*, cf. *A Frank by dale supra*); *Innome clos* 1537-38 (*v.* **innām** 'piece of land taken in or enclosed'); *Joshua Farm* 1723 (no doubt named from the surn. *Joshua*); *domus voc' a Kel'hous in Wathall'* 1497-98 (probably for *Kilnhous*); *langmore, - hill, - Lease* c.1650 (from **lang**, **mōr**^{1}, with **hyll** and **lǣs**); *Linlands end* c.1650 (*v.* **līn** 'flax', **land**); *litelhoupe Close* (sic) 1656; *Atteloft 1327, atte Loft'* 1332 both (p) (*v.* ON **lopt** 'a loft'); *Long close* 1715; *the long land* c.1650 (*v.* **land**); *the Marsh, the Marsh Leas* (*v.* **lea (lēah)** 'meadow, pasture' in the pl.), *the middow in -, the swath in the Marsh* c.1650 (*v.* **mǣdwe**, **swæð**, **mersc**); *ye apertin' ... in þe towne & feldes of Wathe callid Mawdelayn* 1477; *Mawing Close* 1687; *le Mere* 1436 (*v.* **(ge)mǣre**); *Michell farme* 1565, *Mitchel farm* 1723 (named from the *Mitchell* family, cf. Richard *Mitchell* 1637 *Wills*); *litle Moigne clos, Moigne South close* 1537-38, *Moines Close* 1656 (named from the *Moigne* family, cf. Thomas *Moygne* of *Wyfflingham* (i.e. North Willingham LNR) named in the 1537-38 document); *the Pinder nookeing* c.1650 (*v.* **pindere**, **nooking** and cf. Higher Nooking in (a) *supra*); *Phillips farm* 1723 (Robert *Phillips* is mentioned in the same document); *the Pitt, ye Pitts* 1723 (*v.* **pytt**); *the plowed gutter that draynes the Towne* c.1650; *the Poose puding* 1723 ('pease pudding', *v.* **pise**, **peosu**, a fanciful name doubtless referring to sticky soil); *place called Pottams* c.1650; *a forland called Runfurs, Runfurs forland* c.1650, *Runnfurrs* 1656 ('running furrows', *v.* **furh**); *a forland called ... Scalla Cow* c.1540 (for *Scalla* cf. The Scallow Hall, PN L **3**, 4, but for a revised etymology, *v. Scallow* in Covenham St Bartholomew f.ns. (b); *Cow* is unexplained); *Seggarthe* 1537-38, *Seggarthes* 1656 (*v.* **garðr**; the first el. is **secg**, in a Scandinavianized form); *Sharpthorne hedg* c.1650 (*v.* **þorn**, **hecg**); *the little sheep nooke* c.1650 (*v.* **nōk**); *Wid. Smith farm* 1723; *South Fen(n)* c.1650 (*v.* **sūð**, **fenn** and cf. Waith Fen Side in (a) *supra*); *Southindale* 1436, *Southan daile, a forland called ... Southan* c.1650 (probably '(place) south in the valley', *v.* **sūð**, **in**, **dalr**); *Springclose, Spring garth or little close or garth* 1715 (*v.* **spring**, **garðr**, **clos(e)**); *longe stone Rage, short stong stong Rages* (sic) c.1650; *the streete or commonway* 1602; *the swath lea* c.1650 (*v.* **swæð** 'a swathe', **lea** (OE **lēah**)); *Tharolds farm* 1723 (Christopher *Tharold* is named in the same document); *thorn close, forland called by the name of Thorn, thorneforland* c.1650 (*v.* **þorn**, **furlang**); *Thorpcroft* 1472, *thorp close, thorp' closse* 1537-38, *the thorpe closes, the Thorpe hedg(e), the thorpes* c.1650, *the great thorps* 1666, *thorpe* 1668[2], *Great Thorps* 1702, 1717, *great thorps* 1705, *That close of pasture ... called and knowne by the name of (Great) Thorps* 1717 (*v.* **þorp** 'a secondary settlement', but the significance here is not known, **croft**); *a forland called three oures* c.1650 (perhaps *v.* **ofer**[2] 'a slope, a hill, a ridge', in the pl.); *atte Touneshend* 1332 (p), *att the Towne end, the banke att the Townes end* c.1650 (self-explanatory); *Water Garthes* 1537-38, *the water garth* c.1650 (*v.* **wæter** 'wet', **garðr**); *the watering dyke* c.1650; *Wathe Feild* c.1577, *Wathe fielde* 1601, *Wathe field* 1611, *wath fielde* 1612, *Wath-feild* 1638, *the Feild* c.1650, *Wayth feild* 1664, 1668[1], *wath field* 1664, *Wath field* 1671, 1703, *Waishe field* (sic) 1690, *Wath Field* 1706, *Waith field* 1724, *ye field of Waith* 1715[1] (*v.* **feld**); *the Wathleake bracke* 1608-9; *Wath Towne meadowe* 1608-9; *west dailesike gutter* c.1650 (*v.* **west**, **deill**, **goter**, and *Daile sicke supra*); *the West hedg* c.1650; *the windinges, the windinesse* c.1650 (probably 'place where there are bends', *v.* **winding** and the discussion under *two wyndinges* in f.ns. (b) of Binbrook, PN L **3** 16).

Waltham

WALTHAM

Waltham (4x) 1086 DB, c.1115 LS, Hy2 (1409) Gilb, 1177, 1178, 1188 P (p), 1190, 1191 ib, 1192, 1193, 1194, 1195 ib (p), 1196 ChancR, 1197 P (p), 1201 ib, 1202 *HarlCh*, 1202 to 1207 all P, 1214 Cur (p), 1217 Pat, 1230 ChancR (p),

1231 Ch, 1231, 1232, 1235, 1237 Cl, 1238-41, 1242-43 Fees, 1254 ValNor, 1258 FF, 1275, 1276 RH, 1284 *HarlCh,* 1290 Misc, 1290 Pat, 1291 Tax, 1297 AD, 1303 Cl, 1311 Ipm *et freq, - juxta Barnolbi, - juxta Grimesby* 1308 Inqaqd, - *juxta Grymesby* 1309 Orig, 1436 IBL, - "near" *Grymesby* 1308 Pat, - "by" *Grymesby* 1367 Cl, 1437 Pap, - "by" *Grymmesby* 1497 Cl, - *iuxta Scarthou* 1328 *FF,* - "by" *Scarthou, - in Lyndesheymerssh* 1400 Pat, - *in Lyndesey* 1409, 1416 ib, *-hame* 1219 Welles, 1454 Cl, *Walteham* 1275 RH

Wautham(') 1230 P, 1234 FF, 1249, 1252 Cl

'The wold estate', *v.* **wald, hām**. All the known examples of Waltham have been studied by Rhona Huggins, "The Significances of the Place-Name Wealdhām", *Medieval Archaeology,* xix 1975, who has convincingly argued that they comprise a coherent group of names and, further, that they were used in an early period of the settlement of the districts in which they occur for royal administrative centres in forest areas. It may, of course, be pure coincidence, but the name of Jordan *le Forester* is recorded in Waltham in 1323 Pat. It is referred to as near Barnoldby le Beck, Great Grimsby and Scartho.

WALTHAM SOKE, *Socha de Waltham* 1188, 1191 P, 1196 ChancR. R1 Cur, 1202 *HarlCh,* 1212 Fees, *soca* - 1204, 1206, 1207 P, 1210-12 RBE, 1230 Cl, 1237, 1238-41 Fees, 1244 Cl, 1275, 1276 RH, 1320 Orig, *socna de Wautham* 1230 Cur, *soka de Waltham* 1205 OblR, 1206 Ass, 1212, 1226-28 Fees, 1227 Pat, 1228, 1234, 1235 Cl, 1242-43 Fees, 1260 Cl, 1281 QW, *sokna* - 1226 ClR, "soke of" - 1229, 1259, 1260 Ch, 1299 Pat, 1300 Cl, 1315 Pat, 1315 ChancW, 1319 Ch, 1327 Cl, 1328 Ipm *et passim,* from **socn,** ME *soke* 'a district over which a right of jurisdiction was exercised, an estate', cf. Caistor Soke PN L 2 88.

NEW WALTHAM, 1933 Kelly; New Waltham was created a Civil Parish out of Waltham in 1961, 1 April, Ministry of Housing Local Government Order 8987. A part of the new parish was transferred to Great Grimsby in 1968.

ALBION HO. BARNOLDBY HO is apparently *Phillipsons F.^{m}* 1828 Bry, from the family name *Philipson*, cf. Henry *Phillipson* 1824 *BT*. BUCK BECK, 1771 *EnclA*, 1828 Bry, *a certain Drain called* - 1822 *Terrier*, *v.* **bekkr**. CHEAPSIDE (local), 1771 *EnclA*, 1839 *Td'E*, no doubt a transferred name. THE FIRS. FLETCHER'S FM, named from the *Fletcher* family, cf. *Fletcher & Dales* (*Farmers*) 1842 White. GREAT ROWSEY HOLT, cf. *Rowsoe dyke*, - *hill* 1601, *Rowsodik'* (sic), *Rowsay hill* 1606, *Rowsou* hill (sic) 1625, *Rowsey hill*, - *dyke* 1638, *Rowsay Dyke* 1715 all *Terrier*, *Rowsie Close* 1654 *Nelthorpe*; the forms are too late and too varied to suggest an etymology for Rowsey. GREENLAND FM, *Greenland* 1842 White, 1852 *Padley*; since the name has not been noted till the mid 19th century it is tempting to associate this with Greenland Fm in Great Limber, PN L 2 222. There, it was suggested that there was a link between the Great Limber name and Grimsby whaling activities in the early 19th century, though no such historical connexions between Grimsby and Great Limber have so far been discovered. The same is the case with Waltham. GROVE FM. HACKCROSS HILL (lost), 1828 Bry, *Hackerous hill* 1601, 1606, *hacheres hill* (sic), *Hackerosse* Hill 1715, cf. *Hackerous* 1606, *Hackerous street syde* 1601, - *strete syde* 1606, *hackerous strete* 1625, *Hackerosse street* 1715, *hakris* (*gate*) 1638 all *Terrier*, *East* -, *West Hackross Hill* 1852 *Padley*; Dr Insley suggests that this is 'Hacker's house', *v.* **hūs** with **hyll** added, the first el. being ME *hakkere* 'a hacker, a chopper, a cutter (of wood); a maker of hacks' or the derived surn. For the occupational surn. *v.* Thuresson 34. The area was north of Buck Beck and Fletcher's Fm and the old parish boundary. HOLTON CROSS, 1771 *EnclA*, *Houlton Crosse* 1606, *Holton Crosse* 1715, cf. *howton crosse furlonge* 1625 all *Terrier*, *Great* -, *Little Holton Cross* 1769 *LCM*, *Holton Cross Cover* 1824 O, 1831 *Monsom*, 1838 *Brace*, from the neighbouring parish of Holton le Clay and **cros**. INGS LANE, - *lane* 1771 *EnclA*, 1822 *Terrier*, *the Inges gate* 1606, *thinges yate* (sic) 1625, *the Inges gate* 1638, - *Ings Gate* 1715 all *ib*, from **eng** 'meadow, pasture' in the pl. and **gata** 'a path, a road' and cf. *the Inges* 1601, 1606, 1625, 1638, - *Ynges* 1601, 1606, - *ynges* 1635, - *Ings* 1715 all *Terrier*. KING'S HEAD, 1842 White, *Kings Head Inn* 1828 Bry. LINGMARES GRANGE (lost, TA 031 272), *Grange F.^{m} or Lingmares Grange* 1828 Bry, *Lyngmeares* 1601, *Ling-* 1606, -

meares 1625, 1638, - *meres* 1715 all *Terrier*, 'the boundary, land on or forming a boundary where heather grows', *v.* **lyng**, **(ge)mǣre**. LOW FM. MOUNT PLEASANT, presumably a complimentary nickname, but occasionally one used ironically. NORMAN CORNER, cf. *Normangate* 1601, 1606, 1638, *norman-* 1625 all *Terrier*, on the boundary with Brigsley, *v.* **gata** 'a road'. Presumably, the first el. is the surn. *Norman*. PEAKS LANE, *Peake Lane* 1771 *EnclA* and cf. Peaks Fm in Weelsby in Bradley Wapentake. PORTUS FM, presumably from the surn. *Portus*. RECTORY, *The Parsonage house* 1606, *A* - 1674, 1697, 1712, *One* - 1686, *Parsonage House* 1703, *The* - 1715, *Rectory House* 1822, *A large Dwelling House Erected in the year One Thousand eight hundred and Sixty-four* 1864 all *Terrier*. SHOT MILL (lost, TA 032 258), 1828 Bry.. SKINNER'S LANE, from the surn. *Skinner*. SPRING HEAD HOLT, cf. *the Springes head* 1601, 1606, *Spring heades* 1625, *-head* 1638 all *Terrier*, *v.* **spring**, **hēafod**. STERLING COTTAGE, from the surn. *Sterling*. TOM HOLT. TAILPOKE LANE (local). WALTHAM GRANGE, *Grange* 1828 Bry, no doubt a late use of **grange** found frequently in L and recorded in EDD s.v. 2 as 'a homestead, small mansion or farm-house, esp. one standing by itself remote from others', a sense quoted there from L. WALTHAM HO, 1842 White, *Walthamhus* 1275 RH (p). WALTHAM OLD HALL, *Hall* 1842 White, cf. *Mr Skearne hall-close, the hall Low Close* 1606, *the Hall Close, - Land* 1715 both *Terrier*. WALTHAM WINDMILL, *the mill* 1601, 1625, 1715, *Mill* 1606 all *Terrier*, *Wind Mill* 1771 *EnclA*, cf. *the mill pitt hill* 1601, - *pit Hill* 1606, 1715, - *mill poste* 1601, *milne post* 1638, *the Mill Post* 1715, *mill post furlonge* 1606 all *Terrier*. WESTPORT. YARNACRES (lost, TA 278 045), 1828 Bry.

Field-Names

Forms dated 1234 are FF; 1275 RH; 1327, 1332 *SR*; 1373-4 IpmR; 1396 Peace; 1505[1] Ipm; 1505[2] AASR xxiii 38; 1531 Wills iii; 1535-46 *MinAcct*; 1554, e17, 1634 *Nelthorpe*; 1601, 1606, 1625, 1638, 1671, 1674, 1686, 1697, 1703, 1712, 1715, 1822, 1864 *Terrier*; 1649 *Td'E*; 1738, 1792, 1793, 1801, 1805, 1830, 1832, 1839 *PT*; 1769 *LCM*; 1771 *EnclA*; 1782, 1787 *MiscDon 492*; 1829 *MiscDep 18*; 1852, 1854 *Padley*; 1860 *Daubney*.

(a) Barnoldby Rd 1771 (*Barnolby gate* 1601, 1606, *Barnalby gate* 1625, *Barnolbie* - 1638, *Barnolby Gate* 1715, 'the road to Barnoldby le Beck (an adjacent parish)', *v.* **gata** 'a road'); Bradley Rd 1771 (*Bradley Yate* 1715, 'the road to Bradley (an adjacent parish)', *v.* **gata**); Brigsley Hedge 1771 (*Brigesley Hedge* 1715, cf. *Brigsley meare* 1601, - *mear* 1606, *Brygsley meare* 1625, - *Meare* 1638, *Brigesley Mere* 1715, 'the hedge, the boundary of Brigsley (an adjacent parish)', *v.* **hecg, (ge)mǣre**)); Brigsley Rd 1771 (*Brigesley Gate* 1715, *v.* **gata**); the Cow Cl 1787; Damis land 1860; East Fd 1769, the - 1771 (*the East feild* 1601, - *Feilde* 1606, - *feilde* 1625, *the east* - 1638, *le Eastfeild* 1649, *ye East field* 1671, 1697, *the East* - 1703, - *Feild* 1712, - *Field* 1715, *v.* **ēast, feld**, one of the great fields of the parish, cf. the West Fd *infra*); Far Cl 1829; North -, South Fisher Hole 1852; Great Grimsby Rd 1771 (*Grimsby gate* 1601, 1606, 1715, *Grymsby* - 1625, *Grymsbie* - 1638, *Grimsby Gate* 1715, 'the road to Great Grimsby', *v.* **gata**); a place called the Heads 1771 (*v.* **hēafod**); Holton Rd 1771, an old fence next of Holton Lordship 1822, Holton Cl 1852 (cf. *Howton Cow Pasture* in (b) *infra*); Home Cls 1852; Humberston lane End, Humberston Rd 1771 (*Humberston gate* 1601, 1606, *humberston* - 1625, *humberstone* - 1638, *Humberstone Gate, Humber stone Street* 1715, 'the road to Humberston', *v.* **gata**); Langmares 1769 (*Langmeres, further langmeres, hither Langmeres* 1601, (*farther*) *Langmeares* 1606, *further* -, *hither langmeres* 1625, *the farther* -, *Hither Lengmeres, further* -, *hither Lengmeares* 1638, (*further* -, *hither*) *Langmeres* 1715, *Lankenmeares* 1625, *Lankenmares* 1638, 'the long boundaries, boundary fields', *v.* **lang, (ge)mǣre**); New Well 1852; North Furze 1769, the - 1771 (*v.* **fyrs**); the Paddock 1792; Plantation Cl 1852; that cottage Tenement or Farm ... formerly called or known by the name of Rearesby Fm and afterwards of short-house 1801, that Messuage ... formerly called or known by the name of Rearesby Fm and afterwards of Short House 1805 (the earlier name was that of the *Rearesby* family, cf. Arnold *Rearesby* 1606; the later forms may represent the surn. *Shorthouse*); Team Gate 1771 (*v.* Team Gate Drain in Barnoldby le Beck *supra*); Short Thornhills 1852; Toll Bar 1852; the Town Street 1854; Waith Rd 1771 (self-explanatory); Waltham Hedge 1771 (*v.* **hecg**); the West Ditch 1771; the West Fd 1771, 1793, 1801, - of Waltham 1792, the late West Fd - 1805, the late West Fd 1830, 1832, 1839 (*the West feilde* 1601, 1638, - *west feild* 1606, *The* -, *the west feilde* 1625, *le Westfeild* 1649, *ye West field* 1671, *the west* - 1686, *the Westfield* 1702, *the west Feild* 1715, *v.* **west, feld**, one of the great fields of the parish, cf. the East Fd *supra*), West Fd Ings 1769, the West - 1771 (*v.* **eng**).

(b) *Abbot lande* 1531, *Abbottes closse, Abottes close* 1535-46 (*v.* **land,**

clos(e), referring to the abbot of Humberston); *Acres* (*hill*) 1601, *Ackris* (*hill*) 1625, 1638 (*v.* **æcer**); *the Arme* (sic) 1601, *the Carr Arme* 1606, 1638 (*Arme* is obscure; *v.* also **kjarr**); *Edward Allisons house* 1712; *Arabridge greene* 1601, *Arabridge* (*grene*) 1606, *Arabridge grene* 1625, *arrabrige* - 1638, *Arrabrigs Green* 1715 (*v.* **brycg**, **grēne**[2]; the first el. is obscure); *Aslakemeares* 1601, 1606, *aslake meares* 1625, *Haselocke Mares* 1638, *Allakemeres* (sic) 1715 (*v.* **(ge)mǣre**; the first el. is the ON pers.n. *Áslákr*); *Bargh hill* 1606 (*v.* **beorg**, of which *bargh* is a common dial. form); *Barley holme* 1601, 1606, 1625, 1638, *barly* - 1606, *Barleholme* 1638, *Barley Holm* 1715 (*v.* **bǣrlic**, **holmr**); *Barnalbye meare* 1601, *Barnolby mear* 1606, *Barnalby meare* 1625, *Barnolbie Meare* 1638, *Banolby Mere* 1715 ('the boundary with Barnoldby le Beck (an adjacent parish)', *v.* **(ge)mǣre** and cf. Barnoldby Rd *supra*); *Bastwelles* 1601, 1606, *bast well* 1625, *Bastwells* 1638, *Barsthill* (sic) 1625, 1638 (the first el. *Bast-* is perhaps **bæst** 'bast, the bark of the lim-tree'; the second is **wella** 'a spring'); *Bawkocc thyng* 1531 (from the surn. *Bawcock* with **þing** 'property, premises'); *the becke* 1601, 1606, 1638, *the Becke* 1606, *the beck* 1625, *common Issuer or becke* 1606, *the Beck* 1715 (*v.* **bekkr**); *Bleaman sike* 1601, 1625, - syke 1601, *Bleamansike* 1606, *bleaman syke* 1625, *bleamonsike, Bleamon sike* 1638, *Blemen Syke* 1715 (*v.* **sík**; Dr Insley suggests that *Bleaman* is a surn. formed from ME *blē* 'brightness, brilliance, lustre; skin colour' etc. and *man(n)*. He thinks the sense might be 'one with a shining face, or with a bright countenance'); *Blowlande* 1601, *Blow landes* 1606, 1638, *blowlandes* 1625, *Blowlands* 1715 (*v.* **land**); *Boulons hoorne* (sic) 1606 (*v. the east hedge infra*); *the Bowling Green* 1703; *Bowmer* 1601, 1625, 1638, 1715, *Bowmer grene* 1606 (*v.* **grēne**[2]); *Brabeck well* 1601, *Brabecke well* (sic) 1606, 1625, *brabeck* 1625, 1638, *Brabeckwell* 1638, *Brabeck, Brabeck well* 1715, *Brabecke* 1601, *Brabecke grene* 1606 (*v.* **bekkr** and **wella**, **grēne**[2]; the etymology of *Bra-* is uncertain); *Bradley feildes meare* 1601, 1606, *Bradley feild* - 1625, *Bradley feilds* - 1638, *Bradley Mere* 1715 ('(the boundary of) Bradley common fields', *v.* **(ge)mǣre**, **feld**; Bradley is an adjoining village); *Brakens* 1601, *Brackenes* 1625, *Braken* 1638 (*v.* **brakni**); *in the broad merfar* 1601, *the broade merfor* 1625 (*v.* **marfur** 'a boundary furlong'); *Buccoe* (sic) 1601, *Buckey* (sic) 1625, *Buccow, Bucko* 1638, *Buccow hill* (sic) 1625, 1638, *Buccho Hill, Burcho* (sic) 1715 (perhaps 'the mound, hill where bucks are found', *v.* **bucc**, **haugr**); *the Bull merfar* 1601, - *Marfar* 1606, *Bull merfor* 1625, *bull* - 1638, *the Bull Merfer* 1715 (*v.* **bula**, **marfur** 'a boundary furrow'); *Burrow(e)*, *Burrow hill* 1606 (this may be the same as *Bargh hill supra*); *Candesby thyng* (sic) 1505[1], *Candelsby thyng* 1505[2] (named from the *Candelsby* family, cf. Simon *de Canelesby* 1332 *SR*, with **þing** 'property, premises'); *the Carres* 1601, 1606, 1625, *One land under the Carre* 1625, *the Carre* 1638, - *Carrs* 1715, - *longe Carre* 1601, - *Long Carr* 1606, - *longe carre* 1625, - *Longe Carre* 1638, *long Carr* 1649, *the* - 1715 (*v.* **kjarr** 'marsh'); *Castor gate* 1606 ('the road to Caistor', *v.* **gata**); *Chantrie land* 1601, *Chantrie* - 1638, *Chauntry* - 1625 (*v.* **chaunterie**; the Ravenser Chantry in Waltham was founded in 1374 when the lapsed chantry at Belleau LSR was transferred to Waltham; for details *v.* ChancCert. AASR xxxvi, 269-73); *the church Furlong* 1715; *Cockethorne* 1601, 1606, *Cocthorne* 1625, 1638 (presumably self-explanatory, and for the same name cf. Cockthorne Fm PN L 3, 116); *George Coulbeck Close* 1674, *John colebecks close* 1712, - *Colbecks Close* 1715, - *Colebeck's house* 1712; *Cowelles* 1601, 1606, 1625, *Cowels* 1638, *Cowell grene* 1601, 1606, *Cowell* - 1625, *Cowells greene* 1638, - *Green* 1715 (*v.* **grēne**[2]; *Cowel(l)* is probably a surn.); *Cowgath hoole* (sic) 1606 (*v.* **garðr**); *Crake greene* 1601, 1625, - *grene* 1601, 1606, *-grene* 1638, *Crakegreen* 1715, *Creykegrene* 1625, *Grey-* (sic) 1638 (*v.* **kráka** 'crow, raven', **grēne**[2] 'a green, a grassy place'); *Crakemeare* 1601, 1625, 1638, *Crakemere* 1715, *Crakemer gate* 1601, *Crakemear* - 1606 (*v.* **gata**), *Crakemer Hill* 1715 (*v.* **hyll**), *Crakemeare hole* 1601, 1638, *Crakemear* - 1606, *Crakemer holl* 1625 (*v.* **hol**[1]), *Crakemear Linges* 1606 (*v.* **lyng**), *Crakemear Trough* 1638 (*v.* **trōg**), *the well in Crakemeare* 1601, 1625 ('the pool frequented by crows or ravens', *v.* **kráka**, **mere**[1], presumably a body of water, giving name to topographical features nearby); *Curtis headland* 1638 (from the surn. *Curtis*, with **hēafod-land**); *the dam* 1625; *diccon brigewathe* 1601 (*v.* **vað** 'a ford'), *diccon bridge* 1606, *dicconbridge* 1625, *dicken brydge* 1638 (*v.* **brycg**; *diccon* and *dicken* are diminutives of *Dick*, the hypocoristic form of the ME pers.n. *Richard*); *doucemear* 1601, *doucemear grene* 1606 (*v.* **grēne**[2]), *duucemere* (sic) 1625, *duusmare* (sic) 1638 (*douce* etc. may be from the ME surn. *Douce* (Reaney s.n.) and perhaps **mere**[1]); *Dove* -, *dove wonge* 1606 (*v.* **dūfe**, **vangr**); *Douermere* (sic) 1715; *in The Dyke* 1327, *in the dike* 1332 both (p) (*v.* **dík**); *the east hedge* 1601, 1625, 1638, - *East hedges* 1606, - *East Hedge or Bowlands Hude* 1715 (*v.* **ēast**, **hecg**; the 1715 alternative form is probably the surn. *Bo(w)land* perhaps with **hōd** 'a hood, a shelter', found in a corrupt form in *Boulons hoorne supra*; note the similar surn. *Bowlam* in Bowlam Green, in North Thoresby f.ns. (a) *supra*); *Elvyn greene* 1601, - *grene* 1606, *Elvin* - 1625, 1638, *Elwin Green* 1715 (named from *the Elvin* family, cf. John *Elvin* 1765 *BT*, with **grēne**[2]); "the field of" *Wautham* 1234, *in campis de Waltham* 1275, *Waltham felde* 1601, - *field* 1624, 1634, 1638, all *Terrier* (Barnoldby le Beck), *the feild meare* 1601, *the feildes* - 1606, 1625, 1638, *the feild mere* 1715 ('(the boundary of) the open fields of Waltham', *v.* **feld**, **(ge)mǣre**); *the fore garth* 1638 (*v.* **fore**, **garðr**); *Fowler fee* 1505[1], *fowler Close* 1638 (named from the family of Thomas *Fowler* 1505[2]); *furwell grene* 1601, *Furwell* - 1606, *furwells* - 1625, *Furwelles-* 1638 (*v.* **grēne**[2]), *Furwell dale* 1601, - *Dale* 1715 (*v.* **deill**), *Furwelles* 1606; *Gautres* 1601, 1606, *Gautryes* 1601, 1625, *Gawtres* 1625, *Gautrie*, *Gautris* 1638, *Gawterys*, *Gawtreys* 1715 ('the gallow-tree(s), gallows', *v.* **galga, trēow**); *Glew land* 1625 (named from the *Glew* family, cf. Thomas *Glue* 1563 *BT*, Agnes *Glew* 1589 *ib*, with **land**); *Goodericke holme* 1601, 1606, *goodrick* - 1625, *in Gooderick* (sic) 1715 (probably from the surn. *Goodrick* with **holmr**); *Gosling Gutter* 1715 (perhaps from the surn. *Gosling* and **goter**); *Grafurthe* 1601, *the grafurth* 1625, *longe* -, *shorte Grasfurthe* 1601, *longe* -, *Shorte Grasfurth* 1606, *the longe* -, *short grafurth* 1625, *the Longe, the Short graforth* 1638, *Grasfurth* 1715 (the etymology of *Grafurthe* etc. is obscure, unless, as Dr Insley suggests it means 'the grey ford', from ME *grā* (ON **grá**) 'grey' and **ford**. Forms in *Gras-* would then show the influence of **græs** and final *-th* would be the result of Scandinavianization); *Grafurthe Bydle* 1601, 1606, *Grafurth Bydell* 1601, - *bidle* 1625, *the grayforth bidell* 1638, cf. *the bydell ground* 1625, 1638 and *Vincent Bydle infra*. *Bydle, Bydell, bidle* are no doubt variants of *bydale, Bidale* in *A Frank by dale, the Isbel Bydale* etc. in Waithe f.ns. (b) *supra*. It probably means 'the share of land belonging to the village' from **bȳ** 'a village' and **deill** 'a share of land', a Scand. compound not noted previously in this survey); *Grassemere well* 1715 (*v.* **gærs, (ge)mǣre**); *great stone gate* 1601, 1625, 1638, *great-stone* - 1606, *Great Stone Gate* 1715 (*v.* **gata**) (evidently alluding to a local feature called *The Great Stone*, cf. *the wyndinges at great stone infra*); *atte Grene* 1332, *othe Grene de Waltham* 1396 both (p) (*v.* **grēne**^{2}); *Grewell close* 1601, 1625, *Gruell* - 1606, *Grewell Close* 1638 (the first el. may well be the surn. *Grewal* (Reaney s.n.), the second being **clos(e)**); *the Groopes* (sic) 1601, *the groopes* 1625, 1638, *the Groops* 1715; *Grosmer furlonge* 1601, 1606, *grosemer furlonge* 1625, 1638, *grosener furlong* (sic), *Grosmere Furlong, Grosmare* 1715 (obscure); *Mr Hansarte close* 1601, *M^r hansard* - 1625; *Hardmear greene* 1601, - *grene* 1606, *hardmer* - 1625, *Hardmeare* - 1638, *Hardmere Green* 1715 (probably 'the hard boundary, land on or forming a boundary', *v.* **heard** probably in the sense 'hard to till', **(ge)mǣre**, with **grēne**^{2} 'a green, a grassy place'); *the hither furlonge* 1606 (*v.* **furlang**); *Howsam greene, hawsome greene* 1601, *Howsam grene, -grene* 1606, *hawsom grene* 1625, *Hawson* - 1638, *Hawsome greene* 1638, - *Green* 1715, *Houesom Green* 1715 (named from the *Howson* family, cf. Richard *Howson* 1606, Simon *Howson* 1642 LPR, with **grēne**^{2}); *Howton Cow pasture* 1601, *Houlton cowe* - 1606, *houlton cow* - 1625, *Houlton Cow* - 1638, *Holten Cowpasture* 1715; *Howton Dyke* 1601, *Houlton dyke* 1606, 1638, *howton* - 1625, *Holten Dyke* 1715 (*v.* **dīk**) (named from Holton le Clay, an adjoining village); *the houdes* 1625 (perhaps from **hōd** 'a shelter' and cf. *the East Hedge or Barlands Hude supra*); *Huggameres* (sic) 1715; *Humberston meare* 1601, - *Meare* 1625, *Humberstone* - 1638, - *Feild* 1715 ('the boundary, the open fields of Humberston' the adjoining village to the east, *v.* **(ge)mǣre, feld**); *the Inge dytche,* - *dyke* 1601, - *Inges dike* 1606, 1638, *The Inges dyke* 1625, *the Ings dicke* 1638, - *Ing(e)s Dyke* 1715 (*v.* **dīc, dīk**), *the Ynges furlong* 1601, *the Inges furlonge* 1606, 1625, 1638, 1715, - *Ings Furlong* 1715 (*v.* **furlang**), *the Ynges noke* 1601, *the west noke of the Inges* 1606, *the inges nocke* 1625, - *Ing Nook* 1715 (*v.* **nōk**), *the Inges syde* 1606, 1715, cf. Ings Lane *supra*); *Jockomer* 1601, *Jockemear, -mer* 1606, *Jockmar* (sic) 1625, *Jockmer* 1638 (*v.* **(ge)mǣre**; the first el. is perhaps the pers.n. *Jock*); *kirke furlong* 1601, *the Kyrk Furlonge* 1606, *Kirke furlonge* 1625, *the* - 1638 (*v.* **kirkja**, **furlang**); *Leusemear, Leusemer greene* 1601, *Leusemear -, Leucemear -, Louse mear grene* 1606, *Leuksemere* (sic) 1625, *Lewse mares, lewsemer* - 1638, *Lews mere Green* 1715 (*v.* **(ge)mǣre**, **grēne**[2]; the sense of *Leuse* etc. is uncertain unless, as Dr Insley suggests, it is the ME fem. pers.n. *Luce* or a surn. derived from it, *v.* Reaney s.n. *Luce*); *one lime garth* 1625; *litlawe* 1601, *Litlawe, Litlaw hill* 1601, *Litlawe, Litlaw* (*hill*) 1606, *litlow* (*hill*) 1625, *littlow* 1625, *Little how* 1638, *little how* (*hill*) 1638, *Litlaw, Littlelow* (*Hill*) 1715 ('the small mound or hill', from **lytel** with **haugr**); *the long furlonge* 1601, 1606, *the longe* - 1625, 1638 (*v.* **furlang**); *the Lordes headland* 1601, - *headlande* 1606, *the Lords headland* 1638 (self-explanatory, *v.* **hēafod-land**); *the lowe close* 1601, *the low* - 1625, 1638, - *Close* 1715; *uppermore furlonge, the lower furlonge of little peaslandes* 1601, *the lower furlonge -, the uppermore furlonge of little pease landes* 1625, 1638, *the lower Furlong* 1715 (*v.* **furlang** and *Peaslandes infra*); *Luckameres* 1601, *Luckemeares grene* 1606 (obscure, *v.* **grēne**[2]); *Manbrigges* 1601, 1606, *Manbridges* 1625, *Manbrydge* 1638, *Manbriggs* 1715 ('the communally-held bridges', *v.* **(ge)mǣre**, **brycg**); *the Marshe* 1601, 1606, - *Marsh*, - *Marshe syde* 1606, - *Marsh*(*e*) 1625, 1638, - *Marshe* (*syde*) 1638; - *Marsh*, - *Furlong*, - *side* 1715 (*v.* **furlang**); *the medow* 1601, - *Medow* 1625; *the common merfar, the merfor* 1601, *the marfer* 1606, *the common merforth* 1625, *the Common merfer* 1638, *the Merfour* 1625, *the Merfor, the Marfer, the Merfer* 1638, *The Merfer, the Merfor* 1715 (*v.* **marfur** 'a boundary furrow'); *Micklemer, Micklemore* 1601, *Miclemear* 1606, *-moor* 1625, *Mickelmore* 1625, *Micklemere, Micklemore* 1638, *Micklemere, Micllemere* 1715, *Micklemer hill* 1601, *Mickelmor hill* 1625, *Micklemer hill* 1638, *Micklemere Hill* 1715 (probably from **mikill**, and **mōr**[1] 'marsh', confused in some spellings with **mere**); *de Medeby* 1327 (p), *Midbye Lane* 1606, - *lane* 1625, *Midbie* - 1638, *Midby well* 1715 (this name has been noted as Midby PN L 2, 19, and as a surn. *de Middeby* in Ludborough f.ns. (b) *supra*. It is probably a partial anglicisation of Scand. *miðr í bȳ*, literally 'middle in the village', comparable to *Northiby* and *Suthiby* recorded frequently as a surn. in L. It clearly survived in Waltham as such to give name to a lane and well); *the middle furlonge* 1601, 1606, *the Middle* - 1625, 1638, *the midle Furlong* 1715 (*v.* **furlang**); *Millerdale* 1601, 1606, *Miller* - 1625, *Miller Dale* 1715 (probably from the surn. *Miller* and **deill**); *Milner Gate* 1638 (*v.* **gata**; the first el. is presumably the surn. *Milner*); *le more de Waltham* 1554; *Morewell gate* 1715 (*v.* **gata**); *the nether furlonge* 1601, 1606 (*v.* **furlang**); *newbridge gate* 1601, 1625, *Newbridge* - 1606, *newbrydge* - 1638 (*v.* **gata**), *new bridge Ley* 1606, *New bridge Leye endes* 1601, 1625, *new brydge* - 1638 (*v.* **ley, lea** (OE **lēah**) 'meadow, pasture', **ende**), *new Bridge, - or borden Bridge* 1715 (self-explanatory; the alternative name in 1715 means 'the bridge made of boards, planks', 'the wooden bridge', from ME *borden* (MED s.v.) and **brycg**); *the new well Furlong* 1715 (*v.* **furlang**); *Norcotes thyng* 1505[2] (from the surn. *Northcotes* (from North Coates *supra*) with **þing** 'property, premises'); *the north banke* 1625; *the North Field of Waltham* 1738; *North Sleigthes* (sic), *north Sleightes* 1601, *North* - 1606, *north Sleigts* 1625, - *sleygte, northsleyttes* 1638, *North Sleights* 1715 (*v.* **norð, sléttr** 'a level field' in the pl. and cf. (*the*) *Sleights infra*); *Ogle Springarth* 1625 (*v.* **spring, garðr,** *Ogle* is a surn., cf. William *Ogle* 1610 *BT*); *Owle nest* 1601, 1715, *the* - 1606, *the owle nest* 1625, 1638 (self-explanatory); *the oxgange* 1649 (*v.* **oxgang**); *the Parsonnes headland* 1601, *the Parsons* - 1606, *the parsonage* - 1625, 1638 (*v.* **persone, hēafod-land**); *Peaslandes, great Peaseland greene* 1601, - *grene* 1606, - *Green* 1715, *little Peaseland* 1606, - *peaselands* 1638, - *Peaselands* 1715, *peisland grene* 1625, *peaselandes* - 1625, 1638, *peaselands* - 1638 (from **pise** 'pease' and **land** 'a selion' with **grēne**[2]); *peperdike* 1601, *Peper dyke* 1606, 1715, *pepper* - 1625, *peperdicke* 1638 (*v.* **dík**; the significance of *peper* is not clear); *Pickaro* (sic) 1601, 1625, 1638 (obscure); *Pickard headland* 1638 (from the surn. *Pickard* and **hēafod-land**; the similarity to the preceding f.n. is probably coincidental); *Preistmer* 1601, *Preist mear, Preistmear* 1606, *preistmore* 1625, *preistmere* 1638, *Preistmer hill* 1601, *preistmer* - 1625, *prest meare* - 1638, *Preist mere Hill* 1715 ('the priest's boundary land', from **prēost, (ge)mǣre**, with **hyll**); *Ravemworth* -, *Ravinworth* -, *Ravynsworth thyng* 1505[2] (no doubt from the surn. *Ravenworth* and **þyng**); *Rowmer grene* 1601, 1638, *Rawmer* - 1606, *Raumer* - 1625, *Rowmer Green* 1715 (*v.* **grēne**[2]; *Rowmer* is obscure); *Sawter gate* 1601, 1625, 1638, *-gate* 1715 ('the salters' road', *v.* **saltere, gata**); *Scarthow meare* 1601, 1606, *Scarthoe* - 1625, - *Meare* 1638, *Scarthe mere* 1715 ('the boundary with Scartho (formerly a separate parish)', *v.* **(ge)mǣre**); *Scolebrothe* (sic) 1601, 1625, *Scalbrattes* (sic) *Scolbrothe* 1606, *Scalbrath* (sic) 1625, *a place called Scabbrath* 1638 (although the forms are varied and erratic, it may be suggested that this is a Scand. compound of **skáli** 'a temporary hut, shed' and the pl. of **brat** 'a small piece of land'; **skáli** is an OWScand, word common in north-west England, but for which at least half a dozen examples have now been noted in north L, cf. PN L 2, 132); *Scropsmeare* (sic) 1601, *Scropsmear* (sic) 1606, *Scopsmer* 1625, *Scopsmor* 1638, *Scopsmere* 1715 (*v.* **(ge)mǣre**; the first el. is probably as Dr Insley suggests, the surn. *Scrope*, for which *v.* Reaney s.n.); *Seghole* 1601, 1606, 1715, *Segdhole* (sic) 1625, *Sedghole* 1638 ('the hollow place where sedge grows', *v.* **secg, hol**[2]; the forms in *Seg-* are Scandinavianized); *Mr Skearne close, Mr*

Skerne - 1601, *Mr Skearne close* 1625 (for the *Skerne* family, cf. Henry *Skerne* 1505[2]); *Skittle furlonge* 1601, 1625, - *Furlonge* 1606, *Skitt Furlong* (sic) 1715 (*v.* **furlang**; *Skittle* may be from *Skithill* 'the dung-hill', *v.* **skítr**, **hyll**, as Dr Insley suggests, with **furlang**); (*the*) *Sleightes* 1601, *Sleightes* 1606, *Sleigts* 1625, 1638, *Sleygtes* 1638, *the Sleights* 1715 (*v. North Sleigthes supra* and cf. *southe Sleightes infra*); *Small grenes* 1601, - *greenes* 1606, 1625, *Smallgrenes* 1638, *Small Greens* 1715 ('the narrow grassy places', *v.* **smæl**, **grēne**[2]); *the South Feild* 1738; *the southe hedge* 1601, *the South* - 1606, 1638, *the south* - 1625, *the South Hedge* 1715 (*v.* **hecg**); *southe Sleightes* 1601, *South* - 1606, *southe Sleigts* 1625, *South sleygtes* 1638, *the South Sleights* 1715 (cf. *North Sleigthes* and (*the*) *Sleightes supra*); *Sowmer* 1601, 1606, 1625, *Sowmere* 1638, *Sawmer, Sawmare* 1715, *Sowmer greene* 1601, - *green* 1606, - *grene* 1625, 1638, *Sowmer grene* 1606 (*v.* **grēne**[2]), *Sowmer hill* 1601, 1606, 1625, 1638, *the nether end of Sowmer* 1638 (perhaps 'the southern boundary land', *v.* **sūð**, **(ge)mǣre**); *standales* 1601, 1625, *Standales* 1606, 1638, 1715 ('stony portions of land', *v.* **stān**, **deill**); *Stanlandes* 1601, *Standlandes* 1606, *standlandes* 1625, *standlands* 1638 (*v.* **stān**, **land**); *Stanmear grene* 1601, *stonmer* - 1625, *stanmer-* 1638, *Stanmere Green* 1715 ('the stony boundary', from **stān**, **(ge)mǣre**, with **grēne**[2]); *attestaynes* 1332 (p) (*v.* **steinn**); *the Stonye furlonge* 1601, *the stony Furlong* 1715 (*v.* **stānig**, **furlang**); *the stret* 1625 (*v.* **strǣt**); *Styvell* (*greene*) 1601, *Styvell* (*grene*) 1606, *Stivell* 1638, *the Stivel, Stivel* (*Green*) 1715, *Stywell, stiuell greene* 1625, *Stivell* (*grene*) 1638 (obscure); *Suthcurle in Waltham maner* 1373-4 (obscure); *longe* -, *shorte Thicke dales* 1601, *Long* -, *Short Thickdales* 1606, *longe* -, *short thickedales* 1625, *Thicke dales, Short Thikdales* 1638, *long* -, *short thick Dales* 1715 (*v.* **deill**; the significance of *Thick* is not clear); *Thirspitts* 1601, *Thirspittes* 1606, *Thruspites* 1638 ('the demon-haunted pits', *v.* **þyrs**, **pytt**); *Thornemare* 1601, *-mear* 1606, *thornemaer* 1625, *Thornemer* 1638, *Thornmere* 1715 ('the thorn-tree boundary', *v.* **þorn**, **(ge)mǣre**); *Thornye lees* 1601, - *Leas*, - *Leys* 1606, *thornye leys* 1625, *thorne leys, Thorneleys* 1638, *Short thorny Leys Furlong* 1715 (*v.* **þornig**, **lea** (OE **lēah**) 'meadow, pasture' in the pl., with **furlang**); *Rich. Todde Close syde* 1638; *Tofte hill* 1601, *Toft* - 1606, 1638, (*the*) *tofte* - 1625, *Toft Hill ore the Holds* 1715 (*v.* **toft** 'a messuage, a curtilage', **hyll**), *Toftmeares* 1601, 1606, *Tofte* - 1601, *Toft* - 1606, 1638, *toft* - 1625, *tofte meres*, - *meares* 1625, *Toft mares* 1625, - *meres* 1715 (*v.* **toft**, **(ge)mǣre**); *the Town meare* 1715 (*v.* **(ge)mǣre**), *the Town Spring Garth* 1715 (*cf. Ogle Springarth supra*); *one Land under the Towne* 1601, *One land under the towne* 1625, - *Towne* 1638; *the Trough* 1715 (*v.* **trōg** in the sense a hollow resembling a trough); *the upper furlonge* 1601, 1606, 1638, *the uper* - 1625, *the upper Furlong* 1715; (*in the*) *Vincent* (sic) 1601, *Vincent Bydle, Vinson Bydell* 1601, *Vinsent Bydell* 1606, *vincen bidle, vincen bydle* 1625, *the vinson bidell* 1638, *Vincent Bidle* 1715 (cf. *Grafurthe Bydle supra*), *vinson land* 1625,

Vinson land 1638 (*v.* **land**, named from the *Vincent* family, cf. Henry *Vincent* 1332, Thomas *Vyncent* 1531, Henry *vincent*, - *vinson* 1628); *Waltham feild* e17, *campos de Waltham* 1634 (*v.* **feld**); *Waltham holme* 1601, 1625, 1638 (*v.* **holmr**); *de la Ward'* 1332 (p) (*v.* **weard**, if this is a local surn.); *Waterfulgote* (sic) 1601, 1606, *Waterfill gate* (sic) 1625, 1638, *Waterful Gote* 1715 (this presumably is 'the waterful sluice', *v.* **gotu**; *waterful* does not seem to be recorded in NED); *Well hill* 1601, 1606, 1625, 1638; *Wellow Hill* 1715 (from Wellow in Great Grimsby); *the west hedge* 1601, 1606, 1625, 1638, - *Hedge* 1715 (*v.* **west**, **hectg**); *Whilghe hoole* 1601, *wylghe hole* 1625, *wilghe* - 1638, *Whilghe Hole* 1715 ('the willow hollow', *v.* **wilig**, **hol**[1]); *Whishemear* 1601, *Whishmear grene* 1606, *-mare* 1625, *-mere* 1638, *Whismere* 1715; *White cake* (sic) 1601, *Whyte Cocke* (sic) 1606, *White Cocke* 1625, - *tocke* (sic) 1638, *the White Cock* 1715 (obscure); *wilfre acres* 1601, *Wilfor Acres furlonge* 1606, *wilfer acres* 1625, 1638 (*v.* **æcer**, *wilfre*, *wilfer* may be the surn. *Wilfer*); *Wrangmeres* 1601, 1715, *-meares* 1606, *wrangmeares* 1625, *wrengmares* 1638, *Wrangmere* 1715, (*over*) *wrangmers* 1601, *-meare furlonge* 1606, *-mer furlonge* 1625 (*v.* **furlang**), *Wrangmer headinges* 1606, *wrangmer headinges* 1625, *Wrengmeares* (*headinge*) 1638, *wrangmer mouthe* 1601, *Wrangmear mouthe* 1606, *wrangmer Mouthe* 1625, *wrengmeare mouthe* 1638 ('the twisted boundaries or boundary lands', *v.* **wrang**, **vrangr**, **(ge)mǣre**; *mouthe* seems to be used in some topographical sense not associated with river-estuaries etc.); *wray dike* 1601, - *dik* 1606, *Wray dyke leys* 1625, - *dicke leys* 1638, - *Dyke* 1715 (*v.* **dík**, **lea** (OE **lēah**)), *Wraye greene* 1601, *wray grene* 1606, *Way grene* (sic) 1625, *Wray* - 1638 (*v.* **vrá** 'a nook or corner', **grēne**[2]); *the wyndinges at great stone* 1601, *the Wyndinges at the great stone* 1606, *the Windinges at the great stone* 1625, 1638 (cf. *great stone gate supra*; for *wyndinges*, *v.* *wynedyngs* PN L **2**, 173); *attyattes of Waltham* 1508 *GrimsCB* (*v.* **geat** 'a gate').

INDEX

This index is based on the following principles:

(a) It includes all the place-names in the body of the work.
(b) It covers only the main reference to each place and no cross-references are noted.
(c) Street-names are included.
(d) "Lost" names are printed in italics.
(e) In grouping names together no distinction has been made between those written in one word or two, e.g. Windmill and Wind Mill have been grouped together.
(f) Only very few field-names (of special historical or philological interest) have been included.

THE ENGLISH PLACE-NAME SOCIETY

COUNTY VOLUMES

I, Part 1: Introduction to the Survey of English Place-Names
Part 2: The Chief Elements Used in English Place-Names
(Reprinted as a single volume)
II. The Place-Names of Buckinghamshire.
III. The Place-Names of Bedfordshire and Huntingdonshire.
IV. The Place-Names of Worcestershire.
V. The Place-Names of the North Riding of Yorkshire.
VI,VII. The Place-Names of Sussex, Parts 1 and 2.
VIII,IX. The Place-Names of Devon.
X. The Place-Names of Northamptonshire.
XI. The Place-Names of Surrey.
XII. The Place-Names of Essex.
XIII. The Place-Names of Warwickshire.
XIV. The Place-Names of the East Riding of Yorkshire & York.
XV. The Place-Names of Hertfordshire.
XVI. The Place-Names of Wiltshire.
XVII. The Place-Names of Nottinghamshire.
XVIII. The Place-Names of Middlesex.
XIX. The Place-Names of Cambridgeshire and the Isle of Ely.
XX-XXII. The Place-Names of Cumberland, Parts 1, 2, and 3.
XXIII-XXIV. The Place-Names of Oxfordshire, Parts 1 and 2.
XXV,XXVI. English Place-Name Elements, Parts 1 and 2.
XXVII-XXIX. The Place-Names of Derbyshire, Parts 1, 2, and 3.
XXX-XXXVII. The Place-Names of the West Riding of Yorkshire, Parts 1-8.
XXXVIII-XLI. The Place-Names of Gloucestershire, Parts 1-4.
XLII,XLIII. The Place-Names of Westmorland, Parts 1 and 2.
XXLIV-XLVIII. The Place-Names of Cheshire, Parts 1-4, 5(1:i).
XLIX-LI. The Place-Names of Berkshire, Parts 1-3.
LII,LIII. The Place-Names of Dorset, Parts 1 and 2.
LIV. The Place-Names of Cheshire, Part 5(1:ii).
LV. The Place-Names of Staffordshire, Part 1.
LVI/LVII. Cornish Place-Name Elements.
LVIII. The Place-Names of Lincolnshire, Part 1.
LIX/LX. The Place-Names of Dorset, Part 3.
LXI. The Place-Names of Norfolk, Part 1.
LXII/LXIII. The Place-Names of Shropshire, Part 1.
LXIV/LXV. The Place-Names of Lincolnshire, Part 2.
LXVI. The Place-Names of Lincolnshire, Part 3.
LXVII/LXVIII/LXIX. The Place-Names of Rutland.
LXX. The Place-Names of Shropshire, Part 2.
LXXI. The Place-Names of Lincolnshire, Part 4.

ENGLISH PLACE-NAME SOCIETY, DEPARTMENT OF ENGLISH
UNIVERSITY OF NOTTINGHAM, NOTTINGHAM NG7 2RD